COORDINATED COMPUTING
TOOLS AND TECHNIQUES FOR
DISTRIBUTED SOFTWARE

McGraw-Hill Series in Artificial Intelligence

COORDINATED COMPUTING
TOOLS AND TECHNIQUES FOR
DISTRIBUTED SOFTWARE

Robert E. Filman

Hewlett-Packard Laboratories
and
Indiana University

Daniel P. Friedman

Indiana University

McGraw-Hill Book Company

New York St. Louis San Francisco Auckland Bogotá Hamburg
Johannesburg London Madrid Mexico Montreal New Delhi
Panama Paris São Paulo Singapore Sydney Tokyo Toronto

This book was set in Almost Computer Modern Roman by the authors using TEX.
The editors were Eric M. Munson and Linda A. Mittiga.
The production supervisor was Joe Campanella.
The drawings were done by J & R Services, Inc.
Halliday Lithograph Corporation was printer and binder.

COORDINATED COMPUTING
Tools and Techniques for Distributed Software

1234567890 HALHAL 8987654

ISBN 0-07-022439-0

Library of Congress Cataloging in Publication Data

Filman, Robert E.
    Coordinated computing.

    (McGraw-Hill series in computer organization and
architecture) (McGraw-Hill computer science series)
    Bibliography: p.
    Includes index.
    1. Electronic data processing—Distribution processing.
2. Electronic digital computers—Programming. I. Friedman,
Daniel P. II. Title. III Series. IV. Series:
McGraw-Hill computer science series.
QA76.9.D5F55 1984   001.64   83-22226
ISBN 0-07-022439-0

To Myrna, Muriel, and Seymour
and
Mary, Bert, and Dorothy

CONTENTS

Traditional computer systems are built around the solitary central processor—an omnipotent agent that executes instructions and commands peripheral devices. Traditional programs reflect this monolithic orientation; programs describe a single instruction stream, with instructions evaluated sequentially. It is now possible to build systems with many active computing agents—independent processors that execute concurrently but can nevertheless communicate. We need to develop new software technology to control such systems. In this book we explore some of the tools and techniques that have been proposed for programming systems composed of many independent agents and for focusing these systems on single tasks. We give the name *coordinated computing* to this study of organizing multiple, independent, and loosely connected computing systems to perform coherent problem solving.

Historical Perspective

The historical patterns of use and cost of computing systems have changed dramatically. Early computers were extremely expensive, physically large, and computationally slow. They were designed for use by a single programmer at a time, who had the entire machine devoted to his or her use. Such systems did not have an operating system to protect against malice or mistake. Instead, the user's program controlled the computer directly. Since computers were expensive, they were shared — one user at a time. Users "signed up" to reserve time on the computer.

Clearer understanding of computation, cheaper machines, and a desire for improved system utilization led to the batch/stream computer. Here the computer scheduled its work, running each user's task in turn. Typically, a programmer submitted a program on a deck of punch cards in the morning and returned later that afternoon for the output. Better systems provided two or three runs a day. Primitive operating systems were developed primarily to order the batch stream and to arrange for each program's tapes. In these systems, security was limited to ensuring that programs used the correct files and tapes. Since only a single program was running at a time, programs did not interfere with each other's address spaces.

Interactive timesharing systems have replaced batch systems, at least in those environments devoted to program development. A timesharing computer is a complex system. Instead of sequencing the tasks of a series of users, it interleaves them. With timesharing, productivity increases dramatically. Timesharing systems provide facilities such as interactive database access and text editing. However, timesharing requires a more complicated operating system than batch. A timesharing system must provide each concurrent program with a secure address space of its own; the system must switch rapidly between user contexts. Timesharing is possible because of large, fast machines. With these machines, a fraction of the computer's resources is enough to accomplish a single user's work.

This is the age of microprocessors—computers so cheap that their processor cost has almost ceased to matter. Today, a few hundred dollars can purchase more computational power than millions could buy in the 1950s. We are seeing the beginning of the "personal computer" age, where every worker has a computer of his or her own. These machines are usually connected by a network that provides intermachine communication and shared data. In a sense, we are coming full circle: The computer is no longer a shared device, but is being returned to the individual user.

The trend toward cheaper, smaller, and faster machines continues. As fabrication techniques continue to improve, the single processor on a chip will give way to a phalanx of processors on a chip and an army of interconnected chips. We believe that the next generation of computer architectures will provide each user with not just one but many computers—the *megacomputer*. However, improved computational productivity is not achieved by processing power alone. Special problems arise in coordinating systems of independent, asynchronous agents. Along with multiple processor architectures must come the software facility to exploit that computing power. A *coordinated computing system* successfully integrates multiple processing elements for problem solving. This book is a compendium of ideas about the software issues involved in programming coordinated computing systems.

Building a timesharing system is a difficult task. Interleaving computations, arranging to switch contexts between programs, and ensuring the security of each individual process requires proficient engineering. Nevertheless, the problems of timesharing are well understood. Creating a timesharing system is no longer a research endeavor, but an engineering activity. We see the next intellectual step in the development of computing systems as that of harnessing the power of the megacomputer.

Coordinated Computing Systems

A coordinated computing system distributes the work of a single task among many processing agents. Building a coordinated system is much harder than constructing a timesharing computer. Coordinated computing is like timesharing in that we must arrange to do many activities simultaneously. However, unlike timesharing, coordinated computing requires the ability to focus multiple, simultaneous activities on a single goal.

How does coordinated computing differ from conventional programming? To understand the differences we must make several distinctions. We need to distinguish processors and processes. A *processor* is a physical box that *computes*—executes the instructions of a program, moves pulses of electricity around wires, etc. Processors execute instructions. Processors use a fixed and permanent storage.

A *process* is a logical processor. Like a conventional processor, a process executes a program and possesses storage. Unlike a processor, a process is not tied to any particular physical object. Analogically, a process is to a processor as software is to hardware.*

Often systems associate several processes with a single processor. For example, in timesharing systems each user (or user task) gets a process. The timesharing system tries to make that process appear to be running on its own (almost) independent processor. Many of the systems that we describe in this book are based on the synchronization of and communication among independent processes.

Though processes must have some independence, they should not become too isolated. Processes must be able to communicate—to transfer information among themselves. After all, coordinated problem solving requires communication. One crucial dimension of communication is *bandwidth*—the amount of information that communicators can exchange in a given time. We classify multiple processor systems by their communications bandwidth. Systems that allow sharing of much information are *multiprocessors*. Such systems can be thought of as providing shared memory to their processes. We use the term *shared memory* to describe this close information coupling because such systems are usually implemented by sharing primary memory between the multiple processors. With shared memory, communication is inexpensive.

Only a limited set of architectures provide inexpensive communication. More generally, communication has its costs. Systems that incur higher communication costs are *distributed systems*. In this book, we focus on software techniques for controlling and exploiting distributed systems.

A final distinguishing attribute of coordinated computing is a requirement for coherent problem solving. We are not interested in just getting computers to communicate (the study of computer networks), nor are we interested in providing the software foundation for application program communication and synchronization (the study of distributed operating systems). We want our processes to cooperate in the partitioning and resolving of tasks. An appropriate technique

---

* Here we use "process" for what is conventionally called a "logical process" in operating systems.

for the study of coordinated computing would be case studies of such systems. Since distributed problem solving systems have not yet been built, we cannot follow that path. Instead, in this book we take various proposals for the appropriate organization of multiprocessor and distributed systems that have appeared in the scientific literature and develop their themes. We emphasize the theoretical organizing principles of these ideas instead of the engineering decisions of particular implementations.

Building a coordinated computing system involves two primary activities: constructing and connecting the system's hardware and programming the system's software. This book is about software. Clearly, developing hardware is crucial to building coordinated systems. Nevertheless (except for a few definitions and pointers to the literature), we virtually ignore hardware. Instead, we take the point of view that such physical systems will come into existence; the technology to build inexpensive processors and to get them to communicate already exists. We are interested in the effective use of these emerging systems— programs that can use a coordinated system as something more than a complicated sequential processor. This book is an investigation of possible alternatives for constructing coherent multiprocess systems.

Models, Languages, and Heuristics

We believe that building coordinated computing systems requires understanding of three different facets of system organization: models, languages, and heuristics.

Models capture the abstract relationships between the important components of systems. To evaluate a system, one must know the parameters of its construction: how long particular instructions take to execute, the effects of specific statements, and so forth. Modeling is particularly important when considering emerging technologies. Such technologies need models both to guide the system development process and to substitute for observations of system performance. Models are used in system design, validation, and analysis. In Part 2 we discuss several models that apply to the problems of coordinated computing.

The usual way to give directions to a computer is with a *program* written in some *programming language*. Coordinated systems need programming languages that can describe concurrent activity and communication. Some of our experiences with traditional programming systems are an impediment to designing languages for coordinated systems. Traditional programs are executed sequentially. Their control structures can specify only serial activities: "First, do this; next, do that." The primary advantage of coordinated systems is the increased processing power of concurrent computation. However, if system components are to execute concurrently, then they must be able to determine the (potentially) concurrent activities. In general, this can be done in one of two ways: either (1) the programmer can indicate parallel actions with specific programming language constructs, or (2) the system can infer opportunities for parallelism on its own.

The programs one writes reflect the facilities of one's programming system. Classical sequential programming languages (such as Pascal, Cobol, and Lisp) are inadequate for programming coordinated systems. These languages do not treat important problems such as concurrency, communication, synchronization, security, and failure. In Part 3, we consider several different language proposals that address some of our requirements. These languages are primarily *distributed languages* — concurrent languages that recognize the cost of communication.*

Typically, models address the formal, mathematical understanding of systems, while programming languages mediate directions to a computer. Programming languages have a complete syntax and semantics. Models usually express only the simplest of relationships between a system's elements. The systems we consider are usually describing the control of decentralized computer systems. Hence, many systems blend elements of language and model, often taking the form of a few additional concepts to be added to a standard language like Pascal or Lisp.

Programming in sequential languages has taught us about sequential solutions to problems. Coordinated systems provide the opportunity to program concurrent solutions. However, except for the simplest cases, the exercising of such concurrent power is an intellectually demanding task. This is especially true when there are many active processes. *Heuristics* for coordinated computing are ideas on the "organizational" or "social" architecture of coordinated systems— techniques for getting processes to work together and for exploiting potential concurrency. In Part 4 we discuss heuristic organizations for coordinated problem solving systems.

Motivations for Coordinated Computing

This book promotes the idea of coordinated computing. Clearly, organizing a distributed, asynchronous system is harder than organizing one that is centralized or synchronous. So why bother? There are two major motivations for studying coordinated computing: economic and intellectual. On one hand, taming concurrent computation promises virtually cost-free processing. The massive amount of computing cycles that a coordinated system will provide will make many currently intractable computational problems solvable. (These include problems drawn from domains such as large system simulation, database access, optimization, and heuristic search.) On the other hand, organizing and understanding a

---

* We distinguish distributed languages and concurrent languages. Concurrent languages assume concurrently executing processes. However, these processes share storage (can communicate cheaply). Concurrent programming languages are better understood, more specific, and, in our opinion, less interesting than distributed languages. In Chapter 13 we discuss a concurrent programming language, Concurrent Pascal. We include this language for both historical and pedagogical reasons. Concurrent programming languages are also called multiprocessing languages.

set of independent agents is a challenging intellectual task. We find this combination of intellectual challenge and economic reward a compelling argument for the relevance of studying coordinated computing.

Book Overview

Our original title for this book was "Models, Languages, and Heuristics for Distributed Computing." In the course of our research, we came to the conclusion that there was some "whole" of distributed control greater than these three parts. We chose to call that whole *coordinated computing*. Nevertheless, our book structure still reflects our original triad. This book has five parts: "Foundations," "Models," "Languages," "Heuristics," and "Contrasts and Comparisons." The first part, Foundations, covers the minimal required background material and definitions. The next three parts survey proposed models (Part 2), languages (Part 3), and heuristic organizations (Part 4) for computation that we feel bear on coordinated computing. We compare and contrast these models, languages, and heuristics in Part 5, presenting a taxonomy of systems.

Having neither a general theory of coordinated computing nor a large pool of implementation experience, we chose to approach the problem by discussing relevant ideas from the computing literature. These ideas center on programming languages. However, the discussion in the rest of the book touches on many fields besides programming languages (and mentions some programming language concepts that may not be familiar to every reader). We therefore devote the first four chapters to developing background material: Chapter 1, Computation Theory (automata theory, lambda calculus, and the analysis of algorithms); Chapter 2, Programming Languages (syntax and semantics, and pragmatics); Chapter 3, Concurrency (concurrency, resource conflict, and synchronization); and Chapter 4, Hardware. Our intention is that the reader only marginally acquainted with a subject can, by reading the introductory section, learn all he or she needs to know to understand the rest of the book.

The last chapter of Part 1, Chapter 5, forms the introduction to Parts 2, 3, and 4. It outlines the nature of models, languages, and heuristics and touches on some of the difficulties faced by concurrent and distributed systems. This chapter introduces the dimensions of distribution by which we classify the various systems.

Part 2 surveys models for coordinated computing. Each chapter (6 through 12) in that part describes a different model (or a related set of models). For each, we describe the model and present several examples of its use. Part 3 (Chapters 13 through 16) is a similar survey of programming languages.

Part 4 discusses heuristics for organizing coordinated computing systems. Its first chapter, Chapter 17, discusses algorithms for distributed databases. Its other chapter, Chapter 18, develops some of the more interesting ideas for organizing distributed systems for coherent problem solving. Though much of the work described in that chapter has its roots in artificial intelligence research, no particular background in that field is needed to understand the material.

Our final part, Part 5, contrasts and compares these systems, both in terms of the dimensions outlined in Chapter 5, and when appropriate, by similar and contrasting features. We conclude with a section discussing the characteristics of basis and ideal systems.

We tried to write the chapters in Parts 2, 3, and 4 so that each is (by and large) conceptually independent. While this independence is not complete, we feel that readers will be able to read just those chapters that interest them. More specifically, the reader interested in just one system [for example, Communicating Sequential Processes (Chapter 10) or tasking in Ada (Chapter 14)] can skip to that chapter; the reader who finds a chapter too difficult [as many not familiar with the lambda calculus may find Concurrent Processes (Chapter 8)] can omit that chapter at first reading.

Every chapter includes a few exercises. These exercises form three classes: (1) brief *mention* exercises that draw the reader's attention to a tricky point in one of the examples, (2) *homework* problems that request the straightforward programming of a conventional problem in a new system, and (3) *research* exercises that describe a difficult problem. Some of these exercises are suitable for term projects; others are open research questions. Problems of this last type are marked by a "†". Each chapter ends with a bibliography of relevant papers. We have annotated those references when appropriate. There is a cumulative bibliography at the end of the book.

Audience

We have tried to write this book so that it can be understood by someone acquainted with the construction of programming languages—roughly the material in a junior level course on programming languages. A reading knowledge of Pascal (or the equivalent) is essential; a reading knowledge of Lisp is useful for understanding certain sections. The mathematical sophistication of the junior-level computer science student is also required at times. We have tried to avoid demanding a greater background of the reader. However, this material ranges over a wide territory — programming languages, operating systems, database systems, artificial intelligence, complexity theory, and computational theory. We attempt to explain, briefly, each potentially unfamiliar idea and to provide references to more complete descriptions. We urge the reader who finds him or herself in a familiar section to skip to more challenging material. In particular, much of Part 1 will be familiar to many readers.

We anticipate two audiences for this material. The first is the academic community. We use this book as the text in a graduate seminar on concepts of programming languages and include some material (particularly exercises) specifically for classroom use. The second audience is professional programmers.

We believe that coordinated computing will come to have profound economic importance. We have searched the scientific literature for important ideas applicable to coordinated computing and have expressed those ideas in an accessible form. We hope that this volume proves to be a sourcebook of ideas for the people who will actually develop coordinated computing systems.

Instructional use

We use this book as the text for a graduate seminar on advanced concepts of programming languages at Indiana University. Our approach is first to develop the concept and implementation of a process scheduler and then to introduce concurrency. We proceed to discuss most of the systems, describing the material in Part 1 as needed.

In that class, the term project is to implement the important semantic aspects of a distributed model or language. The students build their chosen language or model in Scheme [Steele 78]. We use Scheme because its powerful core and extensible nature make it well-suited for language design and implementation. Several Indiana University technical reports describe particular student projects ([Wolynes 80, Dwyer 81]).

Most classes will not be able to cover the entire book in a single term. In our opinion, every class should read this Preface, Chapter 5, and Chapter 19. The instructor should select a representative set of the important systems, covering those systems and the material in Part 1 needed to understand them. For example, one curriculum would include Shared Variables (Chapter 6), Exchange Functions (Chapter 7), Communicating Sequential Processes (Chapter 10), Actors (Chapter 11), Ada (Chapter 14), PLITS (Chapter 15), and the heuristic material in Part 4.

Structural Choices

In writing a book that covers such a broad territory we made many choices about which material to include and how to present it. We know that some of these choices will displease some people; clearly, we could have emphasized different aspects of our subject or described it differently. We have been driven by an interest in (1) the organizational requirements of coherent distributed computing, and, more particularly, (2) the underlying run-time structure of our various systems. We have deliberately avoided providing either formal semantics or correctness proofs. Though such formality has its research virtues, we feel that it would obscure the content of the book for most readers.

Another choice we faced was whether to preserve the original languages of the systems or to invent a new language, describing the systems in Parts 2, 3, and 4 in that language. We chose (by and large) to keep the originals for the following reasons: (1) By seeing the original language, the reader can get a sense of the real structure and pragmatics of each system; (2) The reader who is familiar with the original can pursue that system in the literature without having to translate mentally to a new language. We made exceptions to this rule when the original model did not have a language, the full language was too obscure, or the particular language was undergoing rapid revision. In all such cases we invented an appropriate syntax to describe the system. One of our current research interests is a tractable universal language that can adequately describe the operational behavior of all these systems.

We use several examples in the description of each system. We might have selected a common example (or set of examples) to be used throughout the book. Instead, we vary the examples but use some repeatedly. We made this decision because the systems cover a wide range of facilities; an interesting example for a model is often too low-level an example for a programming language, while an interesting program is often far too complicated to express in most models. Instead, we have a common set of base examples and use some of these examples (and some others) in each section. Since most of these systems are theoretical, we have not been able to debug the programs on implementations.

Our apologies go to those system designers whose systems have been omitted. We have not been trying to write an encyclopedia of distributed systems. Instead, we selected those systems we feel are representative or important and described them in depth. This has, of course, meant that many systems have been left out. Some of these systems are briefly described in the bibliographic annotations of the appropriate chapters.

Acknowledgments

The help of many individuals and organizations has been important in completing this book. We thank Greg Andrews, David Bein, Gary Brooks, Jim Burns, Will Clinger, Gray Clossman, Dan Corkill, Jack Dennis, Scot Drysdale, Jerry Feldman, David Gries, Cordy Hall, Chris Haynes, Carl Hewitt, Tony Hoare, Eugene Kohlbecker, Steve Johnson, John Lamping, Bob Leichner, Egon Loebner, Barbara Liskov, John Lowrance, Nancy Lynch, George Milne, Robin Milner, Fanya Montalvo, John Nienart, Ed Robertson, Vlad Rutenberg, Rich Salter, Bob Scheifler, Avi Silberschatz, Mitch Wand, Peter Wegner, David Wise, and Pam Zave for discussions and comments. We would particularly like to thank Steve Muchnick and Peter Thiesen for their comprehensive comments. This book is much easier to understand and more accurate for the help of these people.

A paper by David MacQueen [MacQueen 79] originally inspired our interest in the subject of distributed models and languages. This interest led to our teaching a seminar. The ideas of that seminar evolved into the concept of coordinated computing and this book.

Several people and organizations have allowed us to quote or adapt their previously-published material. We would like to thank:

Prentice-Hall for permission to adapt Figure 4-1 from Figure 1-5, p. 11 of *Computer Networks* by Andrew S. Tanenbaum, Copyright 1981. Adapted by permission of Prentice-Hall, Inc. Englewood Cliffs, N.J.

Prentice-Hall for permission to adapt Figure 9-6 from *Petri Net Theory and the Modeling of Systems*, by James L. Peterson, p. 67, Copyright 1981. Adapted by permission of Prentice-Hall, Inc. Englewood Cliffs, N.J.

Jack Dennis and Springer-Verlag for permission to adapt Figures 9-8 through 9-14 and 9-16 from Figures 1 through 5 of the article "First Version of a Data Flow Language," by Jack Dennis in *Proceedings, Colloque sur la Programmation*, B. Robinet, ed., Lecture Notes in Computer Science vol. 19, Copyright 1974, Springer-Verlag.

The ACM for permission to adapt Figures 8-1 through 8-5 and 8-9 from the article "Concurrent Processes and Their Syntax," by George Milne and Robin Milner, *JACM*, vol. 26, no 2, April 1979, Copyright 1979, Association for Computing Machinery, Inc., reprinted by permission.

Steven D. Johnson for permission to adapt Figures 12-5 and 12-11 from *Circuits and Systems: Implementing Communication with Streams*, TR 116, Computer Science Department, Indiana University.

Springer-Verlag for permission to adapt Figures 12-6 through 12-10 from Figures 8 and 10 of the article "An Approach to Fair Applicative Multiprogramming" by Daniel P. Friedman and David S. Wise in *The Proceedings of the International Symposium of Concurrent Computation*, Gilles Kahn, ed., Lecture Notes in Computer Science vol. 70, Copyright 1979, Springer-Verlag.

Daniel Corkill for permission to reprint the quote in Exercise 18-1 from *Cooperative Distributed Problem Solving: A New Approach for Structuring Distributed Systems*, by Victor Lesser and Daniel Corkill, TR 78-7, Department of Computer and Information Science, University of Massachusetts, May, 1978.

The ACM for permission to reprint the quote in Chapter 19 from "High level programming for distributed computing," by Jerome Feldman, *Communications of the ACM*, vol. 22, no. 6 (June 1979), Copyright 1979, Association for Computing Machinery, Inc, reprinted by permission.

We thank the Computer Science Department of Indiana University and the Computer Research Center of Hewlett-Packard Laboratories for their support and the use of their facilities. We also thank the National Science Foundation for its support over the years, and Charles Smith and the System Development Foundation for support for a California visit to complete this project.

Myrna Filman, Kim Fletcher, Peg Fletcher, and Nancy Garrett have provided administrative, organizational, and artistic help. The output of a program by John Lamping was the basis of the jacket design. We typeset this book at Stanford University using Don Knuth's TeX system. The expertise of Bob Ballance, David Fuchs, and Rich Pattis greatly facilitated the typesetting process. They all have our gratitude.

And finally, our love and thanks to our wives, Myrna Filman and Mary Friedman, whose emotional support and understanding were crucial for a project of this magnitude.

Robert E. Filman
Daniel P. Friedman

ONE

FOUNDATIONS

Computers are complex systems, difficult to understand, construct, and manipulate. The decentralization and coherence required by coordinated computing exacerbate the usual problems. It should be no surprise that the study of coordinated computing draws on almost all branches of computer science. This generates a predicament for the organization of this book (and, for that matter, the organization of any interdisciplinary book): What fraction of the background material can we assume the readers already know? Four domains bear directly on coordinated computing: theory of computation, programming languages, operating systems, and hardware. Our approach is (1) to superficially develop the theory of computation, describing only those concepts required by the remainder of the material; (2) to assume that the reader is already familiar with programming language issues to the level of an undergraduate course, expounding on programming languages only to specify definitions, emphasize possibly unfamiliar concepts, and clarify frequent misconceptions; (3) to discuss in greater depth the operating systems issues of concurrency and distribution; and, in keeping with the software spirit of the book; (4) to devote only minor attention to the physical machinery (hardware) needed to build a coordinated computing system. Our intention is that a reader familiar with the material in an undergraduate course on programming languages will find Part 1 to be sufficient background to understand all but the most subtle issues raised in the rest of the book. The reader seeking a deeper understanding of the material discussed in this part can explore the references described at the end of each chapter.

In the last chapter of this part, Chapter 5, we discuss the nature of models and languages for coordinated computing. In that chapter we introduce our dimensions of comparison: 12 key decision points in the design of coordinated computing systems.

CHAPTER ONE

COMPUTATION THEORY

1-1 AUTOMATA THEORY

What is a computer? Physically, certain boxes are computers. These boxes frequently have electrically elaborate internals. Abstractly, a *computer* is a transducer that takes inputs, performs some transformations, and produces outputs. The study of abstract computation is *automata theory*. This section is a brief introduction to automata theory.

Ignoring issues of device control and peripherals, there are several different classes of real computers. Readers are certainly familiar with general-purpose mainframes and know many examples of the complex input-output behavior such systems can exhibit. But four-function pocket calculators are also a variety of computer, albeit less powerful. Correspondingly, automata theory recognizes different classes of automata. In this section we describe two important classes of automata, finite-state automata (FSA) and Turing-equivalent automata (metaphorically, the pocket calculators and mainframes of the automata world). We discuss FSA because we use their notation in several places in the book. We discuss Turing machines as an introduction to two important results: (1) Often different architectures are fundamentally equivalent. (2) Even the most powerful systems have limits on what they can compute.

The classical von Neumann computer is a machine that progresses through a discrete cycle of fetching instructions and executing them. Both fetch and execution usually change the machine's state. Sometimes the instruction execution results in receiving input to the machine from the external environment or placing output to the environment from the machine.

Many abstract models of computation share these themes of state, state transition, input, and output. We call such an abstraction an *automaton*. Each automaton is always *in* some state. It progresses from state to state in discrete steps. At each step it reads an input symbol. Based on the automaton's state and the value of that symbol, it then may write an output symbol (or symbols) and enter a new state. Such a step is a state transition. Specifying an automaton is describing the function from ⟨current state, input⟩ pairs to ⟨new state, output⟩ pairs. This specification must also indicate the automaton's initial state and can declare that certain states are *halting states*. An automaton in a halting state takes no further steps.

Limitations on the kind of functions that can describe the automaton divide the possible automata into classes. (This is how the model separates the mainframes from the pocket calculators.) The most important distinction is between finite automata and unbounded automata. Finite automata can be in only a finite number of different states, much as a memory cell in a computer can hold only a finite number of different values. Hence, their description functions are limited to range over that finite set. Unbounded automata can assume an unbounded number of different states, much as one can select an arbitrarily large integer.

As an example of a finite-state automaton, we consider the *triple machine automaton* described in Table 1-1. The triple machine reads a number, encoded in binary, least significant digit first, and writes, in binary, the value of three times that number.

The triple machine has five states: carry0, carry1, carry2, clear, and halt. The machine's alphabet (the symbols it reads and writes) is the set $\{0, 1, E\}$ (where E stands for empty). The table describes the machine's output symbol and new state for each possible combination of its current state and symbol read. Thus, if the machine is in state carry1 and reads a 1, it writes a 0 and goes into

Table 1-1 The triple machine state table

The table shows the ⟨output, new state⟩ pairs for each combination of current state and input for the triple machine.

		Symbol read	
Current state	0	1	E
carry0	⟨0, carry0⟩	⟨1, carry1⟩	⟨ϵ, halt⟩
carry1	⟨1, carry0⟩	⟨0, carry2⟩	⟨1, halt⟩
carry2	⟨0, carry1⟩	⟨1, carry2⟩	⟨0, clear⟩
clear	⟨ϵ, halt⟩	⟨ϵ, halt⟩	⟨1, halt⟩
halt	- - - - - - - - - -	*automata is halted*	- - - - - - - - -

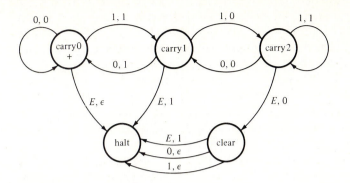

Figure 1-1 The triple machine.

state carry2. We adopt the conventions that reading past the end of the input yields E symbols and that states with output symbol ϵ do not write.

An alternative notation for FSA is the state-transition diagram. Figure 1-1 shows a state-transition diagram of the triple machine. Each node in this diagram represents a state. Each arc is labeled by a pair: the symbol which when read causes that arc to be taken, and the symbol written in taking it. The arc leads to the system's next state. The "+" indicates the initial state. State-transition diagrams are a concise way of describing the behavior of systems that assume a finite number of discrete states, where most states are not potential successors of many other states.

For a typical input, 1 1 0 0 1 E, the machine writes 1 0 0 1 1 1 and halts. Figuratively, we could think of the triple machine as a machine with an input tape and an output tape; it reads the input tape and writes the output tape. Figure 1-2 illustrates this relationship.

If the machine input x is interpreted as a binary number, then the triple machine computes $f(x) = 3x$. Its behavior is *functional* — for each input, the machine writes one specific output and halts. Many automata compute *partial*

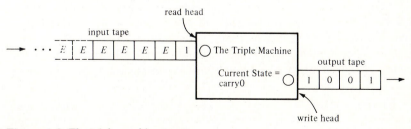

Figure 1-2 The triple machine tapes.

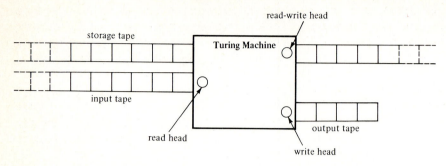

Figure 1-3 Turing machine tapes.

functions. An automaton that computes a partial function does not halt for at least one input. However, for a given input, if the machine halts then it has written a specific output.*

The triple machine is a *finite-state automaton* or *FSA*. That is, it can achieve only a finite number of different internal states (five in our example). As such, it is not an adequate model of computation. For example, no FSA can compute the function $f(x) = x^2$. The deficiency of FSAs lies in their finiteness—interesting functions over unbounded inputs require machines with an unbounded number of different states. An unbounded number of states is usually achieved by adding a storage mechanism to the automata and extending the state-transition function to also rely on the value of storage.

One class of automata with state transitions and storage is represented by the Turing machine, named for its inventor, Alan Turing [Turing 36]. A *Turing machine* is an automaton similar to the FSA described above that also has an unbounded sequential store (conceptually, a *tape*) that can be read, tested, and written. The state transitions of a Turing machine are based not only on the symbol read and the machine's current (internal) state but also on the symbol under the storage tape's read-write head. The possible actions of a Turing machine include not only entering a different (internal) state and writing output but also writing on the storage tape and moving it to the right or left. The values on the tape are part of the state of the Turing machine. Since the tape is unbounded, the machine can assume an unbounded number of different states. Figure 1-3 illustrates the tape relationships of one variant of Turing machine.

In addition to Turing machines, many other models of computation have been proposed. The possible classes of automata form a hierarchy, with the classes higher in the hierarchy able to compute all the functions that the lower

---

* In our description of automata theory, we ignore the many variations of automata that have been proposed. For example, some systems provide multiple input tapes, erasable output, and a large variety of storage mechanisms.

classes can, and some others. Interestingly enough, all attempts to describe a class of automata that maximizes the set of functions computed result in automata that compute the same set. In 1936, Alonzo Church proposed that set is the set of *effectively computable functions.* He showed that any function in the set can be computed by some Turing machine. This assertion is called Church's thesis [Church 36]. We call this class of automata *Turing-equivalent automata.*

What properties distinguish Turing-equivalent automata? Loosely speaking, such automata can (1) perform tests and base actions on the results of those tests, (2) repeat an action until some condition is satisfied, and (3) reference an unbounded storage mechanism, where any particular storage element can be accessed without destroying the information in the rest of the storage.

The class of effectively computable functions includes the familiar arithmetic functions and all functions representable by computer programs. However, not all possible input-output relationships are effectively computable. Two of the important limitations involve the functional nature of automata and the problems of self-reference. Turing-equivalent automata always compute partial functions, yielding at most one output for any input. Systems that have random-number generators or asynchronous elements (like distributed systems) often have a set of possible results for a given input. No single Turing machine can imitate this behavior.

One important theorem about systems, illustrated by automata theory, is that one cannot build a sufficiently complex system that "completely understands itself." For example, no computable function can solve the halting problem. The halting problem requests a function that takes as input (1) the description of any Turing-equivalent automaton and (2) an input for that automaton, and decides if that automaton halts (enters a halt state) when given that input. A function that solves the halting problem is a decision procedure. Decision procedures always yield an answer; they never fail to return or return the equivalent of "I don't know."* The proof of the incomputability of the halting problem relies on encoding the description of programs (such as the state-transition function of a Turing machine) as the input to another program (such as a Turing machine). This is similar to programs that read programs on conventional computers. For example, Pascal programs are strings of characters; strings of characters are acceptable inputs to Pascal programs. Hence, it is possible (and, in fact, common) to write programs whose inputs are themselves (encodings of) programs. (Compilers are examples of such programs.)

Turing proved that no Turing-equivalent automaton can decide the halting problem for Turing-equivalent automata [Turing 36]. Exercise 1-2 requests a

---

* An automaton that merely simulates the behavior of another (Turing-equivalent) automaton is not a decision procedure; if the simulated automaton does not halt, the simulating automaton will not halt either. In general, the simulating automaton cannot distinguish between the indefinite looping of the simulated automaton and a sufficiently complicated state that eventually simplifies and halts.

proof of this theorem. Hoare and Allison present a readable discussion of incomputable functions in their *Computing Surveys* paper [Hoare 72].

We frequently use variants of the word "determinate" in describing programs and automata. A *determinate* automaton traverses one specific path for each possible input. An *indeterminate* automaton has points where it chooses one of several execution paths. This choice is not just a function of the original input—instead, we imagine an indeterminate automaton as sometimes "flipping a coin" and following the path implied by the coin flip. A *nondeterminate* automaton reaches choice points and traverses them all, looking for one to "succeed." Indeterminate automata can therefore produce the "nonfunctionlike" behavior described above. Sometimes a class of nondeterminate automata can compute functions that the corresponding determinate automata cannot; sometimes the nondeterminate and determinate classes are the same. For example, the class of nondeterminate Turing machines computes the same functions as the class of determinate (ordinary) Turing machines, while the class of nondeterminate push-down automata (FSA extended by a stack) computes a larger class of functions than the determinate push-down automata.

In general, when we describe a system as a Turing-equivalent automaton, we wish to emphasize the range of things that the system can do without specifying the details of its internal behavior. This is the same range of abilities that programmers usually ascribe to programs.

1-2 LAMBDA CALCULUS

Automata compute functions. What is a computational theory of functions? One such system is the *lambda calculus*, described by Church in 1941 [Church 41]. Abstractly, the lambda calculus is a string-rewriting system. An expression is a string; the lambda calculus specifies rules for rewriting strings and substrings. At each step, the expression (or some subexpression) is rewritten by one of these rules. The computation terminates when no further rewriting is possible; the resulting expression is the output. As a rewriting system, the lambda calculus expresses computation in a purely syntactic form, without reference to an underlying semantics.

Both logic formulas and programs include the notions of binding and substitution. Quantifiers bind variables in formulas; inference rules allow substitution for these bound variables. In programs, the formal parameters of a procedure are bound in that procedure. One way of interpreting a procedure is to substitute the actual calling parameters in the procedure body and then to evaluate the body itself. Lambda calculus reflects these notions of binding and substitution. Lambda calculus *expressions* are programs. There are three subclasses of expressions: variables, applications, and abstractions. *Variables* are primitive symbols like x, y, and z. An *abstraction* is an expression of the form $\lambda x.E$, where E is itself an expression. This expression binds variable x in expression E. We call variable x the *bound variable* of the expression, and expression E the *body* of the lambda expression. A variable that occurs unbound in an expression is *free* in that expression; variable x is free in the expression $\lambda y.x$.

Syntactically, an *application* is the concatenation of two expressions. Semantically, the first of these expressions is a function and the second an argument to that function. We use parentheses to distinguish $(ab)c$ from $a(bc)$. $(ab)c$ applies function a to the argument b, yielding a new function, which is then applied to c. $a(bc)$ applies function b to the argument c; function a is applied to the result. The first of these may seem odd but (ab) could yield a function; function-valued functions are a key theme of the lambda calculus.

We write the substitution of an expression E for all the free occurrences of a variable x in an expression M as $[E/x]M$.* More formally, $[E/x]M$ is defined as follows:

$[E/x]M \equiv$

(1) For M a variable:
   a. if $M = x \Rightarrow E$
   b. else $\Rightarrow M$

(2) For M an application (PQ):
   $\Rightarrow (([E/x]P)([E/x]Q))$

(3) For M an abstraction $\lambda q.Q$
   a. if $q = x \Rightarrow M$
   b. else if $\neg(\text{occurs-free?}(x, Q) \vee \text{occurs-free?}(q, E))$
      $\Rightarrow \lambda q.[E/x]Q$
   c. else pick a variable y such that
         $\neg(\text{occurs-free?}(y, E) \vee \text{occurs-free?}(y, Q))$
      $\Rightarrow \lambda y.[E/x]([y/q]Q)$

where predicate occurs-free? is

occurs-free?$(v, E) \equiv$

(1)   For E a variable: $\Rightarrow v = E$

(2)   For E an application (PQ): $\Rightarrow$ occurs-free?$(v, P) \vee$ occurs-free?(v, Q)

(3)   For E an abstraction $\lambda q.Q$: $\Rightarrow (v \neq q) \wedge$ occurs-free?(v, Q)

The lambda calculus has two rules for simplifying expressions: α-conversion and β-conversion.

---

* The notation $[E/x]M$ substitutes E for x in M. This parallels the notation for division, where the x's in M are "canceled out."

α-conversion: If $\neg(\text{occurs-free?}(y, M))$ then $\lambda x.M \Rightarrow \lambda y.[y/x]M$

β-conversion: $(\lambda x.M)E \Rightarrow [E/x]M$

The α-conversion rule (the *renaming* rule) states that the bound variable of an abstraction can be changed if the change is made uniformly throughout the body of the abstraction. This corresponds to the programming language idea that the names of the parameters of a procedure can be uniformly changed without affecting the meaning of the program (except when these new names conflict with some other name). The β-conversion rule (the *reduction* rule) encompasses the ideas of application, binding, and substitution. It corresponds to the programming language idea that calling a procedure with some arguments is like executing the body of that procedure with the calling arguments substituted for the procedure's parameters. That is, the application of a function $\lambda x.M$ to an argument E yields the body of function M with every occurrence of x that is free in M replaced by E. This conversion is legal only if it does not cause a free variable of E to become bound in M. Thus, typical sequences of β-conversions are:

(1) $(\lambda x.x)y \Rightarrow y$

(2) $((\lambda x.x)(\lambda y.y))z \Rightarrow (\lambda y.y)z \Rightarrow z$

(3) $(\lambda x.xx)y \Rightarrow yy$

(4) $((\lambda x.\lambda y.xy)(\lambda z.zz))w \Rightarrow (\lambda y.(\lambda z.zz)y)w \Rightarrow (\lambda y.yy)w \Rightarrow ww$

(5) $((\lambda x.\lambda y.xy)(\lambda z.zz))w \Rightarrow (\lambda y.(\lambda z.zz)y)w \Rightarrow (\lambda z.zz)w \Rightarrow ww$

(6) $(\lambda x.xx)(\lambda x.xx) \Rightarrow (\lambda x.xx)(\lambda x.xx) \Rightarrow (\lambda x.xx)(\lambda x.xx) \Rightarrow \ldots$

(7) $((\lambda x.\lambda y.x)w)((\lambda x.xx)(\lambda x.xx)) \Rightarrow (\lambda y.w)((\lambda x.xx)(\lambda x.xx)) \Rightarrow w$

(8) $((\lambda x.\lambda y.x)w)((\lambda x.xx)(\lambda x.xx)) \Rightarrow ((\lambda x.\lambda y.x)w)((\lambda x.xx)(\lambda x.xx)) \Rightarrow \ldots$

Sometimes it is impossible to perform a β-conversion on a lambda expression (and no further α-conversions will allow a β-conversion). Such an expression is in *normal form*. The *Church-Rosser theorem* asserts that if a lambda expression is reduced by two different reduction sequences to normal forms, the two normal forms are the same except for renamings (α-conversions). This implies that if we reach a normal form, it does not matter what path we took to get there. Examples (4) and (5) above are different paths to the same normal form; example (6) has no normal form, and examples (7) and (8) show that it is possible for an expression to have a normal form by one reduction path, but no normal form by another.

The lambda calculus is a formal mathematical notation for describing functions, just as our informal $f(x) = 3x$ is a notation for describing functions. The lambda calculus is particularly useful for describing functions whose values are themselves functions. For example (relaxing the notation slightly), function

$\lambda y.y + 3$ is the function that adds 3 to its argument; function $\lambda x.\lambda y.y + x$ is the function that when applied to 3, yields the "add 3" function (and when applied to 5, yields the "add 5" function).*

Let us tie the lambda calculus back to programming with a final simple example. A standard programming construct is the if-then-else expression. To achieve a similar effect in the lambda calculus, we define two functions, *True* and *False*, each of which, when applied to an argument, returns a function. Each of these functions, when applied to another argument, returns either that argument or the original argument. *True* returns the first argument; *False* the second. That is†

$$True \quad \equiv \quad \lambda x.(\lambda y.x)$$

$$False \quad \equiv \quad \lambda x.(\lambda y.y)$$

Using these functions, we can encode the form "**if** a **then** b **else** c" as "$(ab)c$." More particularly, if we assume the existence of a function to test for equality with 0, then

$$(=0\ 5) \quad = \quad False$$

$$(=0\ 0) \quad = \quad True$$

then function F (where "$-$" is the subtraction function and "$\times$" the multiplication function)

$$F \quad \equiv \quad \lambda x.(((=0\,x)\,1)\,(\times x\,(F\,(-\,x\,1))))$$

computes factorials. More specifically:

$F\,3 \Rightarrow$
$(\lambda x.(((=0\,x)\,1)\,(\times x\,(F\,(-\,x\,1)))))\,3 \Rightarrow$ -- definition of F
$(((=0\,3)\,1)\,(\times 3\,(F\,(-\,3\,1)))) \Rightarrow$ -- β-conversion
$((False\,1)\,(\times 3\,(F\,(-\,3\,1)))) \Rightarrow$ -- value of $(=0\ 3)$
$(((\lambda x.(\lambda y.y))\,1)\,(\times 3\,(F\,(-\,3\,1)))) \Rightarrow$ -- definition of *False*
$((\lambda y.y)\,(\times 3\,(F\,(-\,3\,1)))) \Rightarrow$ -- β-conversion
$(\times 3\,(F\,(-\,3\,1))) \Rightarrow$ -- β-conversion
$(\times 3\,(F\,2)) \Rightarrow$ -- value of $(-\,3\,1)$

---

* Here we use "$+$" as an abbreviation for the addition function. In general, we can let free variables have external meanings, effectively treating them as constants. Stoy [Stoy 77] describes the standard mappings between functions and arithmetic in detail.

† The lambda calculus has mechanisms for associating the body of a function with the name of that function. For recursive functions, one such mechanism is the Y combinator: $Y \equiv \lambda h.(\lambda x.h(xx))(\lambda x.h(xx))$. Since suitable organizations of these mechanisms allow these associations, we use these associations without developing the details. Our $\equiv$ operator may be regarded as syntactic sugar for such expressions.

$(\times 3 \, ((\lambda x.(((=0\,x)\,1)\,(\times x\,(F\,(-\,x\,1)))))\,2)) \Rightarrow$ -- definition of F

$(\times 3 \, (((=0\,2)\,1)\,(\times 2\,(F\,(-\,2\,1))))) \Rightarrow$ -- β-conversion

$(\times 3 \, ((False\,1)\,(\times 2\,(F\,(-\,2\,1))))) \Rightarrow$ -- value of $(=0\,2)$

$(\times 3 \, (((\lambda x.(\lambda y.y))\,1)\,(\times 2\,(F\,(-\,2\,1))))) \Rightarrow$ -- definition of $False$

$(\times 3 \, ((\lambda y.y)\,(\times 2\,(F\,(-\,2\,1))))) \Rightarrow$ -- β-conversion

$(\times 3 \, (\times 2\,(F\,(-\,2\,1)))) \Rightarrow$ -- β-conversion

$(\times 3 \, (\times 2\,(F\,1))) \Rightarrow$ -- value of $(-\,2\,1)$

$(\times 3 \, (\times 2\,((\lambda x.(((=0\,x)\,1)\,(\times x\,(F\,(-\,x\,1)))))\,1)))) \Rightarrow$ -- definition of F

$(\times 3 \, (\times 2\,(((=0\,1)\,1)\,(\times 1\,(F\,(-\,1\,1)))))) \Rightarrow$ -- β-conversion

$(\times 3 \, (\times 2\,((False\,1)\,(\times 1\,(F\,(-\,1\,1)))))) \Rightarrow$ -- value of $(=0\,1)$

$(\times 3 \, (\times 2\,(((\lambda x.(\lambda y.y))\,1)\,(\times 1\,(F\,(-\,1\,1)))))) \Rightarrow$ -- definition of $False$

$(\times 3 \, (\times 2\,((\lambda y.y)\,(\times 1\,(F\,(-\,1\,1)))))) \Rightarrow$ -- β-conversion

$(\times 3 \, (\times 2\,(\times 1\,(F\,(-\,1\,1))))) \Rightarrow$ -- β-conversion

$(\times 3 \, (\times 2\,(\times 1\,(F\,0)))) \Rightarrow$ -- value of $(-\,1\,1)$

$(\times 3 \, (\times 2\,(\times 1\,((\lambda x.(((=0\,x)\,1)\,(\times x\,(F\,(-\,x\,1)))))\,0)))) \Rightarrow$ -- definition of F

$(\times 3 \, (\times 2\,(\times 1\,(((=0\,0)\,1)\,(\times 0\,(F\,(-\,0\,1))))))) \Rightarrow$ -- β-conversion

$(\times 3 \, (\times 2\,(\times 1\,((True\,1)\,(\times 0\,(F\,(-\,0\,1))))))) \Rightarrow$ -- value of $(=0\,0)$

$(\times 3 \, (\times 2\,(\times 1\,(((\lambda x.(\lambda y.x))\,1)\,(\times 0\,(F\,(-\,0\,1)))))))\Rightarrow$ -- definition of $True$

$(\times 3 \, (\times 2\,(\times 1\,((\lambda y.1)\,(\times 0\,(F\,(-\,0\,1))))))) \Rightarrow$ -- β-conversion

$(\times 3 \, (\times 2\,(\times 1\,1))) \Rightarrow$ -- value of $(\times 1\,1)$

$(\times 3 \, (\times 2\,1)) \Rightarrow$ -- value of $(\times 2\,1)$

$(\times 3\,2) \Rightarrow$ -- value of $(\times 3\,2)$

6

1-3 ANALYSIS OF ALGORITHMS

Two important themes run through theoretical computer science, *meaning* (semantics) and *efficiency* (complexity). In the first two sections of this chapter we explored the ideas surrounding the meaning of computations. In this section, we briefly survey some of the ideas relating to the analysis of program efficiency.

The analysis of algorithms is the study of the efficiency of algorithms and programs. Algorithmic analysis divides into two main themes, low-level and high-level analysis. *Low-level analysis* is concerned with "counting" the number of times a particular instruction is executed in a given algorithm or program. For example, we consider the following program segment for performing a bubble sort of an array, a[bottom .. top]:

```
for i := top to bottom − 1 do
    for j := i + 1 to bottom do
        if a[i] > a[j] then
            begin
                temp := a[i];
```

```
    a[i]  := a[j];
    a[j]  := temp
end
```

In this program, the outer **for** loop is executed $(bottom - top)$ times. On the first iteration of that loop, the second **for** loop is executed $(bottom - top)$ times; the second time, $(bottom - top - 1)$, the third time, $(bottom - top - 2)$, and so forth, until the last iteration, when it is done only once. Thus, since

$$n + (n-1) + (n-2) + (n-3) + \cdots + 1 = n(n+1)/2$$

the condition of the **if** statement of this program is executed exactly

$$(bottom - top)(bottom - top + 1)/2$$

times.

Of course, this is a trivial example. A more typical low-level question one might ask is, "How many times is the swapping operation inside the begin-end block executed?" Analysis reveals that in the *best case* (the array already sorted) this algorithm never swaps. In the *worst case* (the array sorted in reverse order), every comparison requires a swap. The *average-case* or *expected* complexity assumes that each possible permutation of the elements of the original array is equally likely. Average-case complexity is usually considerably more difficult to establish than the best- or worst-case complexity. Exercise 1-11 asks how many times the bubble sort algorithm swaps in the average case.

In some sense, counting statement executions measures the *time complexity* of a program. Complexity analysis can also be applied to the use of other resources. A common topic for analysis is *space complexity*—the amount of storage required by a particular program or algorithm. For distributed systems one can also analyze other metrics such as the number of messages sent, the information volume of these messages, or the degree of concurrency an algorithm allows.

High-level analysis of algorithms is concerned not so much with exactly counting statement executions as with approximating an algorithm's asymptotic behavior as its input grows large. For example, if the size of the array in the example is n (where $n = bottom - top + 1$), then the program requires $(n^2 - n)/2$ executions of the **if** statement. This is *on the order of* n^2, written $O(n^2)$. Conceptually, O captures the dominant term in the complexity measure. More formally, a function $g(n)$ is $O(f(n))$ if there is some constant, c, such that for $n > 0$, $g(n) \leq cf(n)$. O is thus a measure of the asymptotic program behavior.

High-level analysis often reveals a lower bound on the work required to do some task, without specifying a particular algorithm for that task. For example, using the techniques of high-level analysis we can show that no sorting algorithm (that relies on only pairwise comparison of elements) can sort a set of n items in the worst case with fewer than $O(n \log_2 n)$ comparisons. This is because a set of n elements can be permuted in $n!$ different ways; each comparison can, at best, exclude half of the possible permutations. We let k be the number of pairwise comparisons in the best sorting algorithm. Thus, k comparisons can distinguish at most 2^k different states. By Stirling's formula $n!$ is approximately

$$n! \approx n^n \sqrt{2\pi n}/e^n$$

Setting 2^k approximately equal to this expression and taking the base two logarithm of each side yields

$$\log_2 2^k \approx \log_2 n^n \sqrt{2\pi n}/e^n$$
$$k \approx n\log_2(n) - n\log_2 e + \log_2\sqrt{2\pi n}$$

As n grows large, the first term of this expression swamps the others. Hence

$$k \approx cn\log n$$

Thus, no pairwise comparison algorithm can sort n objects using fewer than $O(n\log n)$ comparisons. However, this proof does not indicate which algorithms achieve this lower bound (or if it can be achieved at all).*

PROBLEMS

1-1 Show that no FSA can compute $f(x) = x^2$.

1-2 Show that no Turing-equivalent automaton can solve the halting problem. (Hint: Imagine that there were a program, $H(P, I)$, that decides if the "program" P halts when given input I. Consider the result of applying this program H to some variant of itself.)

1-3 Give an algorithm that decides the halting problem for FSAs.

† **1-4** Determining if even a simple program always halts is often a nontrivial task. Prove that for any positive integer n, the following program always halts

```
program nnn1 (n: integer);
begin
      while n ≠ 1 do
          if even(n)
              then n := n/2
              else n := 3 * n + 1
end
```

1-5 Give an example of an indeterminate program or automaton that always yields the same answer.

1-6 Implement the substitution algorithm ($[E/x]M$) for the lambda calculus.

1-7 Why does the α-conversion rule require that y not be free in M?

1-8 Why is the following not a legal α-conversion?

$$\lambda y.\lambda x.xy \Rightarrow \lambda x.\lambda x.xx$$

1-9 Which of the following lambda expressions have normal forms? What are they?

(a) $((\lambda x.\lambda y.xy)(\lambda x.\lambda y.x))w$

(b) $((\lambda x.\lambda y.y)(\lambda x.\lambda y.y))(\lambda x.\lambda y.x)$

(c) $(w(\lambda x.y))z$

(d) $(\lambda x.(xx)x)(\lambda x.x(xx))$

---

* Volume 3 of Knuth [Knuth 73] describes many such algorithms.

1-10 Is there a reduction sequence by which the factorial example does not converge to a normal form?

1-11 How many times, in the average case, does the bubble sort program execute the swapping operation?

REFERENCES

[**Aho 74**] Aho, A. V., J. E. Hopcroft, and J. D. Ullman, *The Design and Analysis of Computer Algorithms*, Addison-Wesley, Reading, Massachusetts (1974). This book is both an excellent text for a first course on algorithmic analysis and a useful reference volume for the practicing computer scientist.

[**Church 36**] Church, A., "An Unsolvable Problem of Elementary Number Theory," *Am. J. Math.*, vol. 58 (1936), pp. 345–363.

[**Church 41**] Church, A., *The Calculi of Lambda Conversion*, Annals of Mathematics Studies 6, Princeton University Press, Princeton, New Jersey (1941).

[**Cook 83**] Cook, S. A., "An Overview of Computational Complexity," *CACM*, vol. 26, no. 6 (June 1983), pp. 400–408. In this Turing award lecture, Cook surveys the history of computational complexity, emphasizing which classes of problems have been solved and which remain open.

[**Hoare 72**] Hoare, C.A.R., and D.C.S. Allison, "Incomputability," *Comput. Surv.*, vol. 4, no. 3 (September 1972), pp. 169–178. "Incomputability" is an entertaining introduction to incomputable functions. Hoare and Allison rely on common sense reasoning and programming more than formal mathematics in their proof of the insolvability of the halting problem.

[**Hopcroft 79**] Hopcroft, J. E., and J. D. Ullman, *Introduction to Automata Theory, Languages and Computation*, Addison-Wesley, Reading, Massachusetts (1979). This book is an excellent introduction to automata theory. It is primarily concerned with the relationship between automata, formal languages, and computability.

[**Knuth 73**] Knuth, D. E., *The Art of Computer Programming*, vol. 3: *Sorting and Searching*, Addison-Wesley, Reading, Massachusetts (1973). *The Art of Computer Programming* is both the encyclopedia of the analysis of algorithms and the book that defined the field.

[**Minsky 67**] Minsky, M., *Computation: Finite and Infinite Machines*, Prentice-Hall, Englewood Cliffs, New Jersey (1967). Minsky develops the machine-like themes of automata theory, including discussion of neurological models such as McCullough-Pitts neural nets.

[**Stoy 77**] Stoy, J. E., *Denotational Semantics: The Scott-Strachey Approach to Programming Language Theory*, M.I.T. Press, Cambridge, Massachusetts (1977). This book is a comprehensive introduction to denotational semantics. Chapter 5 is an excellent introduction to the lambda calculus.

[**Turing 36**] Turing, A., "On Computable Numbers, with an Application to the Entscheidungs-Problem," *Proc. London Math. Soc.*, ser. 2-42 (1936), pp. 230–265. In this paper, Turing describes Turing machines and shows the insolvability of the halting problem.

[**Wegner 68**] Wegner, P., *Programming Languages, Information Structures, and Machine Organization*, McGraw-Hill, New York (1968). Section 3.5 of this comprehensive book is a less formal introduction to the lambda calculus than Stoy's. Wegner presents the lambda calculus as part of a development of the theory and practice of programming languages.

TWO

PROGRAMMING LANGUAGES

We assume the readers of this book are familiar with material covered in a typical undergraduate course on programming languages. Texts for such classes include Pratt [Pratt 75], Organick, Forsythe, and Plummer [Organick 75], and Ledgard and Marcotty [Ledgard 81]. However, not all readers have identical backgrounds. This chapter reviews two aspects of programming languages that are critical for the remainder of our discussion: the formal structure of languages (syntax and semantics) and the practical aspects of programming (pragmatics).

2-1 SYNTAX AND SEMANTICS

Programming languages are defined by their syntax and semantics. The *syntax* of a programming language specifies the strings of symbols that are legal programs. The *semantics* specifies the meaning of each syntactic structure—the action to be taken when that structure is encountered. Thus, the string of characters "3+5" might be a syntactically legal program segment. This string uses *numerals* "3" and "5" and a *plus sign*. Semantically, it might assert that the operation *addition* is to be performed on the *integers* 3 and 5.

Syntax

Perhaps the most useful broad classification of programming languages divides them into imperative and applicative languages. *Imperative languages* are statement- and sequence-oriented. Such languages associate names (variables) with the program state. A programmer can explicitly change the meaning of a name (and the program state) with assignment statements. Input and output are commands, executed like other commands. Repetition is shown by explicit repetitive statements (such as **for** and **while** loops). In general, imperative languages tend towards a complicated syntax, dependent on keywords and punctuation. These languages draw their inspiration from the architecture of the classical von Neumann computer and parallel the state orientation of automata like Turing machines. Fortran, Algol, Cobol, and Pascal are examples of imperative languages.

Applicative languages express programs through function application and binding. These languages associate names with values by function application and parameter binding. This binding provides just a name for the bound value, not the ability to change it. In an applicative system, inputs are the original arguments to the program/function, and the output is the function's result. Repetition is achieved by recursion. By and large, the syntax of applicative languages is more uniform than that of imperative languages. The classical applicative programming language, pure Lisp [McCarthy 60], is almost keyword-free. Lisp uses parentheses instead of keywords to show syntactic forms. Applicative languages are intellectual descendants of the lambda calculus. Pure Lisp and Backus's FP [Backus 78] are examples of applicative systems.*

The difference between imperative and applicative languages is primarily a difference of style. Modern languages frequently blend elements of each. Algol and Pascal permit functional subprograms and recursion; Lisp includes side effects and iteration. Nevertheless, the difference in appearance (though not necessarily substance) between the two forms is striking enough to merit noting. We will see contrasting examples of applicative and imperative styles in the remainder of the book.

Semantics

The syntax of a programming language describes which strings of symbols are legal programs. Programming languages would not be an interesting subject unless these strings could also effect actions. In general, the semantics of a programming language is the set of actions that programs in that language can perform. The semantics of a programming language associates particular actions (or functions) with particular syntactic structures.

---

* FP is actually a special variety of applicative system, a functional language. FP does not have variables or an abstraction operator (like lambda). It therefore does not need a renaming operation.

We can view the semantics of a particular programming language either with respect to computability theory, *formal semantics*, or with respect to the language's underlying conceptual model, *operational semantics*. Computability theory is concerned with the class of functions that can be computed by a given language. Many common languages, like Lisp and Algol, are computationally Turing-equivalent. The distributed languages we study are more computationally powerful than Turing machines, in that they can compute nonfunctional (multivalued) results. Computationally, such systems are equivalent to Turing machines that can also consult an unbounded random-number generator.

Every language designer has a model of the operational primitives that the language manipulates. In conventional computers, such primitives include arithmetic, logical, and input-output operations. Distributed language designers provide, in addition to these primitives, the primitives of the distributed domain. Typically, these primitives manipulate *processes* (automata), *messages* (communications between automata), and other abstractions. The semantics of any particular system defines what can be done with these objects—for example, how processes are created or how the order of message reception can be controlled.

A key theme in current programming language research is proving the correctness of programs. This involves specifying the meaning of each language construct, formalizing the problem statement, and showing that a given program solves the problem. Paralleling the division between imperative and applicative syntactic styles, there are two major themes in program semantics and verification: axiomatic and denotational. *Axiomatic* formalisms lend themselves to statement-oriented languages. These formalisms describe the state of the program execution by logical assertions before and after each statement. *Denotational* formalisms are oriented towards functional application. These formalisms build the meaning of a function application from the meanings of the function's arguments. Wand [Wand 80] includes a brief introduction to these themes. Thorough discussions of axiomatic semantics can be found in Alagic and Arbib [Alagic 78] and Gries [Gries 81], and of denotational semantics in Stoy [Stoy 77] and Gordon [Gordon 79].

2-2 PRAGMATIC STRUCTURES

Since programming languages are (by and large) formally equivalent, why does anyone bother to invent a new language? Language designers create new languages (and new programming structures) to aid in the practical aspects of programming — programming language *pragmatics*. For example, a programming language may provide both linked record structures and arrays. Pragmatically, arrays are used for direct access to fixed-size structures, while linked records are used for serial or logarithmic access to dynamic structures. However, nothing in the syntax or semantics of a language forces those choices. The choice among programming languages is usually one of pragmatics: the constructs of the favored language simplify the creation of correct and efficient programs. Programming languages are themselves inherently pragmatic systems, designed to replace cumbersome assembly language programming.

In this section we consider the pragmatic aspects of three programming language concepts: data abstraction, indeterminacy, and concurrency.

Data Abstraction

Traditionally, programming languages have divided the world into programs and data. Programs are active; programs do things. Data is passive; data has things done to it. In a classical programming language, the ways of describing and using programs are distinct from the ways of describing and using data. There might be several ways of computing a particular function—for example, evaluating an arithmetic expression or looking up the value in a table. Classical programming languages make the choice of implementation obvious to any user.

Data abstraction provides an alternative to the fully visible programming style. Data abstraction merges the notions of program and data. This results in *objects*—program structures that can act both as program and as data. Objects hide the particular implementation of any given behavior from the user. Instead, a data abstraction system presents only an interface to an abstract object.

Typically, the data abstraction interface is just the set of operations that can be executed on an object. If the abstract object has associated storage, these operations often have side effects on that storage. For example, a data abstraction of finite sets would provide functions for testing whether an element is in a set, returning the size of a set, or generating the union of two sets. The data structure used to encode sets remains hidden. The set abstraction can be programmed in many different ways. For example, one can represent a set by a bit vector, a linked list, a hashed array, or even a program. Data abstraction permits the programmer (abstraction implementor) to choose the appropriate method for each individual set. The same abstraction can support several different implementations of sets simultaneously, with the differences invisible to the "user-level" programs. The implementor of a data abstraction can rely on the fact that routines that use an abstract data type have no access to the underlying representation that encodes that abstraction. One can safely modify the underlying implementation as long as it continues to satisfy the abstraction's specifications. Data abstraction is a cornerstone of many modern programming systems.

The earliest programming language implementation of data abstraction was the class mechanism of Simula 67 [Birtwistle 73]. Languages such as Smalltalk [Goldberg 83], CLU [Liskov 77], and Alphard [Shaw 81] have popularized the ideas of associating program with data and hiding implementation. Other programming language constructs that combine program and data include coroutines [Conway 63a], closures (a combination of environment and lambda-expression, see, for example, [Steele 78]), and thunks (a combination of environment and expression, [Ingerman 61]).

Indeterminacy

Most programming languages can describe only sequential, *determinate* programs. That is, given a particular input, the program has only a single possible execution path. *Guarded commands* is a programming language construct, introduced by Edsger Dijkstra [Dijkstra 75], that allows *indeterminacy*—any of several different execution paths may be possible for a given input.

Obviously, the most primitive way of stating, "do one of these statements," would be to have a disjunctive statement to that effect. Guarded commands take this idea one step further. To provide the programmer with greater control over which statements can be executed next, each of the candidate indeterminate actions is "guarded" by a boolean expression. That statement can be selected only if its boolean expression is true. Thus, a guarded command is both a syntax for indeterminacy and a variant of the conditional statement.

More specifically, we build a guard clause from a boolean guard B and a statement action S as

$$B \to S$$

We create a guarded command by joining several guard clauses with []s

$$B_1 \to S_1 \ [] \ B_2 \to S_2 \ [] \ \cdots \ [] \ B_n \to S_n$$

To execute a guarded command, the system finds a boolean expression B_k whose value is "true" and executes the corresponding action S_k. The system simulates parallel guard evaluation.

Guarded commands whose guards are all false are treated differently in different languages. Some systems interpret this as an error, others as cause for exiting a surrounding loop, and still others as blocking the process until one of the guards becomes true. Of course, this last alternative is viable only for concurrent systems.

A program for computing the greatest common divisor of two numbers provides a simple illustration of guarded commands. We assume that a guarded command with false guards exits its surrounding loop. Euclid's algorithm for the greatest common divisor of two positive integers replaces the larger of the two with the difference between the larger and the smaller until the two are equal. As a program with a guarded command, this becomes

```
loop
      x > y   →   x := x − y
   []
      x < y   →   y := y − x
end loop
```

Variants of guarded commands are common in distributed programming languages. This is because guarded commands provide a concise way of reacting to several possible different events without specifying a preferred or predicted order. Thus, a process expecting a message on one of several channels could have reception commands for each joined in a guarded command.

Concurrency

Guarded commands allow one of several alternatives to be executed, without specifying a preference among them. *Concurrent* statements allow several statements to appear to be executed "at the same time." Another name for concurrency is *parallelism*.

Syntactically, the simplest way to declare that several statements are concurrent is to have a structure that asserts, "execute these statements in parallel." A possible (imperative) syntax for concurrency is to wrap the concurrent statements between special delimiters, such as **parbegin** and **parend**:

> **parbegin**
>   statement$_1$:
>   statement$_2$:
>   statement$_3$:
> $\vdots$
>   statement$_n$
> **parend**

An alternative parallel syntax replaces the statement sequencer (;) with a different delimiter ($\|$):

$$\text{statement}_1 \parallel \text{statement}_2 \parallel \text{statement}_3 \parallel \ldots \parallel \text{statement}_n$$

The corresponding applicative syntax would have a function whose arguments are evaluated in parallel. For the moment, we call the agent that executes an arm of a parallel statement a *process*. In Chapter 5, we present a more complete exposition of the notion of process.*

What does it mean to execute several statements concurrently? Each statement is composed of a sequence of indivisible primitives. For example, the expression

$$x := y + z$$

---

* Other ways of indicating parallelism include fork and join [Conway 63b] and systems based on the explicit declaration of processes. One problem with explicit parallel statements is the limitation of the degree of parallelism to the structure of the program text. A second problem is the lack of an explicit joining point for concurrent activities. Fork explicitly creates parallel processes; join uses counters to determine when a set of parallel activities has completed. Most of the languages for distributed computing discussed in Parts 2, 3, and 4 are based on explicit process declaration.

might be composed of the primitive steps

> Load the value of y into local register reg.
> Add the value of z to reg, keeping the result in reg.
> Store the contents of reg in x.

or, more symbolically,

$$
\begin{aligned}
\text{reg} &:= \text{y};\\
\text{reg} &:= \text{reg} + \text{z};\\
\text{x} \ \ &:= \text{reg}
\end{aligned}
$$

One way of viewing the semantics of concurrent statements is to see them as requiring the execution of some permutation of the indivisible primitives of their component statements, restricted only to keeping the primitives of a component in their original order. For example, if statement S is composed of indivisible primitives s_1, s_2, and s_3, and statement T is composed of t_1 and t_2, then the statement

> **parbegin**
> S;
> T
> **parend**

could be executed as any of the permutations

$$
\begin{aligned}
&s_1, \ s_2, \ s_3, \ t_1, \ t_2\\
&s_1, \ s_2, \ t_1, \ s_3, \ t_2\\
&s_1, \ s_2, \ t_1, \ t_2, \ s_3\\
&s_1, \ t_1, \ s_2, \ s_3, \ t_2\\
&s_1, \ t_1, \ s_2, \ t_2, \ s_3\\
&s_1, \ t_1, \ t_2, \ s_2, \ s_3\\
&t_1, \ s_1, \ s_2, \ s_3, \ t_2\\
&t_1, \ s_1, \ s_2, \ t_2, \ s_3\\
&t_1, \ s_1, \ t_2, \ s_2, \ s_3\\
&t_1, \ t_2, \ s_1, \ s_2, \ s_3
\end{aligned}
$$

However, s_2 cannot be executed before s_1. The permutation mechanism hints at a critical postulate for concurrency: We cannot make any assumptions about the relative speeds of concurrent processes. One concurrent process may be arbitrarily (though not infinitely) quicker than another. Worse yet, the processes may be synchronized in lock step, so algorithms cannot be based on the possible occurrence of an irregular ordering.

Treating the semantics of concurrency as a permutation of events is an assumption about computational metaphysics. It asserts that events do not happen simultaneously (or, similarly, that actions can be divided into atomic primitives). A world that allowed simultaneity would need to develop a semantics of simultaneous actions. In real computers, hardware arbiters minimize the probability of simultaneous events. Nevertheless, such arbiters can never completely exclude the possibility of failure from virtually simultaneous occurrences.

PROBLEMS

2-1 Show how conventional conditional statements could be replaced by guarded commands.

2-2 If statement M is composed of m primitive steps and statement N is composed of n primitive steps, how many different ways can the concurrent statement M‖N be executed?

REFERENCES

[**Alagic 78**] Alagic, S., and M. A. Arbib, *The Design of Well-Structured and Correct Programs*, Springer-Verlag, New York (1978). This book presents the idea of integrating top-down development and correctness in the program development process.

[**Backus 78**] Backus, J., "Can Programming be Liberated from the von Neumann Style? A Functional Style and Its Algebra of Programs," *CACM*, vol. 21, no. 8 (August 1978), pp. 613–641. In this paper, the creator of Fortran describes a style of programs based on functional combination. This was Backus's Turing award lecture.

[**Birtwistle 73**] Birtwistle, G. M., O.-J. Dahl, B. Myhrhaug, and K. Nygaard, *Simula Begin*, Auerbach, Philadelphia (1973). This book is an excellent introduction to Simula. Simula was originally designed as an extension of Algol 60 for systems simulation. Simula is important because its class mechanism is the intellectual ancestor of the current work on abstract data types and object-oriented programming.

[**Conway 63a**] Conway, M. E., "Design of a Separable Transition-Diagram Compiler," *CACM*, vol. 6, no. 7 (July 1963), pp. 396–408. This was the first article to describe coroutines.

[**Conway 63b**] Conway, M. E., "A Multiprocessor System Design," *Proceedings AFIPS 1963 Fall Joint Computer Conference*, AFIPS Conference Proceedings vol. 27, Spartan Books, New York (1963), pp. 139–146. Conway presents the fork and join primitive.

[**Dijkstra 75**] Dijkstra, E. W., "Guarded Commands, Nondeterminacy, and Formal Derivation of Programs," *CACM*, vol. 18, no. 8 (August 1975), pp. 453–457. In this paper Dijkstra introduced guarded commands and provided a formal definition of their meaning. Dijkstra allowed guarded clauses in two different contexts, bracketed by **if, fi** pairs to indicate a single test and by **do, od** pairs for a loop. The **if** construct would signal an error if it encountered all false guards, while the **do** construct interpreted this as the exit condition of the loop.

[**Goldberg 83**] Goldberg, A., and D. Robson, *Smalltalk-80: The Language and its Implementation*, Addison-Wesley, New York (1983). Smalltalk is a programming language based on the metaphor of communicating objects. This book is not only a comprehensive description of the Smalltalk language but also a discussion of implementation issues involved in building Smalltalk systems.

[**Gordon 79**] Gordon, M.J.C., *The Denotational Description of Programming Languages*, Springer-Verlag, New York (1979). This book is a good introduction to the use of denotational semantics for proving properties of programs.

[**Gries 81**] Gries, D., *The Science of Programming*, Springer-Verlag, New York (1981). Gries develops axiomatic correctness and ties it to program development. He argues that these mechanisms are the basis of scientific principles for program development.

[**Ingerman 61**] Ingerman, P., "Thunks," *CACM*, vol. 4, no. 1 (January 1961), pp. 55–58. A thunk is a pair composed of a code pointer and a static-chain (environment) pointer. Thunks are used in imperative languages such as Algol for both call-by-name and for passing labels and functions as arguments.

[**Ledgard 81**] Ledgard, H., and M. Marcotty, *The Programming Language Landscape*, Science Research Associates, Chicago (1981). Ledgard and Marcotty develop the principles of programming language design by studying a series of mini-languages that illustrate particular themes.

[**Liskov 77**] Liskov, B., A. Snyder, R. R. Atkinson, and J. C. Schaffert, "Abstraction Mechanisms in CLU," *CACM*, vol. 20, no. 8 (August 1977), pp. 564–576. CLU is a programming language developed around the theme of abstract data types. CLU was one of the first languages to separate the specification of a data type from its implementation.

[**McCarthy 60**] McCarthy, J., "Recursive Functions of Symbolic Expressions and Their Computation by Machine," *CACM*, vol. 3, no. 4 (April 1960), pp. 184–195.

[**Organick 75**] Organick, E. I., A. I. Forsythe, and R. P. Plummer, *Programming Language Structures*, Academic Press, New York (1975). An introduction to programming languages that develops the run-time structure of systems based on the contour model.

[**Pratt 75**] Pratt, T. W., *Programming Languages: Design and Implementation*, Prentice-Hall, Englewood Cliffs, New Jersey (1975). Pratt first develops the concepts of programming languages and then describes several major languages in terms of these concepts.

[**Shaw 81**] Shaw, M. (ed.), *Alphard: Form and Content*, Springer-Verlag, New York (1981). Shaw presents a collection of research papers and reports on Alphard. Alphard is a language based on abstract data types.

[**Steele 78**] Steele, G. L., Jr., and G. J. Sussman, "The Revised Report on SCHEME, a Dialect of LISP," Memo 452, Artificial Intelligence Laboratory, M.I.T., Cambridge, Massachusetts (January 1978). Scheme is a language that features a lexically scoped Lisp with functions and continuations as first-class objects.

[**Stoy 77**] Stoy, J. E., *Denotational Semantics: The Scott-Strachey Approach to Programming Language Theory*, M.I.T. Press, Cambridge, Massachusetts (1977).

[**Wand 80**] Wand, M., *Induction, Recursion, and Programming*, North Holland, New York (1980). This book is an elementary introduction to the "mathematics" of computer science. After developing the theory of sets and functions Wand presents both a denotational semantics for proving the correctness of Lisp-like programs and an axiomatic semantics for proving the correctness of imperative programs.

THREE

CONCURRENCY

The last chapter described linguistic mechanisms for specifying concurrency. However, naively written concurrent programs produce unexpected results. In this chapter, we introduce the problem of resource conflict, describe synchronization mechanisms to resolve that conflict, and present several problems that illustrate synchronization and control issues.

3-1 RESOURCE CONFLICT

Unstructured concurrent computation produces unexpected results. For example, even the simplest of programming rules, "after assigning a value to a variable, that variable has that value (until that program makes some other assignment)," is not true of concurrent systems. We illustrate this difficulty with a procedure to add a deposit to "bank account" (variable) **MyAccount**:

```
procedure deposit (var amount: integer);
begin
     MyAccount := MyAccount + amount;
end
```

Suppose we try to make two deposits at the same time, as might arise from two simultaneous transactions in different branches of the bank. That is, we imagine that we have $1000 in **MyAccount**, and we execute

```
parbegin
     deposit (100);
```

```
     deposit (50)
parend
```

This is equivalent to executing, in parallel, the statements

```
parbegin
     MyAccount := MyAccount + 100;
     MyAccount := MyAccount + 50
parend
```

But neither of these assignment statements is itself primitive. Instead, incrementing an account is a series of operations such as

```
reg          := MyAccount;
reg          := reg + deposit;
MyAccount := reg
```

where reg is a register internal to the process (equivalent to a hardware register). We assume that each concurrent statement in the **parbegin** has its own register. That is, the parallel deposits expand into the primitives

Deposit 100	Deposit 50
reg1 := MyAccount;	reg2 := MyAccount;
reg1 := reg1 + 100;	reg2 := reg2 + 50;
MyAccount := reg1	MyAccount := reg2

The semantics of concurrent execution allows any possible permutation of primitive elements. One legal execution path is

Deposit100	Deposit50
reg1 := MyAccount;	•
MyAccount=1000 and reg1=1000	•
reg1 := reg1 + 100;	•
MyAccount=1000 and reg1=1100	•
•	reg2 := MyAccount;
•	*MyAccount=1000 and reg2=1000*
MyAccount := reg1	•
MyAccount=1100 and reg1=1100	reg2 := reg2 + 50;
•	*MyAccount=1100 and reg2=1050*
•	MyAccount := reg2
•	*MyAccount=1050 and reg2=1050*
•	

Here the vertical axis represents the progression of time; we see the interleaving of concurrent primitives in the alternation of the statements. This execution path shows that our program intended to deposit $150, but the value of the account has increased by only $50. The problem is that the bank account has been improperly shared. Each deposit function needs exclusive control of the bank account long enough to complete its transaction. Our program does not ensure this mutual exclusion.

In general, a *resource* in a computer system is something needed to complete a task. Resources can be physical objects, such as processors or peripherals, or software objects, such as memory locations, buffers, or files. Resources are shared, in that different concurrent activities can use them at different times, but resources are also private, in that there is an upper bound on the number of processes that can use a particular resource simultaneously. Often this bound is only a single process. For example, at some point many different processes may want to change the resource **MyAccount**. However, they should change it sequentially, one at a time. A concurrent activity is in the *critical region* of a resource when it is modifying or examining that resource. Thus, each of our processes is in a critical region of **MyAccount** when it executes the statement **MyAccount** := **MyAccount** + **Deposit**. The problem of preventing processes from executing simultaneously in critical regions over the same resource is the *mutual exclusion problem*. In general, processes that order their activities to communicate and not interfere with each other are *synchronized*. Synchronization includes aspects of cooperation as well as of serialized access to shared resources. Mutual exclusion is thus one facet of synchronization.

A process that is prevented from entering a critical region because another process is already in its critical region is *blocked*. If a set of processes are mutually blocked, that set is *deadlocked*. In a deadlocked set, no process can make further progress without external intervention. This occurs when several processes each need a resource to complete their tasks and the instances of that resource have been divided so as to preclude any process from getting enough to finish. For example, a system may have two tape drives, $drive_a$ and $drive_b$. Both $process_1$ and $process_2$ require two drives (perhaps to copy tapes); $process_1$ and $process_2$ run concurrently. We imagine them to have the program schema shown in Figure 3-1. At statement (3), $process_1$ is blocked; it needs $process_2$ to release $drive_b$ before it can continue. Similarly, $process_2$ is blocked at statement (4) because $process_1$ has possession of $drive_a$. The system halts, deadlocked.

Deadlock implies that all processes in a set are unable to accomplish useful work. A particular process *starves* if it is stuck, even though other processes continue to progress. We illustrate starvation by modifying our tape drive example to three processes and only a single drive. If after using the drive, $process_1$ "passes" it to $process_2$ and $process_2$ back to $process_1$, they can keep it to themselves, starving $process_3$. In reality, starvation is more often the result of timing and priority relationships of programs. For example, $process_3$ may starve if $process_1$ and $process_2$ both have a large appetite for the tape drive and the system gives higher priority to their requests.

	Process$_1$	Process$_2$
(1)	**request** drive$_a$	•
(2)	•	**request** drive$_b$
(3)	**request** drive$_b$	•
(4)	•	**request** drive$_a$
	the rest of process$_1$'s program	*the rest of process$_2$'s program*
(5)	**release** drive$_a$	•
(6)	•	**release** drive$_b$
(7)	**release** drive$_b$	•
(8)	•	**release** drive$_a$

Figure 3-1 Deadlocking resource demands.

3-2 SYNCHRONIZATION MECHANISMS

In 1968, Dijkstra published a classic paper on synchronization, "Co-operating Sequential Processes" [Dijkstra 68]. In that paper, he developed a software solution to the mutual exclusion problem. We follow his derivation in this section.

Dijkstra began by simplifying the general mutual exclusion problem to the mutual exclusion of two processes, process$_1$ and process$_2$. Process$_1$ and process$_2$ cycle through a loop; in each cycle each enters a critical region. Thus, the general schema for each process is

process$_i$:
    L$_i$: *critical region preparation;*
       critical region;
       critical region cleanup;
       concurrent region;
       goto L$_i$

The mutual exclusion problem is to ensure that only one process is ever executing in its critical region at any time. The processes communicate by reading and writing shared variables. We assume that reading and writing a variable are each primitive (indivisible) operations.

A first attempt at a solution of this problem has the processes take turns entering their critical regions. We have a variable, turn, that indicates which process is to enter next. When a process wants to enter its critical region, it waits until turn has its process identifier.

var turn: integer;
begin
    turn := 1;

```
parbegin
    process1:
        begin
            L1: if turn = 2 then goto L1;
                critical region₁
                turn := 2;
                concurrent region₁
                goto L1
        end;
    process2:
        begin
            L2: if turn = 1 then goto L2;
                critical region₂
                turn := 1;
                concurrent region₂
                goto L2
        end
    parend
end.
```

One way a blocked process can recognize an event is to execute a loop, looking at each iteration for the event. Such a process is said to be *busy waiting*, or *spinning*. Statements **L1** and **L2** implement busy waiting.

This solution ensures mutual exclusion—the two processes are never in their critical regions simultaneously. However, we have achieved mutual exclusion at the cost of synchronization—the processes are sure to enter critical regions in the order 1, 2, 1, 2, 1, 2, ... This synchronization is unpleasant; it should be possible to achieve more concurrency than this lockstep allows. The synchronization implied by this solution reduces the speed of each process to that of the slower (and if generalized to several processes would reduce the speed of every process to that of the slowest). To preclude such solutions, we impose another restriction on acceptable programs: "Stopping one process in its concurrent region does not lead to the other process blocking." We continue to assume that processes do not stop either in critical regions or in the preparation or cleanup for critical regions.

This leads us to the second solution. In this solution, we give each process a flag to show that it is in its critical region. To enter its critical region, a process checks if the other process is flying its flag, and, if not, raises its own and enters its critical region. The program to implement this algorithm is as follows:

```
var in_cr1, in_cr2: boolean;
begin
    in_cr1 := false;
    in_cr2 := false;
```

```
parbegin
    process1:
        begin
            L1: if in_cr2 then goto L1;
                in_cr1 := true;
                critical region₁
                in_cr1 := false;
                concurrent region₁
                goto L1
        end;
    process2:
        begin
            L2: if in_cr1 then goto L2;
                in_cr2 := true;
                critical region₂
                in_cr2 := false;
                concurrent region₂
                goto L2
        end;
    parend
end.
```

This solution avoids the pitfall of synchronization. However, it does have a flaw—it fails to ensure mutual exclusion. Each process can find the other's flag lowered, raise its own, and enter its critical region. More specifically, the sequence

Process$_1$	Process$_2$
if in_cr2 **then** ...	•
•	**if** in_cr1 **then** ...
in_cr1 := true	•
•	in_cr2 := true
critical region$_1$	•
•	*critical region*$_2$

finds both processes simultaneously executing their critical regions.

Reversing the acts of checking the other process's flag and raising one's own ensures mutual exclusion. This gives us the following program:

```
var in_cr1, in_cr2: boolean;
begin
    in_cr1 := false;
    in_cr2 := false;
```

```
    parbegin
        process1:
            begin
                L1:    in_cr1 := true;
                BW1: if in_cr2 then goto BW1;
                       critical region₁
                       in_cr1 := false;
                       concurrent region₁
                       goto L1
            end;
        process2:
            begin
                L2:    in_cr2 := true;
                BW2: if in_cr1 then goto BW2;
                       critical region₂
                       in_cr2 := false;
                       concurrent region₂
                       goto L2
            end;
    parend
end.
```

This solution is safe. A process about to enter its critical region knows: (1) The other process's flag is down. Hence that process is not near its critical region. (2) Its own flag is flying. Hence the other process will not enter its critical region. Unfortunately, this program is susceptible to deadlock. Each process raises its flag and then loops, waiting for the other to lower its flag. Temporally, this is

Process$_1$	Process$_2$
in_cr1 := true	•
•	in_cr2 := true
BW1: **if** in_cr2 **then goto** BW1	•
•	BW2: **if** in_cr1 **then goto** BW2
BW1: **if** in_cr2 **then goto** BW1	•
•	BW2: **if** in_cr1 **then goto** BW2
BW1: **if** in_cr2 **then goto** BW1	•
•	BW2: **if** in_cr1 **then goto** BW2
⋮	⋮

The problem is that the processes have been too stubborn about keeping their flags flying. If a process cannot enter its critical region, it needs to back off, lowering its flag before trying again. This brings us to our penultimate program:

```
var in_cr1, in_cr2: boolean;
begin
      in_cr1 := false;
      in_cr2 := false;
      parbegin
          process1:
                begin
                    L1: in_cr1 := true;
                        if in_cr2 then
                        begin
                            in_cr1 := false;
                            goto L1
                        end;
                        critical region₁
                        in_cr1 := false;
                        concurrent region₁
                        goto L1
                end;
          process2:
                begin
                    L2: in_cr2 := true;
                        if in_cr1 then
                        begin
                            in_cr2 := false;
                            goto L2;
                        end;
                        critical region₂
                        in_cr2 := false;
                        concurrent region₂
                        goto L2
                end;
      parend
end.
```

This solution *almost* works. By lowering its flag, each process gives the other a chance to succeed. However, it is possible that the two processes might follow the sequence

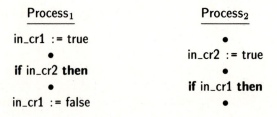

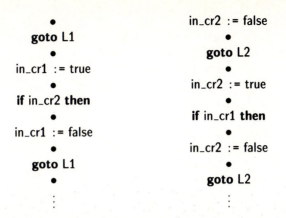

```
        •                          in_cr2 := false
      goto L1                             •
        •                            goto L2
  in_cr1 := true                          •
        •                          in_cr2 := true
  if in_cr2 then                          •
        •                          if in_cr1 then
  in_cr1 := false                         •
        •                          in_cr2 := false
      goto L1                             •
        •                            goto L2
        ⋮                                 ⋮
```

Is such synchronization possible? In systems composed of identical elements, it may even be likely, so we must reject this solution too. This situation, in which a system's processes are not blocked but still fail to progress, is called *livelock*.

Given these constraints, a correct solution to the mutual exclusion problem is surprisingly difficult to program. Thomas Dekker proposed the first such solution. His solution combines elements of the turn variable of the first program with the flags of the later programs. The key idea is to detect potential "after you" situations (when a process has its own flag raised, and sees the other process's flag) and to resolve them by giving priority to the process marked by the turn variable. After each critical region, a process sets the turn variable to the identity of the other process, giving the other priority if there is a conflict the next time around. Unlike the last solution, the processes ignore this priority if there is no conflict.

```
var in_cr1, in_cr2: boolean;
    turn: integer;
begin
    turn    := 1;
    in_cr1 := false;
    in_cr2 := false;
    parbegin
        process1:
            begin
                L1:  in_cr1 := true;
                PW1: if in_cr2 then
                        begin
                            if turn = 1 then goto PW1;
                            in_cr1 := false;
                            BW1: if turn = 2 then goto BW1;
                            goto L1
                        end;
```

```
                    critical region₁
                    turn := 2;    -- give the other process priority
                    in_cr1 := false;
                    concurrent region₁
                    goto L1
        end;
    process2:
        begin
            L2:    in_cr2 := true;
            PW2:   if in_cr1 then
                begin
                    if turn = 2 then goto PW2;
                    in_cr2 := false;
                    BW2: if turn = 1 then goto BW2;
                    goto L2;
            end;
            critical region₂
            turn := 1;
            in_cr2 := false;
            concurrent region₂
            goto L2
        keywordend;
    parend
end.
```

This progression ought to leave the reader with some feeling for the additional complications inherent in programming concurrent systems. We must not only ensure that a particular segment of program is correct, but also that no concurrent activity can jeopardize it. Dekker's solution solves the problem, but the solution itself is complicated and unappealing. Because it is too cumbersome for practical purposes, the search began for alternative mechanisms.*

One reason the problem is difficult is that the actions of reading and writing shared storage are not indivisible primitives. This led to the idea of an instruction that would both read and write storage as a single action. The TS (test-and-set) operation on the IBM/360 was an early implementation of this idea. The instruction both stored a value in a memory location and returned the previous value from that location. To processes running on the machine, the instruction appeared indivisible.

Solutions using test-and-set have the disadvantage of requiring a process waiting for a resource to loop, checking to see when the resource is free. Instead, it would be better to have a primitive that would combine the precise intention

---

* Peterson has demonstrated a simpler solution of the mutual exclusion problem. We present his algorithm in Chapter 6.

of both protecting a resource and waking a waiting process. In "Co-operating Sequential Processes," Dijkstra introduced the semaphore for just this purpose [Dijkstra 68]. A *semaphore* is an (abstract) object with two operations, one to claim the resource associated with the semaphore and the other to release it. The claiming operation on a semaphore s is **P**; the releasing operation is **V**. If the semaphore claimed is busy, the requesting process is blocked until it is free. When another process executes the **V** on that semaphore, a blocked process is released and allowed access to the resource.

Semaphores are typically implemented as nonnegative integers. Executing **V**(s) increments s; executing **P**(s) tries to decrement s. If s is positive, this action succeeds; if it is zero, then **P** waits until it is positive. Instead of a busy wait, the blocked process can be added to a set of processes waiting on that semaphore. These incrementing and decrementing operations must be indivisible. The initial value of s is the number of processes that can simultaneously access the resource. A *binary semaphore* allows only one process to control the resource at any time. A semaphore variable whose initial value is one acts as a binary semaphore. A program for mutual exclusion using semaphores is as follows:

```
var mutex: semaphore;
begin
     mutex := 1;
     parbegin
         process1:
             begin
                 L1: P(mutex);
                     critical region₁
                     V(mutex);
                     concurrent region₁
                     goto L1
             end;
         process2:
             begin
                 L2: P(mutex);
                     critical region₂
                     V(mutex);
                     concurrent region₂
                     goto L2
             end;
     parend
end.
```

This solution has the additional advantage of being able to enforce the mutual exclusion of any number of processes without modification.

Semaphores were a conceptual advance over setting and testing shared memory but failed to provide additional structuring to exclusion and sharing. Other proposed primitives for resource control include locks [Dennis 66] and monitors [Hoare 74]. Locks abstract the simple idea of a resource "lock" with two operations, lock and unlock. A process trying to lock an already locked lock spins until it is unlocked. Monitors combine both data abstraction and mutual exclusion into a single sharable object; access to that object is not only serialized but is also abstract. In Section 13-1, we discuss Concurrent Pascal, a language that uses monitors.

Synchronization mechanisms like semaphores embody the notion of indivisible, primitive actions. Often an action should seem to be indivisible, but is more complex than a single primitive. An *atomic action* is a compound computation that is distributed over time or location, but cannot be externally decomposed into more primitive actions. Following Leslie Lamport, we use angle brackets ($\prec\succ$) to delimit atomic actions [Lamport 80]. Thus, the notation

$$\prec A;\ B;\ C \succ$$

indicates that A, B, and C are to be executed sequentially and atomically.

3-3 ILLUSTRATIVE EXAMPLES

Earlier in this chapter we discussed the issues involved in concurrent access to a bank account variable. We did not select this example as an illustration of what to do if you ever find yourself programming for Chase Manhattan. Instead, the concept of a shared resource with state that can be tested and set is a common theme in programming concurrent systems. The metaphor of a bank account is just an instance of this theme.

Several such "metaphorical" examples have been proposed that summarize particular problems associated with resource control and concurrency. We use five of these as illustrative examples in Parts 2, 3, and 4. We have already described two of them, shared storage and semaphores. We call the shared storage problem the register problem. *Registers* have two operations, one that stores a value in the register and another that returns the last value stored. Of course, semaphores also have two operations, **P** and **V**. A process executing **P** on a depleted semaphore is blocked or refused until another process replenishes that semaphore with a **V**.

Our three other standard examples are the readers-writers, dining philosophers, and producer-consumer buffer problems.

Readers and writers Courtois, Heymans, and Parnas described the readers-writers problem in 1971 [Courtois 71]. This problem illustrates a variety of mutual exclusion that is more complex than simple semaphorelike mutual exclusion but nevertheless realistic. The readers-writers problem posits two classes of users of a resource, readers and writers. Readers *read* the resource and writers *write* it. Readers can share access to the resource. That is, several readers can be reading the resource simultaneously. Writers require exclusive control of the resource. When a writer is writing, no other process can be reading or writing.

The multiple-readers/single-writer pattern of resource control corresponds to a desirable way of accessing shared databases. This pattern allows many processes to be simultaneously reading the database, but restricts database updates to a single process at a time. Many database update transactions involve making several changes in the database. A process that reads the database during an update might obtain an inconsistent view of the data.*

Solutions of the readers-writers problem should maximize concurrent access to the database without starving either readers or writers. Solutions usually allow readers to read until a writer wants to write. Additional readers are then blocked. When the currently reading readers have finished, the system allows the writer to write and then unblocks the waiting readers. The process is then repeated.

Dining philosophers The bank account example illustrated mutual exclusion of two processes and a single resource. Of course, computing systems can have many processes and many resources, with many different patterns of resource exclusion. The readers-writers problem is an example of one such pattern. Dijkstra's dining philosophers problem describes another, more fanciful, exclusion regime [Dijkstra 72a]. Five philosophers live an existence centered around two activities: thinking and eating. In a room is a circular table and in the middle of the table, a serving platter of spaghetti. Each philosopher has her own place at the table; at that place is a plate. A fork lies between each pair of plates. A philosopher's life is a simple one. She thinks. Becoming hungry, she enters the room and takes her place at the table. Since eating spaghetti requires two forks, she picks up first one fork and then the other. She then fills her plate with spaghetti and eats. Satiated, she returns the forks to their places, leaves the room, and resumes thinking, eventually repeating the cycle. Figure 3-2 shows the dining arrangement of the philosophers.

The reader should understand that these philosophers are stubborn characters. Once having become hungry, entered the room, and acquired a fork, they do not relinquish that fork until after they have eaten. And, of course, self-respecting philosophers would rather starve than eat with only one fork.

Given these rules, all five philosophers can become hungry at roughly the same time, enter the room, sit, pick up one fork (say, their left forks), and wait, interminably, for the other fork to become free. At this point, the philosophers are deadlocked and (literally) starve.

A solution to the dining philosophers problem is a program that models this situation. The philosophers are usually modeled as processes. Processes or data structures may be used to model the behavior of the forks and the dining room.

---

* We discuss control algorithms for database systems in Chapter 17.

Figure 3-2 The dining philosophers.

Each philosopher should have virtually the same program, differing only in the philosopher's seat and fork assignments. A deadlock-free solution to the dining philosophers problem is one in which some philosopher eventually eats — that is, some work gets done. A starvation-free solution is one in which no philosopher starves if she waits long enough to obtain forks. Of course, a deadlock-free solution is a more complex program than the simple modeling problem and a starvation-free solution is still more complex.*

The dining philosophers problem reflects the common need of real systems for multiple resources to accomplish their tasks. If five programs share five tape drives and each needs two drives, then an organization that gives one tape drive to each program can starve or deadlock the computer system as easily as poor dining room management can starve philosophers.

---

* Variations on the dining philosopher's problem include generalizing the number of philosophers, changing the possible actions of a hungry, forkless philosopher, and, more whimsically, substituting chopsticks and Chinese food for forks and spaghetti.

Buffers Often two processes are coupled in a "producer-consumer" relationship: the producer process generates data that is used by the consumer process. For example, a producer process might generate output to be printed, while a line printer (consumer) process might take that output and drive the printer to write it.

Clearly, two such processes can be organized procedurally. When the producer has a ready datum it can call the consumer, as a procedure, to handle it. The consumer can return an acknowledgment to the producer when it finishes processing. (Or, conversely, the consumer could call the producer for the next data item.) However, this architecture leaves the producer idle while the consumer computes and the consumer idle while the producer computes. That is, this organization yields no concurrency.

We can obtain concurrency by using an (unbounded) buffer. When the producer has a ready datum, it sends it to the buffer. When the consumer wants the next datum, it asks the buffer for it. If the buffer is empty, the buffer either delays the consumer or informs it of the lack of data. The producer is never slowed; it can always be generating data and adding it to the buffer. The buffer acts as a queue of unconsumed data.

The producer-consumer buffer problem can be generalized to multiple producers and consumers. For example, a system may have several producer processes that intermittently create output for printing and several printer processes capable of consuming that output and creating listings. Producers do not care which printer prints their output. A buffer between the producers and the consumers allows not only the concurrency of data generation and printing but also the delegation of printing tasks independent of printer identity.

We have described an unbounded producer-consumer buffer, where producers never need to be concerned about the availability of buffer space for their output. The bounded producer-consumer problem assumes that the buffer can hold only a fixed number of data items. Solving the bounded buffer problem requires not only an appropriate response to a consumer when the buffer is empty but also an appropriate response to a producer when the buffer is full. A producer that tries to insert an element in a full buffer must be either rejected or delayed until space becomes available.

PROBLEMS

3-1 Generalize Dekker's solution to the mutual exclusion problem from 2 processes to n processes.

3-2 Dekker's solution precludes deadlock. Does it also preclude starvation?

3-3 In Dekker's solution, what happens to the system if a process fails while executing in its critical region? What happens if it fails while executing the code for the critical region preparation or cleanup?

3-4 Program mutual exclusion using the test-and-set operation.

3-5 Program the readers-writers problem using semaphores.
3-6 Program the dining philosophers problem using semaphores.
3-7 Program a bounded producer-consumer buffer using semaphores.

REFERENCES

[**Courtois 71**] Courtois, P. J., F. Heymans, and D. L. Parnas, "Concurrent Control with 'Readers' and 'Writers,'" *CACM*, vol. 14, no. 10 (October 1971), pp. 667–668. Courtois et al. describe and solve the readers-writers problem. Their solution uses semaphores.

[**Dennis 66**] Dennis, J. B., and E. C. Van Horn, "Programming Semantics for Multipro-grammed Computations," *CACM*, vol. 9, no. 3 (March 1966), pp. 143–155. Dennis and Van Horn propose the mutual exclusion mechanism of explicit primitives that lock and unlock a variable.

[**Dijkstra 68**] Dijkstra, E. W., "Co-operating Sequential Processes," in F. Genuys (ed.), *Programming Languages: NATO Advanced Study Institute*, Academic Press, London (1968), pp. 43–112. This paper is an excellent exposition on the difficulties of concurrent pro-gramming. Starting from simple ideas about concurrency, Dijkstra develops the ideas of Dekker's mutual exclusion algorithm and semaphores. He then generalizes the mutual exclusion problem to multiple processes.

[**Dijkstra 72a**] Dijkstra, E. W., "Hierarchical Ordering of Sequential Processes," in C.A.R. Hoare, and R. H. Perrott (eds.), *Operating Systems Techniques*, Academic Press, New York (1972), pp. 72–93. This paper is an introduction to mutual exclusion, including a descrip-tion of the dining philosophers problem.

[**Hoare 74**] Hoare, C.A.R., "Monitors: An Operating System Structuring Concept," *CACM*, vol. 17, no. 10 (October 1974), pp. 549–557. Hoare describes the monitor concept and argues for its value in programming operating systems. We discuss Concurrent Pascal, a language based on a simpler type of monitor, in Section 13-1.

[**Lamport 80**] Lamport, L., "The 'Hoare Logic' of Concurrent Programs," *Acta Informa.*, vol. 14, no. 1 (1980), pp. 21–37. Lamport introduces "$\prec\succ$" pairs to indicate atomic actions.

[**Shaw 74**] Shaw, A. C., *The Logical Design of Operating Systems*, Prentice-Hall, Englewood Cliffs, New Jersey (1974). Shaw develops the issues of concurrency and mutual exclusion within the context of building operating systems. Many of the issues of operating system development apply to coordinated computing.

[**Stark 82**] Stark, E. W., "Semaphore Primitives and Starvation-Free Mutual Exclusion," *JACM*, vol. 29, no. 4 (October 1982), pp. 1049–1072. Stark identifies three different im-plementation techniques for semaphores: (1) queueing processes blocked on a semaphore, (2) keeping processes blocked on a semaphore in a "blocked set," selecting the next proc-ess to be released on a **V** operation from that set, and (3) letting blocked processes spin, with the first to notice that the semaphore has been released being the one that claims it. Stark shows that the first two techniques are more powerful than the third, in that "good" starvation-free mutual exclusion can only be programmed with blocked sets or queues.

HARDWARE

Coordinated computing is concerned with organizing numerous loosely coupled processing agents for coherent action. In this book we emphasize the programming aspects of coordinated computing. However, underlying any computing system is the machinery that performs the computation.

Several multiprocessor (shared-memory) systems have been built (and numerous programming languages designed for them). Siewiorek, Bell, and, Newell's *Computer Structures: Principles and Examples* [Siewiorek 82] contains several articles about such architectures.

Two emerging technologies seem particularly important for the development of coordinated systems. The first is concerned with the inexpensive replication of processing elements—integrated circuit techniques, particularly very large scale integration (VLSI). Perhaps the best survey of this field is Mead and Conway's *Introduction to VLSI Systems* [Mead 80]. VLSI promises to make the price of individual processing elements insignificant, certainly an important development for any system that hopes to exploit many processors.

The study of computer networks seeks optimal ways of connecting computing systems. This field is also called *distributed computing.* Networks connect machines and allow communication. Network technology has matured to the development and product stage. Building a network is no longer a matter of research. Instead, international standards for network communication have been established; several networks are commercially available.

Networks are either local area networks or long haul networks. In a *local area network*, the network manufacturer designs the physical communication channel between computers and can therefore control its performance. Local area networks are used within small areas, such as a single building. *Long haul networks*

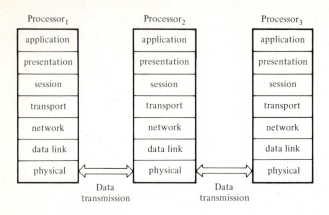

Figure 4-1 Network layers.

use common carriers like telephones and satellites for communication. Long haul networks can transfer globe-spanning messages. Of course, the ultimate local area network is many processors on a single chip.

A common network organization is a series of layers or levels, with each layer supported in every network machine. The layers are hierarchical, each one built on the level below it. The bottommost layer of the machines supports the physical signaling and signal recognition. Logically, the nth layer of each machine communicates with the nth layer of the other machines through a series of protocols—rules that describe their conversation. These layers and protocols support not only the immediate task of information transfer, but also serve to route communications, ensure privacy and security, and handle failures.* Important classes of failures include both the failures of individual processing and communication elements and the failures that result from saturating or flooding the network with too many messages. However, the encapsulation provided by multilayered organizations often has its price—a degradation in communication bandwidth through each layer interface. Figure 4-1 illustrates the layering relationship of a computing network.

Ultimately, the goal of a layered network is to hide the details of the processing of each layer from the layers above it. In such an ideal system, communication and processing failures are invisible to the user program. This goal works against the need of some systems for *real-time response*, where the computing system must react to physical phenomena within some time constraint. For example, the disk spinning under the disk head, the ground approaching an airplane, and

---

* The International Standards Organization (ISO) is in the process of promulgating protocol standards. For example, the X.25 protocol deals with topics such as signaling, transmission errors, addressing, and flow control. Tanenbaum [Tanenbaum 81] is a good source of information about these and other network protocols.

a frustrated user turning off the machine in disgust are all systems that require real-time response (though the time units differ greatly in magnitude). In this book we are concerned both with systems that ignore the problems of response and failure and with languages particularly oriented toward the implementation of real systems.

Good descriptions of the principles and tools of network construction are Ahuja's *Design and Analysis of Computer Communication Networks* [Ahuja 82] and Tanenbaum's *Computer Networks* [Tanenbaum 81].

REFERENCES

[**Ahuja 82**] Ahuja, V., *Design and Analysis of Computer Communication Networks*, McGraw-Hill, New York (1982). Ahuja develops the themes of computer communication networks, starting from the physical connection level, through network design, and on to performance analysis.

[**Mead 80**] Mead, C., and L. Conway, *Introduction to VLSI Systems*, Addison-Wesley, Reading, Massachusetts (1980). This book is a comprehensive discussion of current work on VLSI. Mead and Conway cover material ranging from the physical issues of electron motion through the theoretical issues of circuit complexity.

[**Siewiorek 82**] Siewiorek, D. C., G. Bell, and A. Newell, *Computer Structures: Principles and Examples*, McGraw-Hill, New York (1982). Siewiorek, Bell, and Newell develop the themes of computer architecture both by reprinting important articles and discussing their content.

[**Tanenbaum 81**] Tanenbaum, A. S., *Computer Networks*, Prentice-Hall, Englewood Cliffs, New Jersey (1981). Tanenbaum's book is a comprehensive and well-written discussion of the issues of network design and construction. It is both accessible to the hardware novice and a good reference for the experienced systems architect.

FIVE

MODELS, LANGUAGES, AND HEURISTICS

The next three parts form the heart of this book. In these parts we discuss models, languages, and heuristics for coordinated computing. This chapter lays the groundwork for understanding the various systems, pointing out the critical choices involved in system design. We describe the models in Part 2, the languages in Part 3, and the heuristic systems in Part 4. In Part 5, we summarize our observations, comparing and contrasting the approaches taken by the different systems.

This chapter has three sections. We begin by discussing the differences between programming languages, models of programming systems, and heuristic organizations for programming. Models are used to understand and describe computation, while languages are used to command computers. Often a proposed system has some characteristics of each. Heuristics are organizational frameworks for controlling distributed systems.

Coordinated computing is a field of our invention. The authors of the various proposals wrote papers on subjects such as programming languages, the mathematical theory of computation, and artificial intelligence, not expecting to have these papers packaged together with such distant conceptual cousins. In fact, the systems are very different. This divergence arises primarily because the various proposals address different problem domains. Different domains have different key problems and assumptions; the given of one field is often the critical issue of another. In Section 5-2 we discuss the problem domain "soil" in which these proposals grew, listing the assumptions and issues of each intellectual region.

Designing a programming system involves making many decisions. Some of these decisions are uninteresting: Should the assignment symbol be "=" or ":="? We ignore such issues. On the other hand, some decisions are more important: Should assignment be allowed at all? We have identified 12 crucial dimensions for the language/model designer. We introduce these design dimensions in Sections 5-2 and 5-3. Each of the systems in Parts 2, 3, and 4 chooses one or more of the possibilities for each dimension; the reader should be able to recognize the choices. These decisions determine a large part of the structure of a language or model. In Part 5 we compare the choices used by the various systems. Their variety can then be understood to be a selection in the space of critical choices.

5-1 MODELS, LANGUAGES, AND HEURISTICS

Models are used to explain and analyze the behavior of complex systems. A model abstracts the salient properties of a system. Models of concurrent systems usually specify the interprocess communication and synchronization mechanisms. The model is then used to derive properties and predict the behavior of the system. For example, a model of the communication patterns of a set of processes can be used to analyze algorithmic efficiency; a model of the information transfer between processes can be used to prove algorithmic correctness.

Programming languages are used to provide exact directions to computers. In Chapter 2 we observed that programming languages are characterized by their syntax and semantics. The syntax describes the surface appearance of a language, while the semantics is the set of actions that can be effected. The key issue in programming language design is not syntax but semantics. The semantics of a programming language reveals the choice of ontology (set of things that exist) and the set of things that can be done with them—in some sense, computational metaphysics.

The formal semantics of concurrent languages is a complicated subject. Concurrent languages are almost always more powerful than Turing machines. This is because Turing machines are deterministic—they always produce the same output for the same input. Concurrent systems can take advantage of asynchronous processes to produce many different answers for the same input. Similarly, there are differences in operational semantic power among the concurrent languages. Some systems provide primitives for synchronization and timing that are difficult or impossible to imitate as nonprimitives. Except for the presence of such primitives, usually (but not always) the behavior exhibited by one system can be obtained by the other systems. However (like conventional languages), the equivalent of a short program in one language may be a long program in another. In Section 19-3, we discuss a model that can describe the behavior of all the systems in Parts 2, 3, and 4.

Some of our systems are model-language hybrids. A *hybrid* has some languagelike features (typically the critical ones for distributed computing) often with a minimal syntax. The language/model designer then glosses over the remainder of the proposed language, asserting that it is a standard sort of system. The archetypical hybrid adds a few programming constructs to any of a class of languages. This is a good way to express new programming concepts. The syntax and semantics of ordinary programming languages are well understood. By concentrating only on the extensions for distribution, hybrid designers focus on the critical issues.

Heuristic systems are proposed organizations for distributed problem solving. Megacomputing presents both a challenge and an opportunity to programming. On one hand, large distributed systems will provide almost unlimited processing. On the other hand, it may be difficult to organize such a system to actually get anything useful done. Heuristic organizations are often based on taking a particular algorithm or metaphor and projecting it into a system organization. A simple example is taking the idea of committing or terminating a group of actions simultaneously, allowing a programmer to be sure of a distributed consistency. A more grandiose heuristic organization would be a programming system built around the theme: "the agents of a distributed system are individuals in a *laissez faire* economy, buying and selling goods and services to reach their individual goals." Such a system would provide agents, goods (perhaps computing cycles and memory allocations), services (the solutions of subtasks), and currency and a market to structure their interactions. A programmer who can express a task in terms of these objects would find that task easily programmed in such a megacomputing system.

5-2 PROBLEM DOMAINS

The systems we consider in the next three parts are a diverse group. One might be curious about the origin of their variety. Some of this variety arises from the natural inclination of people to find different ways of doing the same thing. However, most of the differences have a more fundamental source—the plethora of different mechanisms arises from a plethora of different problem domains. That is, the designers of these systems are building tools to solve different classes of problems. Thus, each invents a different set of tools. We have included this variety of systems because we believe that these problem domains and solutions are relevant to coordinated computing.

Problem Domain The system designers have their own perspective on the problems of distributed computing and have designed their systems to address just those issues. We identify five major perspectives in these proposals: operating systems, pragmatics, semantics, analysis, and distributed problem solving.

Each system focuses on some combination of these. Often a construct that is meant to solve the problems of one domain implies a set of unacceptable assumptions for another. For example, an elaborate algorithm for choosing processes to communicate is inappropriate for a system directed at implementing underlying communication mechanisms. On the other hand, a system that provides no communication control may be too primitive for describing complex problem-solving architectures.

Some languages address the immediate control of the distributed system. We call this the *operating systems* approach. Such systems emphasize matching the constructs of the distributed language to the physical machines. Key issues in the operating systems approach are the ease of effecting this control and the efficiency of the resulting system. Operating systems approaches sometimes treat processes and processors as synonymous. In such systems communication structure—which processes can communicate with which other processes — often remains static throughout program execution. We frequently use the synchronization problems discussed in Chapter 3 to illustrate operating systems languages.

The *pragmatic* approach is concerned with providing tools to aid the programming process. Pragmatic systems emphasize ease of program expression. Pragmatic languages often include constructs that are not necessarily easy to implement but that the designers feel are important for structuring or aiding programming. Typical examples for pragmatic systems are difficult algorithms simplified by the special constructs of the language.

Some researchers study concurrent computing systems as mathematical objects, hoping to clarify the semantics of concurrent computation and to prove the correctness of programs. We call this perspective the *semantic* approach to coordinated computing. From this perspective, the key metric for appraising a proposal is mathematical elegance. (Of course, a connection to practice provides a sound basis for theoretical work. Thus, the generality of the selected model and its correspondence to elements of real systems are also important.) The proposer of a semantic model displays its virtues with proofs. However, such proofs are beyond our present scope; we remain aware of mathematical grace without directly experiencing it.

Models developed from the *analytic* perspective are concerned with analyzing algorithmic efficiency. The ease of performing that analysis is an important criterion for success of such systems. Like semantic models, analytic models require a close correspondence between the model and the system being modeled.

Some systems are *heuristic organizations* for problem solving. These systems seek to harness concurrent computing systems to work together on difficult symbolic tasks. The natural expression of problems and problem domains and the translation of this expression into efficient distributed programs are the goals of heuristic approaches.

Often a proposal addresses several of these problem areas simultaneously. For example, a pragmatic approach might assert that program verification is an important tool; programs in "good" languages must be easy to prove correct. Similarly, languages for building real systems should have at least a peripheral concern for programming pragmatics.

5-3 PRIMITIVES FOR DISTRIBUTED COMPUTING

Our survey of systems reveals several common themes. We have already examined one such theme, the problem-domain perspective. In this section, we indicate several other key choices for designers of coordinated systems. The description of each system (in Parts 2, 3, and 4) shows how it approaches each dimension.

Explicit Processes The primary characteristic of a coordinated computing system is the simultaneous activity of many computing agents. The first decision for the designer of a coordinated model or language is whether to make the user (programmer) aware of the existence of these agents or to conceal the systems's underlying parallel nature. Systems that provide such agents to the user level have *explicit processes*. Typically, processes have program and storage. Often, processes have names (or addresses). Every system with explicit processes provides some mechanisms for interprocess communication; some explicit process systems treat processes as allocatable objects that can be created (and destroyed) during program execution.

Alternatively, a system can be organized around implicit processes. With implicit processes, computation is performed on request. The user does not specify "who" is to satisfy the request. The theme of these systems is that the user defines what is to be done and the system arranges for its concurrent computation. In general, a part of a system that can accomplish computation is an *agent*. Processes are examples of agents.

Almost all the systems in Parts 2, 3, and 4 use explicit processes. Many of the remaining dimensions of coordinated language and model design deal with interprocess communication and control. Often these issues must be interpreted differently for implicit-process systems.

Process Dynamics In a system with explicit processes, the set of processes can be fixed for the lifetime of the program or the system can allow processes to be created and destroyed during program execution. We say that a system that allows the creation of new processes during program execution supports *dynamic process creation*. A system that treats the set of processes as fixed has *static process allocation*.

Systems with dynamic process creation usually create processes in one of two ways—either by explicitly allocating new processes in an executable statement (comparable to the **new** statement for storage allocation in Pascal), or by the lexical expansion of program text. That is, if process P declares (as one of its variables, so to speak) process Q, then creating a new copy of P lexically creates a new copy of Q.

Many systems give names to newly created processes. These names can be passed between processes; communications can be addressed to processes by their names. Systems with static processes sometimes require that the system be able to determine the interprocess communication structure ("who talks to whom") before program execution ("at compile time").

Systems that allow dynamic process creation usually provide dynamic process destruction. A process that has finished executing has *terminated*. Processes can terminate in several different ways. Almost all systems allow processes to terminate by completing their program. Some systems have more elaborate schemes for process termination, including mechanisms that allow some processes to terminate other processes. One alternative to explicit termination is garbage collection of the resources of inaccessible or useless processes.

Synchronization Those systems that do not have explicit processes communicate through shared storage. Some systems with explicit processes also allow shared storage for interprocess communication. Communication without shared storage is *message* communication.

The two kinds of message transmissions are synchronous and asynchronous messages. The sender of an *asynchronously* transmitted message initiates the message and is then free to continue computing. These are *send-and-forget* communications. With *synchronously* transmitted messages, the communicating parties both attend to the communication. A process that starts a synchronous transmission waits until the message has been both received and acknowledged. We say that a process that is waiting for a synchronous communication to be accepted is *blocked*.

Synchronous communication resembles a procedure call since the caller transfers control and waits until the called agent returns an acknowledgment.* Asynchronous communication is uncommon in conventional programming languages. Metaphorically, synchronous communication can be compared to a telephone call—it requires the attention of both communicators and allows two-way conversations. Asynchronous communication is like mailing a letter—one is not idle until a dispatched letter is delivered, but there is no direct mechanism for achieving an immediate response. Communications are generally requests. A *request* is an attempt by one agent in a computing system to elicit a particular behavior from another.

Whether synchronous or asynchronous communications provide a better structure is a longstanding issue among operating systems designers. In a controversial paper, Lauer and Needham [Lauer 78] argue that (at least for operating

---

* The term *remote procedure call* has been used to describe the concept of calling a procedure on another machine. Nelson's dissertation [Nelson 81] examines this concept in detail.

systems on conventional uniprocessors) synchronous and asynchronous communication primitives are duals: there is a direct transformation from a system designed around one to a system designed around the other. Whether this duality extends to coordinated computing systems remains an open question.

Buffering One dimension of interprocess communication is the number of messages that can be pending at any time. In synchronous communication, each process has only a finite number of pending messages. Such systems have *bounded buffers*. In asynchronous communication, the system can allow an unlimited number of messages (*unbounded buffers*), provide a finite buffer that can be overwritten (*shared storage*), or halt a process that has created too many unresolved requests. These last two are also examples of systems with bounded buffers.

Information Flow The content of a message is its *information*. When processes communicate, information "flows" between them. This information can either flow from one process to the other (*unidirectional information flow*) or each process may transmit information to the other (*bidirectional information flow*). Bidirectional flow can be either simultaneous or delayed. With *simultaneous* flow, processes receive each other's communication at the same time. With *delayed* flow, first one process transfers information to the other, the recipient processes the request, and then sends an answer back to the original requester.* The classical procedure call is thus an example of bidirectional, delayed information flow. Systems with asynchronous communication invariably have only unidirectional information flow, as the sending process does not automatically receive a response.

We can imagine more complicated schemes, where information is transferred back and forth several times in a single communication. (This idea parallels virtual circuits in communications networks.) However, none of the systems we discuss support such a mechanism. One reason for this is that multiple exchanges can be imitated by repeated single exchanges.

Communication Control The dimension that has the largest variety of mechanisms is *communication control* — the rules for establishing communication. Most systems are concerned with focused communication—communications directed at particular recipient processes or "mailboxes." Some of these systems treat communicators *symmetrically*—each performs the same actions to achieve communication. However, most systems are *asymmetric*. These systems prescribe

---

* Our definitions of unidirectional and bidirectional information flow parallel similar concepts in the design of communication networks: a *simplex* connection transfers data in only one direction; a *half-duplex* connection, in both directions but not simultaneously (a version of our bidirectional delayed); and a *full-duplex* connection, in both directions simultaneously (similar to our bidirectional simultaneous).

a *caller-callee* relationship between communicators. In such an organization, one process makes a request to another. The called process can be *passive*, accepting all calls unconditionally, or it can be *active*, choosing between classes of requests. This selection takes many forms, which include named queues, guarded commands, pattern matching, time-outs, filters, and searches. Occasionally a system provides some of these mechanisms to the calling task.

Several heuristic systems use a pattern-invoking, broadcast form of communication. Here, the system conveys messages to their appropriate recipients, based on the contents of the messages and the interests of the recipients.

Communication Connection Communication can either be organized around a name external to the communicating processes (a *port*), a name associated with a particular process, or as a broadcast to interested tasks. Ports are most common in symmetric organizations. In asymmetric systems, communication is usually associated with either the called process as a whole (a *name*) or a particular label within the called process (an *entry*). In some heuristic systems, processes *broadcast* information. Recipients describe their interests by patterns and the system forwards appropriate messages to them.

Time A process that initiates communication may have to wait for its correspondent process. Such a process is blocked. Systems have various mechanisms for escaping this blocking. A few systems provide a mechanism for *timing-out* a blocked communication, permitting the process to register that the communication attempt failed. The most powerful such time-out mechanisms allow the programmer to specify an amount of time before the failure; weaker mechanisms provide only instantaneous time-out, where a process can check only if communication is immediately available. Although many models and languages do not support any time-based constructs, such constructs are vital for actual system implementations.

Fairness Intuitively, a *fair* system is one that gives each agent its rightful turn. Fairness is prominent in two places in coordinated computing—the fair allocation of computing resources and the fair allocation of communication opportunities among processes.

Formalizing the notion fairness is difficult. Oversimplifying, we say that there are three varieties of fairness: antifairness, weak fairness and strong fairness. An *antifair* system makes no commitments about the level of any process's service. In an antifair system, a process can make a request and be ignored for the remainder of the computation. In a *weakly fair* system, each process eventually gets its turn, although there is no limit on how long it might have to wait before being served. In a *strongly fair* system, processes with equivalent priorities should be served in the order of their requests. However, in a distributed system it is often difficult to establish the ordering of several concurrent events. Strong fairness is usually implemented by keeping an explicit queue of waiting requests.

Of course, all fairness criteria are modified by a model or language's explicit priority structure. If process A has higher priority than process B, then A may receive service arbitrarily more frequently than B in what is nevertheless a fair system.

The most common way to implement strong fairness is with queues. Frequently, every process entry in a strongly fair system has an associated queue. Processes accept requests on these entries in the queue order.

Failure One key issue of distributed computing is coping with failure. Several of the languages and models have features directed at dealing with particular kinds of failures. These mechanisms vary from language to language; they include time-outs, exception handlers, redundancy, atomic actions, and functional accuracy. *Time-outs* specify that a lack of response within a specific time period is to be treated as the failure of the correspondent process. In that case, a specified alternative action is to be executed. *Exception handlers* generalize this idea to other classes of failures, attaching programs to each variety of failure that the system can detect. *Redundancy* provides mechanisms for repeatedly attempting a fragile action in the hope that it will occasionally succeed. *Atomic actions* are a linguistic mechanism for encapsulating a group of more primitive actions, asserting that all are to fail if any fails. *Functional accuracy* embeds sufficient redundancy in the processes, programs, and data of a problem that even errorful intermediate results do not alter the system's overall performance.

Heuristic Mechanisms Several systems include heuristic mechanisms to aid in distributed control. These include atomic actions, pattern-directed invocation, and negotiation-based control. Part 4 discusses systems that focus on heuristic control issues.

Pragmatics Many of the proposals (particularly the languages) are intended as real programming tools. As such, they include features to ease the task of programming. These features include strong typing, symbolic tokens, and data abstraction. These constructs do not change the semantics of the underlying systems—whatever can be programmed with such aids can be programmed without them. However, there is considerable feeling in the programming language community that such features are essential to the design and construction of viable programming systems. When appropriate, we describe the pragmatic aspects of systems.

PROBLEMS

5-1 What other task domains could use a coordinated computing model or language?

5-2 Analyze a natural (human) organization, such as a company, school, or government, for the interactions described by our dimensions.

REFERENCES

[**Lauer 78**] Lauer, H. C., and R. M. Needham, "On the Duality of Operating Systems Structures," *Proc. 2d Int. Symp. Oper. Syst.*, IRIA (October 1978). Reprinted in *Operating Systems Review*, vol. 13, no. 2 (April 1979), pp. 3–19. This paper divides operating systems into two classes, those with a set of independent processes that communicate by messages and those with a set of processes that communicate with procedure calls and shared data. The paper asserts that a system organized by either method has an equivalent dual organized the other way. Furthermore, the dual is as efficient as the original.

[**Nelson 81**] Nelson, B. J., "Remote Procedure Call," Ph.D. dissertation, Carnegie-Mellon University, Pittsburgh (1981). Reprinted as Technical Report CSL-81-9, Xerox Palo Alto Research Center, Palo Alto, California. Nelson argues that remote procedure call is an appropriate basis for organizing distributed systems.

TWO

MODELS

Models capture the essence of a subject in a few simple observations. In this part, we describe seven models for coordinated computing: (1) Shared Variables, (2) Exchange Functions, (3) Concurrent Processes, (4) Data Flow, (5) Communicating Sequential Processes, (6) Actors, and (7) Indeterminate Applicative Programming. An understanding of Data Flow requires that we also develop the seminal themes of Petri Nets.

CHAPTER SIX

SHARED VARIABLES

Most of the models and languages we discuss in this book use explicit processes for the primitive, concurrent-processing object. These systems package the communications of these processes into some form of message and arrange the delivery of these messages to the right destinations. But what lies below messages? Nancy Lynch and Michael Fischer argue that sharing is the foundation of interprocess communication. They base their Shared Variables model on communication through reading and writing of shared variables. They claim three major advantages for their approach: (1) Variable sharing is a close reflection of computer hardware; (2) The frequency of reading and writing shared variables is an excellent metric of the complexity of distributed algorithms; and (3) Shared variables are primitive — all other "realizable" distributed models can be described in terms of shared variables. Lynch and Fischer's primary concerns are the complexity and correctness of distributed algorithms. Their system can be used to model not only the information-transfer aspects of distribution but also the protocols of communication.

Processes and Shared Variables

The Shared Variables model has two kinds of objects, processes and shared variables. Processes compute independently and asynchronously. They communicate only by reading and writing shared variables. A process that reads a shared variable obtains its value; a process that writes a shared variable changes its value. A variable may be shared by two or more processes. Figure 6-1 shows the variable sharing of several processes. In the figure, processes P and Q share variable w, R and S share variable x, P, Q, and R share variable y, and all four processes share variable z.

A model based on shared storage would seem to be inappropriate for coordinated computing. After all, the criterion that distinguishes distribution from mere concurrency is the absence of shared state. Nevertheless, this is a distributed model. Lynch and Fischer argue its relevance by stating [Lynch 81, p. 19]:

> At the most primitive level, something must be shared between two processors for them to be able to communicate at all. This is usually a wire in which, at the very least, one process can inject a voltage which the other process can sense. We can think of the wire as a binary shared variable whose value alternates from time to time between 0 and 1. . . . setting and sensing correspond to writing and reading the shared variable, respectively. Thus, shared variables are at the heart of every distributed system.

Shared Variables is an attempt to model distributed systems at the most primitive level. It explicitly rejects the high-level facilities that programming languages provide. Operations such as implicit synchronization, clock interrupts, and message and process queueing are important for building real systems. However, such facilities are not primitive—they can all be described by a more fundamental mechanism, the shared variable. Describing an algorithm without the aid of such high-level facilities forces the writer to make the algorithm's protocols explicit; it permits the inherent costs of particular communication patterns to be quantitatively analyzed. Furthermore, shared variables are a known technology—the construction of a system described solely in terms of shared variables is straightforward.

A typical shared variable in the Lynch-Fischer model stores only a single, small value. In using this model for analyzing distributed systems, one ought to be limited to only a few such variables. However, nothing in the system design precludes modeling a large shared memory using many shared variables.

Each process in the Shared Variables model is a countably-infinitely-branching, nondeterminate, Turing-equivalent automaton. We explain the meaning of this phrase later in this section. For the moment, we assume that each

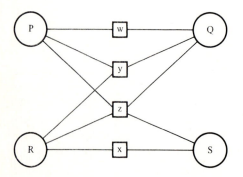

Figure 6-1 Processes and shared variables.

process is running some high-level language on a machine with an infinite memory and an unbounded random-number generator.

Like a Turing machine, each process has an internal state. At each computational step, a Turing machine reads its input tape, writes a value on its output tape, and enters a new state. Changes in the storage tape reflect changes to the Turing machine's state. Similarly, at each computational step a Shared Variables process selects a shared variable to read, reads that variable, writes a new value for that variable, and enters a new state. This entire operation is an atomic action—no other process can access the variable during the update, and this process cannot access any other variable in determining the update value. The process of checking the value in a variable and then updating it is called *test-and-set.*

Test-and-set allows the computation of an arbitrary function between the reading of the test and the writing of the set. For example, a process can read a numeric shared variable, compute its largest factor, and write that value back into the variable. Computing this factor may be a complex computation. Nevertheless, no other process can access that shared variable during the update.*

Despite the similarity of names, the Lynch-Fischer test-and-set is a much more powerful instruction than the standard test-and-set instructions found on many computers. In conventional computers, reading and writing of storage are performed on separate cycles. Other processes or interrupts can interleave with these actions. Some computers combine a limited form of reading and writing in instructions that perform actions such as "increment this location and skip the next instruction if the result is zero." Allowing an arbitrary computation between reading the shared variable and writing the new value may seem too unrealistic. The Lynch-Fischer test-and-set requires a semaphore or lock on each variable to keep other processes from accessing it during the computation of the update.

The full test-and-set instruction is too powerful to faithfully model conventional computers. For such systems we use a subset of the full class of shared variable processes, the read-write processes. If a read-write process reads a value, it must write back that same value. If such a process writes a value, both its new state and the value written must be independent of the value read. That is, in a single, indivisible step, a read-write process can appear to either read or write a variable, not both. Hence, every read-write process is a test-and-set process, but not every test-and-set process is a read-write process.

In the Lynch-Fischer model, processes never fail. More specifically, a process that starts to update a variable finishes that update. Thus, every process has a valid response to every possible value it might read from a shared variable. Furthermore, every shared variable eventually unlocks. Though processes cannot stop in the middle of updating a shared variable, they can stop between updates. These restrictions parallel the limits that mutual exclusion problems place on

---

* However, as this model lacks a notion of time, this use of "during" is somewhat misleading.

stopping inside a critical region. Just as Dijkstra assumed in his development of Dekker's solution (Section 3-2) that processes do not stop in critical regions, Lynch and Fischer assume that processes do not stop while updating.

This model is time-independent. A process cannot refer to the amount of time it has been waiting for a variable to change. It can only intermittently check to see whether the variable really has changed—somewhat akin to busy waiting. Of course, lacking "time," processes do not compute at any particular speed. One is sure only that a process that has not halted will eventually execute its next step.

The model's exclusion of time-dependent behavior is both a limitation and an advantage. Time is important in real systems. For example, clocks and interrupts are fundamental to operating systems. Therefore, relationships such as mainframe/terminal communications (where the two processes depend on having similar clock speeds) and time-outs (where a computation can be aborted after a specified duration) cannot be described in the Shared Variables model. On the other hand, results based on this model are, in some sense, stronger results because they do not depend on temporal assumptions.

As we have said, each process in the Lynch-Fischer model is a countably-infinitely-branching, nondeterminate, Turing-equivalent automaton. A Turing-equivalent automaton is a general computing device (Section 1-1). It can compute any function that can be coded in a high-level language like Pascal or Lisp. A bounded nondeterminate automaton can take each of several paths at a given choice point. An infinitely-branching nondeterminate system can also take several paths. However, it can select an infinite number of different paths at a single choice point. A countably-infinitely-branching automaton is restricted to having choice points with only a countably infinite number of choices.* Each of these extensions allows us some behavior [the computation of some (multivalued) functions] that the earlier class did not have.

Unbounded nondeterminacy is a mathematically unorthodox assumption. Most mathematical models of computation that allow nondeterminacy place a finite bound on the branching factor. Lynch and Fischer chose unbounded branching for their model because they wanted a single process to be computationally equivalent to a set of processes.

Lynch and Fischer prove two fundamental theorems about concurrent computation (given the assumptions of the model). The first is that two asynchronous, determinate automata together can produce infinitely-branching, nondeterministic behavior. This is achieved by having the first send a message to the second, counting until it receives a reply. Since the model does not limit the relative speed of processes, we cannot bound the delay between sending the request and receiving the answer. However, since the second process will *eventually*

---

* A countably infinite set can be placed in a one-to-one correspondence with the integers. This is a small infinite set. Larger infinite sets include sets such as the real numbers and the set of all functions from the reals to the reals.

progress and answer our request, the algorithm always terminates. This varying delay is effectively an unbounded random number and is sufficient to make the system unbounded and nondeterminate.

The second theorem states that any finite set of unbounded nondeterminate processes is equivalent to some single process. This is true because a single process can simulate the set of processes by interleaving their steps. Given the unbounded delay between process steps, this theorem would be false if the automata were not infinitely-branching nondeterminate.

Lynch and Fischer also give a formal definition of what it means for a distributed algorithm to *solve a problem*. Their definition treats the actions of a set of processes as a permutation of the actions of the individual processes. A system solves a problem if every possible permutation yields a *solution state*.

Examples

The Shared Variables model is a perspective on distributed computing. Our examples illustrate the effect of this perspective. Models are not programming languages. Therefore, we cloak the semantics of the Lynch-Fischer model in the syntax of a programming language. We extend Pascal to describe shared-variable algorithms with the following conventions: A process that shares an external variable declares that variable as a **shared** variable. The declaration can specify an initial value for the variable. We create processes with a **process** declaration. We take liberties with the syntax of **const** definitions and with the evaluation of expressions in type declarations.

Semaphores As an example of the full test-and-set capability of the Shared Variables system we model a general semaphore. This semaphore controls a resource that can be simultaneously shared by up to ConcurrentUsers different processes. The semaphore is a shared variable semvar. Process Q executes the P or V operations on semvar. The brackets ≺≻ denote atomic actions. Each process that uses the semaphore has its own copy of the code for P and V.

```
process Q:
shared var semvar: integer (initial ConcurrentUsers):     -- imported variable
var resourcebusy: boolean (initial false):     -- Resourcebusy, a local variable
                                               (not shared) of process Q, is true
                                               when the resource is both sought
                                               and unavailable.


procedure P:
    var local_semvar: integer:
    begin
        local_semvar := semvar:
```

```
              if local_semvar = 0 then          -- read the shared variable
                  begin
                      resourcebusy := true;
                      semvar       := 0         -- write a new value
                  end
              else
                  begin
                      resourcebusy := false;
                      semvar       := local_semvar − 1   -- write a new value
                  end
          end;

procedure V;
    begin
        semvar := semvar + 1
    end

- - - - - - - - - - - - - - - - - - - main program - - - - - - - - - - - - - - - - - - -
begin
      ⋮
    repeat ≺P≻ until not resourcebusy;    -- request the resource
      ⋮
    ≺V≻                                    -- release the resource
      ⋮
end -- process Q
```

We use local procedures P and V to emphasize that the Lynch-Fischer model allows the reading and the writing of the shared variable to be separated by an arbitrary computation (except that these procedures cannot access any other shared variables). Q can inspect its own variable, resourcebusy, to determine if it has gained access to the resource controlled by the semaphore.

The full test-and-set primitive is unrealistically powerful. We have confined the remaining examples of the Lynch-Fischer model to read-write processes: processes that cannot both read and update a shared variable in a single atomic step.

Our next example demonstrates that read-write processes suffice for process synchronization. We describe a solution by Gary Peterson [Peterson 81] of the fair mutual-exclusion problem. His solution is simpler than Dekker's algorithm (Section 3-2). Peterson has the two processes, P and Q, communicate through three shared variables: turn, p_enter, and q_enter. Turn is a priority flag. In case of conflict, turn contains the process identifier of the next process to enter the critical region. The processes use p_enter and q_enter to show readiness to enter the critical region. Variable turn is read and written by both processes while each

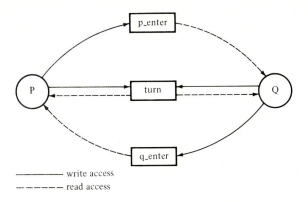

———— write access

– – – – – read access

Figure 6-2 Shared variables for mutual exclusion.

process sets the value of its enter variable and reads the value of its partner's enter variable. Figure 6-2 shows the information flow between the processes through the shared variables. P_enter is true when either P is in its critical region or wants to enter its critical section. A corresponding program specifies Q.

```
process P;
shared var
          turn               : process_id (initial p_id);      -- imported variables
          p_enter, q_enter : boolean (initial false);
begin
     while true do
     begin
          p_enter := true;     -- declare intention to enter
          turn     := q_id;     -- ensure that Q can enter its critical region when
                                        P's turn is over
          while q_enter and turn = p_id do
               skip;                -- wait until P's turn or Q is not in its critical
                                        region
          p_enter := false;     -- withdraw intention to enter concurrent region
     end
end
```

Protocols One feature of Shared Variables is that it can model primitive protocols for interprocessor communication. A *protocol* is an organizational framework for communication: a mapping between the ordering of symbols and their interpretation. In computer systems, typical protocols specify that certain strings of bits are to have meanings such as "I want to send a message" and "Do you have a free buffer?" and replies to such requests. Protocols are particularly important when the communication channel is shared between several logical connections. In that case, the protocol identifies and orders the pieces of a message, keeping it from being scrambled with other messages.

Our next example presents a message transmission protocol that uses a single shared variable. Lynch and Fischer describe some of the difficulties of shared-variable communication [Lynch 81, p. 24]:

> The way in which processes communicate with other processes and with their environment is by means of their variables ... Unlike message-based communication mechanisms, there is no guarantee that anyone will ever read the value [in a variable], nor is there any primitive mechanism to inform the writer that the value has been read. (Thus, for meaningful communication to take place, both parties must adhere to previously-agreed-upon protocols. ...)

The key idea is that any pattern of communication can be achieved by reading and writing a shared variable according to appropriate protocols. To illustrate this idea we consider the problem of message communication between two read-write processes, P and Q. Assume that P and Q share variable pq_var that can store integers between $-n$ and n. P and Q wish to imitate a bidirectional message transmission system, where messages can be up to message_limit words long.

P and Q communicate by obeying the following protocol. P assigns only positive numbers to pq_var; Q only negative numbers. Both processes can set pq_var to 0. The numbers $n - 1$ and n [respectively $-(n - 1)$ and $-n$] are the "message initiation header" (pm_header) and the "end of message" (p_eom) for P (respectively, Q). We use the $n - 2$ remaining values for encoding the message.

P stores the number $n - 1$ (pm_header) in pq_var to show that it wishes to send a message. Q responds by writing a 0 (okay_to_send), indicating readiness to accept the communication. After seeing the value okay_to_send, P writes the body of the message in the variable, one word at a time. After each word, Q responds with a -1 (q_acknowledge). That is, P writes the first value in the message and Q replies with q_acknowledge. When P sees the q_acknowledge, it writes the second word and waits for Q's next acknowledgment. This continues until P has sent the entire message. At that point, P stores p_eom in pq_var. Q responds with okay_to_send. On seeing okay_to_send, either process can start another communication by placing its message initiation header into the variable. P and Q execute the corresponding protocol to send messages from Q to P. Variable pq_var is initially okay_to_send.

Problems arise when both processes try to write the message initiation header at about the same time. P and Q must recognize that writing the header does not guarantee the right to transmit. A process that writes the header and then reads the header of its partner does not send, but instead accepts the next message. When a process writes the header, it waits until its partner either accepts transmission (okay_to_send) or demands the channel for itself (the partner's message initiation header).

We present the program for P. The program for Q is analogous.

```
const
    qm_header       = −(n−1);      -- Q's message header
    pm_header       = n−1;         -- P's message header
    q_eom           = −n;          -- Q's end of message
    p_eom           = n;           -- P's end of message
    q_acknowledge   = −1;          -- Q's response to message data
    p_acknowledge   = 1;           -- P's response to message data
    okay_to_send    = 0;
type message = array [1 .. message_limit] of integer;
        -- Messages can be up to message_limit words long.

process P;
    shared var pq_var: integer (initial okay_to_send);    -- imported variable
        ... <local declarations> ...

    procedure receive;
    var
        in : message;       -- the message
        k  : integer;           -- the number of the words in the message
    begin
        if pq_var = qm_header then              -- Q has signaled that it wants
        begin                                        to send a message.
            pq_var := okay_to_send;
            k       := 0;
            while pq_var ≠ q_eom do             -- repeat until Q signals it is
            begin                                   done
                while pq_var ≥ 0 do skip;       -- wait for response from Q
                if pq_var ≠ q_eom then
                begin
                    k       := k + 1;
                    in[k]   := pq_var            -- get the value
                    pq_var := p_acknowledge;
                end
            end;
            pq_var := okay_to_send;             -- Acknowledge that the entire
                                                    message has been received.
            act(in,k);                          -- act on the message
        end
    end; -- receive

    procedure send (var out: message; k: integer);    -- send a message,
                                                          out[1..k]
```

```
    var
        i                    : integer;
        ready_to_send : boolean;    -- Have we requested communication yet?
    begin
        ready_to_send := false;
        while not(ready_to_send) do
        begin
            while pq_var ≠ okay_to_send do receive;    -- Q wants to send.
            pq_var := pm_header;
            while pq_var = pm_header do skip;           -- waiting for
                                                           acknowledgment

            if pq_var = qm_header then receive          -- cannot send until
            else ready_to_send := true                     okay_to_send is in
                                                             pq_var
        end;

        for i := 1 to k do
        begin
            pq_var := out[i];                           -- write the next word
            while pq_var ≠ q_acknowledge do skip        -- wait for signal
        end;
        pq_var := p_eom;                                -- specify end of
                                                           message

            while (pq_var ≠ okay_to_send) and           -- wait for
                  (pq_var ≠ qm_header) do skip             acknowledgment
    end; -- send


begin
                ⋮

    -- the code for P, including occasional checks to see if a message is waiting
    and calls to send messages as needed.

                ⋮

end -- process P
```

This example emphasizes the fact that the only way to tell if a value has been read from a shared variable is to receive an acknowledgment of that reading.

We measure program efficiency by considering the quantity of a resource that it uses (proportional to its input) (Section 1.3). For example, the protocol program uses a shared memory cell that can accommodate $2n$ different values; the system writes more than $2k$ n-bit messages to transmit kn words of information. These bounds can be improved. For example, Burns [Burns 80a] has shown that a subtle extension of the work of Cremers and Hibbard [Cremers 79] allows the variable to be limited to as few as three values. Exercise 6-9 asks for an improved

Figure 6-3 A long distance communication.

protocol that uses fewer writes to send the same amount of information. The Lynch-Fischer model is particularly well suited for use in this kind of analysis.

Communication delay Shared variables provide failure-free communication between processes. Of course, many real world applications are difficult precisely because individual messages can become garbled or lost. One technique for modeling noisy communication between two shared-variable processes is to use a *channel process*. Imagine two distant processes, P and Q, that communicate through the shared variable x (Figure 6-3). Of course, with this arrangement P and Q have errorless communication. Anything one writes in the shared variable can be correctly read by the other. To model noisy communication, we introduce a *channel process* C that shares variable y with P and variable z with Q (Figure 6-4). C's task is to take the values written by P in y and to write them into z for Q, and to take the values written by Q in z and to write them into y for P. C is programmed to be noisy. That is, now and then it "makes a mistake"— writes the wrong value for a communication, drops a message, or inserts a spurious message. C's pattern of misbehavior can model the channel's intended noise pattern.

We assume that C has a function noise from channel values (integers) to channel values. Noise(x) is usually x, but sometimes it is something else. The code for this function reflects the particular pattern of noise being modeled. The program for the channel is as follows:

```
process channel;
shared var y , z: channel_value (initial 0);      -- imported variables
var yrecent, zrecent: channel_value;
begin
     yrecent := y;
     zrecent := z;
     while true do      -- using a guarded command
```

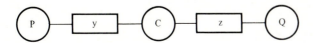

Figure 6-4 A channel process.

```
        y ≠ yrecent →
            z := noise(yrecent);   yrecent := y;   zrecent := z
  ◻
        z ≠ zrecent →
            y := noise(zrecent);   yrecent := y;   zrecent := z
  ◻
        y = yrecent and z = zrecent →
            skip
end -- channel
```

Election algorithms One use of the Lynch-Fischer model is to analyze the complexity of algorithms for distributed systems. In this next example we present a simple analysis of a distributed algorithm.

A common architecture for small distributed systems is a ring. In a ring, processes are arranged in a circle. Each process communicates directly with its left and right neighbors. Figure 6-5 shows a seven-element ring network. Each process in the ring shares a variable with each of its "next-door neighbors."

Sometimes a ring of processes must establish a chief (king) process. This process manages some aspect of the general system function. We assume that each process has a unique positive integer (its *rank*) and that the process with the largest rank ought to be the *king* (Figure 6-6). Process ranks are independent of the number of processes in the ring and the location of the process in the ring. These numbers are not necessarily consecutive; the individual processes do not know a priori how many processes are in the ring.

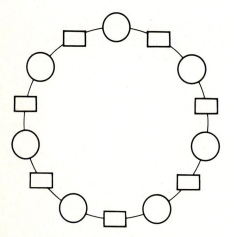

Figure 6-5 A ring network.

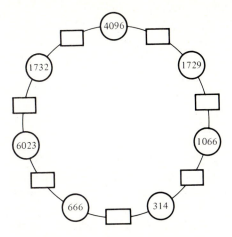

Figure 6-6 A ring network with ranks.

The ring is not static. Instead, processes enter and leave the ring dynamically. The logical ring is automatically (through the underlying hardware) patched to handle changes in the ring's configuration.

The departure of the king process from the ring requires an election to crown the new king. An *election* is an algorithm that determines the process that ought to be the king by passing messages containing the ranks of the active processes around the ring. For the sake of simplicity, we assume that no process leaves or enters the ring during an election.

Our naive election algorithm has each process assign its own number to the variable shared with its "left" neighbor and read from its "right" shared variable its right neighbor's rank. Processes forward, from right to left, any rank that is larger than anyone they have already seen. When a process receives its own rank back through its right variable, it knows that that value has passed all the way around the ring, making that process the legitimate chief—the lord of the ring. The new king process announces its election by circulating the negative of its rank around the ring. The program for election algorithm is as follows:

```
process candidate;
shared var left, right: integer (initial 0);    -- imported variables
const MyNum = 1729;

function election: boolean;    -- returns true if this process is elected king
var best, last: integer;
begin
    left   := MyNum;
```

```
            best  := MyNum;     -- the best this process has seen so far
         while (right ≥ 0) and not (right = MyNum) do
             if (right > best) then
             begin              -- a new, higher rank
                 last  := right;
                 left  := last;
                 best  := last
             end;
         election := (right = MyNum);
         if election
             then  left := −MyNum
             else  left := right;
   end; -- election


                      ⋮
   -- the rest of process candidate

                      ⋮

end -- candidate
```

If there are n processes in the ring, this algorithm may make $O(n^2)$ assignments to the shared variable. Figure 6-7 shows an example of an arrangement of process ranks that can yield this worst case. In the figure, the ranks are sorted in decreasing clockwise order. The worst-case behavior happens when each process sends its value as far as possible to the left without sensing the higher rank on its right. That is, the lowest ranking process sends its message one step to the left. Then the second lowest process sends its message two steps left. This continues until the king process finally awakens and transmits its rank. This requires $1 + 2 + 3 + \cdots + n = n(n+1)/2$ messages to be sent.*

This is not the most efficient possible solution. Hirschberg and Sinclair [Hirschberg 80] have shown an algorithm that solves the election problem in at worst $O(n \log n)$ writes. Their algorithm relies on writing values that contain a limit on how far around the ring they can travel. The processes send these messages around the ring in alternating directions until two messages from the same source meet.

Continuous display The strongly asynchronous nature of the Shared Variables model makes the system ideal for modeling Kieburtz and Silberschatz's continuous display problem [Kieburtz 79]. The *continuous display problem* hypothesizes a system of two processes, the generator and the display. The system tracks and displays. The *generator* continuously discovers the current location of some moving object, the *target*, and passes that location to the display process. The

---

* Our algorithm requires another n writes to circulate the announcement of the election.

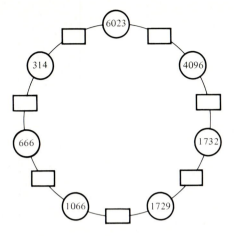

Figure 6-7 The worst case of the election algorithm.

display process uses that value to show the "most current" location of the object on a display device. This idea of using the most recently generated value (and disregarding earlier values) is appropriate for many real systems, such as tracking systems. Synchronous communication would slow the system down to the speed of the slower process; separating the two processes by a producer-consumer buffer ensures that the stalest data is always the next read. However, shared memory obtains precisely the desired behavior. The generator repeatedly writes the current target location in the shared variable; the display just reads the shared variable's current value.

Perspective

Lynch and Fischer assert that some analysis and correctness problems are best attacked by modeling a set of distributed processes as if they shared a small amount of common storage. They argue that this model is primitive; that other more complicated communication mechanisms (such as messages and procedures) can all be expressed with shared variables.

Lynch and Fischer are concerned with formal programming semantics. Their work is heavily mathematical (principally the situation calculus over automata, expressed in predicate logic) and only marginally concerned with programming practice. The shared-variable concept is a low-level approach. It requires that every detail of an interaction be explicit. As such, it is good for modeling low-level activity and for deriving complexity results. The model is an "automata theory" of distributed computing. However, just as Turing machines are not a good basis for sequential programs, shared variables are not an appropriate foundation for practical coordinated computing.

The techniques that have been used to analyze the time complexity of shared-variable programs can also be used to analyze of the complexity of other aspects of programs. For example, Burns et al. [Burns 80b] present an analysis of the shared space requirements of various algorithms.

PROBLEMS

† **6-1**   Extend the election algorithm to allow processes to be added or deleted during the election. Take particular care to handle the deletion of the king process. Assume that if a process leaves the ring, the ring is patched around its place.

6-2   How do the solutions to the previous problem change if all processors have (roughly similar) clocks and failures can be detected through time-outs?

6-3   Does the election program need variable last?

6-4   What is the best case of the naive election algorithm and when does it occur?

6-5   Program a solution to the dining philosophers problem using shared variables.

6-6   Modify the protocol of the message transmission program so that instead of sending an end-of-message symbol, messages are transmitted with their length.

6-7   Modify the protocol of the message transmission program so that neither processor can starve, unable to send a message.

6-8   In the message transmission program, why must processes read an okay_to_send before beginning message transmission? Why is shared variable pq_var initialized to okay_to_send?

6-9   The protocol program is relatively inefficient for the number of bits of information that are written for the size of message transmitted. Improve it.

6-10 Show how the card reader of Chapter 8 can be done using the Lynch-Fischer shared-variable model.

REFERENCES

[Burns 80a] Burns, J. E., personal communication, 1980.

[Burns 80b] Burns, J. E., P. Jackson, N. A. Lynch, M. J. Fischer, and G. L. Peterson, "Data Requirements for Implementation of N-Process Mutual Exclusion Using a Single Shared Variable," *JACM*, vol. 29, no. 1 (January 1982), pp. 183–205. This paper shows how the shared-variable model can be used to analyze the space requirements of communication.

[Cremers 79] Cremers, A., and T. Hibbard, "Arbitration and Queueing under Limited Shared Storage Requirements," Forschungsbericht 83, University of Dortmund, Dortmund, Germany (1979). Cremers and Hibbard prove minimal space requirements for shared variable communication.

[Hirschberg 80] Hirschberg, D. S., and J. B. Sinclair, "Decentralized Extrema-Finding in Circular Configurations of Processors," *CACM*, vol. 23, no. 11 (November 1980), pp. 627–628. This paper contains an optimal election algorithm.

[Kieburtz 79] Kieburtz, R. B., and A. Silberschatz, "Comments on 'Communicating Sequential Processes,'" *ACM Trans. Program. Lang. Syst.*, vol. 1, no. 2 (January 1979), pp. 218–225. This paper is the source of the continuous-display problem.

[**Lynch 81**] Lynch, N. A., and M. J. Fischer, "On Describing the Behavior and Implementation of Distributed Systems," *Theoret. Comp. Sci.*, vol. 13, no. 1 (1981), pp. 17–43. Lynch and Fischer describe their model. While most of the paper is quite formal, the introduction and overview are a good, nontechnical introduction to their system.

[**Peterson 81**] Peterson, G. L., "Myths about the Mutual Exclusion Problem," *Inf. Proc. Lett.*, vol. 12, no. 3 (June 1981), pp. 115–116. Peterson presents a simple solution to the mutual-exclusion problem.

SEVEN

EXCHANGE FUNCTIONS

Exchange Functions is a specification mechanism for designing and a model for describing distributed and embedded systems.* Exchange Functions assumes explicit processes that communicate by calling functions that exchange values. Communication with exchange functions is bidirectional, simultaneous, and symmetric. That is, in an exchange (communication), information transfers between both communicators simultaneously; each communicator has an equal role in establishing the communication. The model has mechanisms for both blocking and nonblocking communication. Exchange functions are a particularly elegant integration of communication and communication failure. Pamela Zave and D. R. Fitzwater developed the Exchange Functions model [Fitzwater 77].

Varieties of Exchange Functions

Exchange Functions is based on synchronous, simultaneous, and bidirectional communication on a static, predetermined set of processes. Each process is a state automaton, described by a current state and a function for reaching its next state. With Turing machines, state progression is determined by the machine's internal state (tape), state-transition function, and input. Similarly, state transition in Exchange Functions is defined by the process's state, state transition function (its *successor function*), and the value received in a communication exchange. For

---

* An *embedded system* is a computer system that is incorporated in a larger device. For example, a computer used to monitor and control a manufacturing process is an embedded system.

example, the even process (which does no communication) has as its successor function:

$$\text{successor(even)} \equiv \text{even} + 2$$

If this process's initial state is 0, it successively takes as its states the even numbers: 0, 2, 4, ...

Successor functions are built up by functional composition from other, more primitive functions. Besides the usual kinds of primitives (such as arithmetic, conditional, constructor, and selector primitives), Exchange Functions introduces a new set of communication primitives—the exchange functions. Two processes that call corresponding exchange functions communicate. Each exchange function takes a single argument (the value to be sent to another process) and returns a single value (the value received from the other process). Exchange functions thus unify input and output.

Each exchange function refers to a particular channel. Two exchange functions can communicate only if their channels match. Calls to exchange functions on different channels do not result in communication. We let E_α indicate a call of exchange function E on channel α. If process P executes an $E_\alpha(1)$ and process Q executes an $E_\beta(2)$, no exchange occurs (as α and β are different channels). If Process R then executes an $E_\beta(3)$, then a 3 is returned as the value of Q's call, and a 2 as the value of R's call. P remains blocked, waiting for a call on channel α.

The model defines three varieties of exchange functions, distinguished by their matching and temporal characteristics. The simplest is X. Evaluating X (on some channel) causes the process to block until another process evaluates any other exchange function on the same channel. When this happens the two processes exchange arguments and return. Thus, X is a waiting, synchronous primitive.

Calling X blocks a process until another process executes a matching exchange function. Sometimes a process needs to check whether another process is trying to communicate, but wants to avoid blocking if no communication is available. Primitive function XR serves this purpose. If a process executes an XR and some other process is currently waiting on the same channel, they exchange and return. If no process is waiting on that channel, the argument of the XR is returned. A process issuing an XR distinguishes between successful and unsuccessful communication attempts by calling XR with an argument that could not be the result of a successful exchange. That is, if P executes $XR_\alpha(4)$, and no communication is waiting on channel α, then the value of $XR_\alpha(4)$ is 4. The R in XR stands for real time. Zave and Fitzwater assert that this exchange behavior is essential for real-time systems.

Metaphorically, we compare the XR primitive to a "flashing" liquid crystal display (LCD) clock. Each second, the clock offers the time. A person looking at the clock (waiting for the time) sees the time when the clock flashes. The clock flash is instantaneous. The clock never waits for the time seeker; the time seeker always waits for the clock. This parallels real-time sensing, where the sensor misses events if it is not watching for them.

Any X_α can communicate with any other X_α. This uniform matching makes it awkward to program some algorithms that use a many-to-one communication pattern. For example, many processes may share a single buffer. They need to communicate with the buffer, not each other. The **XM** exchange function provides the needed "directionality" to communication. Briefly, calls to **XM** do not exchange with other calls to **XM**. **XM** calls can still exchange with Xs and XRs on the same channel. The **M** in **XM** stands for many-to-one.

One example of the use of **XM** is Zave's description of a real-time clock [Zave 82]. The clock is a process that executes XR_{clock}(current_time) each "tick." This offers the clock's time to any process that desires it. To get the time, processes execute XM_{clock}(time_please) (where time_please is any arbitrary value.) This call waits for a matching XR_{clock}. If instead of **XM**, time-desiring processes execute X_{clock}(time_please), then two processes requesting the time could communicate with each other (sending each other a time_please), instead of receiving the time from the clock. If the clock updates the value of current_time between calls to XR_{clock}, then no two processes ever receive the same time.

The check marks in Table 7-1 show the possible communication matches between the three exchange primitives. The variety of exchange function primitives (**X**, **XR**, and **XM**) selects all useful possibilities in a two-by-two grid. An exchange function can exchange with itself, like **X** (self-exchange) or exchange only with other functions, like **XR** and **XM**. An exchange function can be blocking (waiting) like **X** and **XM** or it can be instantaneous (nonwaiting), like **XR**. An instantaneous primitive is available only for an instant. Therefore, an instantaneous primitive never exchanges with another instantaneous primitive. Table 7-2 illustrates this relationship.

Zave and Fitzwater assert that the channel of any particular call to an exchange function must be a compile-time constant [Zave 77]. This has two ramifications. The first is that one cannot subscript channel names in an Exchange Functions program. The second is that channels cannot be dynamically created

Table 7-1 Potential exchanges

	X	XR	XM
X	√	√	√
XR	√		√
XM	√	√	

Table 7-2 Exchange function dimensions

	Waiting	Instantaneous
Self-exchange	X	*Impossible*
No self-exchange	XM	XR

and transferred between processes. In practice, this restriction is just a syntactic impediment—one can achieve subscripting on channel names (over a known set of channels) by a sufficiently complicated program structure. We believe that it is a mistake not to include subscripted channels in the model. So we ignore this restriction in our examples.

Implementing Exchange Functions in a distributed network requires *conflict resolution*—the matching of interacting pairs. Zave and Fitzwater specify that this conflict resolution be weakly fair—that is, no pending exchange (from an X or XM) should be indefinitely denied [Zave 77].

Zave suggests that when more than two processes communicate on the same channel, the communication pattern is almost always many-to-one (though the particular application determines which of the pairs XM/XR or XM/X is appropriate [Zave 83]). Later in this section we present a fanciful counterexample to this hypothesis, a program with a completely unfocused communication pattern.

Sometimes one has a choice of several possible exchange patterns for a particular application. For example, an X–X communication between two processes can just as easily be performed with an X–XM pair; the effect of an X can sometimes be achieved by performing an XR in a loop. (However, one does not achieve an X–X communication pattern using two looping XRs!)

The communication mechanisms of Exchange Functions parallel, to some extent, the communication facilities provided by shared-loop bus systems such as the Ethernet [Metcalfe 76]. The shared buses of Ethernet correspond to the channels of Exchange Functions.

Successor Functions

In Exchange Functions, processes have state. The state of a process changes, stepwise, through the life of the process. Each process has a successor function that describes this change. This function, given the state of a process, returns the new state of the process. The evaluation of this function may block, pending completion of its communications. Notationally, we indicate the successor function for a process by applying the successor function to the name of that process.

The process identifier names the state of the process. For example, if F is the successor function of process P, we write

$$\text{successor}(P) \equiv F(P)$$

Viewing the process identifier as a variable, this sequence of states is analogous to the program

while true do $P := F(P)$

Following Zave [Zave 82], we use functional notation to describe successor functions.*

Binary semaphore A binary semaphore is a process with communication capabilities on two channels, Psem and Vsem. When the semaphore is free, it executes X_{Psem}. When the call on Psem returns, the semaphore calls X_{Vsem}. The semaphore alternates calls to X_{Psem} and X_{Vsem}. The state of the semaphore is expressed entirely by the channel on which it is waiting. A simple program for a binary semaphore is

$$\text{successor (semaphore)} \equiv X_{Vsem}(X_{Psem}(\odot))$$

Shared Variables The Lynch-Fischer model (Chapter 6) is based on shared variables. In that model, the only communication mechanism between processes is the reading and writing of shared variables. The processes of the general Lynch-Fischer model are powerful automata. In a single atomic step they can read a shared variable, compute a new value for that variable, and write that value back into the variable.

We model shared variable communication in Exchange Functions by creating a register process. For each register we have two channels, read, to be used in reading the register value, and write, to be used in writing it. Like the semaphore, the register forces an order on these operations: the alternations of reads and writes. Unlike the semaphore, the register retains its state between reads and writes. The program for the register is

$$\text{successor(register)} \equiv X_{write}(X_{read}(\text{register}))$$

---

* Briefly, the notation $F(G(H(x), y))$ is equivalent to the sequential program
function FGH (x);
begin
    tempH := H(x);
    tempG := G(tempH, y);
    answer := F(tempG);
    return (answer)
end

Operationally, the register responds to a call on X_{read} by sending the current value of the register. The value returned (a synchronization signal like $\odot$) is used as the argument to X_{write}; the value returned by the call on write becomes the new value of the register. Thus, the call on read sends the register's value and receives a synchronization signal; the call on write sends a synchronization signal and receives the register's new value.

Processes that access the register include the sequence

$$\ldots \; \mathsf{XM_{write}} \; (\mathsf{F} \; (\mathsf{XM_{read}} \; (\odot))) \; \ldots$$

as part of their successor function. To be true to the pure Lynch-Fischer model, function F should not read or write any other shared variables.

Unbounded buffer Our unbounded producer-consumer buffer executes the following algorithm: At each step the buffer calls XR on the producer channel and XR on the consumer channel. The buffer changes its state if either call is matched. If neither channel has a waiting call, the buffer retains the same state. Let

Buffer	The ordered list that represents the state of the buffer process.
nil	The null (empty) buffer.
Ack-from-C	The acknowledgment from the consumer.
Ack-to-P	The acknowledgment to the producer.

We represent the state of a buffer as a list L of elements $\mathsf{L}_1, \mathsf{L}_2, \ldots, \mathsf{L}_k$ (where k is the length of L). We then define the following functions (with their Lisp equivalents, of course, in parentheses):

first (L)	$\equiv$	L_1	-- *(car L)*
rest (L)	$\equiv$	$\mathsf{L}_2 \ldots \mathsf{L}_k$	-- *(cdr L)*
first-insert (e, L)	$\equiv$	**if** (e = Ack-from-C) **then** L	
		else e $\mathsf{L}_1 \mathsf{L}_2 \ldots \mathsf{L}_k$	-- *(cons e L)*
last-insert (L, e)	$\equiv$	**if** (e = Ack-to-P) **then** L	
		else $\mathsf{L}_1 \mathsf{L}_2 \ldots \mathsf{L}_k$ e	-- *(append L (list e))*

The successor function of the buffer is

```
successor (Buffer) ≡
    if Buffer = nil then last-insert (Buffer, Xₚ(Ack-to-P))          -- (*)
    else last-insert (first-insert (XRᶜ (first (Buffer)),
                        rest (Buffer)),
            XRₚ(Ack-to-P))
```

This buffer provides two communication channels: $\mathsf{XR_c}$ for communication with consumers and $\mathsf{XR_p}$ for communication with producers. An empty buffer is receptive only to messages from producers. The then clause of the conditional handles this possibility (∗). Steps of the buffer process fit into one of four different patterns: no messages sent to the buffer, messages only from producers, messages only from consumers, and messages from both producers and consumers. If no messages are sent on either channel, then the XR_c is first (Buffer) and the value of XR_p is Ack-to-P. The computation proceeds as

successor(Buffer)
> ⇒ last-insert (first-insert (first(Buffer), rest (Buffer)), Ack-to-P)
> ⇒ first-insert (first (Buffer), rest (Buffer))
> > -- *as last-insert* $(B, Ack\text{-}to\text{-}P) = B$
> ⇒ Buffer

If a process tries to consume, XM_c(Ack-from-C) and XR_c(first (Buffer)) exchange. Ack-from-C is ignored by first-insert (when Buffer is nil) and the buffer shrinks. If a process tries to produce, XM_p(value) exchanges with an XR_p(Ack-to-P), this last-insert (Buffer, value) successfully adds a new element at the end of the buffer. These two exchanges can occur on the same successor step; the buffer shrinks at the front and extends at the rear. No matter how many consumers or producers wish to communicate, the buffer accommodates at most one of each on each full step of the successor function.

Process control Our final example of Exchange Functions is a process control program. We imagine that during some manufacturing process it is necessary to maintain a certain temperature distribution in a vat of liquid over a long period of time. The vat contains several controllers, several sensors (thermometers), and several heating elements at fixed locations. Each controller communicates directly, over its own specialized channels, with its own thermometer and its own heater. The controllers communicate with each other over a single, common channel.

Each controller's position is indicated by its $\langle i, j \rangle$ coordinates (Figure 7-1). The controller's state is a finite buffer in which it maintains the last few readings it has received. A reading is an ordered pair of the form ⟨position, temperature⟩. By the analysis of these values, the controller decides which instructions to send to its heater. The controller's program is a five-state loop. (1) It gets a reading from its own thermometer. (2) It offers its ⟨position, reading⟩ pair on the common controller channel, world. (3) When it receives a ⟨position, reading⟩ pair from some other controller, it adds it to its finite buffer. (4) It analyzes the updated data and decides what instructions to send to its heater. (5) Finally, it deletes its oldest datum, leaving room for a new reading on the next step.

The heating element repeatedly receives instructions and adjusts its control to follow those instructions. Each sensor (like the real-time clock) continuously offers the temperature to its controller. We use function proj-2, that evaluates both of its arguments and returns the second. This example uses exchange function X in a many-to-many organization.

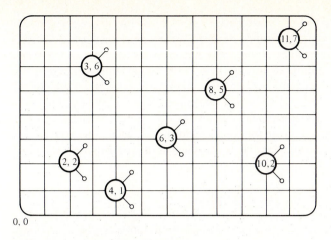

0, 0

Figure 7-1 The process control bath.

successor (controller[i,j]) ≡
        process[i,j] (last-insert (controller,
                    $X_{world}(\langle\langle i, j\rangle, X_{sensor[i,j]} (ack)\rangle)))$.

process[i,j] (controller) ≡
        proj-2 ($\langle X_{heater[i,j]}$ (decide-what-to-send-to-heater (controller)),
           rest (controller)$\rangle$).

successor (sensor[i,j]) ≡
        $XR_{sensor[i,j]}$ (current-temperature-register[i,j]).

successor (heater[i,j]) ≡
        adjust-control[i,j] ($X_{heater[i,j]}(ack)$).

Guarded Exchange Functions

These next two sections describe some possible extensions to the Exchange Functions model.

Many systems use a variant of Dijkstra's guarded commands (Section 2-2) to combine indeterminacy and communication selection. The original exchange functions definition has no mechanism for requesting an exchange on one of several channels. Let us consider the effect of extending exchange functions to include a primitive with the power of guarded commands.

In 1963, John McCarthy introduced the operator **amb** for effecting nondeterminism [McCarthy 63]. McCarthy's **amb** is a binary operator. Its value is whichever of its two operands is defined. If both are defined, then **amb** can return either one; if neither is defined, then **amb** is also undefined. Operationally, amb (f, g) can be thought of as "start both f and g, returning whichever finishes 'first.'" Of course, undefined operands never finish. Since these systems are formally time-free, a complex computation may finish before a simple one. For this section, we restrict the operands of amb to be calls to exchange functions. For any two exchange calls, E_α and E_β, we let amb (E_α, E_β) be whichever of the two exchanges matches first. If there are waiting exchanges on both channels, then we let amb choose indeterminately which one to match. We allow amb to range over any variety of exchange function. Additionally, we extend amb to take an arbitrary number of arguments. Thus, a typical subexpression of a successor function using our amb is:

$$\text{amb } (E_\alpha(1), E_\beta(2), E_\gamma(3), E_\delta(4))$$

The evaluation of this expression sends communication offers out along channels α, β, γ, and δ. When one is accepted, the other three offers are rescinded and values are exchanged on the successful channel.

One peculiarity of this naive introduction of amb is that unlike guarded commands, the calling function cannot find out which amb branch was selected. All that is returned is the resulting value. This difficulty can be overcome by having each sending process decorate its message with the identity of its communication channel. A second artifact is that since XR exchanges always return immediately, an XR in an amb may dominate the other arguments. This implies that XRs inside ambs are of limited utility.

Delaying Exchange

Calling an exchange function produces communication exactly when the function returns. Let us assume that process A wishes to exchange on channel α. If no process is waiting to exchange on α, A either waits for a match (if it executed X or XM) or immediately returns, reporting failure (if it did an XR).

One could imagine other possible timing arrangements for exchanges. A process might expect to have a use for an exchange value, but have another useful computation to do in the meantime. Doing this other computation might reveal that the information requested in the original exchange was not really needed after all. We consider the possibility of allowing the process to initiate an exchange and continue with its computation, pausing only when the value is really needed. This variation is inspired by the theme of *call-by-need*: delaying parameter evaluation until use. This pattern can also be viewed as treating message communication as a fork operation, where using the returned value is the occasion to do the join. We call this mode of communication *join-by-need*.

Starting an exchange and completing it later has different meanings for the waiting (X, XM) and instantaneous (XR) functions. For the waiting exchange primitives, the desired implementation is a simple fork and join. When the interpreter sees a call to an X or XM exchange function, it initiates the exchange.

The process is free to continue its processing. Only when the value returned by the exchange function is used in the computation is there a potential for delay. If the exchange has not been completed by that time, the process waits for the value.

Sometimes the value of the exchange function is never used. For example, acknowledgments (such as the acknowledgment in the buffer insertion example) are frequently not examined. Here the forking acts like a send-and-forget message-passing system. Even if the value is not examined, the exchange is still deemed to have taken place.

The semantics of programs incorporating this fork-and-join primitive differ from those of the original waiting system. Most significantly, exchange no longer effects synchronization. For example, an unchecked semaphore no longer synchronizes. To restore the synchronization aspect of the exchange, we would need an "exchange and immediately access primitive."

The instantaneous exchange function (XR) presents an opportunity to introduce a new primitive. In the original call-by-value semantics, the XR exchange function implied an "instantaneous" exchange. If one considers the intent of XR as an exchange without waiting, the delayed evaluation metaphor can provide a different meaning. A call to XR signifies an exchange offer that can later be withdrawn. If the offer is not accepted before the answer is needed, then the usual failure response (return of the original argument) is given. The notion of a time-out is a traditional one in operating systems theory. Our new primitive allows a "compute out." If further computation reveals that the value would not be useful unless it were immediately present, then the exchange is aborted.

The following analogy may prove helpful. Imagine (process) Joe in his office. He is researching some problem (computing) and decides he needs to go to the library (obtain some resource). Joe can take a cab or a bus to the library (Joe has the choice of two different ways of obtaining the resource). Cabs are preferable, but the taxi company is unreliable and sometimes does not respond to requests. Joe decides that he might want to take a cab to the library later, so he sends out an XR_{cab}(request for cab) and continues his research (computes). At some point he may decide that he really does not need to go to the library (the computation never needs the value in the library). He can then just forget to see if any cab ever responded to his request. The cab may or may not eventually appear.* Or Joe could find himself stuck, with no choice but to go to the library. If no cab appears (the XR responded with his original argument), he can give up and take the bus.

The delayed exchange system can be integrated with the amb operator of the previous section. Joe could then call a cab, call a bus, and compute. When his computation became limited by the need to visit the library, he could then wait for either the cab or the bus to arrive.

---

* This attitude on the part of their customers may explain why the cabs are so unreliable.

As powerful as this extension may seem, it has some limitations. For example, a process cannot discover if an exchange has been completed without either forcing the exchange to complete or abort. This parallels the inability of a function in a delayed-evaluation system (Chapter 12) to find out if a value has been obtained for a delayed evaluation.

Since the XR operator possesses duration in this scheme, we can imagine another exchange function that would fit into the previously barred portion of Table 7-2. This function would be both instantaneous (nonblocking) and able to converse with itself.

Perspective

Exchange Functions provides bidirectional, synchronous communication. The model includes mechanisms for blocking communication, unblocked communication, and broadcast offers of communication. Exchange Functions also extends neatly to other capabilities, such as guarded commands and call-by-need. Syntactically, Exchange Functions has a particularly simple and elegant form: a minimal amount of structure provides a general and flexible facility.

This is not to imply that Exchange Functions handles all synchronization problems. In particular, the static number of exchange channels and the inability to evaluate the exchange channel before use are liabilities for the description of dynamically growing systems. However, these deficiencies are easily remedied. Overall, Exchange Functions allows many interesting communication architectures to be built from only a few simple primitives.

PROBLEMS

7-1 Program a general (n-ary) semaphore in Exchange Functions. Base your program on the binary semaphore program.

7-2 Rewrite the buffer program to be a bounded buffer.

7-3 Rewrite the problem of the constant-temperature liquid bath so that it is more realistic.

† **7-4** A non-empty channel can be in one of two states: either there is a single waiting X or there are one or more waiting XMs. Use this information to design a bounded-time program and data structure to perform the channel operations.

7-5 Exchange Functions hypothesizes three classes of exchange functions with communication capabilities represented by Table 7-1. Invent new classes of exchange functions, describing their possible communication patterns. Present a rationale for your system.

7-6 What is the effect of allowing amb to range over any expression?

REFERENCES

[**Fitzwater 77**] Fitzwater, D. R., and P. Zave, "The Use of Formal Asynchronous Process Specifications in a System Development Process," *Proc. 6th Texas Conf. Comp. Syst.*, The University of Texas at Austin (November 1977), pp. 2B-21:2B-30. This paper contains the first published reference to exchange functions. At that time, they were called XC, XA, and XS (now X, XM, and XR).

[**McCarthy 63**] McCarthy, J., "A Basis for a Mathematical Theory of Computation," in P. Braffort, and D. Hirschberg (eds.), *Computer Programming and Formal Systems*, North Holland, Amsterdam (1963), pp. 33–70. In this paper McCarthy lays the groundwork for many of the ideas that have grown up around the mathematical theory of computation, such as the idea that programs can be proven correct. He also introduces the amb primitive, an idea much copied and insufficiently credited.

[**Metcalfe 76**] Metcalfe, R. M., and D. R. Boggs, "Ethernet: Distributed Packet Switching for Local Computer Networks," *CACM*, vol. 19, no. 7 (July 1976), pp. 395–404. A description of the Ethernet mechanism for local-area networks. Ethernet uses a contention ring, where processors communicate by "yelling" into a shared medium (coaxial cable) until one can be heard by itself.

[**Zave 77**] Zave, P., and D. R. Fitzwater, "Specification of Asynchronous Interactions using Primitive Functions," Technical Report 598, Department of Computer Science, University of Maryland, College Park, Maryland (1977). This paper is a good description of the Exchange Functions model. We adapted the unbounded buffer example from this paper.

[**Zave 82**] Zave, P., "An Operational Approach to Requirements Specification for Embedded Systems," *IEEE Trans. Softw. Eng.*, vol. SE-8, no. 3 (May 1982), pp. 250–269. This paper presents Exchange Functions as a requirements specification mechanism. Zave emphasizes using Exchange Functions as an operational approach to requirements specification. Operational approaches produce executable descriptions of the system specified. (This is in contrast to declarative approaches that specify properties of the system without describing the mechanism for achieving them.) Zave also describes the specification language PAISLey, which is based on exchange functions.

[**Zave 83**] Zave, P., personal communication, 1983.

EIGHT

CONCURRENT PROCESSES

The work of George Milne and Robin Milner is an attempt to describe a mathematical semantics for concurrent computation and communication. Their goal is a formal calculus of concurrent computation, much as the lambda calculus is a formal calculus of uniprocess computation. They are trying to establish the meaning of programs, not to provide a tool for programming per se.

From the title of their paper, "Concurrent Processes and their Syntax," [Milne 79] we adopt the name "Concurrent Processes" for the Milne-Milner model. Their model has explicit processes that communicate synchronously and bidirectionally over labeled channels. The number of processes and their communication connections can change dynamically. Most of this work is concerned with proving that the semantics of their model is specific and unambiguous and that the communication operations provided by the model form an "algebra" with the right properties. This mathematics is heavily dependent on the theory of sets, powerdomains, and functions; it is beyond the scope of this book. Instead, we find their formalism interesting in its own right. We develop examples of that formalism to illustrate its power, reassured by the understanding that the resulting system is mathematically correct.*

---

* This chapter is perhaps the most difficult in the book. It is not essential for achieving an understanding of later material and can be skipped at first reading.

Processes and Nets

The fundamental processing objects of the Milne-Milner model are processes. Formally, a *process* is a set of ports. Each *port* is a triple, formed of a name, a value, and a continuation. We write the port with name α, value u, and continuation f as $\alpha:\langle u,f \rangle$. Two ports are complementary if their names match, one "plain" and the other "barred." Thus, ports with names α and $\bar{\alpha}$ are complementary. Complementary ports can be "joined," providing a path for their processes to communicate.

Milne and Milner have a graphical notation to illustrate processes and communication paths. Figure 8-1 shows the graphic for process r. This process has two ports, α and $\bar{\beta}$. Port α has value u_1 and continuation f_1. Similarly, $\bar{\beta}$'s value is u_2 and its continuation, f_2.

When two processes communicate (compose), they simultaneously exchange information and reconfigure themselves into new processes. Processes communicate through complementary ports. If r communicates through the port α, it sends the value u_1 on the "communication line." It simultaneously receives a value on that line. Let us call that value v_1. The value v_1 becomes the (single) argument to the continuation f_1. The result of this application describes the new process (or set of processes). These continuations capture the state of the process, much as variables and the program counter capture the state of a conventional program. These notions of state and bidirectional communication are a formal echo of the ideas of Exchange Functions.

Milne and Milner use lambda expressions (Section 1-2) to describe the functions f_1 and f_2. They use the lambda calculus because it is a standard for mathematical description of functions, not because it has properties particularly amenable to programming. The important feature of the continuations f_1 and f_2 is that they evaluate to objects that describe processes (or sets of processes).

In Concurrent Processes, communicating processes send each other a value. This value can either include significant information or merely be a synchronization signal. Thus, there are four possible combinations of value transmission in communication: both processes send a signal (*pure synchronization*); a process receives a value, but sends a signal (*input*); a process sends a value, but receives a signal (*output*); or both processes send and receive values (*exchange*).

Concurrent Processes and Exchange Functions (Chapter 7) are the only systems we study that provide simultaneous, bidirectional communication. Most

$\alpha:\langle u_1, f_1 \rangle$ $\bar{\beta}:\langle u_2, f_2 \rangle$

Figure 8-1 A process.

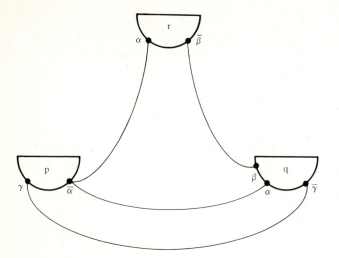

Figure 8-2 A net of processes.

systems permit information transfer in only a single direction at a time. Even Milne and Milner note that the transmission of information (as opposed to signal) in both directions is not used by any of their examples (though it is used in one of ours). We surmise that bidirectional communication is included not so much as a reflection of "reality" but only to make the formalism more elegant.

A group of processes can be composed into a *net*. From the perspective of the external world, that net now acts (almost) like a single process. The compositions of the net then fall into three classes: *input*, in which a value is brought in from the outside environment; *output*, in which a value is sent to the environment; and *covert*, in which information passes between the processes internal to the net. Figure 8-2 shows the graphical description of a net of processes. The visible port names of a process characterize that process. This set is called the *sort* of the process. Similarly, when a group of processes is composed into a net, the port names externally visible from that net are the sort of the net. One operation in the model allows hiding the internal port names of the net.

In Concurrent Processes, the number of processes can grow without bound. The model allows a single composition to create (in a stepwise fashion) an unbounded number of new processes. Since this is a mathematical model, infinite sets are natural objects. The algebra of process composition determines which computations may take place. A "run" of a Concurrent Process system is thus the selection of one sequence of compositions from the many possible.

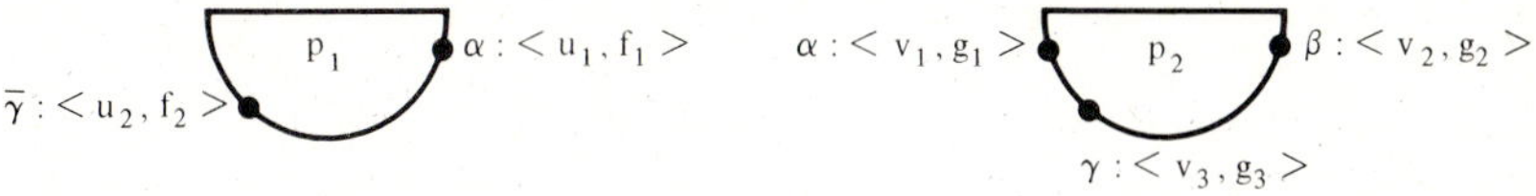

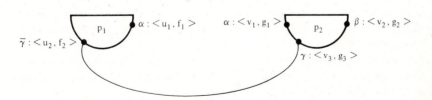

Figure 8-3 A pair of processes.

Mathematics of Composition

Let us assume that we have a pair of processes, p_1 and p_2, as diagrammed in Figure 8-3. Their composition, $p_1|p_2$, is shown in Figure 8-4. Processes p_1 and p_2 connect through the complementary ports, γ and $\overline{\gamma}$. The composition $p_1|p_2$ has five communication capabilities with the external environment: α, $\overline{\alpha}$, $\overline{\beta}$, γ, and $\overline{\gamma}$. One of these is $\alpha:\langle u_1.\ \lambda w.(f_1(w))|p_2\rangle$. If this communication occurs, then u_1 is sent to the environment and a value x is sent to p_1. Process p_1 is transformed into $f_1(x)$. This is called a *renewal* of p_1. Process p_2 is unchanged by this communication; it is then composed with the renewal of p_1.

There is also the possibility of covert communication between p_1 and p_2 through their ports $\overline{\gamma}$ and γ. In that case, their composition also contains the composition of $f_2(v_3)$ and $g_3(u_2)$. This is the result of exchanging the values v_3 and u_2 and applying the continuations to the values received.

As precise as they may appear to be, the diagrams are only illustrative of the process composition relationship. The actual computation is specifically the result computed by the equations that define the model. The most important of these is the equation that defines process composition:*

Figure 8-4 The composition of p_1 and p_2.

---

* In these examples we use the set comprehension operator {}. However, the objects are powerdomains. To be technically correct we should use the powerdomain operators ⦃⦄. A powerdomain is a power set with a partial-ordering relation among its members [Smyth 78].

$$\mathsf{p}|\mathsf{p}' = \quad \{\mu \colon \langle \mathsf{u}, \lambda \mathsf{v}.(\mathsf{f}(\mathsf{v})|\mathsf{p}')\rangle \text{ s.t. } \mu \colon \langle \mathsf{u}, \mathsf{f}\rangle \in \mathsf{p}\} \tag{1}$$

$$\cup \{\mu \colon \langle \mathsf{u}', \lambda \mathsf{v}'.(\mathsf{p}|\mathsf{f}'(\mathsf{v}'))\rangle \text{ s.t. } \mu \colon \langle \mathsf{u}', \mathsf{f}'\rangle \in \mathsf{p}'\} \tag{2}$$

$$\cup \bigcup \{\mathsf{f}(\mathsf{u}')|\mathsf{f}'(\mathsf{u}) \text{ s.t. } \mu \colon \langle \mathsf{u}, \mathsf{f}\rangle \in \mathsf{p}, \overline{\mu} \colon \langle \mathsf{u}', \mathsf{f}'\rangle \in \mathsf{p}'\} \tag{3}$$

The first two lines of this equation define a composition with the external environment. The first line, (1), specifies that process p is to be given a computing step and the result composed with p'. Line (2) is the corresponding stepping of p'. The final line, (3), describes the communication between p and p': the exchange of values and the recomposition of their respective continuations. This is a synchronous exchange.

Milne and Milner also provide mechanisms for renaming labels and for restricting label visibility, much as the lambda calculus provides α conversion for the renaming of lambda variables. Renaming is easier to understand by analogy to hardware design. Each process in the Milne-Milner model is like an integrated circuit and each label is like a pin on that circuit. One would no more want every α label on every process of type r to be connected than one would want every pin 3 on every shift register to share a common wire. Renaming and restricting visibility allow the correct connection of a process/label and its protection from similarly described processes. One wants to be able to bundle a net of processes together, secure that their internal connections cannot be "shorted" by an oddly named external wire. Like Lynch and Fischer, Milne and Milner prove that the behavior of a net of processes is indistinguishable from the behavior of a single process. Without relabeling and hiding this would not be possible.

The operator $\|$ first composes two nets (or processes) and then restricts their shared ports to be externally invisible.

Examples

In the following examples, we present the themes of Concurrent Processes without becoming mired in the mathematical details of formal semantics. Our programs may appear to be forbiddingly symbolic. However, they are usually just the lambda calculus expression of finite state automata or register automata.* In our most complicated example, the card reader, we provide state-transition diagrams of the modeled automata.

---

* Register automata are a variation of finite state automata in which registers that can store integers become part of the automata state and are used in determining state transitions. If the registers can store only a finite number of values, the resulting automata are still FSA; if they can store unbounded values (with the "right kind" of operations on those values), the automata are Turing-equivalent.

Figure 8-5 The initial state of the register.

Register A simple but interesting process in the Concurrent Processes model is a register. We consider a register r. This register responds to two different signals, set and get. Set takes the value sent and sets the register to that value, returning a synchronization signal. Get ignores its input, sends the register's value, and regenerates the register to the same register. "Setting the register to the value" is not exactly the correct description. Instead, sending a 5 to the register makes the register *become* the thing that responds to get with a 5, and to set x by *becoming* the thing that behaves like a register with value x. If the sequence of communications

$$\text{set } 5, \text{ set } 12, \text{ get, get, set } 3, \text{ get}$$

is received, the register replies to the first two get's with **12**, and the last get with **3**. The register responds to the set commands by sending a synchronization pulse $(\odot)$.

The register has ports set and $\overline{\text{get}}$. Since it is meaningless to try to get the value of the register before it has been set, the register initially has only the port set. Figure 8-5 shows the initial state of the register. The register is

$$r \equiv \{\text{set}:\langle\odot, \lambda z.\text{REG}(z)\rangle\}$$

where the definition of REG is:*

$$\begin{aligned}
\text{REG}(z) \equiv \\
\{\text{set}:\langle\odot, \lambda z'.\text{REG}(z')\rangle, \\
\overline{\text{get}}:\langle z, \text{K}(\text{REG}(z))\rangle\}
\end{aligned}$$

Evaluating REG(z) produces a process of two ports, set and $\overline{\text{get}}$. Port set accepts a value z′ and regenerates the register; port $\overline{\text{get}}$ responds with the value z (the value placed there by the last set) and regenerates the same register.

A typical sequence of communications with the register produces the register states shown in Table 8-1. To assign to the register, processes use ports labeled $\overline{\text{set}}$; to retrieve the current value of the register, processes use ports labeled get. Processes that share this register are composed with it.

---

* K is the constant combinator, $\lambda x.(\lambda y.x)$. A constant function is a function that always returns the same value. For example, $f(x) = 5$ is a constant function. The constant combinator K constructs constant functions. What should the constant of these functions be? They take the value given as the argument to K. So K(5) is a function whose value is always 5, $\lambda y.5$.

Table 8-1 Register states

Port	Value received		New register state	Value sent by register
Initial state		$r \equiv$	$\{\text{set: } \langle \odot,\ \lambda z.\text{REG}(z) \rangle\}$	
set	5	$\Rightarrow$ $r \equiv$	$\{\text{set: } \langle \odot,\ \lambda z'.\text{REG}(z') \rangle,$ $\overline{\text{get}}: \langle 5,\ \lambda y.\text{REG}(5) \rangle\}$	$\odot$
set	12	$\Rightarrow$ $r \equiv$	$\{\text{set: } \langle \odot,\ \lambda z'.\text{REG}(z') \rangle,$ $\overline{\text{get}}: \langle 12,\ \lambda y.\text{REG}(12) \rangle\}$	$\odot$
$\overline{\text{get}}$	$\odot$	$\Rightarrow$ $r \equiv$	$\{\text{set: } \langle \odot,\ \lambda z'.\text{REG}(z') \rangle,$ $\overline{\text{get}}: \langle 12,\ \lambda y.\text{REG}(12) \rangle\}$	12
$\overline{\text{get}}$	$\odot$	$\Rightarrow$ $r \equiv$	$\{\text{set: } \langle \odot,\ \lambda z'.\text{REG}(z') \rangle,$ $\overline{\text{get}}: \langle 12,\ \lambda y.\text{REG}(12) \rangle\}$	12
set	3	$\Rightarrow$ $r \equiv$	$\{\text{set: } \langle \odot,\ \lambda z'.\text{REG}(z') \rangle,$ $\overline{\text{get}}: \langle 3,\ \lambda y.\text{REG}(3) \rangle\}$	$\odot$

Binary semaphore In the previous example, the register started with a single port and quickly grew another. Our model of a binary semaphore is a process. It generates and eliminates a port with each step. Synchronization is assured because the semaphore has only a single legal port (P or V) at any time.

$$\text{free} \equiv \{\text{P:}\langle\odot. \qquad\qquad \text{busy} \equiv \{\text{V:}\langle\odot.$$
$$\text{K(busy)}\rangle\} \qquad\qquad\qquad \text{K(free)}\rangle\}$$

When the semaphore is free it has a single port whose continuation takes it to the busy state; when it is busy it has a single port whose continuation takes it to the free state. Processes request the semaphore through their own port $\overline{\text{P}}$; they release the semaphore through port $\overline{\text{V}}$. The semaphore responds with a synchronization signal only, not information. Like the register, this semaphore uses the constant combinator K.

Theorem proving The Milne-Milner model allows the arbitrary growth (and shrinkage) of the process net. As an example of the creation of new processes in the Milne-Milner model, we examine a naive form of theorem proving over the propositional calculus.* This program is a partial decision procedure for tautologies in propositional logic. A *tautology* is a formula of propositional logic

---

* We direct the reader interested in the technology of automated theorem proving to Robinson [Robinson 79] or Loveland [Loveland 78].

(a *well-formed formula* or *wff*) that is true no matter what assignments are made to its variables. Thus, the formula

$$(P \wedge Q) \vee \neg (P \wedge Q)$$

is a tautology.

The algorithm requires first transforming the wff into conjunctive normal form. A formula in *conjunctive normal form* is the "**AND**ing" ($\wedge$) of a group of formulas, each of which is the "**OR**ing" ($\vee$) of a set of literals. A *literal* is either a propositional variable X or its negation $\neg X$. For example, the formula

$$(P \vee Q \vee \neg R) \wedge (\neg P \vee R) \wedge (Q)$$

is in conjunctive normal form. A theorem about propositional logic states that every formula is equivalent to some formula in conjunctive normal form. We call the literal $\neg X$ the *complement* of X, and X the complement of $\neg X$. A *clause* is a set of literals.

A pair of clauses, G and H, *clash* if there is some literal X such that X is in G and the complement of X is in H. The *fusion* of these two clauses is the clause

$$(G - \{X\}) \cup (H - \{\text{complement}(X)\})$$

For example, the fusion of the clauses:

$$\{A, \neg B, E\}$$

and

$$\{\neg C, D, \neg E\}$$

is the clause

$$\{A, \neg B, \neg C, D\}$$

A set of clauses *grows* if there are two clauses G and H in that set that clash. The set of clauses is then extended to include the result of the fusion.

The resolution algorithm takes a wff, negates it, and converts it into conjunctive normal form, revealing a clause structure. The algorithm then fuses pairs of clauses until it generates the *null clause* (the clause with no literals). The null clause indicates success; its appearance shows that the original formula is a tautology.

Real theorem proving systems take great care to avoid doing the same fusion repeatedly. However, we ignore this constraint in our simple program. Our procedure is also incomplete; it does not necessarily recognize that a particular formula is or is not a tautology. Instead, it continues processing, growing new processes at each communication exchange.

In our theorem prover we represent each clause as a process. Each literal in that clause is a port, with negative literals as the barred ports. At each port the

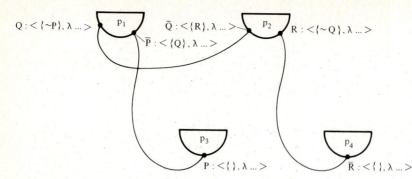

Figure 8-6 The resolution clause processes.

value offered is the clause, less the port literal. Each process regenerates both itself and a new process. This new process's program expresses the fusion of the two clauses. This process is added to the net and commences communicating with the other clauses. The net thereby grows. In general, the clause $G=\{e_1, e_2, \ldots e_n\}$ offers the communications

Clause(G) $\equiv$
    (G = { }) $\rightarrow$
        {answer:$\langle$Done, $\odot\rangle$},
        { e:$\langle$G$-$\{e\}, λG$'$.Clause (G$'$ $\cup$ (G$-$e))$\rangle$ | Clause(G) s.t. e $\in$ G }

where $\neg e$ offers communication on $\bar{e}$ (not shown in the code). **Clause** spawns two processes for the resolvent.* We present a simple example of the theorem prover. Consider the following well-formed formula of the propositional calculus:

$$((P \supset Q) \wedge (Q \supset R)) \supset (P \supset R)$$

We want to show that this formula is a tautology. We transform its negation into conjunctive normal form, yielding

$$(\neg P \vee Q) \wedge (\neg Q \vee R) \wedge (P) \wedge (\neg R)$$

which is rewritten in our set notation as

$$\{\neg P, Q\} \{\neg Q, R\} \{P\} \{\neg R\}.$$

The initial processes for the computation (illustrated in Figure 8-6) are

---

   * The form $p \rightarrow x, y$ is an abbreviation for **if** p **then** x **else** y. This is a shorthand for conditionals (Section 1-2).

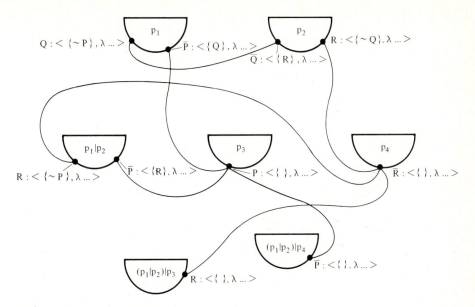

Figure 8-7 An intermediate resolution state.

$p_1 \equiv \{\overline{P}: \langle \{Q\}, \lambda u. \dots \rangle$
    $Q: \langle \{\neg P\}, \lambda u. \dots \rangle \}$

$p_2 \equiv \{\overline{Q}: \langle \{R\}, \lambda u. \dots \rangle$
    $R: \langle \{\neg Q\}, \lambda u. \dots \rangle \}$

$p_3 \equiv \{P: \langle \{\}, \lambda u. \dots \rangle \}$

$p_4 \equiv \{\overline{R}: \langle \{\}, \lambda u. \dots \rangle \}$

Each function regenerates its host process and a new process representing the fusion of its covert communication. If this clause is empty, instead of attempting to continue covert communication, that process has a port to relate the success of the process to the external environment. We leave completing the details of these functions as an exercise (Exercise 8-4).

Figure 8-7 shows a possible state of the net after several computational steps. Even if the original formula is a tautology, there is no guarantee that $p_1 | p_2 | p_3 | p_4$ ever communicates with the external environment.

Card reader Our final example of modeling with Concurrent Processes is the description of the interacting parts of a card reading system [Milne 78]. This example is particularly interesting because it models a system composed of both hardware and software components.

Table 8-2 The status register word

Bit	Status when set
15	Error.
14	Done reading. Another card may be demanded.
9	Card is being read.
8	Reader device off-line.
6	If set when status register loaded, allows the setting of bits 14 and 15 to cause a driver interrupt.
0	If set when status register loaded, causes driver to signal reader to begin reading.

The card reader is a Digital CR11. This reader is used in the PDP-11 series of computers. It follows the PDP-11 system philosophy of "peripheral device control through assignment to and interrogation of status registers." That is, to find out the state of a peripheral device (for example, waiting for a card, reading a card, or mutilating a card), the processor reads the status register associated with that device. Various bits of the register have different meanings. The processor forces the device to particular states by setting values in the status register.

The card reader has four components:

The *reader device* takes the card punches and translates them to numeric information usable by the rest of the system. We treat card reading as a primitive that reads an entire card in a single operation.

The *buffer register* receives the numeric values from the card reader, one at a time, and transmits them to the "outside world."

The *status register* is a 16-bit word. Each bit of the status register can represent some condition in the card reader hardware. Not all the bits in the CR11 status register are used. Table 8-2 lists the significant bits and their interpretation. In Figure 8-8, the significant bits are highlighted.

The *driver program* controls the sequencing of the other components. The driver program is software. This contrasts with the other components of the reader, which are all hardware.

Figure 8-9 shows the net of processes and connections for the card reader. In Figure 8-10, we redraw the connections between the card reader com-

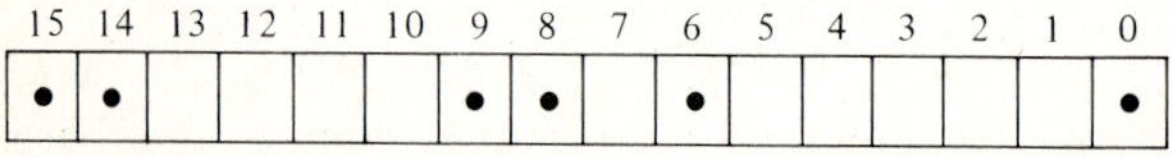

Figure 8-8 The status bits.

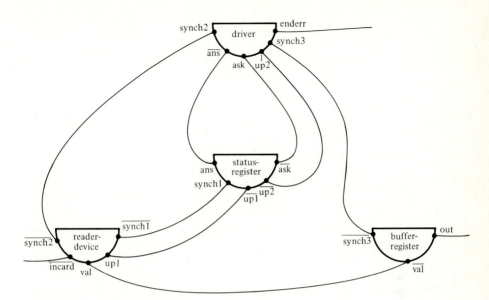

Figure 8-9 The card reader net.

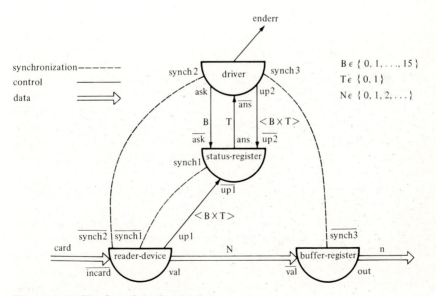

Figure 8-10 The flow of synchronization.

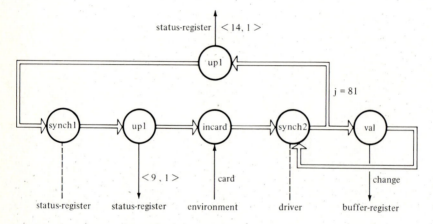

Figure 8-11 The reader device state machine.

ponents to show the flow of synchronization, control data, and information. The connecting links are labeled according to the variety of information transmitted: pure synchronization lines are dotted, control lines solid, and data lines double. The arrowheads show the direction of information flow. The whole net has three communication lines with the external environment: incard, which connects to the card reading mechanism; out, which sends card values to the main computer; and enderr, which signals end-of-card and errors.

The reader device is a six-state automaton. When it receives a synchronization pulse (the 0-bit) from the status register (synch1), it responds by setting the 9-bit in the status register (up1, busy reading). It then inputs an entire card from the environment (incard) and waits for a next character pulse from the driver (synch2). It loops, sending characters to the buffer (val) at each next character pulse, until all 80 characters have been transmitted. It then sets the 14-bit in the status register (up1, ready for next card) and goes back to the synch1 state. Figure 8-11 shows the states of the reader device.

The program for the reader device is as follows:

reader-device ≡
    {$\overline{\text{synch1}}$:⟨⊙.
             K(reader-device2)⟩}

reader-device2 ≡
    {up1:⟨⟨9,1⟩.
             K(reader-device3)⟩}

reader-device3 ≡
    {$\overline{\text{incard}}$:⟨⊙.
             K(countsend(1))⟩}

countsend(j) ≡
    {synch2:⟨⊙.
             K((j=81) →
                    {up1:⟨⟨14,1⟩.
                        K(reader-device)⟩},
                  {val:⟨change(c[j]).
                        K(countsend(j+1))⟩}))⟩)}

where **change** is a function that encodes a card column as an integer and **c** is a card.

The buffer register is a three-state automaton. It simply loops between receiving a character from the reader device (**val**), getting a synchronization pulse from the driver (**synch3**), and sending the character to the outside environment (**out**). Figure 8-12 shows the state-transition diagram of the buffer register. The equations that define the buffer are

buffer-register ≡
    {$\overline{\text{val}}$:⟨⊙.
        λn.{$\overline{\text{synch3}}$:⟨⊙.
                K({out:⟨n.
                        K(buffer-register)⟩})⟩}⟩}

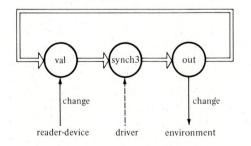

Figure 8-12 The buffer register state machine.

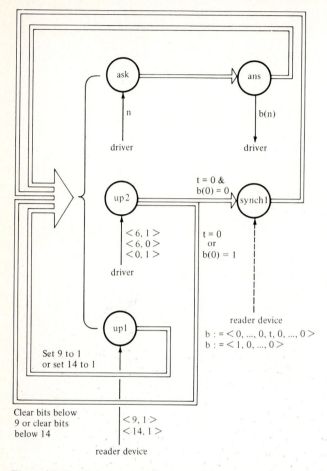

Figure 8-13 The status register state machine.

The status register is initially prepared for any of three different interactions. The driver can have an **ask/ans** dialogue with the status register, requesting the value of a particular bit. The driver can set (or clear) either the 0-bit or 6-bit in the status register, and the reader device can set either the 9-bit (indicating that it is busy reading a card) or the 14-bit (indicating that it has finished and is waiting). Figure 8-13 shows the states of the status register. The large left brace indicates the possible indeterminate interactions. The defining equations for the status register are as follows:

status-register ≡
     status($\langle 0,1,0,0,0,0,1,0,0,0,0,0,0,0,0,0 \rangle$)

status(b) ≡
    {$\overline{ask}$:⟨⊙,
          λn.{ans:⟨b[n+1],
                    K(status(b))⟩}⟩,
      $\overline{up2}$:⟨⊙,
          λm.((m[1]=0 ∧ m[2]=1) →
             {synch1:⟨⊙,
                    K(status(⟨1, b[2], ..., b[8], 0, ..., 0⟩)))},
                status(⟨0, ..., b[m[1]], m[2], b[m[1]+2], 0, ..., 0⟩))),
      $\overline{up1}$:⟨⊙,
          λm.status(⟨0, ..., b[m[1]], m[2], b[m[1]+2], ..., b[16]⟩))}

Here b is a 16-bit vector (the register) and m is an ordered pair. Vector b's elements are indexed from 1 to 16 (not 0 to 15). The first element of m (m[1]) is a bit number (0 ... 15), and the second element (m[2]) is a set/clear (1/0 or true/false) value.

The final component of the card reader is the driver program. The program is a long loop. Most of the time it waits for an opportunity to read a card. When the card reader is no longer busy and is "online," the driver interrupt is enabled and the reading process is started. Reading continues in the embedded loop until the end-of-card message (or read error message) is received from the status register. The driver program then sends a −1 to the environment on the enderr line, disables the interrupt, and prepares to read the next card. Figure 8-14 shows this process. The defining equations for the driver program are as follows:

driver ≡
    {ask:⟨9,
        K({$\overline{ans}$:⟨⊙,
              λt.((t=1) → driver, driver2)⟩})⟩)}
driver2 ≡
    {ask:⟨8,
        K({$\overline{ans}$:⟨⊙,
              λt.((t=1) → driver, driver3)⟩})⟩)}
driver3 ≡
    {up2:⟨⟨6,1⟩,
        K({up2:⟨⟨0,1⟩,
             K(doio)⟩})⟩)}
doio ≡
    {synch2:⟨⊙,
        K(doio2)⟩}
doio2 ≡
    {ask:⟨15,
        K(doio3)⟩}

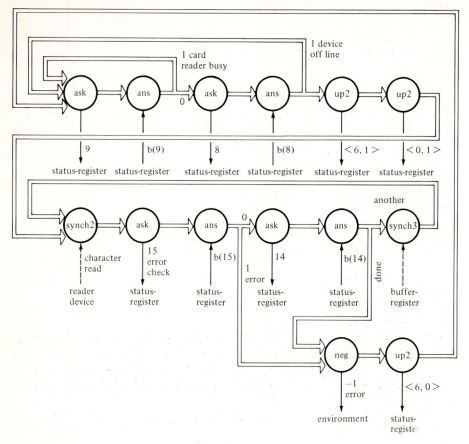

Figure 8-14 The driver state machine.

doio3 ≡
   {$\overline{\text{ans}}$:⟨⊙,
       λt.((t=1) → endcard, doio4)⟩}

doio4 ≡
   {ask:⟨14,
       K(doio5)⟩}

doio5 ≡
   {$\overline{\text{ans}}$:⟨⊙,
       λt.((t=1) → endcard, doio6)⟩}

doio6 ≡
   {synch3:⟨⊙,
           K(doio)⟩}

endcard ≡
    {enderr:⟨-1,
          K(endcard2)⟩}

endcard2 ≡
    {up2:⟨⟨6,0⟩,
          K(driver)⟩}

The composition of these four devices forms the complete card reader device

card reader ≡ reader-device ∥ status-register ∥ buffer-register ∥ driver

where ∥ is the "compose and restrict internal names" operator. It is possible to prove that the driver correctly controls the other components of the card reader (with respect to the appropriate specification).

Perspective

The Concurrent Processes model provides a formal semantics of concurrent computation. Stripped of its formalisms, this model specifies explicit processes that communicate bidirectionally and synchronously. Processes communicate over a set of ports (effectively, channels). Each port has two sides (barred and unbarred). Only processes seeking access from opposite sides of a port communicate. Processes in the Milne-Milner model can be dynamically created and destroyed. The model uses lambda expressions to describe the functional ability of the processes. Lambda expressions are used because they are the standard mathematical way of expressing functions; they have a long-studied and well-understood semantics.

PROBLEMS

8-1 Change the register to respond to set with the last value of the register.
8-2 Can you change the register to respond to set with the value sent?
8-3 Give an expression that represents a general (n-ary) semaphore.
8-4 Complete the code of Clause in the theorem prover.
8-5 Model an unbounded buffer in Concurrent Processes.
8-6 Write a version of the elevator controller of Chapter 14 using the communication mechanisms of Concurrent Processes. Which aspects of the elevator controller does the model capture? Which aspects is it unable to capture?

REFERENCES

[**Loveland 78**] Loveland, D. W., *Automated Theorem Proving: A Logical Basis*, North-Holland, Amsterdam (1978). This book is a detailed exposition on automated theorem proving, with particular emphasis on resolution and its variations.

[**Milne 78**] Milne, G. J., "A Mathematical Model of Concurrent Computation," Ph.D. dissertation, University of Edinburgh, Edinburgh (1978). This is Milne's doctoral dissertation, describing much of the model. Milne presented the original card reader example in this dissertation.

[**Milne 79**] Milne, G., and R. Milner, "Concurrent Processes and Their Syntax," *JACM*, vol. 26, no. 2 (April 1979), pp. 302–321. Milne and Milner present the definitive paper on Concurrent Processes. This paper is formal and difficult to read. The register and semaphore examples are drawn from this paper.

[**Milner 80**] Milner, R., *A Calculus of Communicating Systems*, Lecture Notes in Computer Science 92, Springer-Verlag, New York (1980). CCS is another (and similar) attempt by Milner to develop an algebra of concurrent communicating systems.

[**Milner 83**] Milner, R., "Calculi for Synchrony and Asynchrony," *Theoret. Comp. Sci.*, vol. 25, no. 3 (1983), pp. 267–310. Milner presents a calculus for distributed computation based on four combinators. This paper extends his work on CCS [Milner 80] to include synchronous communication.

[**Robinson 79**] Robinson, J. A., *Logic: Form and Function*, North Holland, New York (1979). Like [Loveland 78], this is a book on automated theorem proving. Robinson places less emphasis on variations of resolution, and greater emphasis on the foundations of logic and semantics. He provides many programmed examples.

[**Smyth 78**] Smyth, M. B., "Powerdomains," *J. Comput. Syst. Sci.*, vol. 16, no. 1 (February 1978), pp. 23–36. Smyth describes the mathematics of powerdomains.

NINE

PETRI NETS AND DATA FLOW

This chapter concerns models inspired by graphs. These models use the nodes of a graph to represent active processing agents that exchange information along paths specified by the edges. We discuss two such models, Petri Nets and Data Flow.

Petri Nets is a formal modeling technique that encodes the states of a dynamic system as the markings of tokens on a graph. Petri Nets expresses in the graph structure the possible state transitions of the system being modeled. Petri Nets has been used to model not only computing systems, but also systems from domains as diverse as neurology, chemistry, and economics. Many theorems have been proved about the formal properties of Petri Nets.

Petri Nets is useful for modeling the states of systems. The tokens passed around a net hold no information. Instead, the number and arrangement of tokens encode the modeled system's state. One can treat a Petri net as a computing mechanism by counting tokens. However, Petri Nets is a weak device for expressing computation. They are not even Turing-equivalent. Data Flow extends the Petri Nets metaphor to associate information with the tokens and to permit computation at the graph nodes. In doing so, Data Flow broadens the limited computational ability of Petri Nets into a mechanism that can compute any computable function. The Data Flow model has excited interest in building *Data Flow machines*, computers whose internal architecture reflects Data Flow's functional nature [Agerwala 82; Treleaven 82]. The designers of these machines hope to avoid the bottleneck of the single-instruction cycle of conventional von Neumann architectures, producing systems that exploit Data Flow's potential concurrency.

Petri Nets is an outgrowth of the 1962 doctoral dissertation of Carl Adam Petri [Petri 62]. Much of the early work on Petri Nets was done by A. W. Holt and his associates at Applied Data Research [Holt 68]. Since then, there has been much interest in both the theory and application of Petri Nets. Peterson's article in *Computing Surveys* [Peterson 77] and his book, *Petri Net Theory and the Modeling of Systems* [Peterson 81], are comprehensive overviews of the subject.

Data Flow models can be traced to Adams' dissertation on data-driven computation [Adams 68], Karp and Miller's work on program schemata [Karp 66], Rodriguez-Bezos's invention of "program graphs" [Rodriguez-Bezos 69], unpublished work by Ivan Sutherland on graphical programming, and the single assignment concept of Tesler and Enea [Tesler 68]. The graph-and-token structure we describe is based on Fosseen's M.I.T. Master's thesis [Fosseen 72]. Early work on Data Flow machines includes the work of Arvind and Gostelow [Arvind 77], Davis [Davis 78], Dennis [Dennis 74], Syre et al. [Berger 82; Comte 79], and Watson and Gurd [Watson 82].

9-1 PETRI NETS

Petri Nets models the states of a system by marking the nodes of a graph with tokens. Petri Nets not only represents states by marking nodes, but also encodes the permissible state transitions in the graph structure.

The graph in Figure 9-1 is a Petri net. This graph has two kinds of nodes, *places*, drawn as circles, and *transitions*, drawn as line segments. Directed edges connect the places and the transitions. Every edge connects one place and one transition. There can be several edges between any pair of places and transitions. If there are k edges going from a place to a transition, we say that the *in-degree to* that transition from that place is k. Similarly, the *out-degree* from a transition to a place is the number of edges *from* that transition to that place.

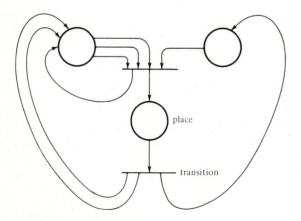

place

transition

Figure 9-1 A Petri Net.

Figure 9-2 The barbershop Petri net.

Formally, a Petri net is a bipartite, directed multigraph. That is, a Petri net is like a conventional graph composed of nodes and edges, but (1) the graph is directed—each edge goes *from* a particular node *to* another node, (2) the graph is a multigraph—there can be several edges from any given node to another, and (3) the graph is bipartite—the nodes of the graph can be partitioned into two sets (the transitions and the places), such that each edge connects an element of one set to an element of the other.*

Petri nets are marked with tokens. A *marked* Petri net is the association of a number with each place, the number of tokens on that place. The number of

---

* There is a natural mapping from Petri nets to multisets. (A *multiset* is a set in which individual elements can appear repeatedly.) In this mapping, the nodes of the graph represent elements of a domain, and the edges of the graph encode functions over multisets of nodes. Peterson presents the details of one such formalization [Peterson 81].

tokens on any place at one time is not bounded but is always finite. Figure 9-2 shows a marked Petri net. This Petri net models the operation of a barbershop. Each token in the *waiting* place represents a customer waiting for a haircut. Each token in the *cutting* place represents a barber giving a haircut. Each token in the *resting* place represents an idle barber. Each token in the *exit* place represents a customer leaving the shop. The figure shows three customers waiting for service, two current haircuts, and one resting barber. In general, the arrangement of tokens on the places of a Petri net represents the state of the system modeled by that net.

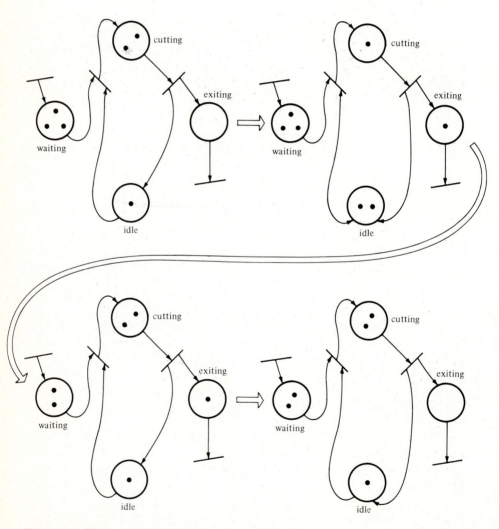

Figure 9-3 States of the barbershop.

Execution of a Petri net is controlled by the number and distribution of tokens on the places of that net. The arrangement of tokens is changed by the *firing* of the transitions. When a transition fires, it removes tokens from the places that have edges running *to* the transition (the input places) and puts tokens on those places that have edges running *from* the transition to them (the output places). More specifically, a transition may fire if it is enabled. A transition is enabled if every place connected to that transition with in-degree k has at least k tokens. For example, let there be three input edges from place p to transition t and five input edges from place q to t. Then t is enabled if p has at least three tokens and q has at least five.

An enabled transition can fire at any time. In firing, a transition consumes one token from (the place associated with) each input edge and produces one token on (the place associated with) each output edge. Thus, firing a transition on a Petri net produces a new marking of the net. Figure 9-3 shows successive firings of transitions of the barbershop net. The successive states of the graph model potential successive states of the (real) barbershop. An enabled transition ceases to be enabled if its enabling tokens are consumed by the firing of some other transition. In Figure 9-4, the firing of transition S disables transition T.

Petri Net models of systems can be used to prove properties such as mutual exclusion (several processes are not engaged in conflicting activities at the same time), liveness (a system of processes does not deadlock; each individual process continues to progress), and reachability (some particular state can or cannot be reached). For example, using the barbershop net we could show that no two barbers ever cut the same customer's hair, that the barbershop as a whole can always make progress in hair cutting, and that the number of customers getting haircuts never exceeds the original number of barbers.

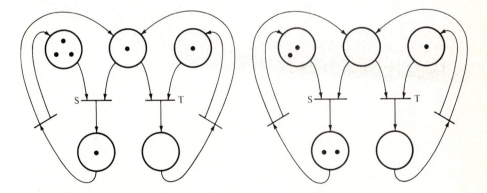

Figure 9-4 Disabled transition.

Modeling with Petri Nets

To design a Petri net to model a system, the parts of that system are classified into events and conditions [Peterson 81]. *Events* are actions, such as a barber beginning a haircut, two chemicals combining to form a third, or a job completing on a computer system. *Conditions* are descriptions of the state of a system. Typical conditions include "idle barber," "sodium ion present," and "computer system running." The *preconditions* of an event are those conditions that must be present before an event can occur. Before a barber can begin a haircut, he must be idle and a customer must be waiting. Before a chemical can form in a reaction, the reactants and catalyst must be present. Before a particular kind of computer job completes, the computer system must be running, the job must have started, and it must have been assigned two tape drives. Events remove some preconditions and assert other *postconditions*. The barber beginning a haircut reduces by one the number of idle barbers and waiting customers and produces the postcondition "a barber is cutting." The occurrence of a reaction removes several units of each reactant chemical and produces the postcondition of an additional unit of reaction chemical. The completion of a computer job ensures the postcondition of an idle processor and two more free tape drives.

The usual technique for system modeling with Petri Nets is to make each possible event a transition and each relevant condition a place. If P is a precondition for an event T, then the place associated with P is an input place of the transition associated with T. If Q is a postcondition of an event T, then Q's place is an output place of T's transition. Thus, in the barbershop net the event "a haircut commences" has the preconditions of a waiting customer and an idle barber and the postcondition of a haircut occurring. It consumes one token from each of "waiting customer" and "idle barber," and puts one token on "haircut occurring." Related events can be counted by having several tokens on a place. Without multiple tokens, we would need separate conditions (places) for "one barber idle," "two barbers idle," and "three barbers idle," and would have no way of specifying an unbounded number of waiting customers.

Mutual exclusion This technique leads to simple models for many of the standard synchronization problems. For example, consider the problem of modeling the mutual exclusion of n processes. For this problem there are $2n$ events: one event for the entry of each process into its critical region, and another for its exit from its critical region. We recognize $2n + 1$ possible conditions: one condition for each process being "in its critical region," another for it being "in its concurrent region" and one condition that "no process is in its critical region." The preconditions for a process to enter its critical region are that it is "in its concurrent region," and that "no process is in its critical region." The event of a process entering its critical region deletes these two preconditions and asserts the postcondition that the process is "in its critical region." Similarly, a process can exit its critical region when it is "in its critical region." This exit deletes the

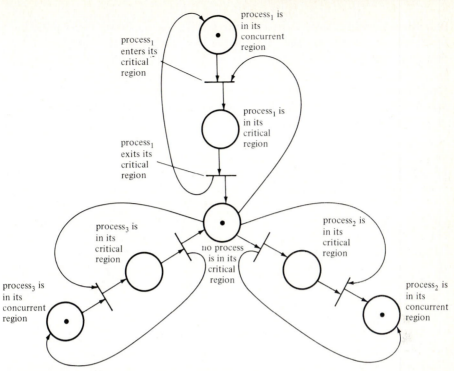

process₁ is
in its
concurrent
region

process₁
enters its
critical
region

process₁ is
in its
critical
region

process₁
exits its
critical
region

process₃ is
in its
critical
region

no process
is in its
critical
region

process₂ is
in its
critical
region

process₃ is
in its
concurrent
region

process₂ is
in its
concurrent
region

Figure 9-5 Three mutually exclusive processes.

is "in the critical region" precondition, and asserts the postconditions that this particular process is "in its concurrent region" and that "no process is in its critical region." Figure 9-5 shows a Petri net for three mutually exclusive processes. The structure of this net is a straightforward consequence of this analysis. That the net is easier to understand than the English description is a good argument for Petri Nets as a modeling tool.*

This Petri net models three mutually exclusive processes. It is not a program for arranging mutual exclusion. We can analyze this net to show, for example, that the processes are mutually exclusive and do not deadlock. However, the model does not indicate how the mutual exclusion it represents is to be accomplished. Petri nets automatically recognize simultaneous conditions and simultaneously effect changes. This ability avoids the major issue in programming synchronization problems, where the atomic actions are at a much less comprehensive level.

Dining philosophers Modeling the dining philosophers problem with Petri Nets is similar to modeling mutual exclusion. Each philosopher cycles through

---

* We could have modeled this situation without the condition "no process is in its critical region," at the cost of a more complex net. Exercise 9-2 asks for such a net.

six states: thinking; having the left fork in preparation for eating; having both forks; eating; having only the right fork in preparation for thinking; having neither fork; and then back to thinking. For each fork, we have a condition that states that it is free. A philosopher can pick up a fork if the fork is free (and she is ready to do so); a philosopher can drop a fork if she is ready to do so. Figure 9-6 shows a Petri net that models the states of the dining philosophers.

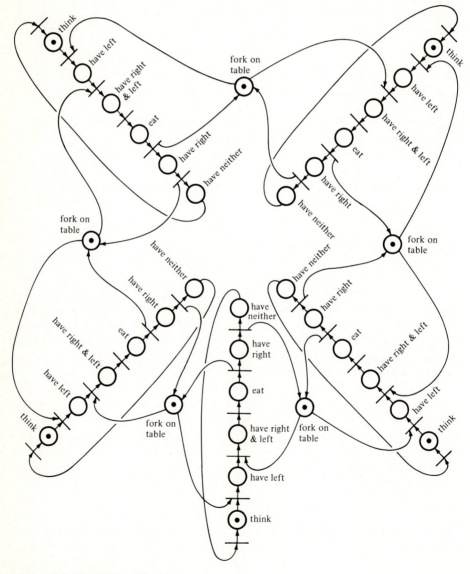

Figure 9-6 The dining philosophers.

This solution is susceptible to deadlock. Our other examples of dining philosopher programs have avoided deadlock by keeping count of the number of philosophers in the room, barring entry to the fifth philosopher. Exercise 9-4 asks for the Petri net that models the deadlock-free solution.

Issues in Petri Nets Theory

A major limitation of Petri Nets is an inability to determine if a place is empty. To overcome this problem when modeling, we must allocate explicit places for negated conditions. For example, "this process is not in its critical region" in the mutual exclusion net is a negated condition. However, this is sometimes inadequate to model situations involving counting. If we can bound the number of tokens that can be in a particular place, then we can count the tokens as they leave that place, recognizing when the count is full. But this does not work when the number of tokens that can be on a place is unbounded.

The readers-writers problem illustrates testing for bounded empty places but not for unbounded empty places. In a system with (at most) three readers, a writer can write if three "can read" tokens are present. The Petri net in Figure 9-7 models the readers-writers problem for three readers and a single writer. The limitation of reader-free writing is enforced by three input lines from the "free

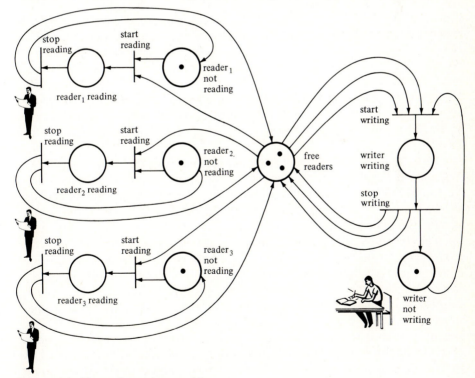

Figure 9-7 The readers-writers problem.

readers" place to the "start writing" transition (and the corresponding three output lines from the "stop writing" transition to the "free readers" place). At any time, the number of tokens in the "free readers" place is the difference between the total number of readers (three) and the number of readers who are reading. A writer can write when the number of readers who are reading is zero—which is equivalent to one token in the "free readers" place for each reader. If there are n readers, we can test for n tokens in the "free readers" place by making the in-degree of the "start writing" transition be n. However, this solution is not practical if the number of potential readers is unbounded.

The inability to test for a specific marking (such as zero) in an unbounded place is the essential weakness of Petri nets. The issue of deciding if a given Petri net with a particular marking of tokens can ever achieve some other marking is the *reachability problem.* There are algorithms that solve the reachability problem for Petri Nets [Kosaraju 82; Mayr 81; Sacerdote 77]. These algorithms are equivalent to solving the Petri Nets halting problem. Thus, Petri Nets is not even Turing-equivalent.

9-2 DATA FLOW

Conceptually, Data Flow takes the Petri Nets theme of modeling state by successive markings of tokens on a graph structure and transforms it into the idea of expressing computation through successive transformations of the values on the tokens of a graph structure. (This is not to imply that Data Flow was directly derived from Petri Nets.) There are many versions of Data Flow systems, all somewhat similar and all unified by the notion of graph-structured computation. We base our description on the work of Jack Dennis and his colleagues at M.I.T., without prejudice to the many other people who have studied Data Flow.

We get the Data Flow model by performing four transformations on the Petri Nets model. The first of these changes the plain, purely marking tokens of Petri Nets to be holders of data values. Every Data Flow token has some value (such as 5 or true or "Hello") in some specific data type (such as integer or boolean or string) "inscribed" on it.

The second transformation takes the synchronizing transitions of Petri Nets and converts them to the computational primitives. We rename the transitions *actors.* Thus, the Petri Nets transition that merely recognized the presence of tokens on each of its input arcs becomes, say, the Data Flow actor that consumes two tokens, computes the sum of the values on those tokens, and outputs a new token whose value is that sum. By and large, Data Flow retains the Petri Nets idea of consuming the input tokens in firing. However, the Petri Nets allowance of explicit multiple outputs from a single transition is replaced by the Data Flow restriction of each actor to a single output. (Some models of Data Flow do not include this restriction.)

The third change replaces the Petri Nets token holders, the places, with Data Flow links. *Links* are the only things that increase the systemwide number of tokens—a link can branch, placing a copy of its input token on each of its output arms. Petri Nets places can store an unbounded number of tokens. In Data Flow, at most a single token can be on any branch of a link at any time. Certain links are designated input or output links for communication with the external environment. Actors and links are the two kinds of *nodes*.

The final difference between Petri Nets and Data Flow concerns the rules for firing. In Petri Nets, a transition can fire as soon as all its input arcs have tokens. Most Data Flow nodes cannot fire unless all their input arcs have tokens, but there are some significant exceptions. Additionally, since only a single token can rest on any arm of a link at any time, a Data Flow node (actor or link) cannot fire until its output arcs are free of tokens.

Like Petri Nets transitions, Data Flow nodes are enabled when their preconditions are satisfied. They do not have to fire immediately. Instead, an enabled Data Flow node is only guaranteed to fire eventually.

Data Flow Graphs

Data Flow graphs are constructed by connecting actor diagrams with link diagrams. In contrast with Petri Nets, the "circles" in Data Flow do the work, while the "lines" (edges) serve as storage. Data flow graphs distinguish data-carrying paths and control paths. *Data paths* carry the data values of the computation: integers, reals, characters, etc. *Control paths* carry control values (booleans) that "open and close valves," regulating the flow of data around the graph. We draw data items with black (filled-in) tokens and arrowheads and control items with white (open) tokens and arrowheads. In Figure 9-8, we see the two kinds of links: data links and control links. We sometimes take liberties in drawing links to pass many copies of a token to distant places on a graph. A *Data Flow program* is a Data Flow graph with an initial arrangement of tokens on its arcs. A link can fire whenever there is a token on its input arc and its output arcs are all empty. Firing copies the input token to each output arc and consumes the input token. Figure 9-9 shows the firing rules for links.

Data Flow has six kinds of elementary actors: operators, deciders, booleans, constants, gates, and simple-merges. Figure 9-10 illustrates the kinds of elementary actors.

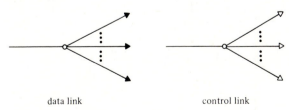

data link   control link

Figure 9-8 Links.

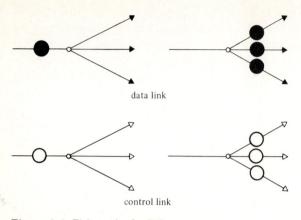

data link

control link

Figure 9-9 Firing rules for links.

Operators compute primitive functions such as addition and multiplication. An operator can fire when all its input arcs have tokens and its output arc is empty. If the input tokens of an operator have values $v_1, v_2, \ldots, v_n$ and the operator computes the function f, then firing the operator consumes these tokens and places a token with value $f(v_1, v_2, \ldots, v_n)$ on the output arc. Figure 9-11 shows the firing of an addition operator.

Deciders are the corresponding actors for primitive predicates, such as $\leq$ (less than or equal to). Figure 9-12 shows the firing of decider $>$.

Boolean actors (and, or, not) are the boolean functions of their control-value inputs. Their firing organization is the same as that of deciders and operators.

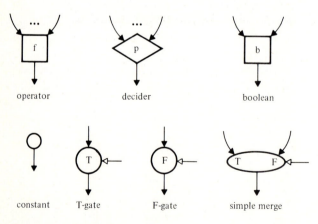

operator   decider   boolean

constant   T-gate   F-gate   simple merge

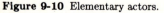

Figure 9-10 Elementary actors.

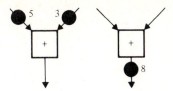

Figure 9-11 Firing an operator.

A *constant actor* produces a stream of its constant as its output and is able to fire whenever its output link is empty. Constant actors have no input arcs.

Gates allow control tokens to regulate the flow of data tokens. Data Flow has two types of gates, T (true) gates and F (false) gates. A gate has two inputs, both of which must be present for the gate to fire. The first input is a data token, the second, a control token. If the type of the gate (T or F) matches the data value of the control token, then (in firing) the data token is passed to the output of the gate. If not, the firing gate consumes the data token and no output token is produced. Firing a gate always consumes the control token. Gates are the only Data Flow nodes that do not always produce an output for every set of inputs. Figure 9-13 shows the possible firings of T gates and F gates.

Simple-merge actors, like gates, allow control tokens to regulate the flow of data tokens. A simple-merge actor has three input lines: a control line and two data lines—a true line and a false line. In firing, a token is taken from the data line that matches the value on the control line and is placed on the output line. The control token is also consumed. The value on the data line that is not selected is not affected. Hence, each firing of a simple-merge actor consumes exactly two tokens. In contrast with the firing rules for the other elementary actors, there need not be a token on the unselected line for a simple-merge actor to fire. If the control token and the "correct" data token have reached a simple-merge actor, the actor can fire. Figure 9-14 shows the firings of a simple-merge actor.

Conditionals One common subgraph of Data Flow programs is to combine a T gate, an F gate, and a simple-merge into a graph that computes a conditional. The Data Flow graph in Figure 9-15 is equivalent to the expression

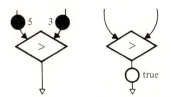

Figure 9-12 Firing a decider.

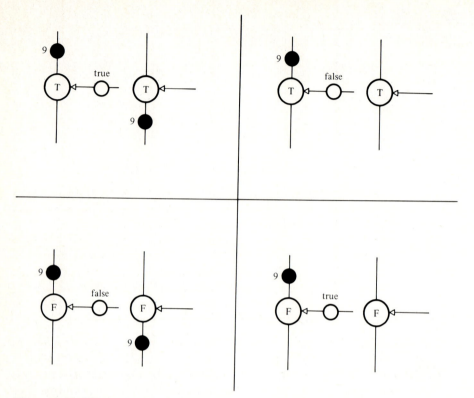

Figure 9-13 Firings of gates.

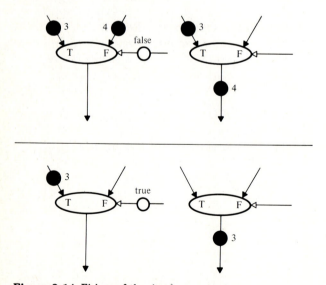

Figure 9-14 Firings of the simple-merge actor.

ThenVal ElseVal

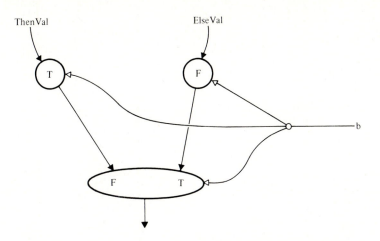

Figure 9-15 The Data Flow graph: **if** b **then** ThenVal **else** ElseVal.

if b then ThenVal else ElseVal

In this example it is critical that the unselected gate consume the unneeded token, preventing it from interfering with the next cycle of the computation. If b is true, then ElseVal is consumed by the F gate; if b is false, then ThenVal is consumed by the T gate.

A simple loop Figure 9-16 shows a Data Flow graph for computing $z = x^n$, adapted from Dennis [Dennis 74]. This Data Flow graph is equivalent to the pseudoprogram

```
function exp (x, n):
begin
      y  := 1:
      i  := n:
      while i > 0 do
            begin
                  y  := y * x:
                  i  := i − 1:
            end:
      z  := y:
      return (z)
end
```

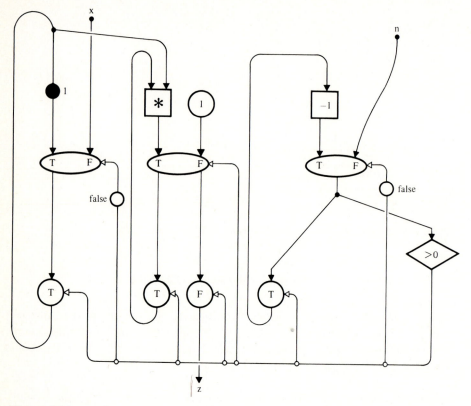

Figure 9-16 $z = x^n$.

This Data Flow computation is driven by the >0 test. This test sends its boolean signal to each of the three simple-merge actors and the four gates. The simple-merge actors serve only to keep the next input data out of the computation after the first time around the loop. Each of the T gates receives the boolean signal, allowing the data tokens to pass through the computational loop again. One T gate serves to iterate the values of x, another y, and the third i. When i is finally reduced to zero, the boolean signal is false and the F gate passes the answer (the current value of y, called z) to the external environment.

Demultiplexer Data Flow diagrams resemble circuit diagrams. This resemblance brings to mind both the circuit designer's repeated use of similar elements and typical circuit design problems. Our next example is a Data Flow demultiplexer (demux) built out of many similar elements. A multiplexer accepts several

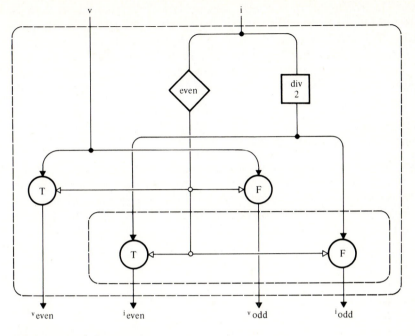

Figure 9-17 A demux unit.

signal lines, typically a power of 2, numbered from 0 through $2^n - 1$, and a control line with an integer in that range, i, and passes the value on the ith control line to the output. (Thus, a conditional expression can be viewed as a multiplexer over true and false.) A demultiplexer performs the inverse function—it takes a value v and a control signal i and places v on the ith output line.

We build our demultiplexer out of a tree of demux units. Each unit has two inputs and four outputs. The inputs are the value v that is to be the eventual output of the demux and the current selection index, i. The four outputs are v_{even}, i_{even}, v_{odd} and i_{odd}. If i is an even number (its least significant bit in binary representation is zero), then tokens are sent to the even lines; otherwise, tokens are sent to the odd lines. The output lines i_{even} and i_{odd} get the value of i (integer) divided by 2, ready to have its next bit tested. A demux unit is illustrated in Figure 9-17.

The full demultiplexer tree has one demux unit at the first level, two at the second, four at the next, and so forth. The tokens for the next level of indices (the interior dotted region of Figure 9-17) are omitted on the bottom level. Figure 9-18 shows the structure of the full demultiplexer.*

---

* This demultiplexer has the disadvantage that its outputs are not in numerical order. If we had tested the high bit of the index at each test, the outputs would be sorted.

Register The availability of feedback loops in Data Flow programs leads to the possibility of building registerlike Data Flow graphs. The Data Flow graph in Figure 9-19 behaves like a register. Our archetypical register responds to two kinds of requests: value "setting" requests and value "getting" requests. This register interprets a token with the special symbol s as a request for its value. Any other token stores the value of that token in the register. In either case, the register places a token with its (new) value on the output line.

Extensions to the Data Flow Model

All Data Flow actors except simple-merge require that all inputs be present before the node is enabled. Even simple-merge requires the presence of the necessary tokens before firing. One extension to Data Flow is the addition of another type of actor, indeterminate-merge [Dennis 77]. An *indeterminate-merge actor* has two inputs. It is enabled when either input line has a token. When an

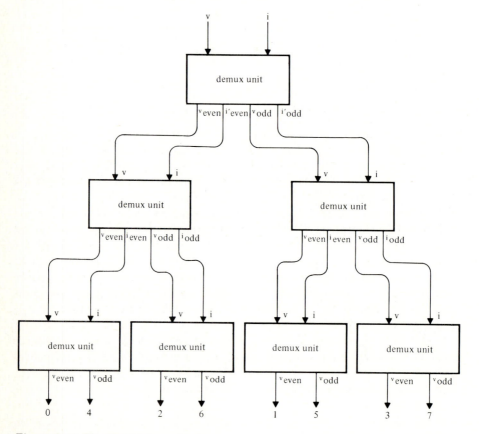

Figure 9-18 The demultiplexer structure.

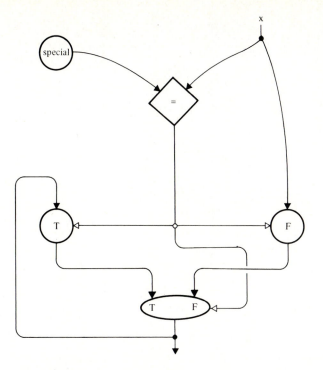

Figure 9-19 A Data Flow register.

indeterminate-merge actor fires, it passes a token from one of its input lines to its output line, leaving the value on the other line unchanged. A possible firing sequence of an indeterminate-merge actor is shown in Figure 9-20. Our example shows new tokens appearing between the firings. The indeterminate-merge actor is antifair; a token on a particular input line can be arbitrarily and indefinitely ignored.

We can build an n-input, indeterminate-merge Data Flow graph by cascading binary indeterminate-merges. Figure 9-21 shows one such graph. Since n-input indeterminate-merge graphs are such a straightforward extension of binary indeterminate-merges, we treat the n-ary case as primitive.

The addition of indeterminate-merge changes the semantics of Data Flow. Without indeterminate-merge, Data Flow is an applicative, Turing-equivalent formalism like the lambda calculus. Indeterminate-merge introduces indeterminacy. Data Flow programs that use indeterminate-merge are no longer functional. However, indeterminate-merge provides Data Flow with a real-world aspect. Just as hardware devices can handle asynchronous interaction on multiple input lines, a Data Flow system with indeterminate-merge can deal with an asynchronous set of inputs.

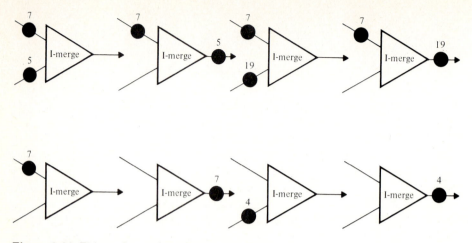

Figure 9-20 Firings of an indeterminate-merge actor.

Data Flow models have been extended to permit a range of possible values for tokens. These extensions include record-structured tokens and tokens that are pointers into a free storage heap.

Our final example of a Data Flow graph brings together several of the elements of the previous examples. We use the feedback idea of the register, the demultiplexer, the indeterminate-merge described above, and structured token values. This example presents a Data Flow graph to solve the airline reservation problem. That problem involves keeping track of the reservations of the seats on an airline flight. Requests come in from travel agents. Each request must be answered, with the answer directed back to the originating agent. The system accepts three different types of requests: reservations, which attempt to reserve seats on the flight; cancellations, which return seats to the flight; and inquiries, which request the number of seats remaining. If there are enough seats left, a reservation of k seats updates the number of seats left (by subtracting k) and responds to the agent with k. If there are fewer than k seats remaining on the flight, the response is 0. A cancellation of k seats adds k to the number of seats left and responds with k; an inquiry leaves the number of seats unchanged, and responds with that number. Specifically, let remaining be the number of seats left on the flight. In the pseudoprogram below, the record accessing functions query-type, size, and agent respectively extract the type of request, the number of seats requested, and the identification number of the inquiring agent.

```
if reservation?(x.query-type) then
    if remaining ≥ x.size then
        ⟨ remaining := remaining − x.size, answer(x.agent) := x.size ⟩
    else
        ⟨ remaining := remaining, answer(x.agent) := 0 ⟩
```

else if cancellation?(x.query-type) **then**
⟨ remaining := remaining + x.size, answer(x.agent) := x.size ⟩
else if inquiry?(x.query-type) **then**
⟨ remaining := remaining, answer(x.agent) := remaining ⟩

In this example, we have paired the consequences of each action. We have done this is because the computation produces two results — one, remaining, to be used in a feedback loop in the program; the other, answer, to be given to the demultiplexer. The demultiplexer takes the agent number and passes this value to that agent's line. The agent's request is on the line labeled x.

Figure 9-22 shows a Data Flow graph of the airline reservation program. In this example, we have used three indeterminate-merges. The one used to receive the requests of the incoming agents must be an indeterminate-merge. The other two could be replaced by several simple actors, at the cost of a more cluttered Data Flow graph. The capacity of the plane, 100 seats, is the value on the initialization token.

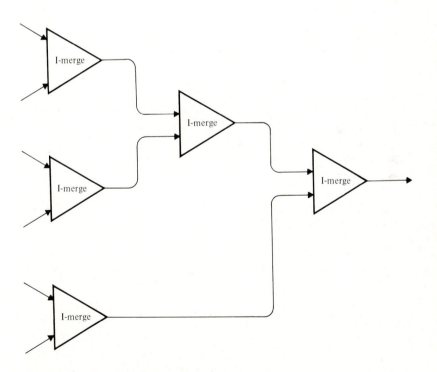

Figure 9-21 Cascading binary indeterminate-merges.

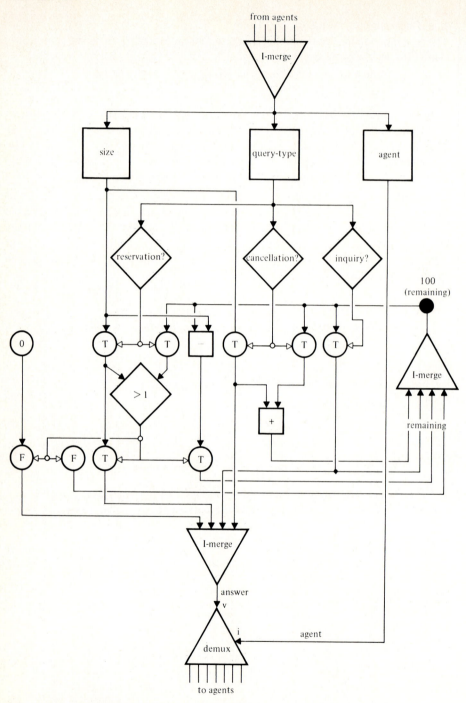

Figure 9-22 The airline reservation Data Flow graph.

Perspective

Petri Nets and Data Flow share the conceptual basis of modeling change through successive markings of a graph structure. Petri Nets is a pure modeling technique. Computing with Petri Nets (by tricks such as counting tokens) is difficult. Data Flow transforms the marked, graph-structured machine to a computing formalism. Data Flow captures some quality of concurrency — if several data values reach actors at the same time, then the computations in those actors can be done in parallel.

Data Flow has proved to be a fertile concept. It has been a source for ideas about both computer hardware and programming languages. Several computers whose internal architectures reflect the concepts of Data Flow have been designed and implemented. Two good surveys of Data Flow are a *Computing Surveys* article by Treleaven, Brownbridge, and Hopkins [Treleaven 82] and an *IEEE Computer* issue on Data Flow edited by Agerwala and Arvind [Agerwala 82].

Programming languages have also been developed to express Data Flow computations. One such language is VAL [Ackerman 79; McGraw 82]. Syntactically, VAL looks like an imperative language with the single-assignment rule — programs must guarantee that each variable is assigned only once during program execution. Semantically, VAL is equivalent to a strongly-typed pure Lisp.

PROBLEMS

9-1   What would an indeterminate transition in a Petri net be like?

9-2   Give a Petri net that models the mutual exclusion of three processes using only six places and six transitions.

9-3   Model a bounded producer-consumer buffer with Petri Nets.

9-4   Modify the Petri net for the dining philosophers problem so that the system is deadlock-free.

9-5   Petri Nets can be extended to produce more powerful automata. Peterson ([Peterson 81]) outlines several possible extensions to the standard firing rules: (*a*) *Constraints* modify the firing rule to specify sets of places that must always retain an empty place. (*b*) An *exclusive-or transition* fires when exactly one of its input places has a token. The transition consumes that token. (*c*) *Switch transitions* use the presence or absence of a token on a special "switch" place to determine which output places get tokens. (*d*) *Inhibitor arcs* lead to places that must be empty before a transition can fire. (*e*) *Priorities* can be associated with transitions. If several transitions are enabled, the transition with the highest priority fires. (*f*) *Time Petri Nets* associates two times with each transition. It requires that every enabled transition wait at least as long as its first time but not as long as its second before firing. Each of these extensions allows for determining empty places and each makes Petri Nets Turing-equivalent.

Devise other possible extensions to the firing rules that allow empty place testing and Turing equivalence.

9-6   Three missionaries and three cannibals come to a river. They want to cross. The only way across the river is in a single rowboat. This boat can hold only two people; it can be rowed by one. Clearly, to cross the river the travelers will have to row back and forth. However, the cannibals are afraid that if some of their group are ever left outnumbered by missionaries (including the people arriving at a river bank) they will be converted, a dire possibility that cannot be allowed to happen.

(a) How can the group cross the river?

(b) Present a Petri net that models this situation, including the constraint on outnumbered cannibals.

9-7 What is the effect of omitting the T gates in the Data Flow program that computes exponentiation?

9-8 Write a Data Flow graph that computes successive Fibonacci numbers.

9-9 What happens to the Data Flow register if the first token sent is the special value s?

9-10 Redo the Data Flow graph of the airline reservation problem using simple-merges instead of the two unnecessary indeterminate-merges.

REFERENCES

[**Ackerman 79**] Ackerman, W. B., and J. B. Dennis, "VAL — A Value-Oriented Algorithmic Language: Preliminary Reference Manual," Technical Report TR-218, Computation Structures Group, Laboratory for Computer Science, M.I.T., Cambridge, Massachusetts (June 1979).

[**Adams 68**] Adams, D. A., "A Computation Model with Data Flow Sequencing," Technical Report TR-CS 117, Computer Science Department, Stanford University, Stanford, California (December 1968).

[**Agerwala 82**] Agerwala, T., and Arvind, "Data Flow Systems," *Comput.*, vol. 15, no. 2 (February 1982). Agerwala and Arvind edited this issue of IEEE Computer devoted to Data Flow systems.

[**Arvind 77**] Arvind, and K. P. Gostelow, "A Computer Capable of Exchanging Processors for Time," in B. Gilchrist (ed.), *Information Processing 77: Proceedings of the IFIP Congress 77*, North Holland, Amsterdam (1977), pp. 849–854. Arvind and Gostelow study Data Flow. This paper reports some of their results. The most interesting difference between the Arvind-Gostelow and the Dennis models is that the former allows multiple, simultaneous tokens on a communications line, while the latter does not. "Coloring" of the tokens distinguishes the tokens created by different function invocations.

[**Berger 82**] Berger, P., D. Comte, N. Hifdi, B. Perlois, and J.-C. Syre, "Le Système LAU: Un Multiprocesseur à Assignation Unique," *Tech. Sci. Inf.*, vol. 1, no. 1 (1982). LAU is the French acronym for single-assignment language. This paper and [Comte 79] describe the micro-architecture of a machine for single-assignment computation, a form of Data Flow.

[**Comte 79**] Comte, D., and N. Hifdi, "LAU Multiprocessor: Microfunctional Description and Technological Choices," *Proc. 1st Eur. Conf. Parallel and Distrib. Proc.*, Toulouse, France (February 1979), pp. 8–15.

[**Davis 78**] Davis, A. L., "The Architecture and System Method of DDM1: A Recursively Structured Data Driven Machine," *Proc. 5th Annu. Symp. Comput. Archit.*, IEEE (April 1978), pp. 210–215.

[**Dennis 74**] Dennis, J. B., "First Version of a Data Flow Procedure Language," in B. Robinet (ed.), *Proceedings, Colloque sur la Programmation*, Lecture Notes in Computer Science 19, Springer-Verlag, Berlin (1974), pp. 362–376. This paper is a good description of Data Flow. It includes sections on building structured data objects in Data Flow and coloring Data Flow tokens.

[**Dennis 77**] Dennis, J. B., "A Language for Structured Concurrency," in J. H. Williams, and D. A. Fisher (eds.), *Design and Implementation of Programming Languages*, Lecture Notes in Computer Science 54, Springer-Verlag, Berlin (1977), pp. 231–242. Dennis presents Data Flow at a workshop devoted to developing Ada. In this paper, Dennis describes the indeterminate-merge actor.

[**Fosseen 72**] Fosseen, J. B., "Representation of Algorithms by Maximally Parallel Schemata," Masters thesis, M.I.T., Cambridge, Massachusetts (1972). Fosseen developed the idea of associating values with the tokens on a Data Flow graph.

[**Gordon 81**] Gordon, M., "A Very Simple Model of Sequential Behavior of nMOS," *Proc. VLSI 81 Int. Conf.*, Edinburgh, Scotland (August 1981), pp. 18–21. Gordon gives an example of the similarity of a Data Flow-like applicative system and computer circuitry.

[**Holt 68**] Holt, A. W., H. Saint, R. Shapiro, and S. Warshall, "Final Report of the Information System Theory Project," Report TRRADC-TR-68-305, Rome Air Development Center, Griffiss Air Force Base, New York (1968). The Information System Theory Project was concerned with methods of modeling and evaluating systems. Much of their work (and much of their report) was devoted to Petri Nets.

[**Karp 66**] Karp, R. M., and R. E. Miller, "Properties of a Model for Parallel Computations: Determinacy, Termination, Queueing," *SIAM J. Appl. Math.*, vol. 14, no. 6 (November 1966), pp. 1390–1411. This is a seminal paper on graph-directed computation.

[**Kosaraju 82**] Kosaraju, S. R., "Decidability of Reachability in Vector Addition Systems," *Proc. 14th Annu. ACM Symp. Theory Comp.*, San Francisco (May 1982), pp. 267–281. Kosaraju presents a simpler proof than Mayr [Mayr 81] or Sacerdote [Sacerdote 77] of the decidability of the reachability problem of Petri Nets.

[**Mayr 81**] Mayr, E. W., "An Algorithm for the General Petri Net Reachability Problem," *Proc. 13th Annu. ACM Symp. Theory Comp.*, Milwaukee (May 1981), pp. 238–246. Mayr presents an algorithm for deciding the reachability problem for Petri Nets.

[**McGraw 82**] McGraw, J. R., "The VAL Language: Description and Analysis," *ACM Trans. Program. Lang. Syst.*, vol. 4, no. 1 (January 1982), pp. 44–82. McGraw provides an overview of the Data Flow programming language VAL. He argues for special-purpose Data Flow languages for Data Flow machines.

[**Peterson 77**] Peterson, J. L., "Petri Nets," *Comput. Surv.*, vol. 9, no. 3 (September 1977), pp. 223–252. Peterson's paper is a good general survey and tutorial on Petri Nets.

[**Peterson 81**] Peterson, J. L., *Petri Net Theory and the Modeling of Systems*, Prentice-Hall, Englewood Cliffs, New Jersey (1981). This book is a comprehensive description of Petri Nets. It emphasizes the theoretical aspects of Petri Nets.

[**Petri 62**] Petri, C. A., "Kommunikation mit Automaten," Ph.D. dissertation, University of Bonn, Bonn (1962). In his dissertation, Petri lays the groundwork for Petri Net theory. His work is directed at issues of automata theory.

[**Rodriguez-Bezos 69**] Rodriguez-Bezos, J. E., "A Graph Model for Parallel Computation," Report MAC-TR-64, Project MAC, M.I.T., Cambridge, Massachusetts (September 1969). In this doctoral dissertation, Rodriguez-Bezos introduces "program graphs."

[**Sacerdote 77**] Sacerdote, G. S., and R. L. Tenney, "The Decidability of the Reachability Problem for Vector Addition Systems," *Proc. 9th Annu. ACM Symp. Theory Comp.*, Boulder, Colorado (May 1977), pp. 61–76. Sacerdote and Tenney present the first proof of the decidability of the reachability problem for Petri Nets.

[**Tesler 68**] Tesler, L. G., and H. J. Enea, "A Language Design for Concurrent Processes," *Proceedings of the 1968 Spring Joint Computer Conference*, AFIPS Conference Proceedings vol. 32, AFIPS Press, Arlington, Virginia (1968), pp. 403–408. In this paper, Tesler and Enea introduce a single-assignment language called "Compel."

[**Treleaven 82**] Treleaven, P. C., D. R. Brownbridge, and R. P. Hopkins, "Data-Driven and Demand-Driven Computer Architecture," *Comput. Surv.*, vol. 14, no. 1 (March 1982), pp. 93–145. Treleaven et al. survey both Data Flow and Reduction Machine architectures.

[**Watson 82**] Watson, I., and J. Gurd, "A Practical Data Flow Computer," *Comput.*, vol. 15, no. 2 (February 1982), pp. 51–57. Watson and Gurd describe a prototype Data Flow machine.

TEN

COMMUNICATING SEQUENTIAL PROCESSES

C.A.R. Hoare's Communicating Sequential Processes (CSP) is a model-language hybrid for describing concurrent and distributed computation. A CSP program is a static set of explicit processes. Pairs of processes communicate by naming each other in input and output statements. Communication is synchronous with unidirectional information flow. A process that executes a communication primitive (input or output) blocks until the process with which it is trying to communicate executes the corresponding primitive. Guarded commands are used to introduce indeterminacy.

CSP is a language fragment; it extends an imperative kernel with guarded and parallel commands. Hoare's primary concerns in the design of CSP have been with issues of program correctness and operating systems description. CSP shows its strong operating systems orientation by prohibiting dynamic process creation, determining the interprocess communication structure at system creation, and excluding recursion.

CSP has inspired both development and response. For example, there have been proposals for a formal semantics of CSP ([Apt 80; Levin 81]), published critiques of the CSP [Kieburtz 79], and suggestions for extensions to the language [Bernstein 80].

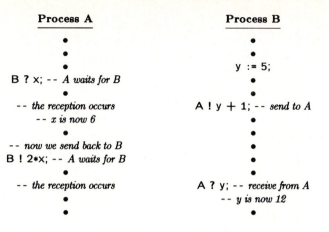

Figure 10-1 The sequencing of communication.

Communications and Processes

Metaphorically, processes in CSP communicate by pretending to do ordinary input and output. More specifically, two processes communicate by naming each other in input and output statements. A process writing *output* specifies an expression whose value is to be sent; one reading *input* names a variable to receive that value. The parallel to writing and reading in conventional languages (perhaps with the reading and writing directed to particular devices) is straightforward. Information flow in communication is unidirectional, from the output process to the input process. Input and output commands that name each other are said to *correspond*.

To illustrate, imagine that we have two processes, A and B. A wishes to receive a value from B and to place it in variable x. A therefore executes the command B ? x ("input a value from B and store it in x"). B wishes to output the value of an expression exp to A, so it executes A ! exp ("output the value of exp to process A"). Communication occurs after both processes have issued their commands. Execution of either B ? x or A ! exp blocks the executing process until the other process executes the corresponding command. Figure 10-1 shows first a transfer from B to A, and then a transfer back from A to B.

Like many other systems, CSP has both parties to a communication participate in arranging the communication. Unlike the other systems we discuss, CSP requires both parties to specifically identify each other. In our other systems, either an anonymous requester calls a named server or anonymous processes communicate through a shared port. CSP is the only system we study that precludes any anonymity in communication.*

---

* Hoare recognizes that this makes it difficult to build subroutine libraries. He suggests extending CSP with a "macroizing" name substitution system to allow libraries of processes.

Of course, computation requires more than just communication. Hoare provides statements that correspond to the commands of conventional imperative languages. These constructs have a few extensions to adapt CSP for indeterminate multiprocessing.

In addition to the communication primitives **?** (input) and **!** (output), CSP has variable declarations, assignment statements, sequencing, concurrent execution, repetition, and conditionals. Despite this variety of constructs, Hoare describes only enough of the language to discuss the communication and concurrency aspects of CSP. The published CSP is a language fragment. Broadening CSP to a full programming language would require significant extension, particularly with respect to data structures.

CSP has its own variations on conventional syntax. CSP joins sequential statements with semicolons and delimits block structure by square brackets ([ ]). Variables can be declared anywhere in a program. Their scope extends to the end of the statement sequence containing their declaration. Thus, the CSP code

```
C:: n : integer;
    n := 1729;
    D ! 2*n;
    n := 3
```

declares process C, gives it an integer n, assigns to n the value 1729, and attempts to send to process D the value of twice n. If D executes a corresponding input statement (one of the form C ? k for its variable k), the output statement terminates, and the program assigns the value 3 to n. Immediately after the communication, the value of k in D is 3458.

CSP provides both primitive and structured (record) data types. Structured types are indicated by an optional structure name and the subfields of the structure (enclosed in parentheses and joined by commas). The composition of a structured data type is to be inferred from its usage.

Assignment and communication require matching structures—by and large, that the structures' field names match. Thus, structures can be used like entry names to control communication patterns. Figure 10-2 gives several examples of matching structures in CSP.

Failure is an important concept in CSP. CSP uses failure both to control internal process execution and to communicate process termination. A process that reaches the end of its program terminates. An input statement that tries to read from a terminated process fails. Similarly, an output statement that tries to write to a terminated process fails. Conditional statements (guarded commands) treat failure as equivalent to false. In other contexts, a failure causes the executing process to terminate.

CSP indicates simple iteration by the form

$$*[\ <test> \ \rightarrow \ <action> \ ]$$

Form	Effect
n := 3*n + 1	Ordinary variable assignment.
x := subscription (name, address)	Constructs a structured record of type subscription, of two fields: the first, the value of name, the second, the value of address.
subscription(name, address) := x	If x is a structured value of the form subscription(i,j), then name := i and address := j. Otherwise, this statement is illegal; it "fails."
semaphore := P( )	A structured record with no fields. Hoare calls such a record a *signal*.
(new, old) := (new+old, new)	An unlabeled structure assignment. Simultaneously, new := new + old and old := new.

Figure 10-2 CSP record structures.

This statement is equivalent to "**while** test **do** action."

CSP processes compute in parallel. Each process has a label (name), denoted by affixing the name to the process program with a double colon (::). Processes joined by the parallel operator (||) compute concurrently. Concurrent processes must not share target (input and output) variables.

Fibonacci numbers We illustrate these operations with a simple triple of pipelined processes (Figure 10-3). The first process, Fibon, computes successive Fibonacci numbers. The second process, Mult, receives these numbers from Fibon. Mult squares and cubes them and passes the results (as a structured record) to process Print. Print communicates with the external environment, which can presumably find something useful to do with the powers of the Fibonacci numbers.

```
[Fibon:: old, new: integer;
        old   := 0;
        new  := 1;
        *[ true → Mult ! new;
                 (new, old) := (new + old, new) ]     ||

Mult:: val: integer;
       *[ Fibon ? val →
           Print ! fibrec(val, val*val, val*val*val) ]      ||

Print:: f, f2, f3: integer;
        *[ Mult ? fibrec(f, f2, f3) →
            environment ! printrec(f, f2, f3) ] ] ]
```

Figure 10-3 The Fibonacci pipeline.

Guarded commands and indeterminacy The → construct of the iterative statement is part of a guarded clause, like the guarded commands discussed in Section 2-2. More specifically, in CSP, a *guarded clause* is a conditional statement. The condition of the clause is the series of boolean expressions before the →. If all these expressions evaluate to true, then the process executes the action of the guarded command (the series of statements after the →). Both boolean conditions and action statements are joined by semicolons.

Alternative commands are built by concatenating guarded statements with ⫿s, and enclosing the result in square brackets ([ ]). An alternative command is thus a kind of guarded command. To execute an alternative command, the system finds a guard clause whose condition is true (all the boolean expressions in the condition are true), and evaluates the actions of that clause. It ignores the other clauses. Since CSP lacks user-defined functions, the evaluation of guard conditions cannot cause any (discernible) side effects.

The above describes just another syntax for guarded commands. CSP introduces an important extension by allowing the last boolean expression in a guard clause condition to be an input statement. This statement is treated as true when the corresponding output statement has already been executed. When combined with the alternative command, this *guarded input command* permits a program (reading input) to select the next available partner for communication. Thus, a process that executes the command

$$
\begin{array}{l}
[\quad X\,?\,k \;\rightarrow\; S_x \\
\quad ⫿ \\
\quad\quad Y\,?\,k \;\rightarrow\; S_y \\
\quad ⫿ \\
\quad\quad Z\,?\,k \;\rightarrow\; S_z\,]
\end{array}
$$

reads into variable k from whichever one of processes X, Y, or Z is waiting to communicate with it. If more than one process is ready to communicate, the system selects one arbitrarily. If no process is waiting, the process that executes this command blocks until one of X, Y, or Z tries to communicate. The process then executes the command list (S_x, S_y, or S_z) associated with the successful communication. Combining the alternative command with the repetitive operator * yields the iterative command. This command repeatedly executes the alternative command. On each repetition, the action of a guard clause with a true guard is executed. When all guards fail, the iterative command terminates. Thus, the process

```
Merge:: c: character;
    *[   X ? c → Sink ! c
      []
         Y ? c → Sink ! c
      []
         Z ? c → Sink ! c
```

receives characters from processes X, Y, and Z and forwards them to process Sink. It repeats this forwarding until X, Y, and Z have terminated.* Although input commands may be included in guard conditions, Hoare specifically excludes output commands in guarded conditions (*output guards*). We discuss the ramifications of this decision later in this chapter.

One can declare an array of processes that execute the same program in parallel. These processes differ only by their array indices. For example, the command

```
transfer (source: 1..limit)::
    val, dest: integer;
    *[ origin(source) ? message(dest,val) → destination(dest) ! val]
```

declares limit processes of type transfer. The sourceth transfer process accepts from the sourceth origin process a message, pair consisting of an address (dest) and a value (val). It forwards that value to the destth destination process. Each transfer process continues this forwarding until its origin process terminates.

Process subscripting can be thought of as a macro operator that generates multiple copies of the text of the process body. In a declaration of process arrays, the size of the array must be a "compile-time" constant. That is, the system must be able to compute the number of processes to create before the program begins executing.† Although the examples only show instances of one-dimensional process arrays, we can declare arrays of parallel processes of arbitrarily many dimensions. In a parallel statement, a reference to process(k: lower..upper) is a request for (upper−lower+1) copies of the text of process, with each of the values from lower to upper substituted for k in one copy of the body of process. A reference to process(k: lower..upper) in an input guard of an alternative command expresses willingness to receive input from any of these processes. Thus, while communication channels in CSP are intended to be somewhat rigid, we can achieve an arbitrary communication structure by evaluating process indices.

To a large extent, processes take the place of procedures in CSP. Unlike many modern programming languages, CSP processes are not recursive—that

---

* This example may remind the reader of the indeterminate-merge of Data Flow (Chapter 9).

† Hoare recognizes that it is just a small step from a bounded array to one that is semantically unbounded (like the stack of Algol or Pascal). An unbounded array could be used to provide CSP with dynamic process creation. However, Hoare chose not to take that step.

is, a process cannot communicate with itself. Clearly, since both parties to a communication in CSP must act for the communication to take place, an attempt at self-communication would deadlock. To get the effect of processes as recursive procedures, we can create a stack (array) of processes and allocate a new process from the stack for each recursive level.

Bounded producer-consumer buffer In this section we present a CSP program for a bounded producer-consumer buffer. This buffer is bufsize elements large. It serves numbcons consumers and numbprod producers. This example illustrates a single process that communicates with an array of other processes. The lack of output guards in CSP complicates the program.

```
[ Buffer::
    buf (0 .. bufsize-1)    : buffer-element;
    first, last             : integer;     -- queue pointers
    j, k                    : integer;     -- process counters
    first := 0;
    last  := 0;
    *[  (j: 1..numbprod)                   -- For each of the numbprod
                                              producers,
            (last+1) mod bufsize ≠ first;  -- if there is room in the buffer,
                Producer(j) ? buf(last) →  -- read an element.
                    last := (last + 1) mod bufsize
        []
          (k: 1..numbcons)                 -- For each of the numbcons
                                              consumers,
            first ≠ last;                  -- if there is something in the
                                              buffer
                Consumer(k) ? more( ) →    -- and a consumer signals a
                                              desire to consume,
                    Consumer(k) ! buf(first);  -- send that consumer an
                                                  element.
                first := (first + 1) mod bufsize ]
    -- The buffer runs concurrently with the producers and consumers.
    PRODUCER is the text of the producer processes; CONSUMER, of the
    consumer processes.
|| (i: 1..numbprod) PRODUCER
|| (i: 1..numbcons) CONSUMER ]
```

The repetition of the loop drives the buffer. The subscripted range implies that this command alternates over the numbprod producers and the numbcons consumers. This buffer can receive input from any producer if there is room in its buffer. In response to a signal of the structured form more( ), the buffer sends the next buffer element to the kth consumer. This signal would be unnecessary if CSP had output guards. With output guards, the buffer could merely have an output guard alternating with an input guard. Without them, the program requires an extra communication step.

Dining philosophers This solution to the dining philosophers problem in CSP is adapted from Hoare [Hoare 78]. There are three varieties of processes: philosophers (Phil), forks (Fork), and the room (Room). Philosophers think, request permission to enter the room, ask first for their left fork and then for their right, eat, drop their forks, and exit. They repeat this sequence interminably. The communications between the philosophers, forks, and room is done purely through labeled synchronization; the input and output commands do not transfer any information. The correct order of communication patterns is maintained because record-structured communication succeeds only when the record structures match. Here we use the "macro" operator $\equiv$ to associate an identifier with program text.

```
PHIL ≡
    *[true →
        THINK;
        room ! enter ( );              -- try to enter the room
        fork(i) ! pickup ( );          -- try to pick up left fork
        fork((i + 1) mod 5) ! pickup ( );   -- try to pick up right fork
        EAT;
        fork (i) ! putdown( );         -- drop the left fork
        fork ((i + 1) mod 5) ! putdown( );  -- drop the right fork
        room ! exit( )]                -- leave the room.
```

The program for a fork is

```
FORK ≡
    *[   phil(i) ? pickup( ) →
                phil(i) ? putdown( )
         ▯
         phil((i − 1) mod 5) ? pickup( ) →
                phil((i − 1) mod 5) ? putdown( ) ]
```

That is, the ith fork can be picked up by either the ith or the $(i-1)^{th}$ philosopher (modulo 5). Then, only that philosopher can put it down.

Somewhat like a fire marshal, the ROOM is concerned with keeping the occupancy of the dining hall at five or fewer. It does this by counting the occupants and refusing requests when four philosophers are already at the table. We enforce this constraint by using a boolean condition in the guarded command.

```
ROOM ≡
    occupancy: integer;
```

```
occupancy := 0;
*[  (i: 0..4) occupancy < 4; phil(i) ? enter( ) →
            occupancy := occupancy + 1

□

    (i: 0..4) phil(i) ? exit( ) →
            occupancy := occupancy − 1
]
```

These elements are set running concurrently with the statement

[room:: ROOM ‖ fork(i:0..4):: FORK ‖ phil(i:0..4):: PHIL]

Since only four philosophers can be in the room at any time, the program cannot deadlock with five single-forked, hungry sophists. On the other hand, the program does not solve the harder problem of precluding starvation—that is, ensuring that every philosopher eventually gets to eat.

Sorting tree Guarded input commands allow input from a variety of different process types. It would seem that output commands, though able to index their destination, would be limited to performing output to only a single kind of process. Our final example shows that restrictions on communication to a single kind of communicator can be overcome by a sufficiently ill-structured program. We recognize that several different process types can be encoded as a single type. Here the index of the process serves as a "big switch," directing processes to the appropriate section of code. Thus, some of the intended limitations on output activity in CSP can be evaded, though at the cost of producing a clumsy program.

We illustrate this idea with a program for sorting. We imagine a binary sorting tree, as in Figure 10-4, which performs a variant of the merge phase of Heapsort [Williams 64]. We use the terms "leaf," "parent," and "child" to describe the relationships of the nodes of the tree. Each of the leaf-level processors is given a number, which it passes to its parent. Each process in the middle of the tree successively reads values from its left and right children, compares these values, passes the larger to its parent, and obtains the next value from the child that gave it the larger value. When a child terminates (runs out of values), its parent transfers the remaining values from its other child until that source is also exhausted. The parent node then terminates, a condition discovered by the grandparent when it next tries to receive input.

In this example, we are sorting 16 items in a 31-node tree; the program naturally generalizes to sorting larger sets of numbers. The program has two kinds of processes. The **source** process receives 16 elements from the environment and feeds them to the leaves of the sorting tree. The **element** processes are the nodes of the tree, including a "sink" process that collects the values (in order, of course) from the root of the tree and sends them back to the environment. There are three classes of **element** processes: leaf processes, intermediate

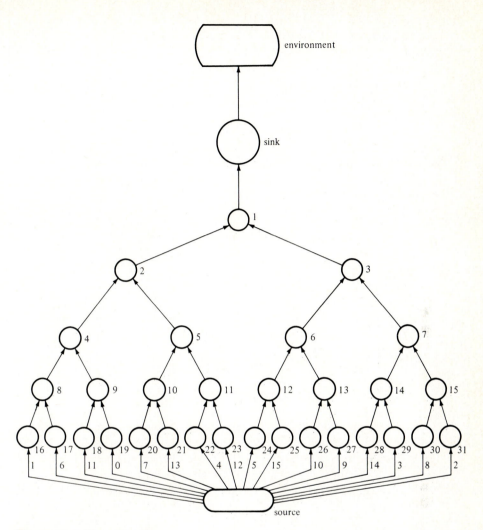

Figure 10-4 The sorting tree.

comparator processes, and the sink. The *leaf processes* just transmit their value
and terminate. The *comparator processes* receive streams of values from their
left and right children, merge them in order, and transmit the values to their
parents. The *sink* passes the values back to the environment. Let us number the
nodes in the tree as illustrated, with the root node as 1, the other comparator
nodes as nodes 2 through 15, the leaf nodes as 16 through 31, and the sink node
as 0.

The program for a source is the CSP version of a **for** loop.

```
SOURCE ≡
    i, val: integer;
    i := 16;
    *[ i < 32;
        environment ? val →
            element(i) ! val;
            i := i + 1
    ]
```

An element's program is more complex. An element recognizes its own class (leaf, comparator, or sink) by referring to its index. The top level of an element is thus a three-way branch.

```
ELEMENT ≡
    [ i > 15 →        -- Leaves transfer and terminate.
        val: integer;
        source ? val;
        element(i div 2) ! val
    □
        i = 0 →       -- The sink node gets values from the root and transfers
                         them to the environment.
            *[ val: integer;
               element(1) ? val → environment!val]
    □
        i > 0; i ≤ 15; → COMPARATOR ]
```

A comparator uses two integer variables, ValLeft (the value from the left child) and ValRight, and two boolean variables, NeedLeft (a value needed from the left child) and NeedRight. NeedLeft and NeedRight are true when a value needs to be "pulled" from that child; when they are both false, a comparison is possible. The result of this comparison is sent to the parent node. The comparator program is thus a two-part procedure; while both children are active, values are merged. After either child has terminated, it pulls the remaining values from the other child and forwards them to its parent. In this scheme, the children of element i are $2i$ and $2i + 1$; the parent of i is i div 2.

```
COMPARATOR ≡
    NeedLeft, NeedRight : boolean;
    ValLeft, ValRight     : integer;
    NeedLeft   := true;
    NeedRight := true;
```

-- *If a value is needed from a side, obtain it. Otherwise, compare the two values in hand and pass the larger to the parent. Continue until one child process has terminated and a value is needed from that process.*

```
*[  NeedLeft; element(2*i) ? ValLeft → NeedLeft := false
  []
    NeedRight; element(2*i + 1) ? ValRight → NeedRight := false
  []
    (not NeedLeft) and (not NeedRight) →
      [  ValLeft > ValRight →
        NeedLeft := true;
        element(i div 2) ! ValLeft
      []
        ValRight ≥ ValLeft →
        NeedRight := true;
        element(i div 2) ! ValRight
      ]
]:
```

-- *Exhaust the remaining values from the child that has not terminated.*
Transfer these values to the parent node.

```
[  not NeedLeft → element(i div 2) ! ValLeft;
      *[ element(2*i) ? ValLeft → element(i div 2) ! ValLeft]
  []
    not NeedRight → element(i div 2) ! ValRight;
      *[ element(2*i + 1) ? ValRight → element(i div 2) ! ValLeft]
]
```

The main program is

[source:: **SOURCE** || (i: 0..31) element:: **ELEMENT** || environment]

Figure 10-5 shows the state of the sorting tree partway through the sorting process.

Perspective

CSP is directed primarily at issues of operating systems implementations and program correctness. Many researchers have used CSP as a basis for describing concurrent programming semantics. For example, Apt, Francez, and de Roever [Apt 80] and Levin and Gries [Levin 81] have studied axiomatic proofs of the correctness of CSP programs; Francez, Lehmann, and Pnueli [Francez 80] have described the denotational semantics of CSP.

Communication in CSP is synchronous. Both parties to an exchange must be ready to communicate before any information transfer occurs. CSP does not have mechanisms for message buffering, message queueing, or aborting incomplete communications. It lacks these features because Hoare believes that they are not

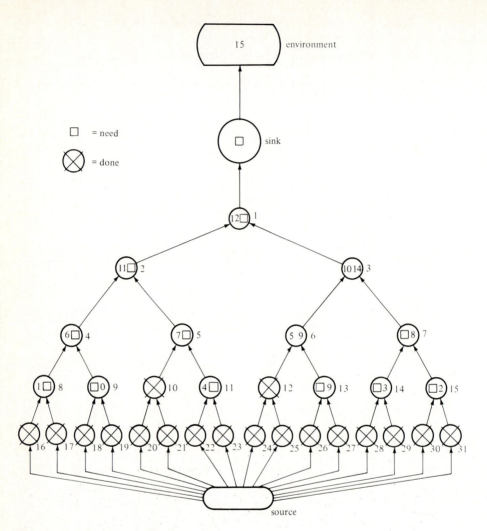

Figure 10-5 The sorting tree while sorting.

primitive—that facilities such as buffering should be provided by higher-level software.

Kieburtz and Silberschatz [Kieburtz 79] dispute this point. They argue that unbuffered communication over memoryless channels is itself an assumption about the nature of computer hardware. This assumption reflects certain implementations in the current technology (such as Ethernet systems). However, not all future hardware will necessarily share this property.

CSP attempts to describe primitives for communication. Naturally, the language is pragmatically weak. If a user wants message buffering, then the user must write the code for that buffering. Some of the other restrictions in CSP are also unpragmatic. The CSP calling sequence precludes recursion, although its effect can be obtained (as Hoare suggests) by programs that use stacks of processes. Limiting interprocess communication structure to those indexed names that can be determined at compilation does not limit the possible varieties of interprocess connections, but (as the sorting tree example shows) only serves to disorganize those programs that require a more complex communication structure. The lack of output guards forces the user to program unnecessary communications in those situations where the action of an output guard is really needed (as the buffer example illustrates.)

Hoare presumably excludes output guards because they complicate the process of matching communicators. Even in his original description of CSP ([Hoare 78]), he recognizes their expressive merits. Kieburtz and Silberschatz [Kieburtz 79] show that CSP, even without output guards, requires a nontrivial interprocess communication protocol. Many now treat output guards as if they were primitive.

Silberschatz [Silberschatz 79] shows that by imposing a strict order among each pair of communication processes, a restricted form of input and output guards can be effectively implemented. In particular, for each communicating pair, one process must be declared the "server" and the other the "user." A *server* process can have both input and output guards with its users. This scheme is appropriate for systems that are hierarchically organized. However, like the original "no output guards" proposal, it suffers from a lack of symmetry between processes.

Bernstein [Bernstein 80] shows that if each process has a static priority, then output guards can be implemented without restrictions. This priority is used only to determine what a process should do if it has sent a request for communication to one process and receives a request for communication from another. Bernstein's implementation does not bound the number of communication requests a process must send before establishing communication. Furthermore, it is possible for two processes to try to communicate indefinitely and never succeed (livelock). To resolve these implementation problems, Buckley and Silberschatz [Buckley 83] propose an implementation which guarantees that two processes attempting to communicate will do so using a bounded number of messages.

PROBLEMS

10-1 Rewrite the program for the producer-consumer buffer using output guards.

10-2 Program the process control bath example of Chapter 7 in CSP.

10-3 Show how recursion can be simulated in CSP with an array of processes.
10-4 Contrast CSP with Concurrent Processes (Chapter 8).
10-5 To what extent can CSP be used to model hardware?

REFERENCES

[**Apt 80**] Apt, K. R., N. Francez, and W. P. de Roever, "A Proof System for Communicating Sequential Processes," *ACM Trans. Program. Lang. Syst.*, vol. 2, no. 3 (July 1980), pp. 359–385. Apt et al. propose an axiomatic proof system for correctness proofs of CSP programs. One of many papers on the formal semantics of CSP.

[**Bernstein 80**] Bernstein, A. J., "Output Guards and Nondeterminism in 'Communicating Sequential Processes,'" *ACM Trans. Program. Lang. Syst.*, vol. 2, no. 2 (April 1980), pp. 234–238. Bernstein shows how static process priorities can be used to implement output guards.

[**Buckley 83**] Buckley, G., and A. Silberschatz, "An Effective Implementation for the Generalized Input-Output Construct of CSP," *ACM Trans. Program. Lang. Syst.*, vol. 5, no. 2 (April 1983), pp. 223–235. Buckley and Silberschatz present an improved priority scheme for implementing output guards.

[**Francez 80**] Francez, N., D. J. Lehmann, and A. Pnueli, "A Linear History Semantics for Distributed Languages," *21st Annu. Symp. Found. Comput. Sci.*, Syracuse, New York (October 1980), pp. 143–151. This paper presents a denotational semantics for CSP.

[**Hoare 78**] Hoare, C.A.R., "Communicating Sequential Processes," *CACM*, vol. 21, no. 8 (August 1978), pp. 666–677. This is the original CSP paper. To illustrate the expressive power of CSP, Hoare presents the solutions to several "standard problems" of concurrency control, such as a bounded buffer, the dining philosophers, semaphores, and the sieve of Eratosthenes.

[**Kieburtz 79**] Kieburtz, R. B., and A. Silberschatz, "Comments on 'Communicating Sequential Processes,'" *ACM Trans. Program. Lang. Syst.*, vol. 1, no. 2 (January 1979), pp. 218–225. This paper discusses some of the limitations of CSP.

[**Levin 81**] Levin, G. M., and D. Gries, "A Proof Technique for Communicating Sequential Processes," *Acta Informa.*, vol. 15, no. 3 (June 1981), pp. 281–302. Levin and Gries present proof rules for the total correctness of CSP programs. They treat output guards as primitive.

[**Reynolds 65**] Reynolds, J. C., "COGENT," Report ANL-7022, Argonne National Laboratory, Argonne, Illinois (1965). COGENT is the source of the CSP-style of structured data type.

[**Silberschatz 79**] Silberschatz, A., "Communication and Synchronization in Distributed Systems," *IEEE Trans. Softw. Eng.*, vol. 5, no. 6 (November 1979), pp. 542–547. Silberschatz shows that segregating sets of input and output processes allows a restricted form of output guards for CSP.

[**Williams 64**] Williams J.W.J., "Algorithm 232 Heapsort," *CACM*, vol. 7, no. 6 (June 1964), pp. 347–348. This paper presents the original definition of Heapsort. The sorting tree example resembles Heapsort's merge phase.

ELEVEN

ACTORS

The Actor model takes the theme of object-oriented computation seriously and to an extreme. In an Actor system, everything is an actor (object). Actors communicate by sending each other messages. These messages are themselves actors.

Carl Hewitt and his colleagues at M.I.T. are developing the Actor model. Their work is devoted to refining the Actor concept, providing a formal semantics for Actor computations, and building programming systems that embody Actor principles. Our discussion of Actors focuses on two of these issues. Our first concern is the Actor metaphor—the philosophical consequences of treating all parts of a programming system uniformly. The remainder of this section deals with the semantics and implementation of Actor systems.

Data Abstraction

In Section 2-2 we introduced the idea of data abstraction—that the logical appearance of a program's data can be made independent of its physical implementation. Most abstraction mechanisms are designed for manipulating general data structures such as stacks, queues, and trees. Within each abstract object, conventional programming techniques are used to describe its behavior. The Actor metaphor extends the idea of abstraction to assert that all programming constructs are objects (actors), be they as simple as "the number 5," as functional as "factorial," or as complex as "this intelligent program."

Actor Theory

There are three kinds of actors: primitive actors, unserialized actors, and serialized actors. *Primitive actors* correspond to the data and procedure primitives of the computer system. For example, integer 5 and function + are primitive actors. Nonprimitive actors combine state and procedure. Serialized actors differ from unserialized actors in that *serialized actors* have local state that the actor itself can change, while *unserialized actors* cannot change their local state. A typical unserialized actor is factorial. Factorial can be implemented in terms of other primitive and unserialized actors, such as true, 1, and, recursively, factorial. A serialized actor associates local storage (state) with function. A typical serialized actor is a register that remembers the last value sent it. Such an actor retains its states between message receptions. Serialized actors process messages serially—one at a time.

Actors communicate by sending each other messages. An actor with a task for another actor to perform composes a *message* describing that task and *sends* that message to the other actor, the *target* of the message. At some time in the computational future, the message *arrives* at the target. At some time after its arrival, the message is *accepted*; its processing commences. An actor's *behavior* describes which messages the actor accepts and how it responds to those messages. Of course, messages are themselves actors, created by the primitive **create-unserialized-actor** actor.

One important class of actors is continuations [Reynolds 72; Strachey 74]. (Hewitt calls these *customer* or *complaint box* actors.) *Continuations* are actors that are sent as part of a message and that are intended (in certain circumstances) to extend part of the computation. Typically, an actor sends the result of its processing to a continuation. Since continuations are actors and all parts of messages are actors, messages can naturally include multiple continuations — perhaps one continuation to be sent the results of an error-free computation, another to be informed of syntax errors, and a third to handle exceptional machine conditions. A primitive, machine-oriented way of thinking about continuations is as a program-counter address combined with a set of registers. Sending a message to a continuation is like jumping to that address— a flexible form of computed-GOTO. Unlike Fortran's archetypical computed-GOTO, the range of possible continuations does not have to be specified before execution. In practice, it is more common to compose a continuation immediately before sending a message than it is to use a predefined one. Continuations are so powerful a control operation that they have been called "the ultimate GOTO" [Steele 77].

Every actor has a *script* (program) and *acquaintances* (data, local storage). When a message arrives at an actor, the actor's script is applied to that message. For example, primitive actor 1 accepts messages like "add yourself to 3, and send the answer to actor G0042." The script for actor 1 includes programs for handling addition messages, subtraction messages, multiplication messages, equality messages, and printing messages. The script for a cell actor would include programs for handling value-setting messages, value-getting messages, and printing messages.

Primitive actors represent the primitive data objects of an actor system. Typical primitive actors include the integers and booleans. Each of primitive actors **true** and **false** has an important line in its script that handles messages of the form "if you are true then respond with **thenval** otherwise respond with **elseval** sending the answer to **continuation**." When actor **true** accepts such a message, it sends **thenval** to **continuation**; actor **false** sends **elseval** to **continuation**. That is, there is no conditional function. Instead, actors **true** and **false** know how to handle messages keyed to if. This parallels the lambda calculus, where true and false are functions (Section 1-2).

Unserialized actors are simply descriptions of functions. They compute their values by sending messages (with the right continuations) to other actors. Serialized actors are more powerful. They have both program (script) and local storage (acquaintances). When a serialized actor accepts a message, it becomes locked against further messages. One thing a locked serialized actor can do is *become* another actor. It unlocks in the process of "becoming." For example, a cell (register) actor might respond to messages of the form get with (actor) **3**. On accepting a message telling it to **set** itself to **5**, it locks. Its script then tells it to become the actor that responds to get messages with **5**. The act of becoming this new actor unlocks the cell. The underlying system ensures that messages do not reach a locked actor. The locking of an actor on receipt of a message causes messages to be processed one at a time, that is, serially. Serialized actors do not behave as functions (in the mathematical sense) — they do not always respond to the same message with the same behavior. In a typical implementation, the underlying actor system would keep a queue of the messages that have arrived at a serialized actor. Hardware arbiters would determine an ordering on this queue. In Actor systems (just as in any postal service), the order in which two messages were sent is not necessarily the same as the order in which they arrive.

Serialized actors are created by sending a message to actor **create-serialized-actor**. This is equivalent to process creation. Sending a message to an actor is process activation. Concurrency in an Actor system arises when, after receiving a message, an actor sends several messages. Concurrency is reduced by an actor that receives a message and does not send any others.

Actor theory has several other rules for actor behavior. All actors have unique names. Actors start processing when they receive a message. Actor languages preclude iteration. Instead, repetition is achieved by having actors send themselves messages or by including themselves in the continuations of their messages. This last restriction has three significant consequences: (1) the evaluation of the code of any actor is finite; (2) the underlying system has the opportunity to interleave the evaluations of different actors and different messages; and (3) no message reception generates an unbounded (infinite) number of messages. Actor systems

(1) If an event E_1 precedes an event E_2, then only a finite number of events occurred between them.

(2) No event can immediately cause more than a finite number of events.

(3) Each event is generated by the sending of at most a single message.

(4) Of any two messages sent to an actor, one precedes the other in arrival order.

(5) The event ordering is well-founded (one can always take a finite number of "steps" back to the initial event).

(6) Only a finite number of actors can be created as an immediate result of a single event.

(7) An actor has a finite number of acquaintances at any time. Acquaintances are the actors to which it can send messages. An actor's acquaintances when processing a message are the union of its own acquaintances and the acquaintances of the message.

Figure 11-1 Laws for Actor systems.

do not guarantee the "prompt" delivery of messages, only their eventual delivery and processing. Thus, Actors support weak fairness.

Hewitt and Baker [Hewitt 77b] call the acceptance of a message by an actor an *event*. The intended semantics of Actor systems can be better understood by examination of their laws for Actor systems, given in Figure 11-1. These laws are meant to restrict Actor systems to those that can be physically implemented. The general goal of the laws is to ensure that Actor systems can be simulated by finite permutation of primitive events. The first, second, third, fifth, and sixth laws preclude possible loopholes to the finite permutation rules. The fourth law precludes simultaneity in Actor systems. The seventh law asserts that the physical storage of an actor is always bounded (though nothing in the Actor laws precludes that storage from growing during processing).

An important goal of the Actor work is universality. The Actor model is intended to be able to model all aspects of a computing system's behavior, from programs through processors and peripheral devices.

Actor terminology is confusing. There is a plethora of new names (such as "actor," "message," "target," "behavior," "script," and "event") for concepts that border on the familiar. The mystery is compounded by the assertion that most of these are members of a single class of object, actors, which all obey the same laws. In reality, the Actor metaphor is not as mysterious as the variety of names would imply. Lisp programmers have long recognized that the same structure can be put to many uses. A particular collection of cells and pointers can serve as a static data structure, as an argument list for a function, or as the code of the function itself. These are all bound together through the common denominator of the cons cell—each is a type of cons cell structure. The Actor metaphor is similar. When it asserts that "a message is also an actor," it is arguing the Actor equivalent of "a function's argument list is built using the Actor equivalent of cons."

Actor Practice

The Actor metaphor is attractive. It promises a uniformity of abstraction that is useful for real programming. One hopes that Actors will provide a release from the atomicity of conventional programming systems. The programmer need not determine the implementation of an object during design, only the form of its messages. No variable or function is so fine that it cannot be dynamically modified to exhibit a different behavior. The granularity of the processing elements in an Actor system is small enough to trace changes in the value of a single cell.

Hewitt and his colleagues have implemented several languages based on actors. The first was called Plasma; current systems include Act-1, Act-2, Omega, and Ether (we discuss Ether in Section 18-3). They developed these languages in a Lisp-based programming environment; their development drew on themes from the lambda calculus, Lisp, and artificial intelligence. The notions of functions as objects, lambda expressions, and continuations come from the lambda calculus. The idea of implementing actors as serialized *closures*—i.e., function code within a specified environment waiting to be applied to (accept) a message, is derived from Lisp.* And the concept of *pattern-matched invocation*—that the script of an actor should be described as a set of patterns instead of a sequential program—originated in artificial intelligence. Strangely enough, since pattern matching is simply another syntax for conditional expressions, the resulting system is remarkably similar to an applicative-order (call-by-value) lambda calculus interpreter (with processes) in Lisp. It is important to ensure in an Actor-like interpreter that the closures are correctly scoped.

Actors and the Lambda Calculus

What is the structure of an Actor implementation? In their description of the programming language Scheme, Sussman and Steele write [Sussman 75, p. 39]:

> This work developed out of an initial attempt to understand the actorness of Actors. Steele thought he understood it, but couldn't explain it; Sussman suggested the experimental approach of actually building an "Actors interpreter." This interpreter attempted to intermix the use of actors and Lisp lambda expressions in a clean manner. When it was completed, we discovered that the "actors" and the lambda-expressions were identical in implementation. Once we had discovered this, all the rest fell into place, and it was only natural to begin thinking about Actors in terms of lambda calculus.

The system that resulted from Sussman and Steele's work was the programming language Scheme—a language that is almost a direct implementation of the lambda calculus (with assignment statements) in Lisp (using lists and atoms

---

* In the past, closures have gone by the name "funargs" in the Lisp community. The "thunks" used to implement call-by-name in languages such as Algol 60 are also versions of closures [Ingerman 61].

instead of the strings of the pure lambda calculus). Scheme also relies heavily on closures. From a Scheme perspective, an actor's script is the closure expression and the set of an actor's acquaintances is an environment. In fact, Scheme is not Actors; even though Scheme can execute code isomorphic to Actor programs, the system does not address the Actor concern for weak fairness.

In Actors, side effects are formalized and given a specific interpretation by primitive serializers. This is particularly important in a distributed environment, where the use of multiple sites obscures the notion of simultaneous state. Steele discusses the mapping between lexically scoped Lisp and Actors in his paper, "Lambda, the Ultimate Declarative" [Steele 76].

Actor Language Features

Hewitt and his colleagues have extended Plasma and Act-1 with several features. They have primitives for delaying the processing of a message that creates an actor until a message is sent to it (**delay**) and for running several actors concurrently, accepting the answer of whichever terminates first (**race**). Act-1 scripts can be written so that message reception is done by pattern matching, instead of sequential conditional expressions. They have also implemented the "description system" Omega [Hewitt 80] that performs pattern matching and type checking based on simple inference mechanisms.

Certain assumptions underlie the implementation of any Actor system. One important concern is the recycling of resources. Actor systems assume the existence of a garbage collector that finds and reclaims the storage of inaccessible actors (as a Lisp system garbage collects inaccessible cons cells). The Actor metaphor also has no explicit notion of time and no facility (except complaint handlers) for handling communication failure. Instead, each actor must trust the underlying system to ensure that all communications are faithfully delivered.

Hewitt and his students have developed the formal semantics of Actor computations. Greif proved results about expressing Actor computations in terms of events and behaviors [Greif 75] and Clinger defined the semantics of Actor computations using power domains [Clinger 81].

Examples

Act-1 is a programming language with a well-defined and complicated syntax. Some of its syntactic goals are intended to aid artificial intelligence research, others to provide helpful functions for the system user. Act-1 is primarily a synthesis of continuation passing, function application, and data abstraction. To illustrate these ideas, we have chosen our own syntax; the commentary clarifies those uses that are unfamiliar programming constructs. We give an example of a syntactically correct, Act-1 program at the end of this section. Act-1's syntax is characterized by its Lisp-like use of parentheses and its keyword-oriented pattern matching. In our examples, we preserve some of the keywords but remove many of the parentheses.

Factorial Our first example presents an unserialized actor, factorial (adapted from Hewitt [Hewitt 77a]). As actors have no loops, factorial is restricted to iteration by recursion—sending a message to itself. The message factorial sends itself has a continuation that embeds the original continuation sent the actor inside the action it performs. Our pseudoactor language is a mixture of Algol, Lisp, and the lambda calculus.

```
factorial ≡ λm.              -- The factorial actor takes a message m.
    match m ⟨n c⟩            -- Pattern-match m with a number n and a
                                continuation c.
      if n = 1
        then (send c ⟨1⟩)    -- If n is 1, then send 1 to c. Send is similar to
                                Lisp's apply, except that in actors, the
                                matching is explicit.
      else
      if n > 1
        then (send factorial ⟨(n − 1) (λk.(send c ⟨n * k⟩))⟩)
                             -- Otherwise, send factorial a message composed
                                of n−1 and a continuation which will multiply
                                n by the result of that factorial, and send the
                                result to c.
```

An actor wishing to have the factorial of 3 computed and the resulting answer sent to continuation wantsanswer would invoke

$$(\textbf{send } factorial \ \langle 3 \ wantsanswer\rangle)$$

This would be successively transformed to (we have primed the successive bound variables for clarity)

$$(\textbf{send } factorial \ \langle 2 \ (\lambda k.(\textbf{send } wantsanswer \ \langle 3 * k\rangle))\rangle)$$

$$(\textbf{send } factorial \ \langle 1 \ (\lambda k'.(\textbf{send } (\lambda k.(\textbf{send } wantsanswer \ \langle 3 * k\rangle)) \\ \langle 2 * k'\rangle))\rangle)$$

When factorial accepts a message whose integer part is **1**, it sends **1** to the continuation.

$$(\textbf{send } (\lambda k'.(\textbf{send } (\lambda k.(\textbf{send } wantsanswer \ \langle 3 * k\rangle)) \\ \langle 2 * k'\rangle)) \\ \langle 1\rangle)$$

Applying that continuation to ⟨1⟩ replaces all occurrences of k′ bound by the outer λk′ with **1** yielding

$$\textbf{(send } (\lambda \textsf{k}.(\textbf{send } \textsf{wantsanswer } \langle 3 * \textsf{k}\rangle)) \ \langle 2 * 1\rangle)$$

Two times one is, of course, two. Sending that value to this continuation produces the result

$$\textbf{(send } \textsf{wantsanswer } \langle 3 * 2\rangle)$$

$$\textbf{(send } \textsf{wantsanswer } \langle 6\rangle)$$

Hence, actor **wantsanswer** is to be sent the message whose only element is **6**. Fortunately, 3! = 6. The factorial actor computes iteratively by passing continuations. This solution avoids the arbitrarily deep stack required by a recursive solution. Instead, it creates an arbitrarily complex continuation. (We have simplified the program by treating multiplication and conditionals as primitive, instead of explicitly detailing their expansion by the primitive actors.)

Bank account A serialized actor can have permanent storage. We present an example of a part of a banking system, a serialized actor called an **account** [Hewitt 79]. An **account** has one permanent storage field, its **balance**. An **account** actor responds to **deposit** messages that add to its **balance** and to **withdrawal** messages that try to decrease it. The **account** actor bounces withdrawals that would leave it with negative funds.

```
account [balance] ≡ λm.
    match m ⟨"withdrawal"        -- A message whose first element is the word
                                    "withdrawal"

               n                 -- second a number n
               c⟩                -- and third a continuation c.
    if balance > n then          -- If the balance is sufficient to cover this
                                    withdrawal,

           parbegin              -- do these things in parallel:
           (send c ⟨"transaction_completed"⟩)
                                 -- send an acknowledgment
           (become account (balance−n))
                                 -- and transform into an account with balance of
                                    (balance−n).
           parend
    else                                        -- If there are insufficient funds
           parbegin
           (send c ⟨"overdraft"⟩)
           (become account balance)    -- perform an identity
                                          transformation.
           parend;
```

match m ⟨"deposit"   -- *If the message matches with a message whose first element is deposit*
    n   -- *second is a number n*
    c⟩   -- *and third is a continuation c, then accept the deposit.*
  parbegin
    (**send** c ⟨"transaction_completed"⟩)
    (**become** account (balance + n))
             -- *This actor becomes one whose new balance is (balance+n).*
  parend

This actor responds to two kinds of messages: Messages of the form ⟨"withdrawal" n c⟩ request that n units be withdrawn from the account, and a confirmation of this action sent to c. The behavior of the actor depends on the balance of the account and the size of the withdrawal. Messages of the form ⟨"deposit" n c⟩ increase the balance by n, and send a confirmation to c. In either case, (serialized) actor account is transformed into an account with the new balance.*
Actor account, written in Act-1 (from [Hewitt 82]), is as follows:

```
(defaction (new account (with balance =b))
    (create
        (is-request (a deposit (with amount =n)) do
            (become (new account (with balance (+ b n))))
            (reply (a deposit-receipt (with amount n))))
        (is-request (a withdrawal (with amount =n)) do
            (if (< b n)
                (then do (complain (an overdraft)))
                (else do
                    (become (new account (with balance (- b n))))
                    (reply (a withdrawal-receipt (with amount n)))))))
        (is-request (a balance) do (reply b))))
```

Perspective

The Actor metaphor provides uniform, independent entities that communicate through message passing and continuations. This is a powerful and rewarding theme. In Section 18-3 we touch on some control organizations that conform to this model.

---

* One creates an account actor by sending a request to create_serialized_actor, the system storage allocation function.

PROBLEMS

11-1 Design an airline reservation system using the Actors model. Have your system keep a waiting list of passengers denied reservations. Inform the appropriate waiting passengers on cancellations.

11-2 Demonstrate how to write standard control structures such as **while**, **repeat**, and loops with multiple-level exits using Actors.

11-3 Write the program of an actor that behaves as a two-field cell, responding to messages that set and return the values of each field. Such an actor is similar to a Lisp cons cell.

REFERENCES

[**Clinger 81**] Clinger, W., "Foundations of Actor Semantics," Ph.D. dissertation, M.I.T., Cambridge, Massachusetts (May 1981). Also available as Technical Report 633, Artificial Intelligence Laboratory, M.I.T., Cambridge, Massachusetts. Clinger gives a denotational semantics for an Actors-like system. His semantics relies on powerdomains. The difficult part of the semantics is combining indeterminacy and weak fairness.

[**Greif 75**] Greif, I., and C. E. Hewitt, "Actor Semantics of Planner-73," *Conf. Rec. 2d ACM Symp. Princ. Program. Lang.*, Palo Alto, California (January 1975), pp. 67–77. This paper describes actor semantics in terms of events and behaviors. Greif and Hewitt justify the use of side effects by arguing that programs with side effects are much more efficient than programs written in a pure, side-effect-free style. However, their argument assumes that computer systems are built with conventional von Neumann architectures.

[**Hewitt 77a**] Hewitt C. E., "Viewing Control Structures as Patterns of Passing Messages," *Artif. Intell.*, vol. 8, no. 3 (June 1977), pp. 323–364. This is one of the most applications-oriented of the Actors papers. Unfortunately, the programming examples are written in Plasma, which is even more obscure than its successor, Act-1.

[**Hewitt 77b**] Hewitt, C. E., and H. Baker, "Laws for Communicating Parallel Processes," in B. Gilchrist (ed.), *Information Processing 77: Proceedings of the IFIP Congress 77*, North Holland, Amsterdam (1977), pp. 987–992. Hewitt and Baker give a set of descriptive laws for the behavior of message-passing systems.

[**Hewitt 79**] Hewitt, C. E., G. Attardi, and H. Lieberman, "Specifying and Proving Properties of Guardians for Distributed Systems," in G. Kahn (ed.), *Semantics of Concurrent Computation*, Lecture Notes in Computer Science 70, Springer-Verlag, New York (1979), pp. 316–336. Hewitt et al. present examples of Actor programs for a checking account and a hardcopy server.

[**Hewitt 80**] Hewitt, C. E., G. Attardi, and M. Simi, "Knowledge Embedding in the Description System Omega," *Proc. 1st Annu. Natl. Conf. Artif. Intell.*, Stanford, California (August 1980), pp. 157–164. Omega is a knowledge representation language that unifies ω-order quantification calculus, type theory, and pattern matching within the Actor metaphor.

[**Hewitt 82**] Hewitt, C. E., personal communication, 1982.

[**Ingerman 61**] Ingerman, P., "Thunks," *CACM*, vol. 4, no. 1 (January 1961), pp. 55–58.

[**Reynolds 72**] Reynolds, J. C., "Definitional Interpreters for Higher-Order Programming Languages," *Proc. 25th ACM Natl. Conf.*, Boston (1972), pp. 717–740. Reynolds demonstrates a sequence of interpreters, progressing to an interpreter that uses continuations. He calls such continuations "escapes."

[**Steele 76**] Steele, G. L., Jr., "Lambda: The Ultimate Declarative," Memo 379, Artificial Intelligence Laboratory, M.I.T., Cambridge, Massachusetts (November 1976). The third section of this paper is a detailed comparison of a continuation-based Lisp programming language, Scheme, and an Actor language, Plasma.

[**Steele 77**] Steele, G. L., Jr., "Debunking the 'Expensive Procedure Call' Myth," *Proc. 30th ACM Natl. Conf.*, Seattle (October 1977), pp. 153–162. Revised as "Debunking the 'Expensive Procedure Call' Myth or, Procedure Call Implementations Considered Harmful or, Lambda: The Ultimate GOTO," Memo 443, Artificial Intelligence Laboratory, M.I.T., Cambridge, Massachusetts, October 1977. This paper demonstrates (among other things) the power of lambda expressions (and continuations) as a programming tool.

[**Steele 78**] Steele, G. L., Jr., and G. J. Sussman, "The Revised Report on SCHEME, a Dialect of LISP," Memo 452, Artificial Intelligence Laboratory, M.I.T., Cambridge, Massachusetts (January 1978).

[**Strachey 74**] Strachey, C., and C. P. Wadsworth, "Continuations—a Mathematical Semantics for Handling Full Jumps," Technical Monograph TRG-11, Programming Research Group, Oxford University, Oxford, England (1974). Strachey and Wadsworth introduce continuations. A continuation is a function that represents the remainder of a computation. They show that continuations are a much more powerful control structure than **goto**s.

[**Sussman 75**] Sussman, G. J., and G. L. Steele, Jr., "SCHEME: An Interpreter for Extended Lambda Calculus," Memo 349, Artificial Intelligence Laboratory, M.I.T., Cambridge, Massachusetts (December 1975). This report documents an attempt to implement Actor concepts. Included in the report is the code for a Scheme interpreter written in Lisp. While Scheme does not deal with every issue of Actor systems, it captures many of the important concepts in a particularly clean fashion.

TWELVE

INDETERMINATE APPLICATIVE SYSTEMS

We have already studied two models that, to some extent, express concurrent computation through function composition. Data Flow (Chapter 9) describes concurrency by a process equivalent to the parallel evaluation of function arguments. In Data Flow, a stream of values computed by a primitive is directed to the inputs of its caller. Input streams can be piped together; parallel streams can be processed concurrently. Similarly, the Actors model (Chapter 11) adds concurrency, side effects, and weak fairness to the lambda calculus. Sending a message to an actor resembles calling a function. The primary source of parallelism in Actors is actors that, on receiving one message, send several messages. This roughly corresponds to functions that evaluate several arguments in a single call.

In some sense, Data Flow and Actors start with unusual ideas (graphical and object-oriented computation) and converge toward classical functional systems. This section discusses Indeterminate Applicative Programming (IAP), a set of ideas centered on extending classical functional environments (like pure Lisp and side-effect-free Scheme) into distributable systems. IAP has mechanisms for constructing infinite objects, indeterminate selection, task generation, and communication.

(1 2 3 4 5 6 7 8 9 10 11 12 13 14 15 ...
       The positive integers.

(2 3 5 7 11 13 17 19 23 29 31 37 41 ...
       The primes.

((1 2 3 4 5 6 7 8 9 10 11 12 13 14 ...
(2 4 6 8 10 12 14 16 18 20 22 24 26 ...
(3 6 9 12 15 18 21 24 27 30 33 36 39 ...
$$\vdots$$
     A stream of streams.

($\perp$ $\perp$ $\perp$ 4 $\perp$ 6 7 $\perp$ 9 10 11 12 $\perp$ 14 15 16 ...
A stream, some of whose elements are undefined.

Figure 12-1 Typical streams.

Infinite Objects

Several inventions led to the development of Lisp-based distributable systems. Clearly, one of the most important was Lisp itself [McCarthy 65]. Another, less well known contribution was Peter Landin's description of streams [Landin 65]. *Streams* are possibly infinite sequences of values. Sequences are a familiar idea in computer science—for example, linked lists are an implementation of sequences. Conceptually, a stream is a sequence with no last element. Streams are typically arguments to functions; those functions act on each element of the stream, producing another stream as output. In a Lisp-like system, the constituent values of a stream can be atomic symbols, finite lists, or themselves streams. One value that might occur in a stream is bottom ($\perp$), the undefined value.* Figure 12-1 shows several typical streams. We use Lisp "parenthesis notation" to show values, with unbalanced parentheses and ellipses suggesting infinite streams.

If the arguments to functions are not simply values but streams, then function composition produces a "graphical" description of computation. For example, the functional expression

$$f(g(x,y), h(y,z))$$

can be thought of as a three-node network, where x, y, and z are the input sources and the value produced is the output sink. Figure 12-2 illustrates this relationship. This view of functional programming is similar to Data Flow.†

---

   * $\perp$ (undefined) should be thought of as the result of performing a nonterminating computation such as finding $f(5)$, when the definition of f is $f(x) \equiv 1 + f(x+1)$.

   † Perhaps the first to notice the equivalence of function composition and graphical computation over infinite sequences was Gilles Kahn [Kahn 74]. He later extended and amplified this work with David MacQueen [Kahn 77].

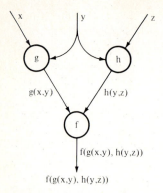

f(g(x,y), h(y,z))

Figure 12-2 $f(g(x,y), h(y,z))$.

Any reasonable implementation of infinite sequences makes certain obvious choices. For example, the same function should return the first element of both finite and infinite sequences. However, there are some obvious difficulties with the a implementation of infinite objects. For example, given that you are going to have an infinite object, where do you store it? The resolution of this problem lies in not creating "too much" of the infinite object. More succinctly, the optimal strategy is to generate the parts of the infinite object as they are used. This *delayed evaluation* requires modifying the underlying programming system. Since Lisp (like virtually every common programming language except the call-by-name feature of Algol 60) evaluates a function's arguments before evaluating its body,* a function whose argument constructs an infinite object would never terminate.

There are two classes of remedies to this problem. The simpler way (from a programming standpoint) is to make the evaluation scheme be normal-order evaluation. *Normal-order evaluation* evaluates functions from the "outside-in." It substitutes the (unevaluated) arguments to the function for the corresponding bound variables in the function body, and then evaluates the function body. Hence, if a particular function parameter is never used, the corresponding actual parameter is never evaluated.

The opposite of normal-order evaluation is applicative-order evaluation. In *applicative-order evaluation*, the function's arguments are first evaluated and the resulting values are substituted into the body of the function. The body of the function is then evaluated. Lisp expr's and Scheme use applicative-order evaluation.

Some expressions terminate when evaluated in normal order, but not in applicative order. In particular, if the evaluation of an argument to a function produces an infinite object, then applicative-order evaluation creates (or at least

---

* At least expr's in Lisp evaluate their arguments in this way.

tries to create) the entire infinite object. On the other hand, normal-order evaluation builds only as much of the object as the computation uses.* Infinite data objects always remain finitely described. However, normal-order evaluation has its drawbacks. If a parameter's value is accessed several times during the evaluation of a function's body, then that parameter is reevaluated each time. A system can waste energy repeatedly evaluating the arguments to functions.† Jean Vuillemin and Christopher Wadsworth discovered resolutions of the problem of multiple argument evaluation in normal-order systems in the early seventies [Vuillemin 74; Wadsworth 71]. We call their idea call-by-need. In a *call-by-need* system, evaluation is done in normal order. However, after computing the value of a parameter, the system remembers that value and does not evaluate that parameter again. Three promising (and similar) approaches have been suggested for embedding call-by-need in a Lisp-like system: Gilles Kahn and David MacQueen's "networks of parallel processes" [Kahn 74; Kahn 77]; Peter Henderson and James Morris's "lazy evaluator" [Henderson 76]; and Daniel Friedman and David Wise's "suspending cons" [Friedman 76].

Kahn and MacQueen recognized that collections of Lisp-like functions over streams are networks that perform a Data Flow-like token passing. Making this token passing demand-driven results in call-by-need. Henderson and Morris modified a Lisp-like interpreter to produce call-by-need. Friedman and Wise found a simple and direct way to have infinite objects in Lisp-like systems, suspending cons.

Suspending Cons

In Lisp, the primary data structure is the list. Lists are constructed with the dyadic function cons. Letting nil denote the empty list ( ), the expression (cons 1 nil) evaluates to the list whose only element is 1, that is, (1). Similarly, the expression

$$\text{(cons (cons 5 nil) (cons 3 (cons 8 nil)))}$$

evaluates to the list

$$\text{((5) 3 8)}$$

---

* The ability of normal-order evaluation to compute some functions that applicative-order cannot is not limited to infinite objects; it extends to infinite computations. For example, if we define $f(x) \equiv f(x + 1)$ and $g(y, z) \equiv$ **if** $y = 0$ **then** 1 **else** z, then $g(0, f(5))$ is defined for normal-order evaluation but not for applicative-order evaluation. Normal-order evaluation of this expression yields 1.

† In a pure system (one without side effects) normal-order evaluation is semantically equivalent to performing call-by-name evaluation and applicative-order evaluation is equivalent to call-by-value. Wand [Wand 80] presents a good development of the theory of evaluation and the differences between call-by-name and call-by-value.

We use the traditional Cambridge prefix notation for describing Lisp functions. In Cambridge prefix, the function name goes inside the parentheses with its arguments (conveniently forming a list). Thus, (f x y) represents $f(x, y)$.

Corresponding to function cons there are functions car (first) and cdr (rest) for retrieving the parts of a cons. By definition [McCarthy 63]

$$(car (cons\ x\ y)) = x$$

and

$$(cdr (cons\ x\ y)) = y$$

Traditionally, cons is implemented by allocating a new storage record (a cell) for each call to cons. This record has two fields. A pointer to the first argument (car) of the cons is stored in one field and a pointer to the second argument (cdr) is stored in the other. The basic Lisp implementation recognizes two major varieties of data objects: cons cells (lists) and atoms (tokens).* The key idea in suspending cons involves making one small change to a pure (side-effect-free) Lisp system. With *suspending cons*, the constructor function, cons, does not evaluate its arguments. Instead, a call to cons builds a cell containing two *suspensions*. When a probing function car (or cdr) is called on a cell that contains a suspension, it *forces* that suspension to become a *manifest* ("real") value. That is, car (cdr) evaluates the first (second) argument of the cons that created that cell, *in the environment of the original call to* cons. The result of this evaluation is then stored back into the car (cdr) field of the cons cell in place of the suspension. It is marked as manifest. The next time the car (or cdr) of that cell is desired, the system recognizes that there is a manifest value in the cell (not a suspension), and returns it without further computation. According to Friedman and Wise [Friedman 78a, p. 931]:

> A "suspension" is a temporary structure planted within the field of a record when it is created instead of the value which rightfully should be there. It contains information sufficient to derive that value at any time it is necessary to the course of the computation. In terms of Lisp, sufficient information is the "form" which specifies the value of the field and the "environment" which retains all bindings necessary to evaluate that form at any time in the future.

Cons builds data structures, and data structures are traditionally understood with diagrams. We diagram cons cells as rectangular blocks, with halves for the car and cdr fields. We draw suspensions as "clouds." Therefore, evaluating

---

* This is just a sketch of a few of the ideas in Lisp. The original Lisp documentation [McCarthy 65] is still a good source for the theory and practice of Lisp. Many books on Lisp have been written in the last few years; Allen [Allen 78] describes Lisp for the system builder, while Winston [Winston 81] provides an introduction to programming in Lisp, particularly for Artificial Intelligence applications.

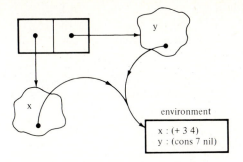

Figure 12-3 ((lambda (x y)(cons x y)) (+ 3 4) (cons 7 nil)).

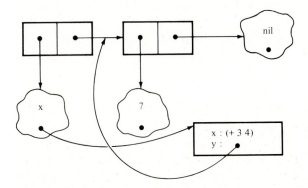

Figure 12-4 After evaluating the cdr.

$$((lambda\ (x\ y)(cons\ x\ y))\ (+\ 3\ 4)\ (cons\ 7\ nil))$$

initially produces the structure illustrated in Figure 12-3. To find the **cdr** of this structure, we force the **cdr**-field suspension to become a value. This forcing progresses only as far as the next call to **cons**. The resulting structure is shown in Figure 12-4. Using suspending cons, we can easily produce infinite structures.

It is important that the reader accept the premise that infinite objects really exist and can be represented in a finite computer system. One can treat an infinite object just like any other object. However, one must be wary of using infinite objects in algorithms that examine the entirety of objects, such as printing or counting the length of an infinite list.

Infinite objects are the children of recursion. We can define infinite objects in two ways: by functional recursion or by data recursion. Recursive function definition should be familiar to most readers. For example, the traditional (recursive) definition of factorial is

$$(\text{factorial } n) \equiv (\text{if } (= n\ 0)$$
$$1$$
$$(\times\ n\ (\text{factorial } (-\ n\ 1))))$$

This is a "good" recursive definition in that (for nonnegative integers n) it always terminates with a well-defined answer. With a suspending cons, we can define function successors as

$$(\text{successors } n) \equiv (\text{cons } n\ (\text{successors } (+\ n\ 1)))$$

This function produces the infinite list of integers, starting with its argument. That is, the successors of a number is that number consed onto the list that is the successors of one more than it. Thus, (successors 4) is the infinite list (4 5 6 7 8 9 . . . .

Data recursion [Ashcroft 77] may be unfamiliar. With data recursion we define an object in terms of itself. The keyword that indicates self-definition is letrec. Thus, the expression

$$(\text{letrec } (\text{suc4} \leftarrow (\text{cons } 4\ (\text{mapcar add1 suc4})))$$
$$<\text{body}>)$$

binds to suc4 the stream of integers starting at 4 in the evaluation of <body>.*

Letrec contrasts with the usual use of self-mention in variable assignment. In most languages, x := x + 1 means that the value of x is to be increased by one. With letrec, the equality implies current substitutivity (as in classical mathematics). That is, the structure being built is used in determining the structure being built. This is useful only if the building process examines only those parts that have already been built. Letrec stands for "let, recursively." We use the simple command let when the definition is not recursive.

We illustrate this idea with a program for generating *all* the primes. Our algorithm is the traditional sieve of Eratosthenes; we repeatedly select the smallest remaining number and discard its multiples.

$$(\text{sieve ints}) \equiv (\text{cons } (\text{car ints})$$
$$(\text{sieve } (\text{removemults } (\text{car ints})$$
$$(\text{cdr ints}))))$$

---

* This example uses functions add1 and mapcar. The expression (add1 x) returns one more than x. Mapcar takes a function and a list of arguments and builds a list of the results of applying that function to each element of the given list. Hence, if m is the list (1 4 7 10), (mapcar add1 m) is the list (2 5 8 11).

Function removemults takes a number and a list and removes all multiples of its first argument from its second argument.*

```
(removemults n l) ≡
    (cond ((evenly-divides (car l) n) (removemults n (cdr l)))
          (t (cons (car l) (removemults n (cdr l))))))
```

The object that is the stream of all the primes, in increasing order, is the value of

$$(sieve\ (successors\ 2))$$

Most recursive Lisp functions have both a base clause (or clauses) and a recursive clause (or clauses). Functions that work with infinite objects usually have only recursive clauses. That is, such programs do not check to see if the problem has been reduced to the empty list because it is never reduced to the empty list. Correspondingly, our sieve and removemults functions only work on infinite lists.

Two-three-five Dijkstra presents the following example, attributing it to Hamming [Dijkstra 76]: Generate, in increasing order, the sequence of all numbers of the form $2^i \cdot 3^j \cdot 5^k$, for natural numbers i, j and k. That is, 1, 2, 3, 4, 5, 6, 8, 9, 10, 12, 15, 16, 18, ... Dijkstra requests only the first 100 elements of the sequence. With suspending cons, we can create the entire sequence [Friedman 78b].
   We define functions scalar-product and join. The expression (scalar-product s v) is a list of the product of s and each element of v; join merges a pair of sorted streams into a single, sorted stream.

```
(scalar-product i m) ≡
    (cons (times i (car m))
          (scalar-product i (cdr m)))

(join l m) ≡
    (cond ((< (car l) (car m))
           (cons (car l) (join (cdr l) m)))
          ((> (car l) (car m))
           (cons (car m) (join l (cdr m))))
          (t (cons (car l) (join (cdr l) (cdr m))))))
```

---

* Cond is the Lisp conditional function. The expression (cond $(b_1\ e_1)$ $(b_2\ e_2)$ ... $(b_k\ e_k)$) is equivalent to the conditional expression **if** b_1 **then** e_1 **else if** b_2 **then** e_2 **else** ... **if** b_k **then** e_k **else** nil. That is, cond successively evaluates the b_i until one is true and then returns the value of the corresponding e_i. Cond treats any value that is not nil as true. In particular, the atom t evaluates to itself and is conventionally used for true.

The Hamming sequence is therefore

```
(letrec (comps ← (cons 1
                    (join (scalar-product 2 comps)
                      (join (scalar-product 3 comps)
                        (scalar-product 5 comps)))))
  comps)
```

Flip-flop Landin observed that once a system includes infinite objects, it is natural to treat a sequential file as an infinite object [Landin 65]. Similarly, we can think of a terminal session as creating an infinite file. Each keystroke adds another element to the terminal stream. This stream has no last element, though all typing after certain sequences may be ignored. Friedman and Wise [Friedman 77] pursued this theme by showing how to write a rudimentary editor as a function of a sequential file stream and a sequential command stream. Their editor produced a sequential file output stream and a stream of responses to the user. In this section we explore the same idea with respect to hardware.

Modeling some situations requires ensuring that the first element of a stream exists before one attempts to examine the rest of the stream [Landin 65]. For example, it is unreasonable to expect to be able to access the character after the next character the user types. For that reason, Friedman and Wise introduce the primitive strictify [Friedman 79]. Strictify is a function of two arguments. It evaluates its first argument and returns the value of its second.

We usually present an example of a simple, state-possessing object (like a register) at this place in the discussion of a model. What does a statelike object look like in a side-effect-free system? In this section, we present a model of a reset/set flip-flop, adapted from a paper by Johnson [Johnson 84].

A *reset/set flip-flop* (RSFF) has two input lines and two output lines. We label the inputs R (reset) and S (set). Figure 12-5 shows the circuit diagram for an RSFF. The RSFF retains its state as long as the inputs are both high. A *pulse* is a sequence of 0s. A pulse on the S line sets the flip-flop (makes $Q_{hi}=1$ and $Q_{lo}=0$) and a pulse on the R line resets the flip-flop (makes $Q_{hi}=0$ and $Q_{lo}=1$). A *spike* (a single 0) on either line makes the flip-flop unstable. The program for the RSFF is as follows:

```
(NAND l r) ≡ (map2car nand l r)
```

```
(nand x y) ≡
    (cond ((= x 0) 1)
          ((= y 0) 1)
          (t 0))
```

```
(two_list x y) ≡ (cons x (cons y nil))
```

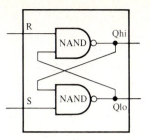

Figure 12-5 Reset/set flip-flop.

$(RSFF\ R\ S) \equiv$
    $(letrec\ (Q_{hi} \leftarrow (cons\ 1\ (NAND\ R\ Q_{lo})))$
            $(Q_{lo} \leftarrow (cons\ 0\ (NAND\ S\ Q_{hi})))$
      $(two\_list\ Q_{hi}\ Q_{lo}))$

where **map2car** maps a two-argument function down two lists.

We include the **1** and **0** in the definition of the RSFF to initialize the output. The output of this function is a list of two streams. The first stream is the behavior of Q_{hi}, and the second is the behavior of Q_{lo}.

Indeterminacy

Coordinated computing systems are naturally indeterminate. Purely functional systems (such as Lisp extended by suspending cons) are determinate. That is, every program always returns the same result. Several mechanisms for the addition of indeterminacy to functional systems have been proposed. We discuss three such extensions, two for purely functional systems and the other for suspending cons.

Merge One way of extending a functional system is to provide additional primitive functions. In Chapter 7 we described McCarthy's **amb** function. This dyadic function indeterminately chooses between its arguments, rejecting undefined arguments in favor of defined ones. Another function for indeterminate processing is **merge**. Merge takes a pair of input streams and produces an output stream of interleaved elements from both input streams. This is much like taking two decks of cards and shuffling them with a standard shuffle: the two decks are interleaved, but the cards of each deck retain their original ordering.* For example, the merge of the streams (1, 2, 3, 4, ... and (A, B, C, D, ... might be the stream (A, B, 1, 2, 3, C, 4, 5, ... But it also might be the stream (1, 2, 3,

---

* We presented an example of an indeterminate merge in the our discussion of Data Flow (Section 9-2).

4, ..., 252, A, 253, ..., 319, B, 320, ..., 461, C, ..., or even the stream (1, 2, 3, ... Different definitions of merge take different approaches to streams that include undefined elements. MacQueen's merge [MacQueen 79] specifies that if a stream has an undefined element, then that element and all future elements from that stream are ignored. Turner's merge [Turner 80] passes undefined elements on to the output. We can characterize the difference operationally by thinking of the MacQueen merge as examining the items in its list before passing them to the output and the Turner merge as passing items without examination. An n-element merge can easily be built from two-element merges. Exercise 12-4 asks for generalized merge functions.

Frons Friedman and Wise adopt a different approach to introducing indeterminacy to functional systems. Their invention is frons, an indeterminate constructor. Cons constructs lists whose element order is determined at "construction time." Thus,

$$\text{(cons 1 (cons 2 (cons 3 nil)))}$$

produces the list (1 2 3). The car of that list is 1 and will always be 1.

Frons also builds listlike objects, in that car and cdr can be used to extract pieces of the result. However, unlike lists that have been created with cons, the order of the elements of a frons list is not determined until the list is probed by car or cdr. For example, let m be the result of (frons 1 (frons 2 (frons 3 nil))). The first call for car of m may yield 1, 2, or 3. If (car m) evaluates to 2 at some time, then it will always be 2. If (car m) is 2, then (car (cdr m)) will be either 1 or 3. In general, car pulls a convergent (not ⊥) element from a frons list; cdr forces a selection of the first element and forms the remaining elements into a frons list. Forcing the evaluation of the entirety of a frons-list produces some permutation of the original elements. This permanence of "found values" is engineered by changing the frons cell into a cons cell when the value of the car is discovered and placing that value in the car of the cons cell.

Frons never selects a divergent element before a convergent one. In this respect, it resembles merge and amb. Thus, the expression

$$\text{(car (frons (cond ((< x 0) ⊥)}$$
$$\text{(t 1))}$$
$$\text{(frons (cond ((> x 0) ⊥)}$$
$$\text{(t 1))}$$
$$\text{(frons ⊥ nil))))}$$

always evaluates to 1, no matter what the value of x (provided, of course, that x has a numeric value).

Determining (in general) whether an element of a frons list will converge is formally undecidable. In implementations of frons, elements are selected by distributing processing resources to successive suspensions until one converges. This (almost) orders the elements of a frons list by their relative computation cost.

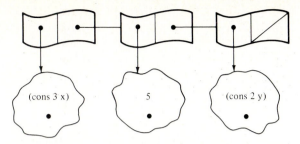

Figure 12-6 (frons (cons 3 x) (frons 5 (frons (cons 2 y) nil))).

Frons, like suspending cons, does not evaluate its arguments. Instead, it builds suspensions. Hence, one can easily build infinite frons structures. For example, the definition

(frsuccessors i) ≡ (frons i (frsuccessors (+ i 1)))

implies that (car (frsuccessors 1)) is going to be a positive integer, though there is no way to tell which one. (IAP therefore supports unbounded indeterminacy.) If n is bound to (frsuccessors 1), and we take (car n), we might get the value 21356. The system decides this once for each frons cell; the next time the (car n) is evaluated, it is still 21356. The value of (car (cdr n)) could be any positive integer except 21356.

In our diagrams, we illustrate frons constructions as wavy boxes. Taking the car of a list of such wavy boxes straightens one of these boxes and moves it to the front of the list. To illustrate this idea, we let I be the list

(frons (cons 3 x) (frons 5 (frons (cons 2 y) nil)))

Figure 12-6 shows the box diagram of I. Of course, the frons cells in the cdr of the cell are originally suspensions; we have drawn the entire frons structure to illustrate the evaluation process.

Taking the car of such a list resembles polling several input lines: we are interested in whichever computation converges first. Let us imagine that it is the second element, 5. This causes a promotion of that value to the head of the list, the solidifying of its wavy box into a rectangular cons cell, and the rearrangement of the rest of the list. Figure 12-7 shows the resulting state.

Sharing of sublists complicates promotion algorithms. For an example of the difficulties involved, let k be the list (frons 1 (frons 2 nil)), and j the list created by (frons 9 k). Figure 12-8 shows this situation. Now, imagine that we evaluate the (car j) and it turns out to be 2. A naive promotion algorithm would rearrange the elements of the frons list so that 2 was the first element, as shown in Figure 12-9. To which element should k now point? By the definition of frons, k must be either the list (1 2) or the list (2 1). It can neither skip one of these

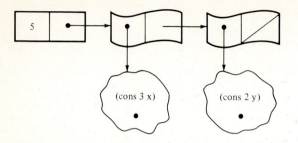

Figure 12-7 After taking the car of l.

elements nor include the spurious 9. One resolution of this problem comes from copying. Figure 12-10 shows a correct promotion. A correct promotion algorithm appears in the original frons paper [Friedman 80].

Multiprocessing The reader may be curious as to why we include IAP in a book on coordinated computing. After all, many of the conventional aspects of distributed computing, such as explicit processes, communication primitives, and distance, are not mentioned by this system. The importance of IAP is that each suspension created by a cons or frons operation is an independent task. A multiprocess system can devote a process to expanding each suspension. When a processor is idle, it can look for a suspension in need of expanding. However, these processes must not get too far ahead of the main computation. We would be unhappy with the diligent process that expanded, say, the first 7 million primes when the program uses only the first seven.*

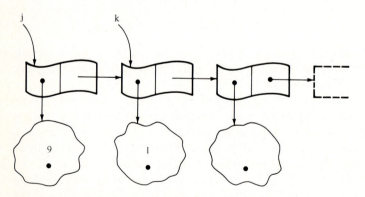

Figure 12-8 Sharing in frons lists.

* Friedman and Wise have identified an algorithm for distributing processing energy among competing suspensions. Their algorithm gives greater energy to computations closer to the main derivation [Friedman 79].

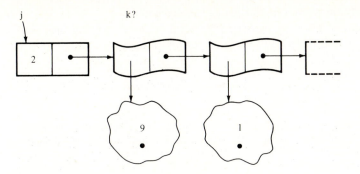

Figure 12-9 Incorrect promotion scheme.

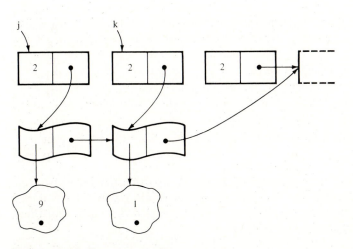

Figure 12-10 Correct promotion.

How can multiple active agents share a lock-free space? To solve this problem, Friedman and Wise invented the operator sting. Sting is a conditional store operation. In the multiprocess model of an IAP system, processes strive to evaluate suspensions, turning suspensions into manifest structures. When an active processor finds the value of a suspension, it "stings" the pointer cell of that suspension with that value. If the cell has already been stung, then nothing happens. Only if that cell has not been stung before does the system insert the value in the cell and mark the cell as stung. The stinging process is not informed if its sting succeeded. If several processors are working on resolving the same suspension (as in the car of a frons list), the first one to finish has a successful sting. Subsequent stings are ignored. Sting combines aspects of send-and-forget and test-and-set instructions. Since IAP is side-effect-free at the processor level, cells progress exactly once from frons cells to cons cells.

The principle underlying the cons and frons functions is turning processes into objects. Johnson and Kohlstaedt describe this philosophy in analogy to Lisp [Johnson 81, p. 4]:

> Returning to the Lisp analogy, we note that one intent of DSI [an implementation of IAP ideas] is to do with *process* what Lisp does with *data*. Lisp "the list processor" is a primeval data management system; it "factors out" some of the complexity of data manipulation by reducing structure to an elemental form — the binary list cell. Similarly, we seek a "lowest common denominator" for the notion of process. The focal point of our discussion is the *suspension*, a kinetic counterpart to the inert list cell. Where, in our view, data is fixed and immutable, suspensions evolve in the presence of processing.

The idea behind frons and cons is to relieve the programmer from worrying about the details of scheduling. A program using frons appears to the programmer like a theater with a single narrow exit door. At some point people (tasks) enter the system. When they leave, it is single file, one at a time. The programmer can remain oblivious to the internal organization of the departure. The exiting patrons can leave in an orderly progression or someone can yell "fire," causing chaos in the theater. The door emits only the next patron. The user of a frons list gets only the next element of the list. The user need not worry how much jockeying for position occurred to get that list in order. The list is in order when needed.

Scheduling

Scheduling freedom is important for applications involving not only operating systems concerns, but also search. To show the scheduling power of frons and cons, we present three examples—a simple search, a selection among algorithms, and a small operating systems scheduler.

Good sequences Dijkstra [Dijkstra 72b] defines a *good sequence* as a sequence of 1s, 2s, and 3s that is not of the form $xyyz$, for any subsequences x, y, and z (y not null). Thus, the sequence

$$1\ 2\ 3\ 2\ 1\ 3\ 2$$

is a good sequence, while the sequences

$$1\ 2\ 3\ 2\ 3\ 1$$

and

$$1\ 3\ 1\ 2\ 3\ 2\ 1\ 3\ 2\ 1\ 2\ 3\ 2\ 1$$

are not.

The good sequences problem asks for a program that, given a length of sequence desired, produces a good sequence of that length. One way of programming the problem is depth-first, recursive search. This algorithm tries extending the current candidate in all possible ways until some sequence reaches the desired length. If all fail, the search backtracks.

Our program for the good sequences problem retains the state of all partial solutions. That way, if we want a different or longer solution, we can extend an earlier partial solution. This avoids starting the search process over from the beginning.

We assume the existence of function good?. The value of (good? x) is true if x is a list whose elements form a good sequence. A recursive program, step, that takes a good sequence, sequence, and extends it in all possible ways with how-many-more additional elements is as follows:

```
(step sequence how-many-more) ≡
    (cond ((good? sequence)
            (cond ((= how-many-more 0) (cons sequence nil)
                  (t (stepper sequence (sub1 how-many-more) 3))))
          (t (frons ⊥ nil))))

(stepper sequence how-many-more k) ≡
    (cond ((= k 0) nil)
          (t (frappend (step (cons k sequence) how-many-more)
                       (stepper sequence how-many-more (sub1 k)))))

(frappend l m) ≡
    (cond ((= l nil) m)
          (t (frons (car l) (frappend (cdr l) m))))
```

A program that needs good sequences of length 5 might bind to a variable x the value of (step nil 5). The value of (car x) is a good sequence. If that particular good sequence proved unappealing, the (car (cdr x)) would also be a good sequence (as would the rest of the elements of x). The first sequence in x would be the first good sequence to be found. If later we decide that we really need good sequences of size 7, we could evaluate (frapcar (lambda (z) (step z 2)) x).*

Algorithmic selection Problems often have several alternative algorithmic solutions. We cannot always decide beforehand which is best (and which are impractical). For example, often many different algorithms solve the same class of numeric problems, but do better over different ranges of input. One algorithm might be good for large values or inexact answers and yet be divergent near zero. It may be difficult to choose, a priori, the best algorithm for a given problem.

---

* Frapcar is the frons analogue of mapcar: (frapcar f l) ≡ (cond ((= l nil) nil) (t (frons (f (car l)) (frapcar f (cdr l))))). The 2 in the function call is the extension of five-element sequences by two to be seven-element sequences.

Frons relieves the programmer from having to make that choice. The programmer can frons together a list of expressions, where each expression represents one possible algorithm. The car of that list would be the answer provided by the first algorithm to converge.

For example, a system to test numbers for primeness might define two functions, say fact and prob-prime. Function fact would seek factors for its argument; function prob-prime would perform a probabilistic test for primeness. Each would return after satisfying its test (and not return if it failed to satisfy). The function (lambda (x) (car (frons (fact x) (frons (prob-prime x) nil)))) would schedule the quicker response.

Terminal controller In "Circuits and Systems," Johnson addresses the problem of a terminal controller [Johnson 84]. He describes a full-duplex message system for two users, u_1 and u_2. Normally, the system echoes the input from each user's keyboard (k_1 or k_2) on that user's screen (s_1 or s_2). However, when a user executes a send command, the input echoes on the other user's screen. The architecture of the message system is shown in Figure 12-11. The MSG function produces an output of two streams, one for each terminal, from an input of two streams, one from each keyboard.[†]

```
(MSG k1 k2) ≡
    (letrec (r1  ← (route k1 m2))
            (r2  ← (route k2 m1))
            (s1  ← (car r1))
            (m1 ← (car (cdr r1)))
            (s2  ← (car r2))
            (m2 ← (car (cdr r2)))
        (two_list s1 s2))


(route k min) ≡
    (let (w ← (wire (cons (two_list (quote ON) (quote #))
                          (select k))))
        (let (mout ← (car w))
             (dplx  ← (car (cdr w)))
            (two_list (merge_input dplx min) mout)))
```

[†] Sometimes we want a convenient way to refer to a list (or atom) in a program without binding or building it from scratch. For that we use function quote. Quote "quotes" its argument. That is, quote does not evaluate its argument. Instead, its value is the literal structure of its argument. The value of (quote #) is #; the value of (quote (1 4 7 10)) is the list (1 4 7 10). For example, evaluating (mapcar add1 (quote (1 4 7 10))) yields the list (2 5 8 11). Since numbers and functions evaluate to themselves, they need not be quoted.

```
(select k) ≡
    (let (ka ← (car k))
         (kd ← (cdr k))
        (cond ((= ka (quote SEND))
                 (let (kda ← (car kd))
                      (kdd ← (cdr kd))
                     (cons (cons (quote #)
                                      (two_list (quote ?) kda))
                           (select kdd))))
              (t (cons (cons ka (quote #))
                       (select kd)))))))

(merge_input l r) ≡
    (let (la ← (car l))
         (ld ← (cdr l))
         (ra ← (car r))
         (rd ← (cdr r))
        (car (frons (strictify la (cons la (merge_input r ld)))
                    (frons (strictify ra (cons ra (merge_input l rd)))
                           nil))))

(ones s) ≡
    (cond ((= (car (car s)) (quote #))
             (ones (cdr s)))
          (t (cons (car (car s))
                   (ones (cdr s))))))

(twos s) ≡
    (cond ((= (car (cdr (car s))) (quote #))
             (ones (cdr s)))
          (t (cons (car (cdr (car s)))
                   (twos (cdr s))))))

(wire s) ≡ (two_list (ones s) (twos s))
```

Function route takes keyboard input and message input and writes screen output and message feedback. Figure 12-11 shows the input-output relationships of route. The (quote ON) in route is for stream initialization. Merge_input indeterminately checks both input lines (using frons) and selects input from the first available line.*

---

* Other examples that use this approach include Henderson's description of an operating system [Henderson 82] and Keller and Lindstrom's functional graph language [Keller 81].

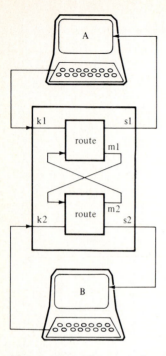

Figure 12-11 The terminal-message system.

Cull

We have already seen several different operators for introducing indeterminacy
into applicative systems — amb, two varieties of merge, and frons. There are
others. In this section we indulge one of our periodic fantasies and consider the
inverse operator to indeterminate merge. This fantasy was prompted by some
remarks by Turner [Turner 80].

Indeterminate merge takes two input streams and interleaves them onto a
single output stream. Every element in each input stream appears in the output
stream (except when merge chooses to ignore the remainder of one stream).
We call the inverse operator of merge, split. Split takes a single input stream and
produces two output streams such that each element in the input stream appears
in exactly one output stream. For example, the expression

```
(let (s ← (split (successors 1))
  (let (a ← (car s))
    (b ← (car (cdr s)))
      <body>))
```

binds both a and b to an ordered subsequence of the positive integers (in <body>). Every integer appears in either a or b, and no integer appears in both a and b.

We can easily obtain this behavior by having split "flip a coin" on each element of the list; "heads" elements going to the first output, and "tails" going to the second. This is unsatisfactory, because we really want a and b's demands to grant them list elements. So we add a further restriction: a and b are to pull elements from the split list as they need them, where need is defined by call-by-need. Hence, if <body> never references a, then the entire list should appear in b; if <body> uses the first 10 elements of a and only the first three elements of b, then the fourteenth element should not appear in either a or b. This restriction precludes the coin flipping solution.

Split is a natural controller for task scheduling. For example, an unbounded producer-consumer buffer of two inputs (producers) and two outputs (consumers) is as follows:

(buffer I m) ≡ (split (my_merge I m))

```
(my_merge I m) ≡
    (let (x ← (frons (strictify (car I) I)
                (frons (strictify (car m) m) nil)))
        (cons (car (car x))
            (my_merge (cdr (car x))
                (car (cdr x)))))
```

We use strictify in this example to ensure that the producer's item exists before it is given to the consumer. Otherwise, this buffer would allocate promises of buffer items that might never exist.

One simple way of introducing split would be to posit a new variety of box (as cons and frons are varieties of boxes). This box would have a mark bit that would be set if its contents had already been taken. A system primitive could filter lists of these boxes, discarding those with marks, and marking and passing those without. Such a mark resembles a lock or semaphore.

This alternative is unesthetic. Another variety of box would require modifying the other primitives of the system to reflect its existence. After all, one ought not multiply entities beyond need.

What are the primitive data types of IAP? In addition to atoms, IAP distinguishes frons cells from cons cells and suspensions from manifest values. Each of these is implemented by a mark/unmark bit. When a frons cell becomes a cons cell, a one-bit field in the cell is updated. Similarly, when a suspension becomes manifest, a different one-bit field is changed. For any given cell, there are two manifest bits, one for each of the car and cdr fields. This implies that there can easily be a function existscdr? that checks if the cdr field of a cell contains a manifest (not suspended) value. Using that as our test for the marking bit, we get function cull*

```
(cull l) ≡
    (cond ((= l nil) nil)
          ((not (existscdr? l))          -- test if the cdr contains a suspension
           (let (x ← (car l))
                (y ← (cdr l))
             (strictify y (cons x (cull y)))))
          (t (cull (cdr l)))))
```

We can then write split in terms of cull as

```
(split l) ≡
    (let (m ← (package l))
       (two_list (cull m) (cull m)))
```

```
(package l) ≡
    (cond ((= l nil) nil)
          (t (cons (car l) (package (cdr l))))))
```

Package is equivalent to a top-level copy of its argument. **Split** passes its argument through **package** to ensure that the entire list is composed of suspensions.

Much like frons, cull plays a restrained havoc with substitutivity. For example, it is usually the case that

$$(\text{cull } l) \neq (\text{cull } l)$$

while

$$(\text{cull (package } l)) = (\text{cull (package } l))$$

And, of course,

$$(\text{strictify (print (cull } l)) (\text{cull } l)) = \text{nil}$$

Perspective

IAP approaches coordinated computing from a different direction than most of the other systems. In IAP, processes become data; tasks are resolved by free processor resources. This shifts the responsibility for indicating concurrency from the user to the underlying system. Nevertheless, IAP remains a programming system; the tasks themselves are expressed as programs, not problem domain expressions.

---

* If cull is used in a multiprocessing environment, the code ((not (existscdr? l)) ...) must be executed indivisibly. This avoids the problem of two processes consuming the same value. For similar approaches see Peterossi [Peterossi 81] and Clark and Gregory [Clark 81].

PROBLEMS

12-1 Write a function that produces the infinite list of even integers.
12-2 What is the result of evaluating (primes (successors 1))?
12-3 Define a five-element merge operator in terms of a two-element merge operator.
12-4 Define the merge operator that takes a stream of streams and produces their merge.
12-5 What are the possible values of the following expressions?

(a) (let (x ← (frons 1 (frons 2 nil)))
         (car x))

(b) (letrec (x ← (frons (cond ((= (car x) 3) 3) (t 4))
                    (frons (cond ((= (car x) 4) 3)
                              (t 4))
                       nil)))
         (car x))

† (c) (letrec (x ← (frons (cond ((= (car x) 3) 3) (t 4))
                     (frons (cond ((= (car x) 4) 4)
                               (t 3))
                        nil)))
          (car x))

12-6 Give an expression whose value is a stream, each element of which is the next digit of the decimal expansion of e (the base of the natural logarithms). That is, the stream begins (2 7 1 8 2 8 1 8 2 8 4 5 9 .... Instead of being an approximation to e whose accuracy is determined at the time the approximation is derived, it is the value of e. The application (by its use), not the generation algorithm, determines the number of significant digits generated. (*Turner*)

† **12-7** Give an expression whose value is a stream that is an infinite good sequence.
12-8 What happens if the 1 and 0 are omitted from the definition of the RSFF?
12-9 What happens if R=1=S at the beginning of the definition of the RSFF? (*Wise*)
12-10 Evaluating y and invoking cons in the definition of cull is expensive. Redefine cull so that these two expressions are not in the atomic portion.
12-11 Write a function, setify, that takes an infinite stream of atoms and returns the set implied by that stream—that is, that stream with multiple elements removed. For example, if list m is

(2 2 4 2 4 6 2 4 6 8 2 4 6 8 10 2 4 6 8 10 12 ...

then the result of (setify m) is some permutation of the even positive integers.
12-12 Write a function that produces the union of two infinite sets of positive integers. Assume that the sets are represented as sorted lists.

REFERENCES

[**Allen 78**] Allen, J., *The Anatomy of LISP*, McGraw-Hill, New York (1978). Allen describes everything you always wanted to know about building a Lisp system.

[**Ashcroft 77**] Ashcroft, E. A., and W. W. Wadge, "Lucid, a Nonprocedural Language with Iteration," *CACM*, vol. 20, no. 7 (July 1977), pp. 519–526. Lucid is a language that combines axiomatic declarations of programs with ease of verification. The last example in this paper, a prime sieve, uses an infinite streamlike data structure.

[**Clark 81**] Clark, K. L., and S. Gregory, "A Relational Language for Parallel Programming," *ACM Proc. 1981 Conf. Func. Program. Lang. Comput. Archit.*, Portsmith, New Hampshire (October 1981), pp. 171–178. This paper adds a notation to Prolog for parallel programming. Clark and Gregory show how to do merge; since programs in Prolog can be run "both ways" this also yields split.

[**Dijkstra 72b**] Dijkstra, E. W., "Notes on Structured Programming," in O.-J. Dahl, E. W. Dijkstra, and C.A.R. Hoare, *Structured Programming*, Academic Press, London (1972), pp. 1–82. Dijkstra presents the good sequences problem (attributing it to Wirth) on pages 63–66.

[**Dijkstra 76**] Dijkstra, E. W., *A Discipline of Programming*, Prentice-Hall, New Jersey, Englewood Cliffs (1976). Dijkstra describes Hamming's "2-3-5" problem on pages 129–134. He wrote his solution imperatively and with guarded commands.

[**Friedman 76**] Friedman, D. P., and D. S. Wise, "CONS Should Not Evaluate its Arguments," in S. Michaelson, and R. Milner (eds.), *Automata, Languages and Programming*, Edinburgh University Press, Edinburgh (1976), pp. 257–284.

[**Friedman 77**] Friedman, D. P., and D. S. Wise, "Aspects of Applicative Programming for File Systems," *Proc. ACM Conf. Lang. Des. Rel. Softw.*, North Carolina (1977), pp. 41–55.

[**Friedman 78a**] Friedman, D. P., and D. S. Wise, "A Note on Conditional Expressions," *CACM*, vol. 21, no. 11 (November 1978), pp. 931–933.

[**Friedman 78b**] Friedman, D. P., and D. S. Wise, "Unbounded Computational Structures," *Softw. Pract. Exper.*, vol. 8, no. 4 (August 1978), pp. 407–416.

[**Friedman 79**] Friedman, D. P., and D. S. Wise, "An Approach to Fair Applicative Multiprograming," in G. Kahn (ed.), *Semantics of Concurrent Computation*, Lecture Notes in Computer Science 70, Springer-Verlag, New York (1979), pp. 203–225.

[**Friedman 80**] Friedman, D. P., and D. S. Wise, "An Indeterminate Constructor for Applicative Programming," *Conf. Rec. 7th ACM Symp. Princ. Program. Lang.*, Las Vegas, Nevada (January 1980), pp. 245–250.

[**Henderson 76**] Henderson, P., and J. H. Morris, "A Lazy Evaluator," *Conf. Rec. 3d ACM Symp. Princ. Program. Lang.*, Atlanta, Georgia (January 1976), pp. 95–103.

[**Henderson 82**] Henderson, P., "Purely Functional Operating Systems," in J. Darlington, P. Henderson, and D. A. Turner, *Functional Programming and its Applications*, Cambridge University Press, Cambridge (1982), pp. 177–192. Henderson presents several examples of implementing operating systems components in a purely applicative language. A key feature of his design is a nondeterminate merge.

[**Johnson 81**] Johnson, S. D., and A. T. Kohlstaedt, "DSI Program Description," Technical Report 120, Computer Science Department, Indiana University, Bloomington, Indiana (December 1981). Johnson and Kohlstaedt provide a good description of the philosophy behind concurrent computation with suspensions.

[**Johnson 84**] Johnson, S. D., "Circuits and Systems: Implementing Communication with Streams," in M. Ruschitzka, M. Christensen, W. F. Ames, and R. Vichnevetsky, R. (eds.), *Parallel and Large-Scale Computers: Performance, Architecture, Applications*, vol. 2 IMACS Transactions on Scientific Computation, North-Holland, Amsterdam (1984), pp. 311–319. This is the source of the flip-flop program.

[**Kahn 74**] Kahn, G., "The Semantics of a Simple Language for Parallel Programming," in J. L. Rosenfeld (ed.), *Information Processing 74: Proceedings of the IFIP Congress 74*, North Holland, Amsterdam (1974), pp. 471–475. This was one of the earliest papers to point out the notion of demand-driven evaluation.

[**Kahn 77**] Kahn, G., and D. B. MacQueen, "Coroutines and Networks of Parallel Processes," in B. Gilchrist (ed.), *Information Processing 77: Proceedings of the IFIP Congress 77*, North Holland, Amsterdam (1977), pp. 993–998. Kahn and MacQueen develop the ideas of turning every edge in a functional graph into a queue and every argument to functions into a stream.

[**Keller 81**] Keller, R. M., and G. Lindstrom, "Applications of Feedback in Functional Programming," *ACM Proc. 1981 Conf. Func. Program. Lang. Comput. Archit.*, Portsmith, New Hampshire (October 1981), pp. 171–178. Keller and Lindstrom show how to model continuous simulation with feedback loops. This paper is a good introduction to their function graph language, FGL.

[**Landin 65**] Landin, P., "A Correspondence Between ALGOL 60 and Church's Lambda Notation: Part I," *CACM*, vol. 8, no. 2 (February 1965), pp. 89–101. This paper demonstrates how Algol programs can be transcribed into an applicative-order lambda calculus. This was one of the earliest uses of streams.

[**McCarthy 63**] McCarthy, J., "A Basis for a Mathematical Theory of Computation," in P. Braffort, and D. Hirschberg (eds.), *Computer Programming and Formal Systems*, North Holland, Amsterdam (1963), pp. 33–70. McCarthy introduces amb.

[**McCarthy 65**] McCarthy, J., P. W. Abrahams, D. J. Edwards, T. P. Hart, and M. I. Levin, *Lisp 1.5 Programmer's Manual*, M.I.T. Press, Cambridge, Massachusetts (1965).

[**MacQueen 79**] MacQueen, D. B., "Models for Distributed Computing," Rapport de Recherche 351, Institut de Recherche d'Informatique et d'Automatique, Le Chesnay, France (April 1979). MacQueen surveys three models for distributed computing. His paper includes a nondeterminate merge.

[**Peterossi 81**] Peterossi, A., "An Approach to Communications and Parallelism in Applicative Languages," *International Conference on Automata, Languages, and Programming*, Lecture Notes in Computer Science 107, Springer-Verlag, New York (1981), pp. 432–446. Peterossi proposes a communication structure to make functional programs more efficient. His structure is a shared message queue, with operators to add to the queue, remove an element from the queue so that no other process sees it, and remove an element from the queue so that other processes continue to see it. Thus, his queues can serve to cull lists.

[**Steele 78**] Steele, G. L., Jr., and G. J. Sussman, "The Revised Report on SCHEME, a Dialect of Lisp," Memo 452, Artificial Intelligence Laboratory, M.I.T., Cambridge, Massachusetts (January 1978).

[**Turner 80**] Turner, D. A., personal communication, 1980.

[**Vuillemin 74**] Vuillemin, J., "Correct and Optimal Implementation of Recursion in a Simple Programming Language," *J. Comput. Syst. Sci.*, vol. 9, no. 3 (June 1974), pp. 332–354. Vuillemin introduces call-by-delayed-value, an independently discovered form of call-by-need.

[**Wadsworth 71**] Wadsworth, C., "Semantics and Pragmatics of the Lambda-calculus," Ph.D. dissertation, Oxford University (1971). Wadsworth describes call-by-need.

[**Wand 80**] Wand, M., *Induction, Recursion, and Programming*, North Holland, New York (1980).

[**Winston 81**] Winston, P. H., and B.K.P. Horn, *LISP*, Addison-Wesley, Reading, Massachusetts (1981). This book is an introduction to Lisp. It emphasizes examples from Artificial Intelligence.

THREE

LANGUAGES

Programming languages are systems for describing commands to computers. This part presents five languages for controlling distributed systems: (1) Distributed Processes, (2) Ada, (3) PLITS, (4) Synchronizing Resources (SR), and (5) Cell. Our discussion of Distributed Processes includes a description of a predecessor language, Concurrent Pascal.

CHAPTER
THIRTEEN
CONCURRENT PASCAL AND DISTRIBUTED PROCESSES

One of the most prolific researchers and implementors of concurrent and distributed systems is Per Brinch Hansen. This chapter describes Brinch Hansen's language for distributed programming, Distributed Processes. For pedagogical purposes, we begin by describing a predecessor of Distributed Processes, Concurrent Pascal.

Concurrent Pascal is a multiprocessing extension of Pascal. It has three important features for structuring concurrency: processes, monitors, and classes. Processes are active computing agents. Monitors synchronize access to shared data. Classes provide structured access to data when synchronization is not required.

Distributed Processes is a language for distributed and real-time systems. It takes the processes, monitors, and classes of Concurrent Pascal and unifies them into a single construct, the process. Its communication mechanism, the remote procedure call, has been copied by several other systems.

These languages focus on the problems of resource management and real-time control. Their "pragmatic" features are the pragmatic features of the system implementor—synchronization and primitive abstraction mechanisms—but not dynamic structures, automatic buffering, and so forth. The primary motivation in the design of Concurrent Pascal and Distributed Processes is to facilitate the programming of powerful, secure, and easily extended systems programs.

183

13-1 CONCURRENT PASCAL

Concurrent Pascal extends the sequential programming language Pascal with mechanisms for structured multiprocessing. Its design was motivated by the observation that the hardest part of concurrent programming is assuring the security of local storage and mutual exclusion in accessing shared storage. Thus, in Concurrent Pascal access rights and synchronization are primitive language structures, enforced by the compiler.

Concurrent Pascal has three structures that combine aspects of active computing and static data storage: processes, monitors, and classes. A *process* is a computing agent. It has three parts: a sequential program, private data, and access rights. Concurrent Pascal rejects the scoping rules of languages like Algol. A process's private data is the only data it can access directly; no other process can access that data. The access rights of a process specify the other system objects (monitors and classes) that this process can call. A *monitor* is a protection and abstraction mechanism for shared data. Monitors ensure that only a single process acts on shared data at any time. *Classes*, like monitors, provide data abstraction. But unlike monitors, the structure of programs guarantees that only a single process will execute the code of any class at any time.

Our first example in Concurrent Pascal is a program for printing the prime Fibonacci numbers. This program has two processes, one that generates successive Fibonacci numbers, and another that tests them for primeness. These processes communicate through a shared buffer—a monitor. This buffer stores a single number. When the prime tester finds that one of the Fibonacci numbers sent it is prime, it calls on a class object, a LinePrinter, to print it. Figure 13-1 shows the parts of this program. We describe each kind of object in a **type** statement, declaring actual instances of each type that the program uses in a **var** statement. The program of the Fibonacci process is as follows:

```
type Fibonacci =
process (buf: buffer)          -- A Fibonacci process has access rights to a
                                  monitor of type buffer.
var this, last, previous: integer;   -- the process's private data
begin
    last  := 0;
    this  := 1;
    cycle                      -- that is, "while true do"
        previous := last;      -- Compute the next Fibonacci number.
        last     := this;
        this     := last + previous;
        buf.add(this)          -- Place this Fibonacci number in the buffer.
    end
end;
```

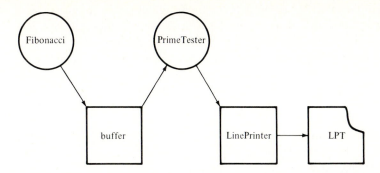

Figure 13-1 Information flow in communication in the prime-Fibonacci system.

Processes do not share data directly. Instead, they share data through calls on monitors [Hoare 74]. A monitor specifies a shared data structure and provides the procedures and functions to manipulate that data structure. A monitor procedure that can be called from another process or monitor is a *procedure entry*. For example, monitor **stack** could have procedure entry **pop**. Processes could pop an element from the stack by calling stack.pop.

Each monitor also has an initial operation. When it creates a new monitor, the system executes that monitor's initial operation. An important use of this operation is to initialize the monitor's data structures. For example, the initial operation of a stack monitor would set the stack to empty. Like a process, a monitor can also have explicit access rights to other monitors and classes.

To enter a monitor, a process calls an entry procedure in that monitor. If no other process is in that monitor, the process begins executing the code associated with that entry. If another process is in the monitor, the calling process waits until the monitor is free. The restriction that only a single process can execute the code of a monitor at any time is a simple mechanism for short-term scheduling.

Monitors serialize access to shared data. However, many programs require a more complex scheduling algorithm than simple mutual exclusion. Concurrent Pascal provides queues for medium-term scheduling. Queues are used to delay processes until it is appropriate for them to continue. There are two operations on queues, **delay** and **continue**. A queue stores a single process-state descriptor. If process A executes **delay** on queue q, then A is blocked on q. The monitor unlocks and allows other processes entry. When another process, B, executes **continue**(q), B returns from its call to the monitor and A continues executing (in the monitor) from the point after the **delay** statement. The monitor remains locked against other processes. Despite the mental image of processes waiting in line that the name "queue" evokes, queues in Concurrent Pascal can hold only a single process. However, Concurrent Pascal allows arrays of queues.

In our example, the buffer is a monitor. Buffers do not have access rights to any other system objects. They have storage for a single buffered value, an integer; a boolean flag that indicates that the buffer is full; and two queues, one which delays a consumer that tries to remove from an empty buffer and another which delays a producer that tries to add to a full buffer. Buffers have two entry procedures: add, called by the producer, and remove, called by the consumer.*

```
type buffer =
monitor;
var
      data                 : integer;
      flag                 : boolean;
      pwaiting, cwaiting : queue;

procedure entry add (invalue: integer);
begin
      if flag then delay(pwaiting);        -- If the buffer is full, delay the
      flag   := true;                          producer.
      data  := invalue;
      continue(cwaiting)
end;

procedure entry remove (var outvalue: integer);
begin
      if not(flag) then delay(cwaiting);   -- If the buffer is empty, delay the
      flag       := false;                     consumer.
      outvalue := data;
      continue(pwaiting)
end;

begin                                      -- initial statement
      flag := false                        -- The buffer is initially empty.
end;
```

The consumer process PrimeTester resembles the producer. It calls the buffer to obtain the next value and tests to see if it is prime. If it is, the consumer process calls the printer, a class object of type LinePrinter, to print it.

```
type PrimeTester =
process (buf: buffer);
var
      num, j : integer;
```

* Variables declared globally in a monitor are permanent and shared by the entry procedures of that monitor. Variables declared in a procedure are allocated afresh for each call to that procedure. Monitors can also have "non-entry" (ordinary) procedures, used by the program of that monitor and not by other system objects.

```
    prime  : boolean;
    printer : LinePrinter;      - - This declaration creates a printer class object, of
                                    type LinePrinter.
begin
    cycle
        buf.remove(num);
        if ((num mod 2) = 1 or (num = 2)) then      - - odd or 2
        begin
            j       := 3;
            prime := true;
            while (j < sqrt(num)) and prime do      - - not the most efficient
                prime := not ((num mod j) = 0);        way to test primeness
                j       := j + 2
            end
        end;
        if prime then printer.show(num)
    end
end;
```

In Concurrent Pascal, a *class* is an abstract data object that is not shared. A class object can be declared only as a permanent variable within another system object. Classes can be passed as (access-rights) parameters to other classes, but never to processes or monitors. Hence, two processes cannot call the same class object simultaneously and class objects do not require scheduling. This permits the Concurrent Pascal compiler to optimize calls on classes, making such calls execute faster than calls on monitors. This optimization is the major reason for including classes in Concurrent Pascal. The difference between classes and monitors is primarily one of efficiency, not functionality.

Peripheral devices are treated as hardware implementations of monitors. They have only a single access procedure, **io**. This procedure delays the calling process until the completion of the input-output process. Thus, a class of type LinePrinter is

```
type LinePrinter =
class;
var parm = record ... end;
    - - The standard procedure io takes arguments of a particular internal
      structure. We omit the details of that structure.


procedure entry show (i: integer);
begin
    io(i, parm, "LPT")
end;
```

begin
  -- LinePrinters do not need initialization.
end;

Each of the above examples is a type declaration. Specifying a description of a monitor or a process does not create one, any more than specifying a type declaration in Pascal allocates storage. A program with such type statements allocates these objects in a **var** statement. The program starts the processes and runs the initialization statements of the monitors and classes with an **init** statement. This **init** statement also provides the names of the other system objects to which this object has access. The entire program is

```
program FibonacciPrimes;
type
      Fibonacci   = process ... ;
      buffer      = monitor ... ;
      PrimeTester = process ... ;
var
      FProd    : Fibonacci;
      FConsum : PrimeTester;
      FBuffer  : buffer;
begin
      init FProd(FBuffer), FConsum(FBuffer), FBuffer;
end;
```

Storage allocation in Concurrent Pascal is completely static. It lacks recursion and has no command to dynamically create new processes or monitors. Concurrent Pascal not only does not dynamically allocate storage, it never deallocates storage. Even if a process has terminated, its storage continues to exist. The system cannot reclaim its storage because that storage may have been passed by reference to another system object.

Must Concurrent Pascal be so static? Brinch Hansen presents the reasoning behind these choices as [Brinch Hansen 75, p. 201]:

> Dynamic process deletion will certainly complicate the semantics and implementation of a programming language considerably. And since it appears to be unnecessary for a large class of real-time applications, it seems wise to exclude it altogether. So an operating system written in Concurrent Pascal will consist of a fixed set of processes, monitors and classes. These components and their data structures will exist forever after system initialization. An operating system can, however, be extended by recompilation. It remains to be seen whether this restriction will simplify or complicate operating system design.

Dining philosophers The dining philosophers problem illustrates processes that share monitors. Our program uses five processes, one for each philosopher; a monitor for each fork; and a monitor for the room. A **philosopher** process thinks, enters the room, picks up the forks, eats, drops the forks, leaves the room, and

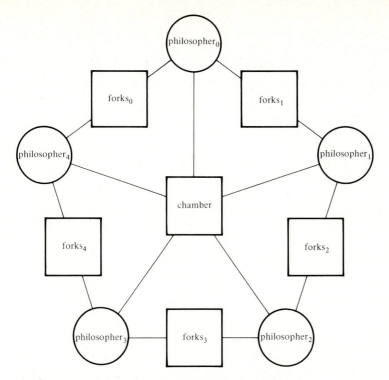

Figure 13-2 The objects in the dining philosophers program.

repeats the cycle. The dining philosophers problem is a pure synchronization problem. Thus, the system components exchange only synchronization, not information. Figure 13-2 shows the communication relationships of the elements of this system.

```
type philosopher =
process (theroom: room; left, right: fork);
begin
    cycle
            -- think;
        theroom.enter;
        left.pickup;
        right.pickup;
            -- eat;
        left.putdown;
        right.putdown;
        theroom.exit
    end
end;
```

Forks are monitors. Each **fork** has a boolean flag that shows if it is taken, a queue to delay the philosopher that tries to take it when it is busy, and two entry procedures, **pickup** and **putdown**. Forks are initially free. A philosopher that tries to pick up a taken fork is delayed in the **pleasewait** queue; each philosopher, as she drops the fork, continues that queue, thereby giving a waiting philosopher her turn.

```
type fork =
monitor;
var
     taken       : boolean;
     pleasewait : queue;

procedure entry pickup;
begin
     if taken then delay(pleasewait);
     taken := true
end;

procedure entry putdown;
begin
     taken := false;
     continue(pleasewait)
end;

begin
     taken := false
end;
```

A **room** is a monitor. It keeps the number of dining philosophers at four or fewer, delaying any philosopher that tries to enter when four of her companions are eating. It has a variable to count the philosophers in the room, a queue for the waiting philosopher, and procedure entries **enter** and **exit**. The room is initially empty.

```
type room =
monitor;
var
     occupancy: integer;
     WithoutReservations: queue;

procedure entry enter;
begin
     if occupancy = 4 then delay (WithoutReservations);
     occupancy := occupancy + 1
end;
```

```
procedure entry exit;
begin
    occupancy := occupancy − 1;
    continue (WithoutReservations)
end;

begin
    occupancy := 0
end;
```

Since processes, monitors, and classes are objects, declared in type state-ments, we can have arrays of them. We pass the objects they access to the philosophers when we initialize them. The program for the dining philosophers problem is

```
program dining;
type
    philosopher = process ... ;
    fork        = monitor ... ;
    room        = monitor ... ;
var
    philosophers : array [0 .. 4] of philosopher;
    forks        : array [0 .. 4] of fork;
    chamber      : room;
    i            : integer;

begin
    init chamber;
    for i := 0 to 4 do init forks[i];
    for i := 0 to 4 do init philosophers[i](chamber, forks[i], forks[(i+1) mod 5])
end;
```

13-2 DISTRIBUTED PROCESSES

Concurrent Pascal provides three different primitives (processes, monitors, and classes) for data encapsulation and parallel processing. Brinch Hansen recognized that this multiplicity was unnecessary. The difference between monitors and classes is primarily an optimization hint to the compiler. And the difference between processes and monitors is just the embedding of active processing in processes. Even so, monitors and classes need some active processing for their initialization statements. In his successor language, Distributed Processes, Brinch Hansen unifies these three concepts into a single entity, the process.

Concern for resource allocation and real-time issues motivated the design of Distributed Processes. A Distributed Processes system has a fixed set of concurrently executing, sequential processes. Processes are determined at compilation and can be neither dynamically created nor destroyed.

A Distributed Processes's process can access only its own local storage. There are no global data structures (like the monitors of Concurrent Pascal) shared by several processes. Instead, processes communicate by calling procedures (*common procedures*) in other processes, sending and returning parameter values. Each process multiprocesses the tasks of executing its own program and handling calls to its common procedures. In some sense, the processes of Distributed Processes act as monitors for each other, though without the specific synchronization rules of monitors. Since Distributed Processes is concerned with distributed processing, values are passed by value, not by reference. A call from one process to another is an *external request*.

Distributed Processes uses Pascal for syntactic foundation. The principal extensions are the constructs for interprocess communication. Each process has four parts: a name, local storage, common procedures, and an initial statement. Syntactically, the verb **call** invokes an external request. Like Concurrent Pascal, a process calls a procedure in another process by referencing the procedure name together with the process name. Thus, the one parameter procedure NextCharacter in process CardReader is invoked by

call CardReader.NextCharacter(C)

Procedure NextCharacter in process CardReader has no input (value) parameters and a single output (result) parameter of type char. The process's input and output parameters are separated in the parameter list declaration by a #. Thus, the declaration of process CardReader begins

```
process CardReader;
    var count: integer;              -- a local variable
    procedure NextCharacter (# ch: char);   -- a single output parameter
        ⋮
```

Distributed Processes includes a variant of Dijkstra's guarded commands (Section 2-2). *Guarded clauses* are formed by joining the guarded condition (a boolean expression) to the guarded action (a statement) with a ":". Guarded clauses are joined with "|"s to form *guarded regions*.* Of course, guarded regions imply an indeterminate choice among the open guarded clauses.

Each process performs two kinds of computations: executing its own program (its initial statement) and handling calls to its common procedures. The

---

* This contrasts with the → and ▯ notation of the original syntax.

Table 13-1 Guards and loops

	Non-waiting	Waiting
Single Execution	**if** $B_1\!:\!S_1 \mid \ldots \mid B_n\!:\!S_n$ **end** If a B_i is true, then execute the corresponding S_i; an error if none of the B_i is true.	**when** $B_1\!:\!S_1 \mid \ldots \mid B_n\!:\!S_n$ **end** Wait for a B_i to be true, then execute the corresponding S_i.
Repeated Execution	**do** $B_1\!:\!S_1 \mid \ldots \mid B_n\!:\!S_n$ **end** Repeatedly find a true B_i and execute the corresponding S_i, until all B_i are false.	**cycle** $B_1\!:\!S_1 \mid \ldots \mid B_n\!:\!S_n$ **end** Repeatedly find a true B_i and execute the corresponding S_i. If no B_i is true, wait until one is. This statement never terminates.

process interleaves these actions. This interleaving is not preemptive; instead, the process executes each task until the task blocks in a guarded command. At that point, the process can execute another task. Specifically, the process begins by executing its initial statement. When this statement terminates or blocks, the process starts some other pending operation. When that operation terminates or blocks, the process starts yet another pending operation. These operations are either resumptions of the initial statement or calls to the process's procedures. Operations blocked in guarded commands become pending when one of their guards becomes true. This interleaving continues for the life of the program. Even if the initial statement terminates, the process continues to exist, handling calls to its common procedures. Distributed Processes does not guarantee any particular ordering on the interleaved operations of a process. We know only that the first statement executed is the process's initialization statement. The interleaving is not preemptive. It is a function of the execution path of the program, not the pseudosimultaneity of simulated multiprocessing.

In Distributed Processes, guarded commands control two dimensions of processing: waiting and repetition. Distributed Processes has two choices for each of these and a language verb for each of the four possible combinations. Waiting concerns the action to be taken when none of the guard clauses is true. In that case, the process can either wait for one to become true (by using the language verbs **when** and **cycle**) or exit the statement (**if**, **do**). Repetition specifies how frequently to evaluate the guarded region: once (**if**, **when**) or repeatedly (**do**, **cycle**). The **do** statement executes until all guards are false; the **if** statement aborts the program with an error if all guards are false. Table 13-1 summarizes the kinds of guarded statements in Distributed Processes.

A process executes the statements of its current program segment until either (1) the program blocks in the guarded region of a **when** or **cycle** statement, or (2) the program blocks, waiting for the return from a call to an external procedure. If the process is in a guarded region, then it is free to interleave the evaluation of the initial statement and other calls to its common procedures. On the other hand, if the process is waiting on an external call, the process pauses until that call returns. That is, a process blocked on a guarded command is waiting to serve and is eligible to handle other calls. A process blocked on a call to another process is presumed to need the results of that call before it can continue. When the external call returns, the process continues executing statements where it left off. This implies that processes must not be mutually recursive; if process A calls a procedure in process B and process B then calls a procedure in process A, they are both blocked, each waiting for the other's return.

Unlike CSP (Chapter 10), guarded commands in Distributed Processes do not specifically control communication. Instead, a process pauses in a guarded command, waiting for changes caused by other calls to this process.

Binary semaphore Perhaps the simplest synchronization primitive is the binary semaphore. In our Distributed Processes program for a semaphore, the semaphore is a process. It has two common procedures, P (get the semaphore) and V (release the semaphore). The semaphore keeps its state in variable s. When s is positive, the semaphore is free; when it is zero, the semaphore is busy. Procedure P waits until s is positive, then decrements it and continues. Procedure V simply increments s.

```
process Binary_Semaphore:
var s: integer:

procedure P:
    when s > 0:
        s := s − 1
    end:

procedure V:
    s := s + 1:

begin    -- initialization statement
    s := 1
end:
```

A general semaphore that permits n processes to share a resource is the binary semaphore with s initialized to n.

Dining philosophers In Distributed Processes, we can declare an array of processes, all executing the same program but each with its own storage. Identifier **this**, when used in the body of a process, is the index of that process in the array. Our program for the dining philosophers problem uses an array of five philosopher processes, five fork processes, and a room process. Figure 13-3 shows the calling relationships in the program. The program for a philosopher is as follows:

process philosopher [5]:   - - *There are five philosophers.*
  - - *Philosophers have no storage. Since they are not called by other
    processes, they do not have entry procedures.*

```
do true:                       - - one way to get an infinite loop
     - - think;
    call room.enter;
    call fork[this].pickup;
    call fork[(this + 1) mod 5].pickup:
     - - eat;
    call fork[this].putdown;
    call fork[(this + 1) mod 5].putdown;
    call room.exit;
end;
```

Forks are also processes. They keep track of their state in boolean variable busy.

```
process fork[5]:
var busy: boolean;

procedure entry pickup:
    when not(busy):
        busy := true
end;

procedure entry putdown;
    busy := false

     - - initialization statement
    busy := false
end;
```

The room keeps the usual counts.

```
process room;
var occupancy: integer;

procedure entry enter;
    when occupancy < 5:
        occupancy := occupancy + 1
    end;
```

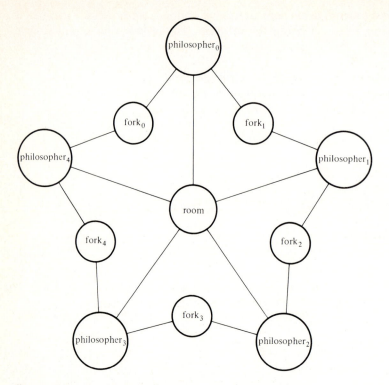

Figure 13-3 The Distributed Processes dining philosophers.


```
procedure entry exit;
    occupancy := occupancy − 1
end;
```

```
    -- initialization statement
        occupancy := 0
end;
```

The last section showed a similar solution to the dining philosophers problem in Concurrent Pascal. That solution relied on explicit **delay** and **continue** statements to schedule the philosopher processes. On the other hand, this solution uses the indeterminacy of guarded commands for scheduling.

Apart from the extensions described above, the syntax of Distributed Processes is just a variant of standard Pascal. However, like Concurrent Pascal, Distributed Processes does not have any constructs (like recursion and explicit allocation) that dynamically create storage. Therefore, storage allocation in Distributed Processes can be done at compilation.

Distributed Processes is a language for implementing resource managers. It requires that the conceptual processes of the programming language must be matched, one for one, with the physical processors of the distributed system.

Bounded buffer A bounded buffer (that stores elements of type BufferItems) is a process with two procedures, Insert and Remove. Insert waits until the buffer is not full; Remove, until the buffer is not empty. They interact by updating pointers into the buffer.

```
process BoundedBuffer;
const Bufsize = 100;
var
      first, last : integer;      -- First points to the next available item; last to the
                                     most recent addition.
      queue     : array [0 .. Bufsize − 1 ] of BufferItem;

procedure Insert (m: BufferItem);              -- one input parameter
    when not (((last + 1) mod Bufsize) = first):   -- queue not full
        last         := (last + 1) mod Bufsize;      -- Put this item in the
        queue[last] := m                                queue.
    end;

procedure Remove (# m: BufferItem);    -- one output parameter
    when not (last = first):                  -- queue not empty
        m     := queue[first];              -- Pull an item from the queue.
        first := (first + 1) mod Bufsize
    end;

begin                                  -- initialization statement
      first := 0;
      last  := 0
end;
```

The system executes the initialization statement of the buffer once. On the other hand, the buffer exists for the entire run of the program.

This is an antifair buffer. A process that wishes to access this buffer can be arbitrarily and indefinitely ignored while the buffer handles other requests.

Perspective

Concurrent Pascal and Distributed Processes lie on the extreme operating systems end of the coordinated computing spectrum. These languages have an imperative, statement-oriented syntax, primitives that implement mutual exclusion, explicit processes that cannot be dynamically created, and predefined connections between processes. They rely on strong typing and other compilation checks to ensure program correctness. Brinch Hansen views such checks as the crucial ingredients for developing efficient concurrent computing systems. He writes [Brinch Hansen 78, p. 934]:

> Real-time programs must achieve the ultimate in simplicity, reliability, and efficiency. Otherwise one can neither understand them, depend on them, nor expect them to keep pace with their environments. To make real-time programs manageable it is essential to write them in an abstract programming language that hides irrelevant machine detail and makes extensive compilation checks possible. To make real-time programs efficient at the same time will probably require the design of computer architectures tailored to abstract languages (or even to particular applications).

The evolution of these languages (from Concurrent Pascal through Distributed Processes and on to Edison, discussed in the bibliography) moves away from language design based on the perceived requirements of compiler construction and towards building generality into the language. Concurrent Pascal explicitly distinguishes between active processing elements and passive shared structures and between synchronized and unsynchronized structures. Distributed Processes eliminates this distinction. It has only a single variety of object, the process. The language that results turns out to be not only simpler and more esthetically pleasing, but also a system for which it is easier to write a compiler. Brinch Hansen states [Brinch Hansen 78, p. 940]:

> The Concurrent Pascal machine distinguishes between 15 virtual instructions for classes, monitors, and processes. This number would be reduced by a factor of three for Distributed Processes. In addition, numerous special cases would disappear in the compiler.

By and large, these languages are designed to be practical, usable tools, instead of simple academic exercises. Many of the decisions in their design and implementation were based on the difficulty of system implementation or requirements for explicit user control. These decisions have resulted in theoretical flaws—the lack of recursion, the static storage allocation, and the fixed process structure being among the most critical. However, it is inappropriate to urge theoretical nicety on someone who must get something to work. The computing world is littered with impractical implementations of ideas that are esthetically pleasing. (Of course, the computing world is also littered with impractical systems that ignored theoretical generality chasing after the chimera of efficiency.)

PROBLEMS

13-1 Rewrite the Concurrent Pascal buffer program to use a larger buffer.

13-2 Rewrite the Concurrent Pascal bounded buffer program to serve more than one producer and more than one consumer.

13-3 Redesign the bounded buffer programs in Concurrent Pascal and Distributed Processes so that a producer and a consumer can concurrently update the buffer. How many monitors or processes does your solution use?

13-4 Can a philosopher starve in the Concurrent Pascal solution to the dining philosophers problem?

13-5 Can a philosopher starve in the Distributed Processes solution to the dining philosophers problem?

13-6 Program a manager for the readers-writers problem in Distributed Processes.

REFERENCES

[**Brinch Hansen 75**] Brinch Hansen, P., "The Programming Language Concurrent Pascal," *IEEE Trans. Softw. Eng.*, vol. SE-1, no. 2 (June 1975), pp. 199–207. This paper is a brief description of the language Concurrent Pascal. Brinch Hansen illustrates the language with examples of the buffer processes of a miniature operating system.

[**Brinch Hansen 77**] Brinch Hansen, P., *The Architecture of Concurrent Programs*, Prentice-Hall, Englewood Cliffs, New Jersey (1977). Brinch Hansen describes the nature of synchronization and the languages Pascal and Concurrent Pascal. He then gives several examples of concurrent systems written in Concurrent Pascal.

[**Brinch Hansen 78**] Brinch Hansen, P., "Distributed Processes: A Concurrent Programming Concept," *CACM*, vol. 21, no. 11 (November 1978), pp. 934–941. This paper describes Distributed Processes. The binary semaphore and dining philosophers programs are derived from this article.

[**Brinch Hansen 81**] Brinch Hansen, P., "The Design of Edison," *Softw. Pract. Exper.*, vol. 11, no. 4 (April 1981), pp. 363–396. The path from Concurrent Pascal to Distributed Processes was marked by reduction and simplification—principally, the unification of the monitors, classes, and processes of Concurrent Pascal into a single, distributable object, the process. In Edison, Brinch Hansen takes this process one step further, omitting most conventional programming statements and synchronization structures.

Edison transforms the processes of Distributed Processes into Modules. Modules can allocate storage and declare procedures and other modules. Each module has an initial operation that is executed when the module is created. However, modules do not enforce mutual exclusion. Several processes can be executing the procedures of the same module simultaneously. Modules achieve mutual exclusion by using conditional critical regions. Only one module can execute in the "global" conditional critical region at any time. Concurrency is indicated with the equivalent of a **parbegin** statement.

Edison attempts to provide the tools for constructing concurrent systems, not to dictate the tools that must be used. The processes of Distributed Processes combine mutual exclusion and data abstraction. Edison separates these notions into explicit mutual exclusion (conditional critical regions) and data abstraction (modules). Applications that require monitors can implement them using modules and conditional critical regions.

Edison makes several linguistic advances over its predecessors. In particular, Edison permits procedures as procedure parameters and allows recursive procedure calls. (This second feature requires Edison to do dynamic storage allocation.) In addition, Brinch Hansen proposes an interesting addition to the syntax of typed languages, retyped variables. If x is a variable and t a type, the expression x:t is the value of the bit string that is x in the type t. The storage size of objects of the type of x and of objects of type t must be the same.

This issue of *Software — Practice and Experience* contains papers by Brinch Hansen describing Edison and giving examples of Edison programs.

[**Hoare 74**] Hoare, C.A.R., "Monitors: An Operating System Structuring Concept," *CACM*, vol. 17, no. 10 (October 1974), pp. 549–557. This paper is Hoare's original description of monitors. He argues that monitors are useful in programming operating systems.

[Li 81] Li, C.-M., and M. T. Liu, "Dislang: A Distributed Programming Language/System," *Proc. 2d Int. Conf. Distrib. Comput. Syst.*, Paris (April 1981), pp. 162–172. Li and Liu propose the language Communicating Distributed Processes (CDP). CDP extends Distributed Processes to be more "distributed." More specifically, CDP supplements Distributed Processes with the following additions: (1) A process can specify an action to be taken on communication time-out. This action can be to retry the communication, to abort the communication, or to transfer control to an exception routine. (2) A process can use one of several different broadcast mechanisms to communicate with several processes in the same step. (3) The language supports both synchronous and asynchronous requests. (4) A program can specify that an operation is "atomic." Failure in an atomic action returns the system to its state before the action was begun. (See Section 17-2 for a language based on atomic actions.) (5) Timestamps are a primitive system data type. The system generates new timestamps on request. (6) The broadcast mechanism allows the creation of several responses to a single request. Programs can specify which of these responses are desired: the first, the last, or all of them. And (7) the system can automatically create replicated copies of data (for replicated databases).

To illustrate the features of the language, Li and Liu propose the "distributed dining philosophers problem." This problem involves families of philosophers that borrow forks from their neighbors, where different families have different responses when forks are not immediately available.

[Wirth 77] Wirth, N., "Toward a Discipline of Real-Time Programming," *CACM*, vol. 20, no. 8 (August 1977), pp. 577–583. This paper discusses the problems of real-time and concurrent programming. Wirth argues that real-time programs should first be designed as time-independent systems and then modified to satisfy temporal requirements.

Wirth introduces the language Modula for describing real-time systems. Modula resembles Concurrent Pascal in both design and intent. In addition to constructs that parallel the classes, processes, and monitors of Concurrent Pascal, Modula has a type of object for performing input and output. Whereas Concurrent Pascal prohibits simultaneous access to a shared variable, Modula does not. Like Edison [Brinch Hansen 81], Modula is a language that can be used to ensure security but does not demand it. Modula also leaves many scheduling decisions to the programmer.

[Wirth 82] Wirth, N., *Programming in Modula-2*, Springer-Verlag, New York (1982). Modula is a complex language. Wirth has designed a simpler successor, Modula-2. This book is the reference manual for Modula-2.

FOURTEEN

ADA

The United States Department of Defense (DoD) is a major consumer of software. Like many computer users, the Defense Department is having a software crisis. One trouble centers on the programming Babel — the department's systems are written in too many different languages. This problem is particularly acute for applications involving embedded systems—computers that are part of larger, noncomputer systems, such as the computers in the navigation systems of aircraft. Since timing and machine dependence are often critical in embedded systems, programs for such systems are often baroque and idiosyncratic. Concerned about the proliferation of assembly and programming languages in embedded systems, the DoD decided in 1974 that it wanted all future programs for these systems written in a single language. It began an effort to develop a standard language.*

Typical embedded systems include several communicating computers. These systems must provide real-time response; they need to react to events as they are happening. It is inappropriate for an aircraft navigational system to deduce how to avoid a mountain three minutes after the crash (in the unlikely event that the on-board computers are still functioning three minutes after the crash). A programming language for embedded systems must include mechanisms to refer to the duration of an event and to interrupt the system if a response has been delayed. Thus, primary requirements are facilities for exception handling, multi- and distributed processing, and real-time control. Since the standard is

---

* Fisher [Fisher 78] and Carlson [Carlson 81] describe the history and motivation of that project in greater detail.

a programming language, the usual other slogans of modern software engineering apply. That is, the language must support the writing of programs that are reliable, easily modified, efficient, machine-independent, and formally describable. A request for proposals produced 15 preliminary language designs. The Defense Department chose four of these for further development. After a two-year competition, it selected a winner. This language was christened "Ada" in honor of Ada Augusta, Countess of Lovelace, a co-worker of Babbage and the first programmer.

Ada was created in the limelight. Many members of the academic and industrial computer science community contributed advice and criticism to the development process. The result is a language whose scope is ambitious. *SIGPLAN Notices* served as a forum for much of the debate surrounding the specification and development process.

Ada is at the far language end of the language-model spectrum.* The entire syntax and most of the formal semantics of Ada have been specified [Donzeau-Gouge 80]. The language is progressing towards standardization [DoD 80]. Its conceptual basis and the foundation of its syntax are derived from Pascal, a language renowned for its simplicity. However, the designers of Ada, in trying to satisfy the numerous requirements of the Ada specification, created an extensive and complicated language.

This section describes the Ada facilities for distributed processing and communication. We do not consider all the intricacies of Ada, since a complete description of Ada would itself fill a book.† Jean Ichbiah led the group at CII-Honeywell-Bull that designed Ada. Several Ada compilers have been completed and the DoD has great expectations for Ada's eventual widespread application. For those who wonder about the effect of U.S. military support on the popularity of a programming language, the last language promoted by the Defense Department was Cobol.

Entry, Access, and Rendezvous

Explicit processes and synchronized communication are the basis for concurrency in Ada. In many ways, Ada builds on concepts from Distributed Processes. Ada borrows Distributed Processes's remote procedure call and extends it in three important ways. (1) The entry procedures of Distributed Processes become objects (entries) with properties such as size and order, accessible from many places

---

* We characterize models as being a simple description of distributed computing, unadorned by syntax, and languages as embedding (and perhaps obscuring) their ideas for distribution in the practical aspects of programming. By that metric, Ada is at the far, far language-end of the language-model spectrum.

† Many books devoted to describing Ada have already been published. One such book is Pyle's *The Ada Programming Language* [Pyle 81]. Similarly, a "self-assessment procedure" in the *Communications of the ACM* was devoted to a tutorial on the nonconcurrent aspects of Ada [Wegner 81].

within a single process. (2) Called processes are not passive—they schedule the order in which they serve their entries. (3) Though calling processes are, by and large, passive, they can abort calls if they do not receive a quick enough response.

Ada is a complete programming language. Its designers intended to provide the programmer with a useful set of facilities (such as process communication, queueing, and abstract data types) while still permitting manipulation of the system primitives (such as interrupt locations, processing failures, and queue sizes). The overall effect is a language that is frightening in complexity but impressive in scope.

Processes in Ada are called *tasks*. Tasks have local storage and local procedures. Ada tasks are objects. The programmer can declare a single instance of a particular task or describe a *task type*, generating instances of that type much as one would create new instances of a Pascal record. Our first few examples deal with individual declarations of tasks. If a subprogram declares three tasks, then the tasks are created when that subprogram is entered. When created, a task commences processing. Tasks can terminate in several different ways, such as reaching the end of their program, being explicitly stopped, or by causing a run-time error. Ada also has a mechanism for synchronizing the termination of a collection of tasks. We discuss synchronized task termination at the end of this chapter.

Ada permits arbitrary nesting of program descriptions. A task can declare other tasks, which in turn can declare still other tasks. Additionally, Ada procedures can be recursive. Thus, a recursive Ada procedure that declares a new task creates a new instance of that task for each recursive call. Tasks can also be created by explicit execution of the task-creation command. Thus, Ada has both explicit process creation and process creation through lexical elaboration. A task that creates other tasks is the *parent* of these tasks; these tasks are *dependent* on the parent and are *siblings*. Thus, if task P creates tasks Q and R, P is the parent of Q and R while Q and R are siblings.

One of Ada's design goals is *encapsulation*—hiding the implementation of a subsystem while exhibiting (to other program segments) the subsystem interface. This intention is realized by breaking the description of a task into two parts, a specification and a body. The *specification* is visible to the other program components. That is, at compilation other components can use the information in the specification. The specification describes the names and formats of the interfaces to this task from other tasks. The *body* contains the task's variable declarations and code. It is hidden from other tasks and subprograms. That is, other program segments cannot reference the internal structure and state described in a task body. The separation of a task into specification and body syntactically enforces intermodule security and protection.

Communication requires syntactic connection—names for mutual reference. We create a communication channel to a task by declaring an *entry* in the task's specification. Syntactically, other tasks treat that entry as a procedure. Within the called task the entry represents a queue of requests. A statement of the form

accept <entry name> <formal parameter list>; is a directive to retrieve the next call from an entry's queue and to process it with the code that follows. The structure of the information exchange is similar to a procedure call: there are named and typed fields for information flow both into and out of the task.*

Our first example is a task, line_block, that assembles lines of 120 characters and forwards them for printing. A line is

type line **is array** (1 .. 120) **of** character;

When a line is full, line_block passes it to the **printer** task. The specification part of line_block defines its name and declares a communication channel, entry **add**. The parameters in this declaration define the shape of communications to this channel, not particular identifiers for actual processing.

task line_block **is**
    entry add (c: **in** character);
end line_block;

To place the character "d" in the line being assembled, another task would execute the command

line_block.add ("d");

The declaration of an entry creates a queue and calls on that entry are placed in that queue. But for an exception discussed below, a task that calls an entry blocks until that call is handled.

Line_block invokes **accept** on an entry to get the next item in a queue. The **accept** call supplies a formal parameter list. Thus, in the *module* (hidden, invisible) body of line_block, a statement of the form

accept add (c: **in** character);

takes the next item from entry **add** and assigns the value of the calling argument to variable c. The scope of this variable is the **accept** statement (discussed below). The completion of the **accept** unblocks the calling task; it resumes processing. If there are no calls waiting in the entry queue, then the **accept** statement blocks until one arrives. Variable c is an **in** parameter because it channels information *into* the task.

Line_block first accumulates a line of 120 characters. It then requests that the line be printed by calling entry **writeit** in task **printer**. It repeats this process for successive lines. The **task body** of line_block is as follows:

---

* Unfortunately, the Ada documentation is deliberately ambiguous about the semantics of parameter passing. Evidently, particular Ada implementations can use either call-by-value-result or, when feasible, call-by-reference for intertask communication.

```
task body line_block is
    thisline : line;
    i       : integer;
begin
    loop
        for i in 1 .. 120 loop
            accept add (c: in character) do     -- The scope of c is the accept
                                                    statement.
                thisline (i) := c;   -- In Ada, semicolons are statement
                                         terminators, not separators.
            end add;     -- Block structure is usually indicated by "<keyword>
                             ... end <identifier>" pairs, instead of "begin ...
                             end" pairs. We usually pick this identifier to be the
                             keyword that began the block or, for accept
                             statements, the name of the accept entry.
        end loop;
        printer.writeit (thisline);
    end loop;
end line_block;
```

Ada provides **out** parameters for communicating responses back to a calling task. To illustrate **out** parameters, we extend line_block to respond to character insertions with a count of the character positions remaining on the line. This requires two modifications to line_block. The first is to include an **out** (result) parameter in entry **add**. This changes both the specification part of the task and the **accept** statement. The second is to add a critical region after the **accept** statement. During this critical region, the calling and called task are synchronized and the called task computes its response. The calling task blocks until after the critical region. Syntactically, the critical region is the sequence **do** <statements> **end**; following the **accept**. The called process returns the value of the **out** parameter at the end of the critical region. The time between the execution of the **accept** and the **end** of the accept statement is called a *rendezvous* between the calling and the called tasks.

```
task line_block is
    entry add (c: in character; left: out integer);
end line_block;

task body line_block is
    thisline : line;
    i        : integer;
begin
    loop
        for i in 1 .. 120 loop
```

```
            accept add (c: in character; j: out integer) do      -- rendezvous
               j := 120 − i;    -- the critical region
            end add;           -- end of rendezvous
            thisline (i) := c;
         end loop;
         printer.writeit (thisline);
      end loop;
end line_block;
```

Indeterminacy Timing, delays, and time-outs are important for real-time systems. Languages for embedded systems need mechanisms to deal with time. In Ada, a process can execute a **delay** command to suspend processing for a specified interval. For example, if the value of current is five, executing the statement

delay 2*current;

causes this task to pause for ten seconds. As we shall see, delay is also an integral part of the Ada communication mechanism.

CSP uses guarded commands to select a process that is ready to communicate from among several possible communicators. Ada's **select** statement generalizes CSP's guarded input command, allowing other alternatives besides blocking until communication. **Select** takes a sequence of select alternatives, separated by the delimiter **or**. Each alternative is an accept alternative, a delay alternative, or a terminate alternative. *Accept alternatives* attempt to read a value from an entry. Delay and terminate alternatives are used when the system cannot immediately accept an input. A *delay alternative* sets an alarm clock. If the alarm goes off before an acceptable request arrives, the task executes the code of the delay alternative instead of accepting. If an acceptable request arrives first, the alarm is disabled and the request accepted. *Terminate alternatives* are used to bring a set of tasks to simultaneous conclusion. We discuss terminate alternatives below. Both accept and delay alternatives can be followed by a series of statements to be executed when that alternative is selected.

Like guarded commands, select alternatives can be conditional on a boolean expression. An alternative of the form **when** b => **accept** e can be selected only if boolean condition b is true. A select alternative is *open* when it has either no guard or a true guard.

In line_block, we might prefer to separate the mechanisms for adding a character to the output line and returning a count of the available character positions. This requires that line_block have two entries, an add entry to add a character and a free entry to request the free space count.

```
task line_block is
   entry add (c: in character);
   entry free (left: out integer);
end line_block;
```

```
task body line_block is
    thisline : line;
    i       : integer;
begin
    loop
        i := 1;
        while i < 121 loop
            select
                accept add (c: in character) do
                                    -- Selection of this alternative first executes
                                       the accept statement and then increments
                                       the counter.
                        thisline (i) := c;
                end add;
                i := i + 1;
            or
                accept free (j: out integer) do
                    j := 120 − i;
                end free;
            end select;
        end loop;
        printer.writeit (thisline);
    end loop;
end line_block;
```

Sometimes we prefer that a task not block if there are no pending requests. An *else alternative* provides this possibility. Syntactically, an else alternative substitutes **else** for the select statement's last **or** and follows the **else** with a series of statements. Semantically, a select statement with an else alternative that cannot immediately accept an entry request executes the statements of the else alternative instead.

Ada has several syntactic restrictions on the arrangement of select alternatives. Every select statement must have at least one accept alternative. If it has a terminate alternative, it cannot have a delay alternative; if it has a terminate alternative or a delay alternative, it cannot have an else alternative.

The syntax of the select statement allows the expression of a variety of control structures. Therefore, the algorithm followed in evaluating a select statement is somewhat complex. Its theme is to select an immediately available, open accept alternative. If no such alternative exists, then the arrangement of waiting, delay, termination, and else alternatives determines the task's behavior. More particularly, evaluation of a select statement proceeds as follows: (1) The task checks the guard of each alternative and discovers the open alternatives. Each open alternative is an accept, delay, or terminate alternative. (2) It determines to which entry each open accept alternative refers. (As we discuss below, entries can be subscripted. Determining the referent entry is equivalent to computing the entry subscript.) We call entries with open accept alternatives and waiting requests in the entry queue the *acceptable* entries. (3) The task determines how long a delay each delay alternative specifies. (4) If there are any acceptable entries, the task executes the action associated with one of them (selecting one arbitrarily). That is, the first choice of a select statement is always to immediately accept an entry call. (5) If there are no acceptable requests waiting, then we might want to wait for one, wait for one but give up after a while, execute some alternative action, or check if it is time to coordinate the termination of a set of tasks. (6) If the select statement has no delay alternatives, no terminate alternative, and no else alternative, then the task waits until a request appears in an acceptable entry queue. This is typical behavior for a passive, "server" task. (7) If the select statement has an else alternative, the process executes that alternative immediately. (8) If the select statement has a delay alternative, the task blocks. It unblocks after the shortest delay. It then executes the statement associated with that delay. If an acceptable request appears before the delay has elapsed, the task executes an accept alternative that refers to that request instead. (9) If the select statement has a terminate alternative, then the terminate alternative may be executed under certain circumstances.

Of course, there may be no open alternatives. In that case, if the select statement has an else alternative, it evaluates that alternative. A select statement with neither open alternatives nor an else alternative has reached an error. It raises the **select_error** exception. Figure 14-1 graphs the decision flow of the select statement.

In our next example, we vary line_block to illustrate the select statement. We assume that line_block no longer forces lines out to the printer, but waits for the printer to ask for them. (Thus, line_block becomes a producer-consumer buffer.) Furthermore, if the internal buffers are full, a line is ready for the printer, and the printer fails to request that line within 5 minutes (300 seconds), line_block calls the routine printer_trouble. We provide line_block with two buffers, one for filling with incoming characters and another to hold a line ready to be sent to the printer. The task has variables that record the state of these buffers: nextfree, the next free character position in the filling buffer; and print_ready, a boolean that is true when the printing buffer is ready to be written.

```
task line_block is
    entry add          (c: in character);
    entry please_print (ln: out line);
end line_block;

task body line_block is
    printer_trouble_time : constant integer := 300;
    print_line, fill_line  : line;   -- a buffer for the printer and a buffer for
                                            filling
```

```
    nextfree              : integer;
    print_ready           : boolean;     -- Is the printing line ready to output?
begin
    nextfree     := 1;
    print_ready  := false;
    loop
        select
            when (nextfree < 121) =>     -- space for another character
                accept add (c: in character) do
                    fill_line (nextfree)  := c;
                end add;
                nextfree := nextfree + 1;
                if (nextfree = 121) and not print_ready then
                    print_ready := true;
                    nextfree    := 1;
                    print_line  := fill_line;     -- By subscripting our two
                end if;                            buffers, we could have
                                                   avoided this copying.
        or
            when print_ready =>     -- full buffer ready for the printer
                accept please_print (ln: out line) do
                    ln := print_line;
                end please_print;
                if nextfree = 121 then
                    print_line := fill_line;
                    nextfree    := 1;
                else
                    print_ready := false;
                end if;
        or
            when print_ready and (nextfree > 120) =>
                delay printer_trouble_time;
                    printer_trouble;     -- waiting for the printer for over five
        end select;                      minutes
    end loop;
end line_block;
```

Ada programs can reference attributes of certain objects. An *attribute* of an object is non-value information about that object. For example, one attribute of an entry is the size of its queue. Syntactically, an attribute of an object is the name of the object, an apostrophe, and the attribute name. For example, the attribute add'count is the size of the add entry queue; line_block'terminated is true when task line_block has terminated.

Ada entries can be subscripted, producing a *family* of entries. If line_block is a buffer for 20 tasks, each with its own printer, then line_block would declare

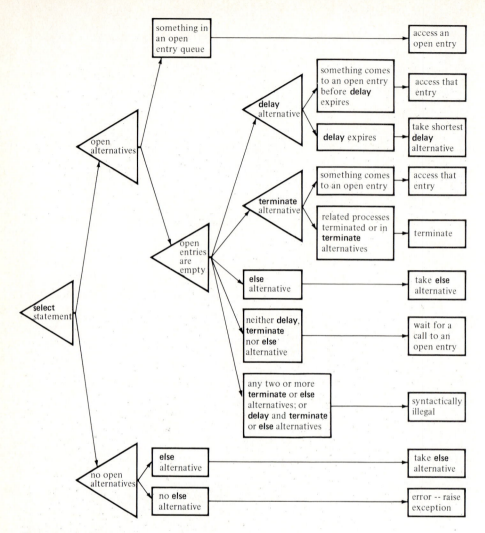

Figure 14-1 Selection statement operation.

a family of entries for each character producer and each printer. We must successively poll the entries to find one with a waiting request. (This contrasts with CSP, where we can check an entire family of processes in a single guarded input command.)

```
task line_block is
    entry add (1..20) (c: in character);    -- a family of entries
    entry please_print (1..20) (ln: out line);
end line_block;
```

```
task body line_block is
     buffers  : array (1..20) of line;     -- no double buffering this time
     bufnext  : array (1..20) of integer; -- pointer into each buffer
     thisone  : integer;                   -- entry currently under consideration

begin
     for thisone in 1..20                  -- initialize the buffers
         loop
             bufnext (thisone) := 1;
         end loop;
     thisone := 1;

     loop    -- This loop polls each entry pair to see if that producer/printer
             pair is ready to interact. If nothing is waiting in the appropriate
             entry, we select the else alternative and proceed to poll the next
             pair.
         select
         when bufnext (thisone) < 121 =>      -- space for another
                                                 character in this buffer
                 accept add (thisone) (c: in character) do
                     buffers (thisone) (bufnext (thisone)) := c;
                 end add;
                 bufnext (thisone) := bufnext (thisone) + 1;
         or
         when bufnext (thisone) > 120 =>      -- full buffer ready for the
                                                 printer
                 accept please_print (thisone) (ln: out line) do
                     ln := buffers (thisone);
                 end please_print;
                 bufnext (thisone) := 1;
         else
             null;    -- If neither is ready, go on to next member of the family.
         end select;
         thisone := thisone + 1;
         if thisone > 20 then thisone := 1; end if;
     end loop;
end line_block;
```

We could specify 20 printers to handle the 20 calls with

```
            task printer (1..20) is
            end printer;
```

The printers are numbered from 1 to 20. Within its task body, a printer can reference its own number as the attribute printer'index.

Task types Tasks can be types, just as records, arrays, and enumerations are types. We can have both statically allocated tasks (such as arrays of tasks) and dynamically created tasks. Processes execute the command **new** to dynamically create new instances of a task type. Of course, one needs pointers to dynamically created objects. Ada calls such pointers *access types*.

We illustrate task types with a program for the dining philosophers problem. The dining philosophers program has three varieties of tasks: philosophers, forks, and the room. Philosophers call the room to enter and exit, and call the forks to pick them up and put them down. Philosophers cycle through thinking, entering the room, picking up the forks, eating, putting down the forks, and leaving the room. To declare a new type, task type fork, we state

```
task type fork is
    entry pickup;
    entry putdown;
end task;
```

A pointer to a fork is an afork.

```
type afork is access fork;
```

Philosophers are also a task type. In our example, we create them dynamically and then send them pointers to each of their forks.

```
task type philosopher is
    entry initiate (left, right: in afork);    -- This is a template for the structure
                                                  of the initiate entry, not a
                                                  declaration of left and right.
end task;
```

We give ourselves a fixed, initial room.

```
task room is
    entry enter;
    entry exit;
end task;
```

The task bodies of the processes are as follows:

```
task body room is
    occupancy: integer;
begin
    occupancy := 0;
    loop
        select
            when (occupancy < 4) =>
```

```
            accept enter;
            occupancy := occupancy + 1;
      or
            accept exit;
            occupancy := occupancy - 1;
      end select;
   end loop;
end task;
task body fork is
begin
   loop
       accept pickup;
       accept putdown;
   end loop;
end task;
```

New does not provide creation parameters for the newly generated object, so we call the initiate entry in the new philosopher to send it the names of its forks. Since the entry parameters (leftparm and rightparm) last only through the scope of the accept statement, we need permanent variables left and right to remember the names of the forks.

```
task body philosopher is
   left, right: afork;
begin
   accept initiate (leftparm, rightparm: in afork) do
       left  := leftparm;
       right := rightparm;
   end;
   loop
       -- think;
       room.enter;
       left.pickup;
       right.pickup;
       -- eat;
       left.putdown;
       right.putdown;
       room.exit;
   end loop;
end task;
```

The entire program is as follows:

```
procedure dining_ps is pragma main;     -- In Ada, the "pragma" (compiler
                                            advice) "main" asserts that this is
                                            the main program.
```

```
task room is ... ;
task body room is ... ;
task type fork is ... ;
task body fork is ... ;
type afork is ... ;
task type philosopher is ... ;
task body philosopher is ... ;

philos    : array (0..4) of philosopher;      -- declarations of global storage
i         : integer;
theforks : array (0..4) of afork;
begin
    for i in 0..4 loop
        theforks (i) := new fork;
    end loop;
    for i in 0..4 loop                        -- Send each philosopher its forks.
        philos (i).initiate (theforks (i), theforks ((i + 1) mod 5));
    end loop;
end dining_ps;
```

This solution avoids both deadlock and starvation. The room's occupancy limit (four philosophers) prevents deadlock and the fork entry queues prevent starvation.

Selective entry call In Ada, an accepting task has some control over ordering the processing of calls to its entries. It can select the next entry for processing, choose the first arrival from among several entries, abort a potential rendezvous if a time constraint is exceeded, and even use the size of its entry queues in deciding what to do. Calling tasks do not have an equivalent variety of mechanisms to control communication. However, Ada does provide calling processes with a way of aborting calls that "take too long." This mechanism is the select/entry call. A *select/entry call* takes one of two forms—either a conditional entry call or a timed entry call. The form of a *conditional entry call* is

```
select
    <entry call> (<parameters>); s1; s2; ... ;
else
    s'1; s'2; ... ;
end select;
```

A *timed entry call* is similar

```
select
    <entry call> (<parameters>); s1; s2; ... ;
```

or

    delay <time-expression>; s'_1; s'_2; ... ;
end select;

In a conditional entry call, a rendezvous takes place if the called task is waiting for a request on this entry. After the rendezvous, the calling task executes statements s_1; s_2; .... If the called task is not waiting for a request on this entry, the calling task executes the **else** statements s'_1; s'_2; .... In either case, this task does not block for long; it either communicates immediately or does not communicate at all. The timed entry call is similar, except that the call aborts if the rendezvous does not begin before the end of the indicated delay. If the delay is exceeded, the call is abandoned and the task executes statements s'_1; s'_2; ....

Unlike the multiple arms of the select/accept statement, a calling task can offer to communicate with only a single other task in any select/entry call. This avoids the potential difficulty of matching several possible communicators. A task executing a conditional entry call offers the called task an opportunity for rendezvous. Either the called task accepts immediately or the calling task withdraws the offer. This organization allows a simple protocol in which only two messages need be sent to accept or reject a rendezvous offer.

The timed entry call is somewhat more complex; its semantics is complicated by the issue of whose clock (which task) is timing the delay. Bernstein discusses the more elaborate protocols involved in many-to-many communication matching in his paper on output guards in CSP [Bernstein 80]. He argues that matching many-to-many requests requires complicated or inherently unfair protocols. Since even the timed entry call allows only many-to-one offers, it is simpler to program the protocols of Ada than of CSP output guards.

Since requests can be withdrawn from an entry queue, programmers cannot (in general) treat a nonzero count as assuring the existence of a call. That is, the statement

    if thisentry'count > 0 **then**
        accept thisentry ...
    end if;

can block if the request to thisentry is withdrawn between the test of the **if** statement and the **accept**.

Ada treats interrupts as hardware-generated entry calls. It provides *representation specifications*, a mechanism for tying specific interrupts to particular entries. A task can disable an interrupt by ignoring requests on that interrupt's entry.

The elevator controller Ada was designed for programming embedded systems. As an example of an embedded system, we present a decentralized elevator control system. This system schedules the movements of several elevators. Due not so much to the wisdom of building decentralized elevator controllers as much as to our desire to illustrate distributed control, many components in this system are processes. More specifically, a task controls each elevator and a task controls each button (up and down) on each floor. An elevator task controls moving an elevator up and down, opening and closing its doors, and stopping at floors. Each floor button task waits for its button to be pressed, then signals the next approaching elevator to stop. Figure 14-2 shows the communication structure of the elevator system.

```
procedure elevator_controller is
pragma main
begin
     basement       : constant integer := 0;      -- elevators for a building of
     penthouse      : constant integer := 40;     -- 40 stories
     num_elevators  : constant integer := 8;      -- There are eight elevators.
     floor_wait     : constant integer := 15;     -- Elevators stop at a floor for
                                                   --   (at least) 15 seconds.
```

-- *The motor procedure accepts commands of the form "up," "down," and "stop." A direction (the ways an elevator can move) is a subtype of a motor_command, either "up" or "down." A floor is an integer from basement (0) through penthouse (40).*

```
     type motor_command is (up, down, stop);
     subtype direction is motor_command range up .. down;
     type floor is range basement .. penthouse;
```

A floor button task has four entries. The press entry is for the line from the real (physical) button. Each time the real floor is pressed, a call is added to this entry's queue. When an elevator approaches a floor from a particular direction, it calls that floor's button for that direction on the coming entry. That is, an upward moving elevator arriving at a floor calls that floor's up button task. This call is a select/entry call. If the button is waiting on coming (someone has pressed it and no other elevator has promised to come) then the tasks rendezvous. The elevator detects the rendezvous and knows that it is sought. (The elevator also stops at floors requested by its internal buttons, the car_buttons.) When an elevator arrives at a floor it announces its arrival with a call to the here entry. The button also has an interested entry for communicating with idle elevators (described below). Floor buttons never initiate communication. Instead, they wait for elevators to call them. Additionally, all communication is between anonymous elevators and floor buttons. No elevator ever communicates directly with another elevator and no floor button knows which elevator will serve it.

Sometimes elevators find themselves with no pressing demands. An elevator with none of its car_buttons on *dreams*—that is, it surveys floors until it finds

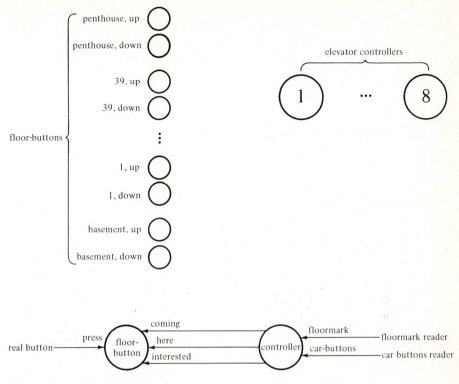

Figure 14-2 The elevator system.

one that needs its services. This survey is done without actually moving the elevator. To distinguish between elevators that are actually going to a floor and the ones that are just considering going, elevators conduct this survey on the interested entry. A floor with waiting passengers responds to a single interested call. However, if another elevator indicates that it can get to that floor first by signaling the floor on the coming line, the floor accepts the offer. Thus, an interested connection is a promise by an elevator to go to a floor but entails no commitment by that floor to save its passengers for the elevator.

```
task type button is
    entry press;
    entry coming;
    entry interested;
    entry here;
end task;

task body button is
    press_on, coming_on, interested_on: boolean;
```

-- *When an elevator arrives at a floor, the button on that floor calls the "arrived" procedure. This procedure clears the button's press queue and delays the departure of the elevator until at least one second after the last press. Thus, a passenger can keep an elevator at a floor by holding down the button on that floor.*

```
procedure arrived is
begin
    delay floor_wait;
    loop
        select
            accept press;
            delay 1;                -- time for another press
        else
            exit                    -- exit the loop
        end select;
    end loop;
    press_on       := false;
    coming_on      := false;
    interested_on  := false;
end arrived;
begin                               -- the main procedure of task button
    loop
        select
            accept here do          -- always respond to arrivals
                arrived;
            end here;
        or
            when not press_on =>
                accept press;       -- Check if the button has been pressed.
                press_on := true;
        or
            when press_on and not coming_on =>
                accept coming;      -- Accept the first "coming" if the
                coming_on := true;     button has been pushed.
        or
            when press_on and not coming_on
                    and not interested_on =>
                accept interested;  -- Accept at most one expression of
                interested_on := true;  interest, and only if no elevator has
                                        promised to come.
        end select;
    end loop;
end button;
```

-- This statement generates 2·(penthouse−basement+1) buttons and sets
them running. (In practice, we might omit the "down" button for the
basement and the "up" button for the penthouse.)
buttons: **array** (floor, direction) **of** button;

Each elevator controller is a task with two entries. The first is for requests
from its own internal floor selection buttons, the car_buttons. The second is
from the floormark_reader. When the elevator is moving, the floormark_reader
interrupts as each floor approaches, signaling the floor's number. This signal
allows enough time to decide whether to stop the elevator at that floor.

```
task type controller is
    entry car_buttons (f: in floor);
    entry floormark_reader (f: in floor);
end task;
```

The controller procedures motor and door_move cause the starting and stopping of the elevator and the opening and closing of the elevator doors. The
motor procedure takes the commands up, down, and stop; the door procedure
takes open and close. The machine hardware ensures that the motor never drives
the elevator through the foundation or roof. Stop stops the elevator at the next
floor. We ignore the internal structures of these procedures, other than the minor
caveats implied in their comments.

```
task body controller is
    type doormove is (open, close);
```
-- Motor returns from a stop call when the floor is reached and the elevator
has stopped. Motor returns from an up or down immediately.
```
    procedure motor (which_way: in direction) is
        ⋮
```
-- This procedure opens and shuts the doors.
```
    procedure doors (how: in doormove) is
        ⋮
```

The elevator's permanent state is stored in three variables. The current_floor
is the elevator's current floor. The current_direction is the elevator's current (or
intended) direction. The array goingto (a two-dimensional, boolean array, indexed by floors and directions) is the elevator's set of intended visits. A ⟨floor,
direction⟩ entry is set in goingto when the elevator promises to visit that floor
with a coming call or when an elevator passenger requests that floor. Variables
found and where are temporaries.

```
type setting is array (floor, direction) of boolean:
goingto            : setting:
current_floor      : floor:
current_direction  : direction:
where              : floor:
found              : boolean:
```

Three simple auxiliary functions on floors and directions are step, limit, and opp_direction. Function step takes a floor and a direction, and returns the next floor in that direction. Thus, a step(up) from floor 5 is floor 6. A step(down) from floor 5 is floor 4. The limit of a direction is the farthest floor in that direction. For example, limit(down) = basement. Function opp_direction reverses directions. The opp_direction(up) = down. For the sake of brevity, we omit the code for these functions.

Initializing the elevator controller consists of moving it to the basement and setting the elements in its goingto array to false.

```
procedure initialize (aset: in out setting:
                      cur_floor: out floor:
                      cur_dir: out direction) is
    f   : floor:
    dir : direction:
begin
    doors (close):
    motor (down):
    loop
        select
            accept floormark_reader (flr: in floor) do
                f := flr:
            end floormark_reader:
            exit when f = basement:
        or
            delay 60:    -- If no new floor mark has shown up in the last
            exit:            minute, we must be at the bottom.
        end select:
    end loop:
    for f in basement .. penthouse
    loop
        for dir in up .. down
        loop
            aset (f, dir) := false:
        end loop:
    end loop:
```

```
    cur_floor := basement;
    cur_dir   := up;
end initialize;
```

Procedure check_carbuttons reads the floors requested from entry car_buttons and sets the appropriate values in array goingto.

```
procedure check_carbuttons (cur_floor: in floor;
                                goingto: in out setting) is
begin
    cbs: loop
        select
            accept car_buttons (f: in floor) do
                if f > cur_floor then
                    goingto (f, up) := true;
                else
                if f < cur_floor then
                    goingto (f, down) := true;
                end if;
            end car_buttons;
        else
            exit cbs;     -- We can exit a labeled loop.
        end select;
    end loop;
end check_carbuttons;
```

An elevator calls procedure arrive_at_floor when it reaches a floor. The elevator does not leave until the floor button returns from the call to here. Since the floor button empties its press entry queue during the here rendezvous, one can keep an elevator at a floor by repeatedly pressing the call button on that floor.

```
procedure arrive_at_floor (cur_floor: in floor; cur_dir: in direction) is
begin
    doors (open);
    buttons (cur_floor, cur_dir).here;
    goingto (cur_floor, cur_dir) := false;
    doors (close);
end arrive_at_floor;
```

Function further_this_way is true when an element of goingto, "further along in this direction," is set. Additionally, further_this_way enforces promises found by dreaming (see below) by ensuring that the elevator goes at least as far as the get_to floor.

```
function further_this_way (cur: in floor;
                           dir: in direction;
                           get_to: in floor) returns boolean is
    answer : boolean;
    f       : floor;
begin
    answer := false;
    if not (cur = limit(dir)) then
        f := step(cur, dir);
        loop
            answer := goingto(f, dir) or (get_to = f);
            exit when answer or (f = limit(dir));
            f := step(f, dir);
        end loop;
        return answer;
    end if;
end further_this_way;
```

The system workhorse is function move_til_stop. It takes the elevator as far as needed in a given direction, calling the procedures that run the motor and open and close the doors.

```
function move_til_stop (dir: in direction; get_to: in floor) returns floor is
    cur: floor;
begin
    motor (dir);              -- An elevator continues until told to stop.
    mainloop: loop
        accept floormark (f: in floor) do
            cur := f;
        end floormark;
        select                -- entry call select
            buttons (cur, dir).coming;
            goingto (cur, dir) := true;
        else                  -- attempt only an immediate rendezvous
            null;
        end select;
        check_carbuttons (cur, goingto);
        if goingto (cur, dir) then
            motor (stop);
            arrive_at_floor (cur, dir);
            exit mainloop
                when not further_this_way (cur, dir, get_to);
            motor (dir);
        end if;
```

```
      end loop;
      return cur;
end move_til_stop;
```

A difficult part of elevator control is deciding what to do when an elevator does not have a currently pending request, such as a pressed car_button. When that happens, our elevators *dream*—pretend to move up and down the building, looking for a floor that is interested in having an elevator visit. A floor that accepts an interested call is promised that this elevator will move to that floor. However, the floor can still respond to a coming call from another elevator if the other elevator gets there first.

```
procedure dream (start, stop, realfloor: in floor;
                 dir: in direction;
                 answer: out boolean;
                 finds: out floor) is
begin
      check_carbuttons (realfloor, goingto);
      answer := false;
      finds  := start;
      loop
          select
                buttons (finds, dir).interested;
                answer := true;
          else
                answer := goingto (finds, dir);
          end select;
          if finds = stop or answer then
                exit;
          end if;
          finds := step (finds, dir);
      end loop;
end dream;
```

- - - - - - - - - - - - - - - - - - *main program* - - - - - - - - - - - - - - - - - -
```
begin
      initialize (goingto, current_floor, current_direction);
```

-- *First dream of going in the current direction until the limit (basement or penthouse) of that direction, then in the opposite direction down from that limit to the other limit, and so forth, until a real request appears. Then satisfy requests until at a limit. Then go back to dreaming of work.*
```
      loop
          dream (current_floor, limit (current_direction), current_floor,
```

```
                        current_direction, found, where);
            if found then
                    current_floor := move_til_stop (current_direction, where);
            else
                    dream (limit (current_direction), current_floor, current_floor,
                            opp_direction (current_direction), found, where);
                    if found then
                            current_floor := move_til_stop (current_direction, where);
                    else
                            current_direction := opp_direction (current_direction);
                    end if;
            end if;
        end loop;
end controller;


    -- Create a controller for each elevator.
vators: array (1 .. num_elevators) of controller;

end elevator_controller;
```

In this example, we periodically call procedure check_carbuttons to examine the elevator's internal buttons. This could be a task running concurrently with the main program. Ideally, such a task would share the array goingto with the controller. In Ada, one can share storage between tasks—tasks created in the same scope share variables declared in that scope and higher scopes. Exercise 14-7 asks that the elevator controller be modified to have a process that checks carbuttons execute in parallel with the process that controls elevator movement.

Pragmatics

Packages Several of Ada's features are of particular pragmatic interest. The first is the inclusion in the language of packages, a form of abstract data type facility. The second is the ability to declare generic program objects. Generic objects reflect Alan Perlis's maxim that "one man's constant is another man's variable" [Perlis 82]. They allow the type information in Pascal-like languages to be instantiated to different values. For example, Pascal requires separate sorting routines to sort integers, reals, and so forth. In Ada, one could build a generic sorting routine and instantiate that routine to particular data types.

Priorities A task may be given an integer-valued priority. A task of higher priority has greater urgency. Thus, a disk-controller task would typically have a higher priority than a terminal-controller task. In a task specification, the pragma

pragma priority <compile-time integer expression>

associates a priority with a task. The Ada standard states the intended effects of a priority as [DoD 80, p. 9-13]:

> If two tasks with different priorities are both eligible for execution and could sensibly be executed using the same processing resources then it cannot be the case that the task with the lower priority is executing while the task with the higher priority is not.

The standard goes on to warn [DoD 80, p. 9-13]:

> The priority of a task is static and therefore fixed. Priorities should be used only to indicate relative degrees of urgency; they should not be used for task synchronization.

Attribute taskname'priority gives the priority of task taskname.

Dynamic exception handling In Ada, certain run-time incidents are *exceptions*. Ada subprograms can have a section of code reserved to deal with each particular variety of exception. A program segment that runs when an exception happens is an *exception handler*. Typical exceptions include numeric exceptions, raised on conditions such as underflow and overflow; select exceptions, raised when a select statement without an else alternative has no open alternatives; and tasking exceptions, raised when intertask communication fails. Programmers can declare their own exceptions. The command raise <exception-name> raises an exception, forcing control to that exception's handler. If an exception occurs and the program segment has no exception handler, the exception propagates back through the run-time calling structure of the task until a handler for it is found. If an exception propagates to the outermost level of a task without finding an exception handler, the task terminates.

Termination An Ada task terminates when it has reached the end of its code and all its dependent tasks have terminated. This is *normal termination*. Selection of a terminate alternative in a select/access statement also causes normal termination (see below). Execution of an **abort** statement causes *abnormal termination*. Any task may abort any task; a task is not limited to aborting only itself or its dependent tasks. Abnormal termination of a task causes abnormal termination of its dependent tasks. Thus, if a system of tasks is floundering, the entire system can be terminated by aborting the parent task. The attribute taskname'terminated is true if task taskname has terminated; the attribute taskname'completed is true if task taskname is waiting for the termination of its dependent tasks before terminating.

A task that terminates while waiting in an entry queue is deleted from that queue. If rendezvous is in progress when a calling task terminates, the called task completes the rendezvous normally. If a task calls an entry in a task that has terminated, the tasking_error exception is raised in the calling task. The termination of the called task during rendezvous also raises the `tasking_error` exception in the calling task.

The terminate alternative of the select/accept statement is designed to co-ordinate the termination of a set of tasks. The idea is that a task may wish to terminate when it is no longer possible for it to receive any further entry calls. This can be the case only if its parent and all its sibling and dependent tasks are either terminated or in this same "potentially dying" state. Algorithmically, we imagine a task that is active as flying a white flag. When a task terminates, it lowers the white flag and raises a black one. A task waiting in a select statement with an open terminate alternative flies a gray flag. If and only if all other tasks that can call the gray-flag task have dark (gray or black) flags does this task terminate (changing gray to black). If a task flying a gray flag receives a call to one of its entries, it changes its flag to white and continues processing. A mostly dark landscape is not an assurance that termination is near—one white flag can eventually cause a sea of gray flags all to turn white. To simplify determining which tasks can still potentially receive communications, creating tasks with the **new** statement precludes using a terminate alternative.

Perspective

Ada is an imperative, explicit process language that provides synchronized com-munication. Communication is a form of remote procedure call. However, unlike procedure calls, the called process keeps multiple entries and the calling process can abort the communication for inadequate service.

Ada is an attempt to deal with the issues of real multiple-processor, dis-tributed computing systems. The facilities for synchronization provided by ren-dezvous, multiple entries, and the temporal constructs provide Ada great opera-tional power. Ada provides a well-developed set of mechanisms for dealing with temporal relationships, such as elapsed time and time-outs. This variety of mech-anisms is not surprising; concepts such as delay and time-out are important for manipulating objects in the real world. By and large, other languages omit these functions because they complicate the language semantics. Explicit time (much like multiple processes) introduces an element of indeterminacy into a program-ming system. For most programming tasks this indeterminacy is a hindrance to the writing of correct programs.

Ada has been criticized for the asymmetry of its communication relation-ships. Calling and called tasks are not equal, though it is not clear where the balance of power lies. A calling task knows with which task it is communicating. However, it can only select its communicators serially, with little more control over the occasion of communication than time delay.* Called tasks can schedule their work with much greater flexibility, choosing indeterminately as requests

* Even this power, embodied in the select/entry call, was a late addition to Ada—it is not in the preliminary manual [SIGPLAN 79], only the later standard [DoD 80].

arrive. However, calls to a task are anonymous. This ignores a potential form of interprocess security.

In providing mechanisms for handling process and communication failure, Ada moves beyond the simpler proposals. In so doing, it has limited the distributed aspects of the language. The visibility of attributes such as task'terminated and the presence of terminate alternatives in select statements does not mean that an Ada program cannot be implemented on a distributed system; only that there is more underlying sharing of information than may be apparent at first glance.

Ada tries to deal with the pragmatic issues in programming. On the other hand, it tries to be all encompassing, to provide a mechanism for every eventuality. This produces a language that is not only powerful but also complex. Ada has been criticized for this complexity (for example, by Hoare in his Turing Award lecture [Hoare 81]). But Ada is also to be praised for its scope and depth. Its future is difficult to predict: It has the potential to soar on the power of its mechanisms, or to become mired in a morass of syntactic and semantic complexity.

PROBLEMS

14-1 Imagine an alarm clock process in an Ada system that can keep time (and, of course, use all the other process communication mechanisms). Can this process be used to replace the delay alternative in the select statement?

14-2 Kieburtz and Silberschatz [Kieburtz 79] cite the example of a "continuous display" system of two processes, one that calculates the current position of an object (the update process) and the other that (repeatedly) displays the object's location on a screen (the display process). The two processes run asynchronously; typically, the update process is faster than the display process. The goal of the system is to display the latest position of the object; when update calculates a new value for the position of the object, the old ones become useless. However, the display process should never be kept waiting for an update. Thus, the information from update should not be treated by display with the usual first-in-first-out (queue) discipline. Instead, it is the most recently received value that is needed. Old values are useless and should be discarded.

This idea of display/update interaction is isomorphic to an organization that shares storage between the two processes. Of course, shared storage is easy to arrange in Ada. This question requests a program for the continuous display problem that does not rely on shared storage.

14-3 To what extent can the effect of **select/accept** be achieved by checking the size of the entry queue with the **count** attribute? What are the pitfalls of this approach?

14-4 Contrast the **select/accept** and **select/entry** call mechanisms with Exchange Functions (Chapter 7) and CSP's guarded input and output commands (Chapter 10).

14-5 Procedure check_carbuttons sets an element in goingto for floors f less than or greater than the current floor. It does not set an element when f equals cur_floor. Why?

14-6 Modify the elevator controller program to turn on and off the lights on the up and down buttons on each floor.

14-7 Program an "elevator button checking task" that runs concurrently with the elevator control and communicates with it by sharing the array goingto.

14-8   Can a passenger on floor 2 be ignored by elevators that are kept busy between floors 5 and 8? (*Clossman*)

14-9   What happens when two elevators arrive at a floor at the same time?

14-10   Improve the program of the elevator controller to run the elevators more efficiently. For example, have a floor serviced by another elevator send a cancellation message to an interested elevator.

14-11   Devise an algorithm that mimics the effect of terminate alternatives without using terminate alternatives.

REFERENCES

[**Bernstein 80**]   Bernstein, A. J., "Output Guards and Nondeterminism in 'Communicating Sequential Processes,'" *ACM Trans. Program. Lang. Syst.*, vol. 2, no. 2 (April 1980), pp. 234–238. This paper discusses the protocol difficulties in dealing with processes that can issue guarded input and output commands. Ada sidesteps much of this problem by allowing only a single destination for a select/entry call.

[**Carlson 81**]   Carlson, W. E., "Ada: A Promising Beginning," *Comput.*, vol. 14, no. 6 (June 1981), pp. 13–15. Carlson's paper is a brief history of the Ada development effort. He combines this history with predictions about Ada's future.

[**DoD 80**]   Department of Defense, "Military Standard Ada Programming Language," Report MIL-STD-1815, Naval Publications and Forms Center, Philadelphia, Pennsylvania (December 1980). This is the current Ada standard. This document will be replaced by future standards as Ada evolves. The standard is about 200 detailed pages long. This is a good measure of Ada's complexity.

[**Donzeau-Gouge 80**]   Donzeau-Gouge, V., G. Kahn, and B. Lang, "Formal Definition of the Ada Programming Language: Preliminary Version for Public Review," unnumbered technical report, INRIA (November 1980). This paper is a formal definition of all aspects of Ada except tasking. The paper presents two kinds of semantics for Ada, "static semantics" and "dynamic semantics." The static semantics performs type checking and the like. The dynamic semantics expresses the run-time semantics of programs in an "applicative subset" of Ada.

[**Fisher 78**]   Fisher, D. A., "DoD's Common Programming Language Effort," *Comput.*, vol. 11, no. 3 (March 1978), pp. 24–33. This article relates the motivations for and historical development of Ada.

[**Hoare 81**]   Hoare, C.A.R., "The Emperor's Old Clothes," *CACM*, vol. 24, no. 2 (March 1981), pp. 75–83. This paper was Hoare's Turing Award lecture. In this paper he warns about the pitfalls of programming languages that are too complicated.

[**Kieburtz 79**]   Kieburtz, R. B., and A. Silberschatz, "Comments on 'Communicating Sequential Processes,'" *ACM Trans. Program. Lang. Syst.*, vol. 1, no. 2 (January 1979), pp. 218–225. Kieburtz and Silberschatz's paper is the source of the "continuous display" problem.

[**Perlis 82**]   Perlis, A. J., "Epigrams on Programming," *SIGPLAN Not.*, vol. 17, no. 9 (September 1982), pp. 7–13. Perlis presents a satirical collection of programming wisdom.

[**Pyle 81**]   Pyle, I. C., *The Ada Programming Language*, Prentice-Hall International, Englewood Cliffs, New Jersey (1981). This book is a good introduction to the complexities of Ada for the experienced programmer. It is both concise and comprehensive. Particularly useful are appendices on Ada for programmers familiar with Fortran or Pascal.

[**SIGPLAN 79**]   SIGPLAN Notices, "Ada Manual and Rationale," *SIGPLAN Not.*, vol. 14, no. 6 (June 1979). This is the original report from the Honeywell Ada group on their language. This report was published as a two volume issue of SIGPLAN Notices and is widely available. The current Ada manual [DoD 80] supersedes it as the Ada standard. SIGPLAN Notices published much of the discussion and many of the proposals that led to Ada. ACM now has a technical group, ADATEC (a "junior" special interest group) devoted to Ada.

[**Wegner 81**] Wegner, P., "Self-Assessment Procedure VIII," *CACM*, vol. 24, no. 10 (October 1981), pp. 647–677. This paper presents a self-assessment procedure on Ada. Because of Ada's novelty, Wegner attempts not only to test, but also to teach the language. He concentrates on the abstraction aspects of Ada, such as modules, types, and packages. He completely excludes discussion of concurrency in Ada.

FIFTEEN

PLITS

The languages we have discussed so far (Distributed Processes and its kin, Ada) use synchronous communication — both the initiator of a communication and the recipient attend to communication. This technique limits the demand for processing resources and simplifies the problem of getting processes to reach synchronous states. Asynchronous communication suggests a greater freedom — the ability to make a request without attending to its completion. Along with this greater freedom comes the risk of unbounded demands for system resources — the possibility that processes will make requests faster than they can be handled.

PLITS (Programming Language In The Sky) is a language based on communication with asynchronous messages. It therefore resembles Actors (Chapter 11). Unlike Actors, PLITS fits the asynchronous mechanisms into an imperative syntax and places a greater emphasis on explicit, interacting processes.

The important primitive objects in PLITS are messages and modules. *Modules* are processes. Modules communicate by sending each other *messages*. PLITS queues and sorts these messages for the receiving process. PLITS also has mechanisms for abstracting and protecting message information, and for selective message reception.

PLITS is the creation of Jerome Feldman and his co-workers at the University of Rochester. Despite its whimsical name, there is an implementation of PLITS. This implementation includes both a high-level language simulator and a distributed system based on message passing and modules.

Messages and Modules

Modules in PLITS communicate asynchronously. PLITS modules enjoy many attributes of true objects: they can be dynamically created and destroyed, and (the names of) modules are themselves a proper data type. PLITS messages are structured association sets. Associated with each module is a queue of messages; modules exercise considerable control over the order in which messages are accepted from the queue.

Communication depends on mutual understanding. To facilitate interprocess communication, PLITS provides a new structured data type, the message. *Messages* are sets of *name-value pairs*. Each such pair is a *slot*. The name field of a slot is an uninterpreted character string and is unique in that message. That is, no name field occurs twice in a given message. The value field is an element of one of a set of primitive unstructured domains, such as integer, real, and module. The value field of a slot cannot be a structured data type, so a message cannot be included in a message. A module declares as *public* the names of the message slots it uses and the types of the slot values. A form of linkage-editing resolves conflicts on slot/types among modules.

PLITS is a foundation on which one can build one's choice of syntax. Following Feldman [Feldman 79], we present a version of "Pascal-PLITS"—PLITS with a Pascal-like syntax. The "." operator of Pascal's record structure extracts message parts, with the slot name serving as the field designator. Name-value pairs (slots) are constructed with operator "∼". Function **message** constructs a message out of slots. Thus, the assignment

$$\text{m} := \textbf{message} \ (\text{day} \sim 135, \ \text{year} \sim 1983)$$

assigns to variable m a message of two slots. The value of m.day is **135**.

PLITS provides many primitives for manipulating messages and modules. The next few paragraphs list these mechanisms. The parenthesized numbers in the text correspond to the lines in Table 15-1, which gives the syntax for each primitive.

A collection of slots can be constructed into a message if their name fields are distinct (1). In PLITS, one can add a slot to a message (changing the value if that slot name is already present) (2), remove a slot from a message (3), change the value of a particular slot (4), and detect the presence (5), or absence (6) of a particular slot in a message. Changing or deleting a nonexistent slot produces an error (3, 4). Modules can manipulate only those message slots to which they have been declared to have public access. Slot names are not a data type so no expression evaluates to a slot name.

Messages can have slots that the recipient of that message cannot access. That is, a module can reference only the slot names that it has declared, but messages may contain other slots. A module can forward an entire message, even if it has access to only a few of its slots. This facility enforces a clever form of se-

Table 15-1 PLITS syntax extensions

1.	**message**$(..., N_i \sim X_i, ...)$	A message constructor function. It returns a message with the given name-value pairs.
2.	**put** $N \sim X$ **in** M	Adds or changes the slot with name N to have value X in message M.
3.	**remove** N **from** M	Deletes the slot with name N from message M. This is an error if M does not have such a slot.
4.	$M.N := X$	Changes the value of slot with name N to X in message M. This is an error if M does not have such a slot.
5.	**present** N **in** M	True if M has a slot with name N.
6.	**absent** N **in** M	True if M does not have a slot with name N.
7.	**new_transaction**	A function that returns a new transaction key.
8.	**send** M **to** V	Sends the message M to module V.
9.	**send** M **to** V **about** K	Sends M to V. Makes the **about** field of M be the transaction key K.
10.	**receive** M	Removes the next message from the message queue, and assigns it to M.
11.	**receive** M **about** K	Removes the next message from the message queue with a transaction key of K, and assigns it to M.
12.	**receive** M **from** S	Removes the next message from the message queue that was sent from module S, and assigns it to M.
13.	**receive** M **from** S **about** K	Removes the next message from the message queue that was sent from module S with a transaction key K, and assigns it to M.
14.	**pending from** S **about** K	True if there is a message in the queue from S about K. Like **receive**, the **from** and/or **about** clauses are optional.
15.	**new**$(ModType, x_1, ..., x_n)$	A function that generates a new module of type $ModType$ parameterized by $x_1, ..., x_n$ and returns its name.
16.	**self destruct**	Causes this module to stop processing and "cease to exist."
17.	**extant** V	Does the module V still exist? (Has it already executed **self destruct**?)

curity, where information can be kept from certain modules, but still transmitted by them without resorting to coding tricks or additional communications.

Different models and languages have different methods of organizing and segregating a process's messages. For example, Ada's tasks have multiple entry queues while CSP's "structured data types" require a form of pattern matching for communication. In PLITS, request structuring can be done with transactions. A *transaction* is a unique key. A module can generate a new transaction at will (7); once generated, these transactions are objects of the primitive transaction data type. Every message contains two specific slots: an **about** slot with a transaction key and a **source** slot which specifies the module that sent the message. If a message does not have an explicit **about** slot the system inserts the default transaction key automatically. The system ensures that **source** slots are correct—that a module cannot "forge" another module's "signature" to a message.

Modules are processes. Each module is the instantiation of a module type. One can have arbitrarily many module instances of that type. Modules have both program and storage. The program portion of a module can execute any of the standard imperative (Pascal-like) control structures. Additionally, modules can compose, decompose, send, and receive messages from other modules. Modules therefore have all the computational power of abstract data types. The data type **module** is the union of all module types.

The message-sending primitive takes a message and destination and delivers that message to that destination (8). In sending, a process can specify a transaction key (9). **Send** is an asynchronous (send-and-forget) operation; the sending process continues computing after sending. Messages are ultimately routed to the destination module's queue. This requires that there be an "unbounded" queue of unreceived messages kept for each module. Messages from a single sender using a particular transaction key arrive in the order sent and are received in the order sent.* Any module can send a message to any other. Messages are sent by value.

Modules can choose to accept messages in a strictly first-come-first-served order (10). However, there are alternative reception orders. Specifically, a module can specify that a particular reception is to be the next message **about** a particular transaction key (11), the next message **from** a particular source module (12), or the next message **about** a particular key and **from** a particular module (13). This mechanism allows modules some control over the order in which they accept messages, but not as much control as one might imagine. A module might want to receive the message with the highest value on some slot, to exclude messages with a particular transaction key, or, more generally, to accept only messages whose content satisfies some arbitrary predicate. PLITS has a primitive language predicate for determining if there are any pending messages. The pending function can be restricted to messages from a specific source, about a specific transaction key, or both (14).

Programs can dynamically create new instances of a module type (15). Modules can terminate, but only by their own action—by executing the command **self destruct** (16). The **extant** function is true if its argument module has not terminated (17).

Fibonacci numbers Our first example, derived from Feldman [Feldman 79], demonstrates the data structuring, message construction, coroutine, and continuation facilities of PLITS. We imagine three varieties of modules: a type of

---

* This contrasts with Actors (Chapter 11), where dispatch-order arrival is not guaranteed. Dispatch-order arrival may be difficult to implement when a distributed system allows messages to take different routes to a destination. To ensure this sequencing, modules need to track the history of their communications with other modules.

Fibonacci module that generates Fibonacci numbers, a Printer module that takes a message and prints part of it, and a Seeker module that directs successive Fibonacci numbers from the generator to the Printer (Figure 15-1). At each cycle, the Seeker prompts the Fibonacci module to send the next Fibonacci number to the Printer. The Printer prints the Fibonacci number and sends a synchronization message back to the Seeker. The system repeats this cycle for 100 Fibonacci numbers.

```
program Triangle (Output);
type
  Printer = mod                          -- A Printer is a type of module.
    public                               -- It has access to two message slots.
        continuation : module;           -- The first, "continuation," is the
                                            module destination of the
                                            synchronization pulse.

        object       : integer;          -- The second, "object," is an
    var                                     integer to be printed.
        m  : message;
        val : integer;
    begin
        while true do                    -- Loop forever, doing:
        begin
            receive m;                   -- Wait for and accept a message.
            val := m.object;             -- Extract the number.
            writeln (output, val);       -- Print it.
            send m to m.continuation     -- Forward message m to the module
        end                                 in the continuation field of m.
    end;

  Fibonacci = mod                        -- A Fibonacci is a module
    public                               -- that has access to
        whonext : module;                -- whonext, a continuation, and
        object  : integer;               -- object, the value to be printed
    var
        this, last, previous : integer;  -- for Fibonacci generation
        m                    : message;
    begin
        last := 0;
        this := 1;
        while true do
        begin
            receive m;                   -- Get the next message. Store it in m.
            previous := last;            -- Compute the next Fibonacci number.
            last     := this;
            this     := last + previous;
```

```
                put object ~ this in m;      -- If there is already a slot of the form
                                                object ~ x in m then replace it;
                                                otherwise, add object ~ this to m.
                send m to m.whonext          -- Send message m to the continuation.
        end
    end;

Seeker = mod
    const size = 100;
    public
        continuation, whonext: module;
    var
        fibgen    : module;
        printput  : module;
        m         : message;
        i         : integer;
    begin
        fibgen    := new(Fibonacci);
        printput  := new(Printer);
        put continuation ~ me in m;         -- "me" is the primitive that returns a
                                                module's own name.
        put whonext ~ printput in m;
        for i := 1 to size do               -- Direct the Fibonacci generator's
                                                continuation to do "size" numbers.
        begin
            send m to fibgen;
            receive m    -- If this receive statement is omitted, the numbers
                            are still printed, but the system is no longer
                            synchronized. Greater concurrency results. In this
                            case, the continuation sent by the printer could be
                            omitted.
        end;
    end;

- - - - - - - - - - - - - - - - - - main program - - - - - - - - - - - - - - - - - -
var s: Seeker;
begin
    -- Creating the Seeker module s initiates s. S creates its own Fibonacci and
        Printer modules.
end.
```

Producer-consumer buffer Our second example is a module that acts as a bounded producer-consumer buffer. This module uses transaction keys to control its acceptance of produced values and its presentation of these values to

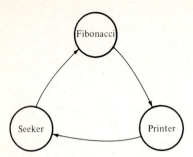

Figure 15-1 The Fibonacci processes.

consumers. Buffers are created with three parameters: **size**, the size of the buffer; **accept**, a transaction key that distinguishes messages that are to be stored in the buffer; and **deliver**, a transaction key for requests for values. When the buffer receives a request for an element, it sends the first item in the queue to the source of that request.

Modules that use this buffer must not only know the buffer's name, but also have been passed the appropriate transaction key. The process that creates the buffer must create it with two different transaction keys; otherwise, the buffer cannot distinguish producers from consumers.

```
type buffer = mod (size: integer; accept, deliver: transaction)
var
      queue     : array [0 .. size − 1] of message;
      first, last : integer;

procedure intake (w: message);      -- Put this message on the queue.
begin
      last          := (last + 1) mod size;
      queue [last] : = w
end;


procedure outplace (w: message);    -- Send the top of the queue to the source
                                       of this message
begin
      first := (first + 1) mod size;
      send queue[first] to w.source
end;

- - - - - - - - - - - - - - - - - - main program - - - - - - - - - - - - - - - - - - -
begin
      first : = 0;
      last  : = 0;
```

```
    while true do
    begin
        if first = last then                -- queue empty (1)
            receive m about accept          -- Here the buffer is empty. We want
                                               only messages that add to it. We
                                               use the "about" option in receive to
                                               restrict access.
        else
        if (last + 1) mod size = first then  -- queue full (2)
            receive m about deliver         -- The buffer is full. We want
                                               only requests that consume
                                               buffer elements.
        else
            receive m;                      -- queue part full (3)
        if m.about = accept
            then intake (m)
            else outplace (m)
    end
end;
```

A program that needs a buffer creates one with **new**, specifying the size of the buffer and transaction keys for accept and deliver. The only action the buffer can take when it is empty is to accept (line 1) and the only action the buffer can take when it is full is to deliver (line 2). When the buffer is partially full, it can both accept and deliver (line 3).

Readers and writers The readers-writers problem requires sharing a resource between two classes of users: readers who can use the resource simultaneously, and writers who require exclusive control. The task is to program a manager that receives requests from readers and writers and schedules their access.

There are two naive ways of approaching the readers-writers problem. The first is to alternate access by a reader and a writer. This solution is unsatisfactory as it excludes concurrent reader access. The alternate extreme is to allow all readers to read and to permit writing only when no reader wants the resource. This scheme has the potential of starving the writers if readers make requests too frequently. (One can give the corresponding priority to writers, threatening the starvation of readers.)

To avoid these pitfalls we take the following approach. We alternate sets of readers and a writer. If both readers and writers are waiting to use the resource, the manager allows all currently waiting readers to read. When they are through, it lets the next writer write. Of course, if only one class of process wants the resource, the manager gives that class immediate service.

Processes must also notify the manager when they are through with the resource. Thus, we imagine that the manager receives three varieties of mes-

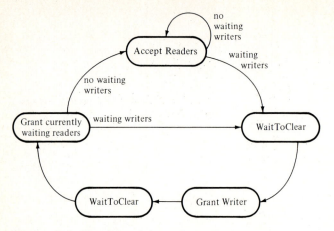

Figure 15-2 The states of the readers-writers manager.

sages: read requests, write requests, and release notifications. When a process wants the resource, it sends a message with a slot of the form want ~ PleaseRead or want ~ PleaseWrite to the manager. When it receives a reply with the slot YouHaveIt ~ CanRead or YouHaveIt ~ CanWrite then it has the corresponding access to the resource. When it is through, it sends a message with the slot want ~ ThankYou back to the manager. Thus, we have the enumerated types Request and Permission, declared as

type
    Request   = (PleaseRead. PleaseWrite. ThankYou);
    Permission = (CanRead. CanWrite);

    The manager keeps two queues of requests, one for readers and the other for writers. It alternates between allowing all readers to read and letting the next writer write. We assume that no more than numqueue reader or writer requests are ever pending at any time. The manager keeps its queue using the same queue discipline as the producer-consumer buffer. The manager also keeps a count, using, of modules currently accessing the resource. Figure 15-2 shows the states of the manager.

type manager = **mod** (numqueue: integer);
    queue = **array** [0 .. numqueue − 1] **of** module;
public
    want   : Request;
    YouHaveIt : Permission;
var
    using : integer   *-- count of current readers*
    m   : message;

```
    readqueue, writequeue    : queue;
    readfirst, readlast      : integer;
    writefirst, writelast    : integer;
```

procedure enqueue (v: module; **var** q: queue; **var** last: integer);
begin   -- *We assume that the queues never overflow.*
    last   := (last + 1) **mod** numqueue;
    queue[last] := v
end;

function dequeue (**var** q: queue; **var** first: integer) : module;
begin   -- *We check for an empty queue before calling dequeue.*
    first   := (first + 1) **mod** numqueue;
    dequeue   := q[first]
end;

procedure Grant (v: module; p: Permission);
begin
    using := using + 1;
    send message (YouHaveIt ~ p) **to** v
end;

procedure WaitToClear;   -- *This procedure enqueues readers and writers until*
begin   *the resource is free.*
    while using > 0 **do**
    begin
        receive m;
        if m.want = ThankYou **then**
            using := using − 1
        else
            if m.want = PleaseRead **then**
                enqueue (m.**source**, readqueue, readlast)
            else   -- *must be another write request*
                enqueue (m.**source**, writequeue, writelast)
    end
end;

procedure AcceptReaders;   -- *This procedure accepts readers until a writer*
begin   *requests the resource.*
    repeat
        receive m;
        if m.want = ThankYou **then** using := using − 1
        else
        if m.want = PleaseRead **then** Grant (m.**source**, CanRead)

```
            else
                enqueue (m.source, writequeue, writelast);
        until m.want = PleaseWrite
end;
```

```
        - - - - - - - - - - - - - - - - - main program - - - - - - - - - - - - - - - - - -
begin
        readfirst  := 0;    - - Initialize the queue pointers.
        readlast   := 0;
        writefirst := 0;
        writelast  := 0;
        using      := 0;    - - Initially, no process is using the resource.
        while true do       - - The manager loops forever.
        begin               - - The manager is a five-state machine.
                - - If there are no writers waiting, accept all reader requests.
            if writefirst = writelast then AcceptReaders;
                - - Now queue readers and writers until all the readers are done
                  with the resource (i.e., using = 0).
            WaitToClear;
                - - Grant access to a writer.
            Grant (dequeue (writequeue, writefirst), CanWrite);
                - - Wait until that writer is done.
            WaitToClear;
                - - Permit all waiting readers to access the resource.
            while not (readfirst = readlast) do
                Grant (dequeue (readqueue, Readfirst), Canread)
                - - And repeat the entire process.
        end
end.
```

Eight queens PLITS supports dynamic creation of new modules. These new modules have no communication restrictions. They can send messages to any other module whose name they come to possess. We use the eight queens problem to illustrate this facility. This problem, investigated by Gauss, requires the placement of eight queens on a chessboard such that no queen can capture any other.* Figure 15-3 shows one solution of the eight queens problem.

One way to solve this problem is to use recursive backtracking. We note that in any solution each row and each column must hold exactly one queen. We place the nth queen on some row of the nth column, check to see if it can be captured by any queen already on the board, and, if it cannot, recursively try

---

* In chess, a queen can capture any (opposing) piece that shares the same row, column, or diagonal with it, provided no other piece lies on the path between them.

Figure 15-3 A solution of the eight queens problem.

to place the remaining queens in the remaining columns. We repeat this process until the eighth queen is successfully placed. If the queen can be captured, or the recursive attempt fails, we move this queen to another row and repeat the process. If we cannot place the queen on any row, we backtrack, reporting failure to the previous column. We imagine three auxiliary functions, (1) **place**, which takes a chessboard, row, and column and returns a new board, updated with a queen at that intersection; (2) **safe**, which is true if its argument board has no mutually attacking queens; and (3) **printanswer**, which given a board prints the problem solution implied by that board. A pseudo-Pascal function that solves the eight queens problem is as follows:

```
function solve (var brd: chessboard; col: integer) : boolean;
var
      row : integer;
      ans : boolean;
begin
      if safe (brd, col − 1) then
          if col = 9 then
              begin
                  printanswer (brd);
                  solve := true
              end
          else
              begin
                  row := 0;
                  repeat
                      row := row + 1;
                      ans := solve (place (brd, row, col), c + 1)
```

```
                until (row = 8) or ans;
                solve : = ans
          end
     else
          solve : = false
end;
```

Our technique is similar, except that instead of trying each queen placement in turn, we try all the possible queen positions in a column concurrently. (Hence, we do not have to report failures.) The agent of this arrangement is a module, Queen, that receives a message with three slots: (1) a column slot that tells it which column to try to fill; (2) a board slot that contains a representation of those squares of the board already filled; and (3) a continuation slot that contains the identity of the module that eventually prints the answers.

The action of a Queen module is as follows: It receives a message m containing a board and a column. It first checks to see if m.board is safe. If not, the module terminates. If it is, the module determines if it has been asked to fill in the ninth (off-the-edge-of-the-board) column. If so, it has an answer, m.board. It sends m.board to the continuation. It then informs its requestor that it is finished, and terminates.

If this is not a terminal search point, then, for each row, row, the queen module copies its board, adds a new queen at ⟨row, m.column⟩, creates a new queen module, and sends that module the new board, asking it to solve the next column. We assume that a chessboard is a primitive data type that can be included in messages.

After all the generated modules of a queen module have reported completion of the task, the current module reports completion (in the slot done) and terminates. Variable children keeps count of the module's currently computing descendant modules.

```
type queen = mod;
public
      column       : integer;
      board        : chessboard;
      continuation : module;
      done         : boolean;
var
      row          : integer;
      m, problem   : message;
      children     : integer;      -- number of extant modules that this module has
begin                                        created
    receive problem;
    if safe (problem.board) then
        if problem.column = 9 then
```

```
                    send message (ans ~ problem.board) to problem.continuation
            else
                begin
                    children := 8;
                    for row := 1 to 8 do
                        begin
                            send message (column ~ problem.column+1,
                                           board ~ place (problem.board,
                                                          row,
                                                          problem.column),
                                           continuation ~ problem.continuation)
                                    to new (queen)
                        end;
                    while children > 0 do
                        begin
                            receive m;      - - This message is for
                                                 synchronization.
                            children := children − 1
                        end
                end;
            send message (done ~ true) to problem.source;
            self destruct
    end;
```

A module with an empty board EmptyBoard and the name of a printing continuation Printing could have the 92 solutions to the eight queens problem sent
to Printing (and a termination confirmation message sent to itself) with the
command

```
                    send message (column ~ 1,
                                   board ~ EmptyBoard,
                                   continuation ~ Printing)
                            to new (queen);
```

Perspective

PLITS is based on processes and messages. Processes are objects; they possess
program and storage and can be dynamically created and destroyed. Process
names can be passed between processes.

Processes communicate by asynchronously sending each other messages.
These messages are transmitted by call-by-value (copying). The underlying system keeps an unbounded queue of unreceived messages for each process. The
process can check the size of its queue or treat it as several subqueues, simultaneously organized by sender and subject.

Turning constant into variable is a boon to most programming activities (though one sometimes trades efficiency for this flexibility). PLITS's treatment of processes as a data type, to be created, referenced, and destroyed is an example of such a generalization. PLITS correctly recognizes that an asynchronous distributed system must treat process names as a proper data type.

Feldman and his co-workers at Rochester are in the process of implementing a distributed system founded on the ideas of PLITS. While their short term goals have been directed at organizing a varied collection of computers, they clearly share many of the long-term goals of coordinated computing.

PROBLEMS

15-1 If PLITS had not provided the primitives **self destruct** and **extant**, how could a programmer achieve the same effect?

15-2 How many elements can fit into the bounded buffer before it is full?

15-3 The program for the readers-writers problem assumed that no more than a constant number (numqueue) of reader or writer requests would ever be pending. Modify that program to remove this restriction. (Hint: Use transaction keys.)

15-4 Similarly, the readers-writers program used two internal, finite queues. Modify that program to use the message queue instead.

15-5 Generalize the eight queens problem to the n-queens problem over an $n \times n$ chessboard.

15-6 The sorcerer's apprentice: The eight queens program generates all solutions to the problem. Modify the program to stop (reasonably soon) after the first solution has been found. (*Muchnick*)

REFERENCES

[**Feldman 79**] Feldman, J. A., "High Level Programming for Distributed Computing," *CACM*, vol. 22, no. 6 (June 1979), pp. 353–368. This paper describes PLITS. It also discusses implementation issues for PLITS-like systems and several pragmatic issues (such as typing, assertions, and verification) not specific to PLITS, but of concern to the general problem of programming.

[**Wirth 76**] Wirth, N., *Algorithms + Data Structures = Programs*, Prentice-Hall, Englewood Cliffs, New Jersey (1976). This book is a good introduction to programming style and data structures. On pages 143–147, Wirth presents an excellent description of the eight queens problem and a Pascal program that solves it.

SIXTEEN

SYNCHRONIZING RESOURCES AND CELL

This chapter describes Synchronizing Resources (SR) and Cell. These two systems use mechanisms similar to remote procedure calls of Distributed Processes and Ada. They extend these concepts by providing new mechanisms for scheduling communications.

Two of the important dimensions of interprocess communication are the size of the communication channel and the synchronization required of communicators. To communicating processes, the interprocess communication channels appear to be either of bounded size (*buffered communication*) or of unbounded size (*unbuffered communication*). Communication either requires the simultaneous attention of all communicators (*synchronous communication*) or allows the sending and receiving of messages to be temporally disjoint (*asynchronous, send-and-forget messages*). All explicit process systems choose some point in this two-by-two space. Buffered, asynchronous communication is shared storage—for example, Shared Variables. In Shared Variables, the size of the variable is the size of the communication channel. Processes freely read and write the variable, independent of the status of other processes. Message-based systems use unbuffered, asynchronous communication. Examples of such systems include PLITS and Actors. Procedure-call systems, such as Distributed Processes and CSP, use buffered, synchronous communication. In synchronous communication, both processes must attend to the communication; a process never sends a second message until after the first has been received.*

The language Synchronizing Resources synthesizes these three possibilities. SR supports both synchronous and asynchronous communication. Additionally, the structure of SR programs allows sharing storage between certain processes. In some sense, SR merges a multiprocessing system into a distributed environment.

SR is a language designed for operating systems implementation. One important problem of systems development is scheduling. To simplify scheduling, SR has a priority mechanism built into its communication primitives.

SR is the work of Gregory Andrews at the University of Arizona.† He has implemented SR on UNIX-based PDP-11 systems.

Synchronizing Resources extends the ability of a called process to schedule its interactions by priorities. Cell, a system proposed by Abraham Silberschatz of The University of Texas, combines SR's priority mechanisms with powerful internal queueing structures to provide the programmer with even greater control of the scheduling of process activities.

16-1 SYNCHRONIZING RESOURCES

Synchronizing Resources distinguishes between processes and resources. A *process* in SR corresponds to our familiar notion of process—program and storage, capable of executing concurrently with other processes. A *resource* is a collection of processes that can share storage, their shared storage, and an initialization program for the shared storage. Each process is in exactly one resource; each resource has at least one process.

Processes communicate either through the common storage of a resource or by requests to named entries in other processes. These requests can be either synchronous requests (calls) or asynchronous requests (sends). Entries are declared in the **define** command. This declaration can restrict an entry to receive only synchronous communications (**call**) or asynchronous communications (**send**). We illustrate the structure of an SR program with the skeleton of a program for a

---

* No one designs a model based on unbuffered, synchronous communication. Unbuffered systems are helpful in that they hold unprocessed messages. Synchronization implies that, from the point of view of the sender, each message dispatch is accompanied by an immediate reception. In an unbuffered, synchronous system there are no unprocessed messages to take advantage of the unbounded size of the communication channel.

† This section is based on the preliminary SR design described in "Synchronizing Resources" [Andrews 81a]. SR has since been modified and extended, principally by the addition of an import/export mechanism, named processes, and minor syntactic improvements. These changes are described in Andrews's 1982 article on the mechanisms, design, and implementation of SR [Andrews 82].

bounded buffer.* Entry names declared in a **define** command are visible outside the resource. In resource stack, the entry pop is called stack.pop.†

```
type item = ... ;              -- declaration of the items stored by the buffer
resource producer_resource;    -- the producer and consumer resources
    process producer;
            ⋮

resource consumer_resource;
    process consumer;
            ⋮

resource buffer;
    define
        insert,                -- entry name for producers
        remove {call};         -- entry name for consumers. This entry
                                  receives only synchronous calls.

        const bufsize = 20;    -- a buffer of size 20
        var
            first, last : integer;
            queue    : array [0..bufsize − 1] of item;
    -- initialization statements
    process intake;
    -- program for process intake
            ... in (m: item) ...
            ⋮

    end intake

    process outplace;
    -- program for process outplace
            ... in (var m: item) ...
            ⋮

    end outplace
end buffer
```

As we mentioned above, requests can be either synchronous or asynchronous. One invokes a synchronous request with the command **call** and an asynchronous

---

* In those cases where the description of SR [Andrews 81a] omits the details of the declarative structure of the language, we have improvised, using a Pascal-like syntax.

† An entry that is the only entry in the program with a given name can be referenced without mentioning its resource. For example, if there are no other push entries in the program, the entry can simply be called push.

request with **send**. **Call** blocks the calling process until its call is handled. Since the calling and called processes are synchronized, a call request allows the called process to reply to the caller. **Send** transmits the request to the entry and allows the sending process to continue. Each takes the syntactic form of a procedure call. Particular entries may be restricted to receiving only **call** or **send** requests. The example above has the remove entry restricted to calls.

A program accepts requests with an **in** command. This command takes a sequence of guarded clauses (Section 2-2). The guards of the **in** command can reference the parameters of the request and sort calls by priority. An **in** command has the form

> **in** <operation_command> [] $\cdots$ [] <operation_command> **ni**

where an <operation_command> is

> <entry_name> <formal_parameter list>
> **and** <boolean_expression>
> **by** <arithmetic_expression> $\rightarrow$
> <statement_list>.

The **in** command is a guarded input command. The boolean expression is the guard. The use of a guard (**and** <boolean_expression>) and a priority (**by** <arithmetic_expression>) are optional. This use of **and** as a keyword is something of a pun. This **and** joins the entry name and the guard. The guard is a boolean expression and can contain **and**s of its own, whose meaning is logical conjunction. The <arithmetic_expression> is an integer expression; SR does not support a primitive floating type.

The operation command does not accept a message from a clause with a false guard. If there are several messages on an entry, then these messages are ordered by their priority—their value under the **by** expression. The smallest value has the highest priority. In our other systems with guarded input commands (such as Distributed Processes, CSP, and Ada) the guards refer to the internal state of the receiving process. For example, the input entry of a buffer has a false guard when the buffer is full. In SR, the guard and priority expressions can examine the parameters of the request. For example, an empty **taxicab** process that wants to respond to the closest (Cartesian-closest) calling customer has the **in** statement

in customer (cust_x, cust_y: integer) **and** cab_free
    by (cab_x $-$ cust_x) $*$ (cab_x $-$ cust_x) $+$
    (cab_y $-$ cust_y) $*$ (cab_y $-$ cust_y) $\rightarrow$
  -- *code for responding to customer call*

where cab_x, cab_y, cust_x and cust_y are the Cartesian coordinates of the cab and the requesting customer, respectively.

SR has four sequential programming constructs: (1) a null statement **skip**; (2) assignment; (3) a guarded alternative statement of the form **if** <guarded_command> [] ⋯ [] <guarded_command> **fi**; and (4) a guarded repetitive command of the form **do** <guarded_command> [] <guarded_command> [] ... **od**. Guarded commands are syntactically identical to Dijkstra's original guarded commands: <boolean_expression> → <statement_list>. The alternative command executes the statement list of one of its clauses with a true guard. If the guards of an alternative command are all false, the process terminates abnormally. The repetitive command repeatedly executes the statement list of a clause with a true guard until all guards are false. It then terminates. SR does not have procedures or functions—processes, though not recursive, are meant to serve instead of procedures. The program for the bounded buffer resource is as follows:

```
resource buffer;
    define
        insert,
        remove {call};
    const bufsize = 20;
    var
        first   : integer;
        last    : integer;
        queue : array [0..bufsize − 1] of item;
    first  := 0;                        -- initialization statements
    last   := 0;


    process intake;
        do true →
            in insert (m: item)
                and not (((last + 1) mod bufsize) = first) →
                    last         := (last + 1) mod bufsize;
                    queue[last]  := m
            ni
        od
    end intake


    process outplace;
        do true →
            in remove (var m: item)      -- Entry call parameters can be either
                                         input parameters (no keyword) or
                                         input-output parameters (keyword
                                         var).
                and last ≠ first →
                    first  := (first + 1) mod bufsize
```

```
                        m  : = queue[first]:
              ni
        od
     end outplace
end buffer
```

This program does not treat requests as permutations of producer and consumer calls. Instead, a process is devoted to producers and another to consumers. Both processes run concurrently when there are both empty slots and available messages. These processes communicate through their shared storage. Processes intake and outplace interact in only one place — each tests in its input guard whether the other has gotten too far behind, leaving it with a full (or empty) buffer. We do not synchronize the shared-variable updates because every shared variable is set by only one process (and read by the other). We repeat the theme of single-writer variables in other examples.

Scheduling Requests An SR process has some control over the order in which it handles requests. The guards on input commands can reference not only the internal state of the process, but also the values of the parameters of the message. The priority mechanism can sort messages by "importance." The major limitation of the guard and priority mechanisms is the absence of functions. The guard and priority expressions must therefore be simple and loop-free. An important consequence of this simplicity is that their evaluation must terminate.

In addition to being able to sort requests by priority, a process can access the size of its request queue. The expression ?entryname is the number of requests waiting on entry entryname.

Readers-writers Our next example is a program for the fair control of a readers-writers resource. This program uses both memory sharing within a resource and priority examination in guarded commands to ensure fairness. The readers-writers problem requires a manager that gives access to a resource to two different classes of users—readers and writers. Many readers can simultaneously access the resource, but writers must have exclusive control. Of course, a solution to the readers-writers problem is better if it precludes starving readers or writers. This solution not only allows all readers and writers to progress, but also serves readers and writers fairly—waiting writers keep all newly arrived readers from commencing reading; writers are served in the order that they request the resource.

This fair discipline echoes the linearity of timing and clocks. We ensure a fair queue with a form of clock. The manager resource has two processes, a time_stamp process and a guardian process.* Processes that want the resource call process time_stamp and get a numbered "ticket." One can think of this

---

* We discuss timestamps and their applications in distributed databases in Section 17-1.

ticket as being stamped with the time of the request. After obtaining a ticket, the potential reader or writer calls process **guardian** to wait for service. Guardian serves callers (roughly) in the order of their ticket numbers, except that the start of a reading cycle entitles all readers with tickets before the current time to read.

```
resource manager;
type request = (wanttoread, wanttowrite);
define
     stamp {call};              -- entry for ticket stamping
     enter  {call};             -- entry for the resource
     exit   {send};             -- When a process is through with the resource, it
                                   sends a message on the "exit" entry.
var
     num_waiting_readers, num_waiting_writers: integer;
                                -- the number of readers and writers waiting to
                                   access the resource
     clock: integer             -- the guardian's timestamp counter


num_waiting_readers := 0;     -- initialization of common storage
num_waiting_writers := 0;
clock               := 0;

process time_stamp;
     do true →
         in stamp (req: request; var ticket: integer) →
             if
                 req = wanttoread →
                     num_waiting_readers := num_waiting_readers + 1
             []
                 req = wanttowrite →
                     num_waiting_writers := num_waiting_writers + 1;
             fi
             clock  := clock + 1;
             ticket := clock;
         ni
     od
end process

process guardian
     var
         num_readers        : integer;   -- the number of readers and writers
         num_writers        : integer;      currently using the resource
         num_readers_done   : integer;   -- the number of readers and writers
         num_writers_done   : integer;      finished with the resource
```

```
last_user           : request;
switch_time         : integer      -- timestamp of the last transition
                                      between readers and writers


num_readers      := 0;
num_writers      := 0;
num_readers_done := 0;
num_writers_done := 0;
switch_time      := 0;
last_user        := wanttoread ;          -- an arbitrary choice
do true →
    in enter (req: request; ticket: integer)
        and
            (num_writers = 0) and          -- conditions under which
                                              a reader can read—no
                                              writer writing and no
                                              writer waiting too long
            ((req = wanttoread) and
                (last_user = wanttowrite) or
                (ticket ≤ switch_time)))
        or
            ((req = wanttowrite) and       -- conditions under which
                                              a writer can write—no
                                              reader reading and no
                                              reader waiting too long
            (num_readers = 0) and
                ((num_waiting_readers − num_readers_done = 0) or
                (last_user = wanttoread)))
        by ticket →
            if
                not (last_user = req) →
                    last_user     := req;
                    switch_time := clock
            []
                last_user = req → skip
            fi;
            if
                req = wanttoread →
                    num_readers := num_readers + 1
            []
                req = wanttowrite →
                    num_writers := num_writers + 1
            fi
    []
```

```
            exit (req: request) →
                if
                    req = wanttoread →
                        num_readers          : = num_readers − 1;
                        num_done_readers  : = num_done_readers + 1;
                []
                    req = wanttowrite →
                        num_writers          : = num_writers − 1;
                        num_done_writers  : = num_done_writers + 1;
                fi
        ni
    od
end guardian
end manager
```

Shared variables num_waiting_readers, num_waiting_writers, and clock do not require mutual exclusion because they are set only by process time_stamp. This process serves as a "secretary" for process guardian, filtering and ordering requests before they reach the "executive's" desk. (Of course, the timestamp counter overflows if the manager is used too long.)

To obtain read access to the resource, a process executes

```
call manager.stamp (wanttoread, my_ticket);
call manager.enter (wanttoread, my_ticket);
    -- access the resource
send manager.exit (wanttoread);
```

Variable my_ticket is of type integer. The protocol for a writer is identical except that it requests wanttowrite.

Initialization, Fairness, and Termination An SR program starts by executing the initialization statement of each resource. Each process begins computing after initialization. SR enforces a weak form of fairness on process scheduling: if a process does not block in a **call** or **in** statement then it eventually gets to execute.

A program terminates when all its constituent processes terminate or are blocked. A process reaching the end of its program terminates *normally*; abnormal termination results when all the guards of an alternative command are false.

Traffic lights A *family* of resources is a set of resources that share the same code. An SR program declares a family of resources by providing a subscripted range declaration for the resource. Similarly, a family of processes can be declared inside a resource. For example, the SR program skeleton

```
type intersection = 1 .. maxlight;
resource light [ intersection ];
    type direction = (north, south, east, west) ;
        ⋮

    process arrival_sensor [direction];
        ⋮
```

declares maxlight resources of type light, each with four processes of type arrival_sensor. Within each resource, myresource is the resource index; within each process, myprocess is the process index.

Our final example SR program is a traffic light control system. The city pictured in Figure 16-1 is installing a distributed system to control the traffic lights at each of the numbered intersections. Each intersection has a traffic light and eight road-sensors. Figure 16-2 shows an intersection. The traffic light has two sets of lights, east-west lights and north-south lights. Each set of lights can be red, yellow, or green. Sensors are embedded in the roadway. They detect and signal the passing of vehicles. The two kinds of sensors, arrival sensors and departure sensors, respectively register cars arriving at and departing from the intersection. For the sake of simplicity, we assume that the roads are all two lanes (one lane in each direction) and that a vehicle reaching an intersection can turn in any direction. The traffic flow is such that a car exiting over a departure sensor is likely (but not certain) to continue to the next controlled intersection in that direction.

When the intersection is busy, we want the traffic lights to cycle in the obvious fashion, letting traffic through first in one direction, then the other. Optimally, when the intersection is not busy the light should go to red-red. This

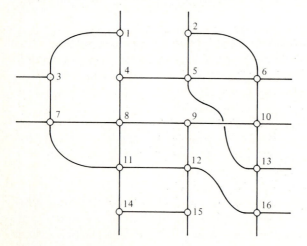

Figure 16-1 City lights.

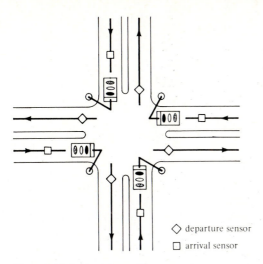

◇ departure sensor

☐ arrival sensor

Figure 16-2 An intersection.

allows the light to turn green immediately for the next car, without requiring a yellow delay. To improve traffic flow at quiet times we send a message from the departure sensors to the next controller. This message informs the controller that there is probably a car coming. If the controller is in a red-red state, it turns the signal green for that car, allowing it to proceed without stopping. If the controller is busy handling real traffic, it ignores the message.

Our traffic light resource consists of ten processes. It has four arrival_sensors, four departure_sensors, a controller, and a secretary. Arrival_sensors detect the arrival of a car at the intersection. Each approach to the intersection has an arrival_sensor. Departure_sensors register the direction of car departure. Each exit of the intersection has a departure_sensor. Process controller coordinates the traffic information and turns the lights on and off, and process secretary receives messages from other intersections about approaching cars. Sensors recognize passing cars as calls over the a_sense and d_sense entries; secretaries receive messages over the approaching entry. The skeleton of our program is as follows:

```
type intersection = 1 .. maxlight;
resource light [ intersection ];
    type
        direction      = (north, south, east, west);
        light_direction = (ns, ew);
    -- shared storage declarations and initializations
    define
        a_sense, d_sense [direction] {call},
        approaching {send};
```

```
    process controller;
            ⋮
    process secretary;
            ⋮
    process arrival_sensor [direction];
            ⋮
    process departure_sensor [direction];
            ⋮
```

Processes controller, secretary, and arrival_sensors communicate by sharing storage. The sensors write variables ns_arriving and ew_arriving when a car arrives from one of those directions; the secretary writes variables ns_coming and ew_coming when it receives messages about approaching cars. Array goingto stores the intersection to which each departure_sensor leads.

```
type goingrec =
    record
        inter : intersection;
        ldir  : light_direction
    end;

var     -- common storage declarations and initializations
    ns_arriving, ew_arriving : boolean;
    ns_coming, ew_coming  : boolean;
    goingto                : array [direction] of goingrec;

ns_arriving  := false;
ew_arriving  := false;
ns_coming    := false;
ew_coming    := false;
    -- initialization of the "goingto" array
```

An arrival_sensor reads its next call from its entry and marks the corresponding arriving variable. The entries in this example are not subscripted because each entry is implemented by exactly one process.

```
process arrival_sensor [direction];
    do true →
        in a_sense →
            if
                (myprocess = east) or (myprocess = west) →
                    ew_arriving := true
            ▯
```

```
            (myprocess = north) or (myprocess = south) →
                ns_arriving := true
        fi
    ni
  od
end arrival_sensor;
```

Departure sensors accept interrupts from the sensor device and send messages to the neighboring intersections.

```
process departure_sensor [direction];
    do true →
        in d_sense →
            send light[goingto[myprocess].inter].approaching
                (goingto[myprocess].ldir)
        ni
    od
end departure_sensor;
```

When the secretary receives a message from another intersection it marks the appropriate coming variable.

```
process secretary;
    do true →
        in approaching (dir: direction) →
            if
                (dir = east) or (dir = west) →
                    ew_coming := true
            ▯
                (dir = north) or (dir = south) →
                    ns_coming := true
            fi
        ni
    od
end secretary;
```

The program gives priority to cars that have arrived at a sensor. It allows no more than **carmax** cars through in a particular direction if cars are waiting in the other direction. If there are no "arrived" cars, the light turns for "coming" cars. The light turns yellow for **yellow_time** seconds and the system allows **car_delay** seconds for each car to pass over the arrival sensors. We hypothesize two procedures, **delay** and **signal**. Delay(n) suspends a calling process for n seconds; **signal**(direction.color) turns the lights for the given direction to the given color.

```
process controller;
    const
        carmax      = 20;
        yellow_time = 15;
        car_delay   = 5;
    type
        color = (green, yellow, red);
    var
        ew_green, ns_green : boolean;
        carcount             : integer;

    ew_green := false;
    ns_green := false;
    signal (ew, red);
    signal (ns, red);
    carcount := carmax;

    do
        ew_green →
            if
                (ew_arriving and
                    ((carcount > 0) or not ns_arriving)) or
                (not ew_arriving and not ns_arriving
                    and ew_coming and not ns_coming) →
                        ew_arriving := false;
                        ew_coming  := false;
                        carcount    := carcount − 1;
                        delay (car_delay)
            □
                (ns_arriving and
                    ((carcount ≤ 0) or not ew_arriving)) or
                (not ew_arriving and not ns_arriving
                    and ns_coming and not ew_coming) →
                        signal (ew, yellow);
                        delay (yellow_time);
                        signal (ew, red);
                        ew_green   := false;
                        signal (ns, green);
                        ns_green   := true;
                        carcount    := carmax;
                        ns_coming := false;
                        delay (car_delay)
            □
```

Table 16-1 Green east-west successor states

carcount >0	ew_com.	ns_com.	ew_arr. ∧ns_arr.	ew_arr. ∧¬ns_arr.	¬ew_arr. ∧ns_arr.	¬ew_arr. ∧¬ns_arr.
true	true	true	−c	−c	NS	red-red
true	true	false	−c	−c	NS	−c
true	false	true	−c	−c	NS	NS
true	false	false	−c	−c	NS	red-red
false	true	true	NS	−c	NS	red-red
false	true	false	NS	−c	NS	−c
false	false	true	NS	−c	NS	NS
false	false	false	NS	−c	NS	red-red

Key: −c Decrement carcount and leave east-west green.
NS Turn east-west red and north-south green.
red-red Turn both lights red.

```
                not ew_arriving and not ns_arriving and
                    (ew_coming = ns_coming) →
                        signal (ew, yellow);
                        delay (yellow_time);
                        signal (ew, red);
                        ew_green    := false;
                        carcount    := carmax;
                        ew_coming := false;
                        ns_coming := false;
            fi
    □
        ns_green →    -- a similar program for ns_green
                    ⋮
    □
        not ew_green and not ns_green →
            if
                ew_arriving or (not ns_arriving and ew_coming) →
                    signal (ew,green);
                    ew_green    := true;
                    ew_arriving := false;
                    ew_coming := false;
                    carcount    := carmax;
                    delay (car_delay)
```

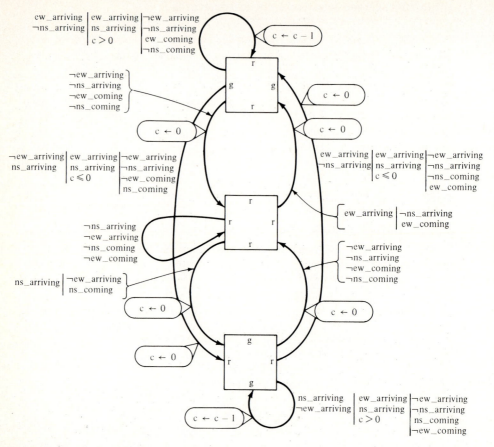

Figure 16-3 The traffic light state machine.

```
        []
                ns_arriving or (not ew_arriving and ns_coming) →
                    ⋮
-- similarly for north-south
        []
                not ew_arriving and not ns_arriving
                    and not ew_coming and not ns_coming →
                        skip
            fi
        od
end controller
end light
```

The convoluted logic used above is really a selection of a point in a state space. This selection is based on the current settings of the arriving, coming, and carcount variables. Figure 16-3 shows the program's three-state automaton [augmented by the register carcount (c)]. Each arc of this automaton is a disjunction of conjunctions of the arriving and coming variables, and the value of carcount. Table 16-1 summarizes the successor-state relationship for a green light shining in the east-west direction. The boolean expressions in the alternative commands of the program are minimizations on this table. This control structure can also be achieved using table-lookup techniques or by assigning numeric values to the arriving and coming variables and computing relative priorities.

16-2   CELL

Cell is a model-language hybrid; a proposal to extend other languages with a few additional constructs for multiple-process communication and control. Cell's theme is the effective and efficient synchronization of processes. To support synchronization, Cell provides processes that are proper objects and several priority mechanisms for scheduling process requests.

A Cell program is a finite (but not fixed) set of concurrent processes. The processes are called, not surprisingly, cells. A *cell* is a structured data type; the programmer describes the cell class and can create specific instances of that class. Thus, the declaration*

```
type register = cell (initial: in integer);
var reg: integer;
begin
    reg := initial;
    while true do
        select
            accept set (setval: in integer) do
                reg := setval;
            end;
        or
            accept get (getval: out integer) do
                getval := reg;
            end;
        end;
end.
```

declares a class of objects called registers. A register responds to two different kinds of requests, set and get. Set stores a value in the register; get retrieves the

---

* Following Silberschatz [Silberschatz 80], we use a form of extended Pascal/Ada for our Cell programs.

last value stored. This declaration does not create any **registers**. A program or a cell that declares

var memory: **array** [1 .. 100] **of** register;

would have (potentially) 100 cells of type **register**, each named by an element of array **memory**. This declaration still does not allocate storage. Instead, when the program executes the statement

init memory[5](7);

a new process (cell) is created, the value of initial in that process is set to 7, that process is set running, and the fifth element of array **memory** is set to that new process. **Init** is a forking statement; the creating cell continues processing after executing **init**.

Cell processes are objects. Both **init** and (recursive) lexical elaboration can create new cells. Cell names are of a data type called **identity**; variables can range over this data type. Any syntactic expression that uses the name of a cell can use a variable of this type. The initial parameter of the register is an example of a cell's *permanent parameters.* Cells can have both **in** and **out** permanent parameters. **In** parameters are passed to the cell at its creation. The cell returns **out** parameters when it terminates.

A simple example of using cell names as values and input and output parameters is an accountant cell. A certain operating system charges jobs for printing by the line and plotting by the vector. These charges vary by the time of day and class of user; for any job these charges are the charges in effect when the job starts. When a job is created it is given the name of an accountant cell. The job routes all its printing and plotting requests through this cell. When the job informs the accountant cell that it is done, the accountant cell returns the total charges to the operating system.

```
type accountant = cell
    (print        : in printer_cell;
    print_cost    : in integer;
    plot          : in plot_cell;
    plot_cost     : in integer;
    total_charges : out integer);
var done: boolean;    -- Done is set when the job is through.
begin
    total_charges := 0;
    done          := false;
    repeat
        select
            accept please_print (ln: in line) do
```

```
            print.act (ln);
            total_charges := total_charges + print_cost;
        end;
    or
        accept please_plot (vec: in vector) do
            plot.act (vec);
            total_charges := total_charges + plot_cost;
        end;
    or
        accept finished do
            done := true;
        end;
        end;
    until done;
end.
```

The operating system, having the declarations

```
type
    prt  = cell ... ;    -- printer cell description
    plt  = cell ... ;    -- plotter cell description
    acct = cell ... ;    -- accountant cell description, above
var
    printer                     : prt;
    plotter                     : plt;
    accountant                  : acct;
    print_price, plot_price     : integer;
    charges                     : integer;
```

could execute the statements

```
init printer ... ;
init plotter ... ;
print_price := ... ;
plot_price  := ... ;
init accountant (printer, print_price, plotter, plot_price, charges);
```

to create an accountant cell. It would pass the name of this cell to the job that needs to print and plot. When the accountant cell terminates (after receiving a finish call from its client) it sets charges to the total charges due.

Scheduling The most significant features of Cell are those that order process scheduling. As should be clear from the preceding examples, Cell bases its communication mechanism on Ada's select and accept statements. Processes direct requests at the entries of other cells. Cell extends the scheduling mechanisms of Ada in four ways: (1) **accept** statements can restrict requests to be from only a specific cell, (2) a queueing mechanism allows cells to delay calls after they have been accepted, (3) the program can specify a partial order on selection from entry and waiting queues, and (4) like SR, requests waiting in delay queues can be ordered by priority. Cell specifies that there is no shared storage between processes and that parameter passing is by value/result. Other than these changes, Cell is a strict generalization of Ada.

The first extension, the **from** clause, makes communication between calling and called cells more symmetric. An accept clause of the form

> **accept** <entryname> (<parameters>) **from** <cellname> **do** ...

accepts calls from only the named cell. This is useful for server-user dialogues— cells that serve several other cells, but whose communication requires a conversation, not just a single request/response exchange. For example, a printer cell would first accept input from any cell and then restrict its input to be from that cell only. This restriction would continue until the end of the printing job. Since the identity of the calling cell is important information to the called cell, the system provides the primitive function **caller**, which (in the scope of an **accept** statement) yields the name of the calling cell.

The second extension introduces the **await** primitive. An **await** statement has the form **await** <boolean-expression>. **Await** statements occur only in the bodies of **accept** statements that are within **select** statements. If a cell executing the body of an **accept** statement reaches an **await** statement, it evaluates the boolean-expression. If the expression is true, it continues processing. If it is false the rendezvous is delayed. The system creates an *activation record* (closure) describing the point of program execution, the request's parameters, and the local variables of the accept clause. It adds this record to a set associated with the **await** statement. (Unlike the accept queue, the **await** set is not ordered.) The cell then executes the program after the **select** statement. The calling process remains blocked. Silberschatz credits the idea for a construct similar to **await** to Kessels [Kessels 77].

What unblocks the calling process? The **select** statement treats requests waiting at **await** statements within its scope as if they were **accept** clauses. If **select** chooses an **await** statement then its processing continues after the **await** statement. Just as **accept** clauses can have boolean guards, the guard of the **await** statement is its original boolean expression. Since this guard can refer to the local parameters of the **accept** statement, the system must potentially evaluate each element of the **await** set in search of one whose local parameters make the guard true. (Silberschatz hypothesizes that in practice, few **await** guards would mention local parameters, and that most of these would be used only for priority scheduling.) If we think of the **select** statement as also accepting clauses from **await** sets, then the program

```
select
    L1: accept queue₁ (<queue₁_parameters>) do
            <statements₁,₁>
        M1: await (<boolean_expression₁>);
            <statements₁,₂>
or
    L2: accept queue₂ (<queue₂_parameters>) do
            <statements₂,₁>
        M2: await (<boolean_expression₂>);
            <statements₂,₂>
end;
```

is equivalent, from the point of view of a call blocked in an **await** statement, to the program

```
select
    L1: accept queue₁ (<queue₁_parameters>) do
            <statements₁,₁> ...
or
    L2: accept queue₂ (<queue₂_parameters>) do
            <statements₂,₁> ...
or
    M1: when <boolean_expression₁> -> await M1_accept do
            <statements₁,₂>
or
    M2: when <boolean_expression₂> -> await M2_accept do
            <statements₂,₂>
end;
```

That is, the **await** statement tries to "continue where it left off."

We use the Exchange Functions model (Chapter 7) to illustrate the **await** statement. Briefly, Exchange Functions supports synchronous and immediate bidirectional communication. Communication is directed over channels. Exchange Functions has three communication operations, X, XM, and XR. A call to X on a channel communicates with any other call to that channel. Calls to XM do not communicate with other calls to XM. Calls to XR communicate only if another communication is waiting. If no other communication is ready for an XR, the input value is returned to the task that calls the XR. The channel's task is to pair possible communicators. We assume that this channel passes values of type item. A cell that does channel pairing is as follows:

```
type channel = cell;    -- no input or output parameters
var
    Xwaiting     : boolean;    -- Is an X call waiting?
```

```
    XMwaiting    : boolean;    -- Is an XM call waiting?
    AnswerReady  : boolean;    -- Is it time to wake a waiting call?
    ansval       : item;

begin
    AnswerReady := false;
    Xwaiting    := false;
    XMwaiting   := false;

    while true do
        select
            when not AnswerReady →
                accept X (inval: in item; outval: out item) do
                    if Xwaiting or XMwaiting then
                        begin
                            outval       := ansval;
                            ansval       := inval;
                            AnswerReady  := true;
                        end;
                    else
                        begin
                            Xwaiting     := true;
                            await (AnswerReady);
                            outval       := ansval;
                            AnswerReady  := false;
                            Xwaiting     := false;
                        end;
                end; -- accept X

        or   -- Never match an XM with an XM.
            when not AnswerReady and not XMwaiting →
                accept XM (inval: in item; outval: out item) do
                    if Xwaiting then
                        begin
                            outval       := ansval;
                            ansval       := inval;
                            AnswerReady  := true;
                        end;
                    else
                        begin
                            XMwaiting    := true;
                            await (AnswerReady);
                            outval       := ansval;
                            AnswerReady  := false;
```

```
                        XMwaiting    : = false;
                    end;
             end; -- accept XM

      or
         when not AnswerReady →
             accept XR (inval: in item; outval: out item) do
                 if Xwaiting or XMwaiting then
                     begin
                         outval       : = ansval;
                         ansval        : = inval;
                         AnswerReady  : = true;
                     end;
                 else
                     outval : = inval
             end; -- accept XR
      end; -- select
end. -- channel
```

Since XR (real-time exchange) is a "real-time" operation, we might want the XR calls to have higher priority than the X and XM calls. Cell provides a mechanism for such priorities: One can label **accept** clauses and **await** statements and specify a partial order on these clauses. When a **select** statement has several such choices, it chooses one of the lowest in the partial order. Syntactically, the **order** statement specifies a partial order on the **accept** and **await** statements. Thus, the program

```
order (L1 < L2; L1 < L3; L2 < L4; L3 < L4);
select
     L1: accept ...;
or
     L2: accept ...
         L3: await ...;
         L4: await ...;
end; -- select
```

specifies that **accept** clause L1 is to be taken in preference to all others, that **await** statement L4 is to be given the lowest priority, and that the system is to choose arbitrarily between **accept** clause L2 and **await** statement L3.

The fourth extension to the conventional select semantics provides that a **by** clause in the **await** statement controls the service order of the elements in the **await** sets. The program

```
var p, q: boolean;
     ⋮
```

```
select
   accept
        this_entry (x, y: in integer ... );
            ⋮
        await (p and q) by (3*x + 4*y);
            ⋮
```

orders the elements in the **await** set by the lowest value of **3*x+4*y**. This use of numeric priorities parallels SR. In SR, priorities are associated with the **accept** clauses; in Cell they are associated with the **await** set.

Termination and calls Cells are created by the declaration and initiation of cell variables. Hence, Cell supports dynamic process creation. A cell *terminates* when (1) it reaches the end of its program, and (2) all the cells it created (its children) have terminated. Cells cannot force the termination of their children. When a cell with **out** parameters terminates, the values of its **out** parameters are returned to its parent.

It is often useful to treat dependent cells not as concurrent processes but as procedures. A cell that executes

call <cell-identifier> (<actual parameters>)

both initiates the cell <cell-identifier> and waits for its termination.

Perspective

SR and Cell are both proposals that extend Ada's synchronization mechanisms. These extensions significantly reduce the difficulty of programming many common resource control problems. Nevertheless, each system has several important deficiencies.

SR's approach to distributed computing has three distinguishing features: (1) SR mixes shared storage and request-based communication, (2) SR has both synchronous and asynchronous requests, and (3) SR uses numeric priorities for scheduling. Each of these ideas is a positive contribution to controlling distribution. Our quarrel is with the failure to carry these ideas to their logical conclusion. What is missing from SR is a recursive Gestalt. Processes are to replace procedures, but processes cannot communicate with themselves. And the fixed, two-level hierarchy of resources and processes is a structure that cannot be embedded in other program segments. We present a few examples to illustrate these limitations.

Memory sharing SR processes can share storage with processes within their own resource. No other storage sharing is allowed. This structure mimics a physical system of shared-memory multiprocessors communicating over distributed connections. Figure 16-4 shows one such architecture. However, we can imagine alternative architectures. One simple example of such a system is a ring of processors separated by two-port memories (Figure 16-5). In this architecture, memory sharing cannot be described simply in terms of sharing processes within resources. Each processor shares memory with two other processors, but these processors do not share memory with each other.

SR neglects other opportunities for sharing. For example, processes in a resource can share memory but cannot share entries. Shared entries would eliminate the need for many programmer-created buffers. If there are several printers, then processes could send their printing requests to the printing resource instead of to particular printers. Each printer could get the next request by pulling an item from this entry. Thus, shared entry queues would, without any additional mechanism, turn every resource into a producer-consumer buffer.

Process names SR recognizes that providing both synchronous and asynchronous communication facilitates programming. However, useful asynchronous message-based communication requires that processes have names that can be included in messages. The original SR definition [Andrews 81a] omitted such names. The full implementation of SR [Andrews 82] rectifies this deficiency and treats process names as a distinct data type.

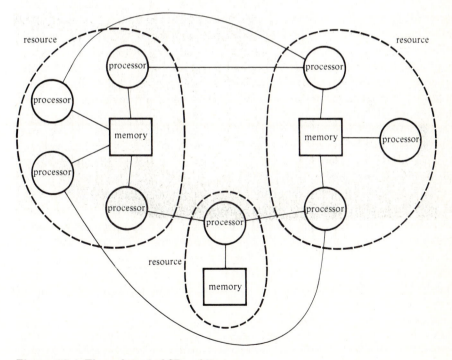

Figure 16-4 The archetypical SR architecture.

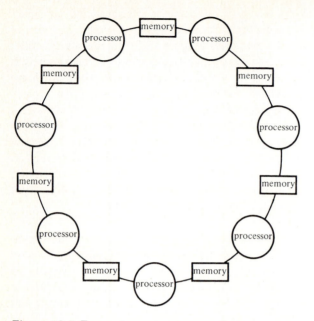

Figure 16-5 Two port memory processor ring.

Scheduling SR allows process guards and synchronization expressions to examine incoming messages. However, it requires scheduling constraints to be described solely by priorities (and messages deferred by guards). SR assumes that scheduling algorithms can be expressed by a single number. One can imagine stronger mechanisms that would allow comparison of pending messages. SR uses numeric priorities because they are easy to compute and provide a quick determination of the next message.* Of course, some problems do not require such a priority mechanism and can simply omit priority clauses. Other programs are clearly simplified by its existence. But numeric priorities are not the ultimate in scheduling description. Presumably, some problems can profitably use mechanisms beyond numbers.

Additionally, SR neglects including key communication information in its priority mechanism. SR requests are anonymous. The receiver of a call does not know its originator. And though SR provides both synchronous and asynchronous calling mechanisms, an SR process cannot determine how it was called. These attributes are fertile material for priority mechanisms. A process might want to provide better service to a certain class of users or to respond more quickly to requests when the caller is waiting (synchronous requests). An SR

---

* Numeric priorities allow determination of the next message by a simple linear search of the message queue. This search requires storing only the lowest priority value (and a pointer to the message with that value). Partial-order mechanisms require more search and more structure.

program is forced to encode these concepts in the message where they are subject to error and abuse.

Cell Cell contributes three key ideas: explicit process objects, delay queues in **accept** statements, and partial ordering of choices. Cell has borrowed the foundation for each of these ideas and cleverly extended the concepts. However, Cell also fails to carry these ideas to their logical conclusions.

More than most languages in the imperative, systems tradition, Cell recognizes the desirability of processes as objects — structures that can be created, destroyed, named, and used. Cell's implementation of this idea is almost complete. The major omission is the dynamic creation of cells outside the recursive process—the equivalent of the **new** function in Pascal. What is novel and interesting is the passing of output parameters on cell termination.

Process initialization parameters (or their equivalent) are a familiar concept. In addition to initialization, terminating cells return parameters to their callers. Thus, the program

```
type this_cell = cell (y: out integer) ...;
var
    j : integer;
    c : this_cell;
        ⋮
    init c(j)
        ⋮
    j := 5;
    write(j);
        ⋮
```

assigns the value computed by terminating cell c to variable j *sometime after cell c terminates*. This happens asynchronously with respect to the creating process. That is, there is no way of telling when it will happen. Thus, one cannot be sure that the write statement will actually print **5**. In practice, one can avoid such pitfalls by not assigning to output variables. However, designing such traps into the language is a mistake.

The **await** statement integrates the monitor delay queue with the indeterminacy of the Ada **select** statement. Cell wisely recognizes that program state is useful for synchronization and scheduling. We object to Cell's limitation of reviving awaiting requests only at the point of the **await** statement. We propose that an explicit queue of awaiting callers (like the entry queue) that could be accessed at any point in the program would provide a more flexible scheduling structure. (Of course, the various SR and Cell proposals for queue ordering can be retained.) We contrast the Cell program for an Exchange Functions channel that requires continuation (as given above) with the same program that treats await queues as entries. In this program, we name the await queue and explicitly mention its parameters.

```
type channel = cell;    -- no input or output parameters
var
    barXMaccept : boolean;    -- The last accept was an XM.
    barXRaccept : boolean;    -- The last accept was an XR.
    ansval        : item;

begin
    while true do
    begin
        barXMaccept := false;
        barXRaccept := false;
        select
            accept X (inval: in item; outval: out item) do
                ansval := inval;
                await MatchCall (inval, outval);
                    -- Wait in the MatchCall queue.
            end; -- accept X
        or
            accept XM (inval: in item; outval: out item) do
                barXMaccept := true;
                ansval        := inval;
                await MatchCall (inval,outval);
            end; -- accept XM
        or
            accept XR (inval: in item; outval: out item) do
                barXRaccept := true;
                outval        := inval;
            end; -- accept XR
        end; -- select

        if not barXRaccept then
        begin
            select
                accept X (inval: in item; outval: out item) do
                    outval := ansval;
                    ansval := inval;
                end; -- accept X
            or
                when not barXMaccept →
                    accept XM (inval: in item; outval: out item) do
                        outval := ansval;
```

```
                        ansval := inval;
                   end; -- accept XM
          or
                accept XR (inval: in item; outval: out item) do
                   outval := ansval;
                   ansval := inval;
                end; -- accept XR
             end; -- select
             accept MatchCall (inval: in item; outval: out item) do
                -- treating the MatchCall await queue as an entry
                   outval := ansval;
                end;
          end; -- not an XR
      end; -- while loop
end; -- end cell definition
```

This program implements a three-step algorithm: Receive a call. If that call is an XR, return its value. Otherwise receive a matching call, respond to it, and then complete the first call.

The partial-order priority of the select statement is a clever idea. Conditional statements originally had one determinate form: **if** ... **then** ... **else** ... **if** ... **then** ... **else** .... The programmer specified an order for the evaluation of the conditions; the program followed that order. Guarded commands, a later invention, took the opposite approach: the programmer does not specify any order. The partial-order priority of the Cell select statement encompasses both of these approaches and all points between. Cell requires that this partial order be fixed at compilation. Programming, compilers, and computer architecture being what they are, this is perhaps an inevitable decision. Certainly a system that allows the priorities to shift based on program experience would be more flexible. Such dynamic rearrangement allows the programmer to easily specify priorities such as "select the entry queue that is the busiest." We also regret that Cell limits partial-order guards to select statements. They are an interesting programming structure for languages in general.

PROBLEMS

16-1   Does SR need both synchronous and asynchronous communication mechanisms? Argue whether synchronous communication can be modeled by asynchronous communication, and conversely, if asynchronous communication can be modeled by synchronous communication.

16-2   The SR readers-writers program is only weakly fair, even with respect to the values presented on the timestamps. Why is it not strongly fair?

16-3   Reprogram the readers-writers problem to allow a few readers that arrive after a waiting writer to access the resource on the current read cycle. What criteria can be used to decide what "a few" is? Be sure that your solution precludes starvation.

16-4   Rewrite the readers-writers program to dynamically adjust the service levels of readers and writers based on the historic access patterns to the resource.

16-5   Rewrite the reader-writers controller to use another secretary process to receive exit messages, instead of routing these messages to the primary guardian process.

16-6   Arrange the sensors and controller of the traffic light problem to permit all communication to be through shared memory. Your program must keep every controller in a different resource.

16-7   The traffic light program specifically tests a large boolean expression to decide what to do. The text hints that an arithmetic expression of the basis variables can be used instead. Rewrite the traffic light program to control the signals by a priority index for each direction. Make sure your program has the same behavior as the original.

16-8   Modify the traffic light program to allow special routing for emergency vehicles. Design a protocol for communication between intersections and a technique for describing the intended path for a fire engine or ambulance. Arrange for green lights all along the emergency path well before the arrival and during the passage of the emergency vehicle.

16-9   Are output parameters in Cell really necessary or can they be imitated by some more conventional mechanism? How could a program obtain the same effect?

16-10   Using the **from** clause, write the Cell controller for a printer that can be initiated by any process but serves that process only until the initiating process's job is completed.

16-11   Write the Cell program for an elevator-algorithm disk scheduler. This scheduler treats the disk head as an elevator, moving it from the edge to the center and back again, always trying to serve calls in its path. Calls to this scheduler specify the track to be read; the scheduler returns the data on that track. The elevator algorithm seeks to minimize disk head movement when there are many simultaneous calls on the disk.

16-12   Write the SR program for the elevator-algorithm disk scheduler.

16-13   Contrast the Cell and SR disk schedulers.

16-14   Cell (like SR and Ada) has an attribute of each entry that is a count of the number of pending invocations of that entry. Cell does not have a corresponding system-defined count of pending calls on **await** statements. Why not?

16-15   Rewrite the SR time-stamped readers-writers program in Cell. Instead of a separate time_stamp process, delay callers in an **await** statement in a single resource.

16-16   Contrast the **await** statement in Cell with queues in Concurrent Pascal.

REFERENCES

[**Andrews 81a**] Andrews, G. R., "Synchronizing Resources," *ACM Trans. Program. Lang. Syst.*, vol. 3, no. 4 (October 1981), pp. 405–430. This paper describes SR. Besides detailing the language and providing a few sample programs, it includes comments on implementing SR and on proof rules for SR.

[**Andrews 81b**] Andrews, G. R., "SR: A Language for Distributed Programming," Technical Report TR81-14, Computer Science Department, University of Arizona, Tucson, Arizona (October 1981). This is the SR manual.

[**Andrews 82**] Andrews, G. R., "The Distributed Programming Language SR—Mechanisms, Design and Implementation," *Softw. Pract. Exper.*, vol. 12, no. 8 (1982), pp. 719–753. Andrews presents both an overview of the SR language and a discussion of the implementation issues involved in creating an SR system.

[**Kessels 77**] Kessels, J.L.W., "An Alternative to Event Queues for Synchronization in Monitors," *CACM*, vol. 20, no. 7 (July 1977), pp. 500–503. Kessels proposes a **wait** statement for monitors. Silberschatz drew his inspiration for the **await** statement in Cell from this paper.

[**Silberschatz 80**] Silberschatz, A., "Cell: A Distributed Computing Modularization Concept," Technical Report 155, Department of Computer Science, The University of Texas, Austin, Texas (September 1980). (To appear March 1984, *IEEE Trans. Softw. Eng.*). This is a concise description of Cell.

FOUR

HEURISTICS

This part discusses the problems of organizing distributed systems — what we call the heuristics of coordinated computing. In Chapter 17 we explore one of the better-mapped regions of distributed computing, distributed databases. We present several of the standard algorithms for concurrency control and recovery for distributed database systems. We discover that the principal concurrency control mechanism for distributed databases is the atomic transaction. We then examine a language, Argus, that integrates atomic actions with conventional programming technology.

In Chapter 18 we travel over the frontier to a more speculative region. In this chapter we consider proposals for heuristic organizations for coherent problem-solving systems. Unlike programming languages and distributed databases, these proposals are still far from mature implementations. We discuss three of these: Distributed Hearsay-II, Contract Nets, and the Scientific Community Metaphor.

SEVENTEEN

DISTRIBUTED DATABASES

A *database system* is a collection of information together with programs to manipulate that information. These programs present the user of the database with a structured interface to the database's information. We are interested in databases because some of them are distributed—they store information in many locations, often spanning great distances. Many advanced algorithms for organizing distributed systems have been developed as a result of the demand for coherent distributed database systems. Distributed databases strive to run programs at optimal locations (minimizing computation and communication costs) and to ensure the correctness of concurrent transactions. Distributed databases are among the most complex real distributed systems.

Database systems is a field in itself, suitable for study in advanced courses. We are not, of course, going to cover the field in its entirety. Instead, we focus on the points of particular interest to coordinated computing: the control of concurrency and distribution, and linguistic mechanisms for achieving this control. We introduce only a few formal database terms and assume no particular background in the field. In the first section of this chapter, we discuss concurrency control, replication, and failure and recovery mechanisms for distributed databases. In the second section, we introduce Argus, a language that incorporates notions of concurrency control, failure, and recovery into a programming language. We recommend that the reader who wishes to understand database systems in greater depth read one of the many texts on databases, such as Date [Date 81], Ullman [Ullman 82], or Wiederhold [Wiederhold 83]. The material in Section 17-1 is developed more thoroughly by Date [Date 83], Kohler [Kohler 81],

279

and Bernstein and Goodman [Bernstein 81]. Argus, described in Section 17-2, is the work of Barbara Liskov and her colleagues at M.I.T. [Liskov 83].

17-1 DATABASE CONTROL

Why distribute a database's data? Distribution greatly complicates constructing a correct database system. Two important motivations for the distribution of databases involve geography and reliability. Often, database users and data are themselves physically distributed. For example, banks keep databases of their customers' accounts. A bank with many dispersed offices may want local or regional processing centers to ease the transport of records and reduce the delay for inquiries. After all, most queries refer to local information and can be most economically processed locally. Nevertheless, the branches still need occasional, immediate access to the other regions' records. For example, if a customer from another region wants to cash a check, tellers must be able to quickly get that customer's records. Ideally, to the tellers, the customers' accounts should seem to be a monolithic whole. They should not be burdened with the details of where particular records are stored.

Second, distribution accompanied by replication can improve database reliability. *Replication* is storing the same information at several network locations. If the computer at the site of one copy of some particular datum is not working, the information can be obtained from another site with the same datum. This replication introduces the problem of ensuring that the multiple copies *appear* to be the same at all times.

Thus, two important aspects of distributed database systems are the location of the data and its consistent replication. A major design criterion for databases is that these two facets remain *transparent* to the database user. That is, the user should remain ignorant of which computer's data is being read, how far away that computer is, and, in general, the existence of other concurrent users of the database.

Transactions and Atomicity

Databases organize information. Let us call the smallest information structure in a database a *record*. We imagine that primitive database operations read and write records. A typical banking database might have a record for each customer's checking account showing the account number, name, and balance; a typical airline reservation system database might have a record for each reservation showing the reserver, number of seats, and flight.

Some database queries or updates access only a single record and access that record only once. For example, a request for an account balance only needs to read the account record. However, most actions combine access to multiple records (find the total balance in a customer's accounts by summing the balance in each), multiple varieties of access (find the balance in a customer's account, increment it by the amount of a deposit, and store the new balance), or a combination of reading and writing multiple records (transfer funds from one account to another).

Optimally, a database should be "correct" at all times. That is, it should always satisfy some consistency constraints. Thus, if a database stores both individual records of flight reservations and the total number of seats remaining on a flight, the total of all reservations and the remaining seats should remain constant (the number of seats on the plane). Unfortunately, this is not possible in general; the steps involved in updating the individual records leave the database temporarily inconsistent. For example, consider the following program which creates a reservation for a seat on flight f for customer c:

```
reserve (f: flight; c: customer) ≡
     avail := read (f, available_seats);
     if avail ≥ 1 then
          begin
               write (f, new_customer_record (c));     -- (1)
               write (f, available_seats, avail − 1)    -- (2)
          end
```

After line (1), the database is inconsistent. The total number of customer reservations and available seats exceeds the plane's capacity. Of course, the program quickly corrects this imbalance on line (2). Since inconsistent program steps are used in writing consistent programs, we cannot expect to have the database consistent at all times. Instead, we define a *transaction* to be an operation that takes the database from one consistent state to another consistent state. During any given transaction the database may be temporarily inconsistent. However, by the end of the transaction the database must be consistent again. For the remainder of our discussion, we assume that all user operations on our example database are transactions (if viewed in isolation from all other operations).

Databases often have many simultaneous users. For the database as a whole to preserve consistency, it is crucial that transactions be atomic—that transactions seem to be indivisible and instantaneous. Other processes should not become aware that a transaction is in progress. The transaction must also appear internally instantaneous—it should not see both the "before" and "after" of any other transaction.

In Section 3-2 we defined atomicity and presented an example of the inconsistency that can result when it is violated. It is helpful to review a similar example in our database context. Let us consider what happens if two different processes (transaction managers) simultaneously try to reserve a seat on flight 132 for customers Smith and Jones. We assume that there is a single remaining seat. As usual, each transaction manager has its own local temporary, avail (avail').

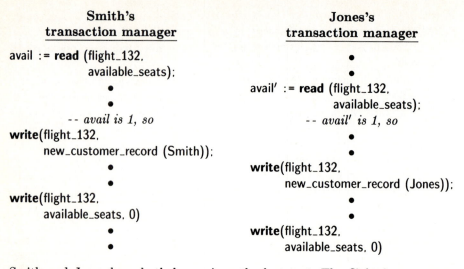

| | Smith's
transaction manager | Jones's
transaction manager |

avail := **read** (flight_132,
          available_seats);
          ●
          ●
    -- *avail is 1, so*
write(flight_132,
      new_customer_record (Smith));
          ●
          ●
write(flight_132,
      available_seats, 0)
          ●
          ●

          ●
          ●
avail' := **read** (flight_132,
          available_seats);
    -- *avail' is 1, so*
          ●
          ●
write(flight_132,
      new_customer_record (Jones));
          ●
          ●
write(flight_132,
      available_seats, 0)

Smith and Jones have both been given the last seat. The flight is now over-booked.*

Of course, the problem is that the steps of the two transactions have been interleaved. Clearly, if we had executed the transactions sequentially (in either order), the database would have remained consistent. However, this is not to imply that transactions cannot be safely executed simultaneously. If Jones had been reserving a seat on flight 538, then the operations of his reservation could have been harmlessly interleaved with Smith's. We call a *schedule* an ordering of the elementary steps of a set of transactions. A schedule is *serial* if whole transactions are executed consecutively, without interleaving of the steps of other transactions. A schedule is *serializable* if its effect is equivalent to *some* serial schedule. In general, the goal in distributed databases is to produce a serializable schedule that maximizes potential concurrency — that is, to give each user the appearance of serial execution while still doing many things at the same time.

A slightly more general description of the previous conflict is that each transaction tried to first read and then update the same record. Schematically, this becomes

Time	Transaction P	Transaction Q
0	Read (r)	●
1	●	Read (r)
2	Write (r)	●
3	●	Write (r)

That is, at time 0, transaction P reads record r. At time 1, Q reads r. Each remembers what it has read. When P writes r at time 2, Q's knowledge of the

---

* No, this is not how airlines really run their reservation systems.

database is now incorrect. Based on that incorrect value, its database update at time 3 can lead to an inconsistent state.

A *concurrency control mechanism* has three places that it could intervene to prevent this inconsistency:

(a) At time 1, it could deny Q access to r, because P has already read it (and is likely to change it).

(b) At time 2, it could refuse to let P write a new value for r, because Q is looking at the old value.

(c) At time 3, it could refuse to let Q write a new value for r, because its update is based on the (now) incorrect value of r.

Many different algorithms for concurrency control have been developed. The two most important and recurring themes are locks and timestamps. Locks are used to ensure the synchronization of methods (a) and (b); timestamps for methods (b) and (c).

Locks Locking associates a *lock* with each database object. A transaction that *locks* an object makes that object inaccessible to other transactions. A transaction that tries to lock an object that is already locked must do one of three things: (1) wait for the object to unlock, (2) abort, or (3) cause the locking transaction to abort. Each of these possibilities has its costs. Waiting for the object to unlock reduces the potential concurrency in the system. More significantly, a pure waiting strategy can produce deadlock (processes waiting for each other). This deadlock must be detected and resolved by aborting one of the deadlocked transactions. Aborting a transaction involves restoring the objects the transaction has changed to their state before the transaction began (*rollback*). In order to be able to rollback, the system must maintain the old versions of records until it is sure that the transaction will not abort. Since the transaction itself is not in error (the problem was its coincidence with another transaction), it should be rerun.

Locking has the advantage of being able to ensure serializability. More specifically, Eswaran et al. [Eswaran 76] have shown that if every transaction is well-formed and two-phase then the resulting system is serializable. A transaction is *well-formed* if (1) it locks every object it accesses, (2) it does not lock any already-locked object, and (3) it eventually unlocks all its locks. A transaction is *two-phase* if it does all of its locking before any of its unlocking. Two-phase transactions pass through the phases of first acquiring locks and then releasing them.

The simplest kind of lock is an *exclusive (write, update) lock*. When a transaction places an exclusive lock on an object, it is the only transaction that can read or write that object. For example, a transaction should obtain an exclusive lock if it intends to read a record, compute a new value for that record, and update the database with the new value. If another process wrote a different value into the record between the transaction's read and its write, that process's update would be overwritten and lost.

A transaction that only needs to read the database (and not update it) does not require such strong protection. For example, a transaction to compute the sum of a customer's accounts (but not store that sum in the database) would need to prevent a transfer of funds from one account to another during its computation. However, no harm results from another transaction reading the value of one of that customer's accounts while the first is processing. To handle this possibility, some systems provide *shared (read) locks*. A process that writes a database record must eventually obtain an exclusive lock on it. However, it can allow shared access until an update phase. Several processes can have shared locks on a record simultaneously. The system must still ensure that lock attempts fail if a transaction tries to get an exclusive lock and another transaction holds any lock on that record, or a transaction tries to get a shared lock and another transaction holds an exclusive lock on that record. Exclusive locks implement concurrency control mechanism (a) (see page 283), while shared locks implement mechanism (b).

Locking requires two steps, requesting the lock and granting it. Requests for a lock on a resource are directed at the resource's *lock manager*. Centralizing the lock management of all records at a single site simplifies the design of a distributed database and reduces the communication required to obtain and release locks. However, this scheme has two weaknesses: the lock manager is a potential communication bottleneck, and the entire system fails when the lock manager fails. Alternative structures involve making each database site the manager of its own data or distributing the management of record copies so that all the copies of any record are managed at a single site, but many sites are managers.

In a locking system, deadlock occurs when transactions are waiting for each other. Deadlock should, by now, be a familiar theme; avoiding the deadlock of five single-forked philosophers has been our goal in several example programs in earlier chapters. Operating systems often avoid deadlock by forcing processes to preclaim the resources they intend to use. That is, if a job requires two forks or five tape drives it must ask for them when it commences, not incrementally as it is running. Unfortunately, such deadlock avoidance techniques are inappropriate for databases. Transactions cannot know ahead of time which records they will access. On the contrary, a transaction often discovers the next search item only by analyzing the data in the last.

Since deadlock is hard to avoid in a locking database, deadlocks must be discovered and broken. The two primary mechanisms for resolving deadlocks are time-outs and deadlock detection. With time-outs, a transaction that has been waiting "too long" on a locked record aborts and restarts. This has the advantage of being easy to implement, but the disadvantage of being somewhat unfocused in its approach. If the waiting period is too short, some transactions may abort that are not deadlocked; if the waiting period is too long, the system stays locked longer than necessary. Similarly, time-outs preclude fairness — a locked-out transaction can be timed-out repeatedly.

Deadlock detection steps above the actual locking processes and examines the *waiting-for* relation. In particular, if transaction A has a lock on record r, and transaction B is waiting for that lock, then B is *waiting for* A. A deadlock is a cycle of waiting transactions, with transaction A_0 waiting for A_1 waiting for ... waiting for A_n waiting for A_0. An algorithm for distributed deadlock detection requires potentially deadlocking transactions to report their waiting-for relationships to the deadlock detector. Practical distributed deadlock detection algorithms are a subject of current research.

Timestamps Locking is a pessimistic strategy. It assumes that transactions will conflict and acts to prevent that conflict. An alternative, "optimistic" approach is to assume that transactions will not conflict and to act only when they do. If this optimism is justified, the system enjoys increased concurrency, as transactions never wait on a lock. However, if this optimism is misplaced, the system performs redundant work, as actions that produce conflict are rerun.

The best way to implement the concurrency control mechanism (c) (see page 283) is with timestamps. (Timestamps can also be used to implement the mechanism (b).) A *timestamp* is a unique number associated with an object or event. This number can be thought of as the "time" the timestamp was issued. Although real times do not have to be used with timestamps, timestamps must be chosen from a strictly monotonic sequence. That is, if timestamp A is assigned after timestamp B, then A should be greater than B.* Since timestamp systems never lock, the only way to prevent other transactions from seeing partial effects of a transaction is to make all the transaction's changes simultaneously, at the end of its execution (at *commit time*). Later in this section we discuss the two-phase commit algorithm which ensures either that all of a transaction's changes take effect or that none of them do.

Conflict occurs when a transaction tries to read a record written by a younger transaction (one with a larger timestamp) or tries to write a record that has already been seen or written by a younger transaction. (Thus, to detect conflict the system must maintain, for each record, the timestamps of the youngest transaction that has read that record and the youngest transaction that has successfully written it. Successful writing is committed writing.) Conflict can

---

* The astute reader may wonder how unique times are to be generated in a distributed system. One awkward way would be to have a centralized timestamp authority. This suffers from all the usual problems of introducing a central point to a distributed system. A better algorithm is to let each process issue timestamps that are the concatenation of that process's real time and its unique identifier. (The real time must be the higher-order bits.) This ensures that no two timestamps are the same (provided each process's clock "clicks" between issuing timestamps). Of course, process clocks may lose synchronization. This problem can be overcome by using the timestamp information of the communications each process receives to update its clock. An algorithm to ensure this synchronization is described by Lamport [Lamport 78].

be resolved by waiting for a conflicting transaction to terminate (*wait*), or by aborting and restarting a transaction. A transaction can decide to restart itself. We call this action *dying*. Alternatively, a transaction could try to cause another transaction to restart. This is called *wounding*, because the wounded transaction may have already begun to commit its database changes and ought not be killed. If a wounded transaction has not already committed, it is aborted and restarted. The particular action taken is based on comparison of the timestamps of the conflicting transactions.

Two of the more prominent timestamp conflict-resolution algorithms are Wait-Die and Wound-Wait [Rosenkrantz 78]. In *Wait-Die*, if the requesting transaction is older it *waits*; otherwise it *dies*. In *Wound-Wait*, if the requesting transaction is older it *wounds*; otherwise it *waits*. (In each case, the first word describes the action of the requester if it is older, and the second word the action if it is younger.) Both protocols guarantee consistency and freedom from starvation. Both give priority to older transactions; in Wait-Die, an older transaction is spared death, while in Wound-Wait, an older transaction can attempt to preempt a younger one. Wait-Die has the undesirable property that a dying transaction can repeat the same conflict; Wound-Wait lacks this fault. On the other hand, a transaction under Wound-Wait can be interrupted at any time before committing, perhaps even during output, while a Wait-Die transaction only aborts at program-defined points (e.g., before accessing a data record).

Summary Locking and timestamps each have advantages. Locks require little space and (as Gray et al. [Gray 75] show) can be used with larger structures than single records. On the other hand, timestamp systems never deadlock and therefore do not have the problem of deadlock detection and resolution. The ultimate practical algorithms will probably combine some aspects of each, perhaps treating the serialization of reading and writing differently. Bernstein and Goodman discuss many of the possible combinations of control strategies, showing that almost all can be described as a selection from a regular framework [Bernstein 81].

Replication

Data in a distributed database is, by definition, spread over several physical sites. One possible database organization is to store each record in one unique location. An alternative scheme is to replicate records, storing copies in several places. Replication can improve both performance and reliability. It improves performance by allowing a process to obtain data from a near copy instead of a distant original. Often, the major computational cost of a distributed query is the communication cost. (Of course, the ultimate near copy is one on the same processor as the requesting process.) Replication improves reliability because the failure of a site does not mean that a data set is inaccessible. Along with these advantages come the problems of propagating changes to all copies of

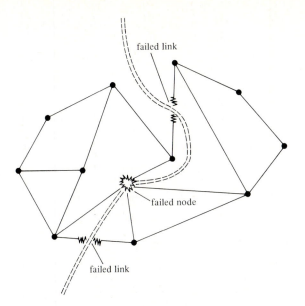

failed link

failed node

failed link

Figure 17-1 Subnet partition through failures.

a record and ensuring that all copies appear to be the same at all times. In general, replicated systems should provide *replication transparency*—the user of the database should not discover which copy has been accessed (or even where or how many copies exist).

The possibility of individual site failures complicates the design of replicated systems. How can a system propagate updates to all copies of a record in the presence of failure? One technique is to update the working sites immediately and to keep a list of updates for the failed sites to read when they resume processing. When a site revives it needs to obtain its update list and perform the requested actions before processing new requests.

However, site failure is not the only kind of failure a system can experience. Both the failure of communication links and the failure of key network sites can break communication connectivity. These failures can partition the network into disjoint subnetworks (as in Figure 17-1) which are unable to communicate. Inconsistency may result if the subnetworks continue processing, updating their versions of the database. For example, two different subnetworks unable to synchronize their transactions might each give the last seat on our hypothetical flight to two different customers.

One replication algorithm that deals with the partitioning problem makes one copy of each record the *primary* copy. Different sites hold the primary copies of different records. The system first directs updates to the primary copy. When this copy has been changed, it propagates the updates to the rest of the database.

(The system must also ensure that if a transaction has written a record its subsequent read operations on that record see an updated copy.) Thus, if the network becomes partitioned, only the sites in the partition with the primary copy can update a record. However, the other sites can continue to read the record's old value. This scheme has the disadvantage that if the primary site for the record fails, the record cannot be updated at all.

Adiba and Lindsay propose an alternative approach to this problem, *database snapshots* [Adiba 80]. They suggest that many applications do not need exact, up-to-the-millisecond accurate views of the database. Instead, the system should periodically distribute copies of records (snapshots). Most applications will find that these copies satisfy their needs. When a program needs the exact value of a field, it can request it from the primary copy. Of course, updates are still directed at the primary copy.

Failure, recovery, and two-phase commit The design of a reliable system starts by specifying the meaning of reliability. This includes analyzing the kinds of errors expected and their probabilities, and defining an appropriate response to each. Kohler's *Computing Surveys* article is a good overview of failure, reliability, and recovery [Kohler 81]. Reliable database systems are built around stable storage that survives system failures (typically disk storage) and holds multiple copies of data records. In the discussion below we assume that the techniques described in that paper are followed and that disk storage is (adequately) reliable. That is, the database that writes a file on the disk will (with a high enough probability) be able to read back that same file.

Transactions are, by definition, atomic. If a transaction intends to change several different database records it must (to preserve its atomicity) either change them all or change none. Because individual sites can fail at any time, the problem of committing all the updates of a transaction together is more difficult for distributed systems. A transaction that does not commit at every site must rollback to the previous state and restart.

Reliability and the ability to rollback depend on keeping an *incremental log* of changes to the database on stable storage. This log must contain enough information to undo any unfinished transaction and to complete any committed transaction. Effectively, the incremental log keeps a record of system intentions. This record is used by the recovery procedure to determine what has been done and what remains to be done. A node runs its recovery procedure when it resumes processing after a failure.*

---

* By and large, the system that intends to do action X must first (1) write to stable storage that it intends to do X and then (2) do X. If it fails while writing its intentions, then the system is still in a consistent state; X has not been done at all. If it fails while doing X, then the recovery procedure can read the intention from stable storage, discover what part of the operation has completed, and continue or rollback. Systems must be sure not to first (1) do X and then (2) write to stable storage that X was done. If such a system fails after (1) but before (2) it cannot determine how to recover (or even if it needs to recover).

The standard algorithm for ensuring that the updates of a transaction either all commit or all abort is *two-phase commit* [Gray 79; Lampson 76]. With two-phase commit, every transaction has a commit coordinator. The *commit coordinator* is responsible for coordinating the other sites of the transaction (the cohorts), ensuring that every cohort either commits or every cohort aborts. As you might expect, two-phase commit has two phases. In the first phase, the commit coordinator alerts the cohorts that the transaction is nearing completion. If any cohort responds that it wants to abort the transaction (or does not respond at all), the commit coordinator sends all the cohorts abort messages. Otherwise, when all cohorts have responded that they are ready to commit, the commit coordinator starts the second phase, sending commit messages to the cohorts. At that point the transaction is committed. More specifically, the algorithms for the commit coordinator and cohorts are as follows:

Phase one

Commit coordinator

(1)   Send a **prepare** message to every cohort.

(2)   If every cohort replies **ready** then proceed to Phase 2. If some cohort replies **quit** or some cohort does not respond (within the time-out interval) then:

(3)   Write an **abort** entry in the log. Send an **abort** message to every cohort. Receive acknowledgments from each cohort and enter in the log. Repeat **abort** message to each cohort until it acknowledges.

(4)   Terminate the transaction.

Cohort

(1)   Receive a **prepare** message from the commit coordinator.

(2)   Choose a response, **ready** or **quit**, and write that response on stable storage. Send that response to the commit coordinator.

Phase two

Commit coordinator

(1)   Write a **commit** entry in the log. (*The transaction is now committed.*)

(2)   Send a **commit** message to each cohort.

(3)   Wait for an **acknowledge** response from each cohort. Enter acknowledgment in the log. Repeat **commit** message to each cohort until it acknowledges.

(4)   Enter **completed** in the log and terminate.

Cohort

(1)   Receive message from commit coordinator. If it is **commit** then:

(2a)   Release locks and send commit coordinator **acknowledge**.

otherwise:

(2b)   Undo actions, release locks, and send commit coordinator **acknowledge**.

If the commit coordinator fails during this protocol, its recovery procedure is as follows:

Recovery procedure

Commit coordinator

(1) If it failed before writing the **commit** entry in the log, continue the commit coordinator at step (3) of Phase 1 (abort the transaction).

(2) If it failed after writing the **completed** entry in the log, the transaction has been completed.

(3) Otherwise, start the commit coordinator at step (2) of Phase 2.

17-2   ARGUS

Atomic actions, recovery, and two-phase commit are clever inventions. This section is an overview of Argus, a language based on these ideas. Argus is concerned with manipulating and preserving long-lived, on-line data, such as the data of databases. Argus builds on the semantic architecture of remote procedure calls with processes whose communication structure resembles Distributed Processes (Section 13-2). Argus draws its syntactic and semantic foundation from CLU, a language developed around the ideas of data abstraction [Liskov 77]. It extends Distributed Processes in several ways, the most important of which is by making each external call part of an atomic action. This involves providing mechanisms to abort the calling structure if part of an atomic action fails and to recover from such failures. This recovery mechanism allows a software representation and resolution of hardware failures.

Actions and Atomicity

The primitive processing object in Argus is a *guardian* — the "protector" of a resource, such as permanent data. Guardians have *handlers* (procedure entries) that can be called by other guardians. Guardians and handlers parallel the processes and procedure entries of Distributed Processes.

A guardian can have two kinds of storage, stable storage and volatile storage. Stable storage survives failures of the guardian (crashes of the guardian's processor) while volatile storage is destroyed by such failures. Therefore, volatile storage can be used only to keep redundant information, such as a cache or an index into a data structure. Atomic actions transform stable storage from one

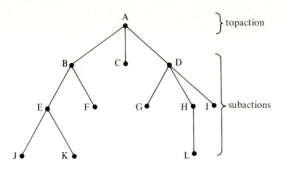

Figure 17-2 A topaction-subaction tree.

consistent state to another. Argus guarantees that atomic actions have the appropriate effect on stable storage — all changes made by an atomic action are seen by other actions as having happened simultaneously; either all the changes of an atomic action take place or none do.

A primitive atomic activity in Argus is an *action*. An action completes by either committing or aborting. Of course, if an action aborts, the effect should be the same as if the action had never begun. Argus achieves serializable schedules by locking and (within the context of locking) keeping versions of stable storage. (However, as we shall see, versions in Argus are not as general a mechanism as the versions of timestamp systems.)

Argus has two kinds of actions, topactions and subactions (nested actions). A *topaction* is an attempt to get the stable storage of a system to achieve a new consistent state. If a topaction fails or aborts, all changes made by that topaction are discarded. While executing a topaction, a program can invoke other subactions.

Subactions play two important roles. The first is that concurrent activities are usually run in subactions. Subactions see the changes caused by their ancestor actions, but appear atomic to their sibling and cousin subactions. The other is that remote procedure calls (calls to the handlers of other processes) are always done in subactions. No subaction runs concurrently with its parent action.

Subactions can themselves have subactions. To another action, the subaction is invisibly part of the topaction. Thus, subaction invocation forms a tree structure, as in Figure 17-2. Like topactions, subactions can either commit or abort. Aborting a subaction does not abort its parent. Instead, the parent can detect the abort and respond accordingly. However, if a parent action aborts, all changes caused by its subactions are rolled back; the subactions are aborted, even if they had already reached their commit points.*

---

* The concept of subactions is not original with Argus. Earlier work on nested actions includes Davies [Davies 78], Gray et al. [Gray 81], and Reed [Reed 78]. Argus's novel idea is to make actions and subactions part of a programming language.

Argus uses a locking protocol to synchronize data access. It allows read locks and write locks. Issuing a write lock creates a new version of the locked object. The action then updates this version. If the action ultimately commits, this version becomes the "real" version of the data record and the old version is discarded. If the action ultimately aborts, the new version is discarded. These versions can be kept in volatile storage because they are temporary until their ancestor topaction commits. Argus uses two-phase commit to ensure that committed versions become permanent. Argus does not detect deadlocks. Instead, user programs can time-out topactions that appear deadlocked.

The introduction of subactions complicates the locking rules. Argus permits an action to obtain a read lock on an object if every holder of a write lock on that object is an ancestor action. An action can obtain a write lock if every holder of any lock on that object is an ancestor. For example, we imagine that the subaction structure shown in Figure 17-3 has evolved, with actions A through L having the indicated read (R) and write (W) locks on objects x, y, and z. Subaction J could now obtain a read lock on z [R(z)] and a write lock on x [W(x)]. However, J cannot obtain a read lock on y [R(y)], as C, a nonancestor, has a write lock; nor can it obtain a write lock on z [W(z)], as F, a nonancestor, has a read lock.

Since several actions could have write locks on a given object simultaneously, Argus must maintain multiple versions of objects. However, as actions with write locks form an ancestor chain and actions do not run concurrently with their descendants, only a single version of any object is active at any time. The versions of any object thus form a stack. All access is directed to the version at the top of the stack. When a subaction with any lock commits, its parent inherits its locks. When a subaction with a write lock commits, its version becomes the new version of its parent. Versions of aborting subactions are discarded.

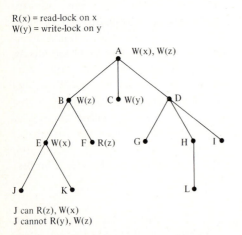

R(x) = read-lock on x
W(y) = write-lock on y

J can R(z), W(x)
J cannot R(y), W(z)

Figure 17-3 Locking rules for subactions.

Argus also permits an action to start a new topaction—a *nested topaction*. Such a new topaction has no particular privileges with respect to its parents. In particular, it does not inherit their locks. When a nested topaction commits, its changes become permanent. Aborting its parent action does not erase them. Nested topactions are useful for benevolent side-effects, such as caching data closer to its user or updating system performance statistics.

Guardians

A guardian type declaration has seven parts: (1) a *name*, (2) *creation routines*, parameterized functions that can be invoked to create a new instance of this type of guardian, (3) *stable storage* that survives process failures and is safely updated by the commit of a topaction, (4) *volatile storage* that does not survive guardian crashes, (5) *handlers* (entry procedures) that other guardians can call to send requests to this guardian, (6) a *background routine* that runs the program of the guardian, and (7) a *recovery routine* that the guardian runs to recover from a crash. Recovery runs as a topaction. It is responsible for restoring the volatile storage of the guardian to a consistent state.

The description of a guardian type can provide several functions to create guardians of that type. The creation operation can specify on which physical node of the distributed system the guardian is to reside. These creator functions can be used to initialize the guardian's storage. They usually return the name of the new guardian. A guardian (being an object on stable storage) can be deleted in only two ways: if the action which created it aborts, or if it specifically self-destructs. The run-time action of Argus resembles Distributed Processes: the background program of each guardian runs and calls the entry procedures of other guardians; the guardian's handlers accept calls from other guardians. Unlike Distributed Processes, Argus spawns a new process for each external request and runs these requests in the guardian concurrently. A guardian's background task starts running and its handlers begin accepting calls immediately after the completion of creation or recovery.

Argus is a language based on objects. Often the referent of local storage is an external object. Certain objects are atomic. Atomic objects are referenced and changed under the rules of atomicity. The stable storage of a guardian should contain only references to atomic objects. For example, an atomic_flag that is a single atomic boolean is declared as follows:

atomic_flag = **cluster is** create, set, test   -- *Cluster defines a new "user" data type. One can create, set, or test an atomic_flag.*

    rep = atomic_record[flag: bool]   -- *An atomic_flag is represented in terms of the primitive atomic_record*

```
    create = proc (flag: bool) returns (cvt)    -- Cvt converts between an
                                                    external, abstract
                                                    representation and an
                                                    internal, concrete one.

    set = proc (af: cvt, flag: bool)
        af.flag := flag
    end set

    test = proc (af: cvt) returns (bool)
        return(af.flag)
    end test

end atomic_flag
```

Argus introduces concurrency with the (**coenter**) statement, a form of **cobegin**. This statement initiates a parallel group of subactions or topactions. Argus provides an iterator (coroutine) construct in the **coenter** statement that generates elements and starts a process for each.

A child subaction of a **coenter** can abort its siblings. Thus, an Argus program seeking the value of a record from several sites of a distributed database could request them all in a single **coenter**, allowing the first subaction that succeeds to terminate the other requests.

In Distributed Processes, processes synchronize by setting the storage of a called process and testing it in guarded commands. Argus dispenses with this indirect mechanism. The primary use of synchronization is to ensure that data updates are consistent. But Argus's *raison d'être* is the consistent update of shared storage. Hence, calls to the handlers of a guardian are scheduled by the system independent of any explicit programmer control.

Dining philosophers We present a program to model the dining philosophers problem as our example of an Argus program. Unlike our other dining philosophers programs, this program does not have a centralized "room" object to prevent deadlocks. Instead (perhaps in keeping with more conventional eating habits), our philosophers try to pick up two forks. If a philosopher cannot get two forks soon enough, she backs off, dropping the forks to try again later. We ensure getting either two forks or none by making fork selection an atomic action. We run this action in parallel with an "alarm clock" action that aborts the pickup operation on time-out. Figure 17-4 shows the subaction structure of a single attempt to take two forks. This example uses the exception mechanism of Argus. A process that *signals* an exception transfers control to the closest (on the run-time stack) *exception handler* that handles that exception. Syntactically, the identifier **except** defines an exception handler, which lists in **when** clauses the various signals it handles.

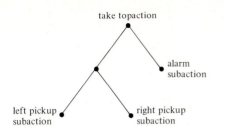

Figure 17-4 The subaction structure of claiming forks.

philosopher = **guardian** -- *the declaration of a process type*
  -- *Argus guardian declarations begin with a specification part that indicates the names of both functions to create new instances of that type and that guardian's handlers (entry procedures).*
   is create -- *This function returns a new philosopher. A philosopher does not have any entry procedures.*

  -- *These variables are on stable storage and survive the failure of the guardian's processor.*
   stable left, right : tableware -- *the two forks passed this guardian on its creation*
   stable taken : atomic_flag -- *set when this philosopher has her forks*

   recover -- *The guardian recovers from crashes by dropping any forks*
      drop *she might have.*
   end -- *Argus eschews semicolons.*

   background
      while true **do** -- *Repeat ad nauseam.*
         -- *think*
         take
         -- *eat*
         drop
      end
   end

  -- *This function takes two forks and returns a new philosopher.*
   create = **creator** (l, r: tableware) **returns** (philosopher)
      left := l
      right := r
      taken := atomic_flag$create(false)
      return (self)
   end create

```
take = proc ( )                      -- to pick up both forks
    while true do
        enter topaction             -- start a top-level action
            coenter                  -- run the fork-getter and the alarm, in
                                        parallel, as subactions
                action               -- fork-getter
                    coenter
                        action left.pickup
                        action right.pickup
                    end
                    atomic_flag$set(taken, true)
                    return    -- abort alarm, commit pickups
                action        -- the alarm process
                    sleep (100 + random( ))
                                      -- Delay some appropriate time. Make
                                         this delay include a varying element.
                    exit timeout -- abort fork-getting
            end
            except
                when timeout, already_taken:
                when failure (*):
            abort leave
            end except when failure(*): end
        sleep (200 + random( )) -- Wait awhile before trying again.
    end
end take


drop = proc ( )    -- We drop the forks in a single topaction, dropping each
                      in its own subaction. Either they both succeed or
                      neither does.
    while true do
        enter topaction
        begin
            if atomic_flag$test(taken)
                then coenter
                    action
                        left.putdown
                        right.putdown
                    end
                    atomic_flag$set (taken, false)
                end
                return
            end except when failure(*): end
        abort leave
```

```
              end except when failure(*): end
          end
      end drop
end philosopher
```

Forks return normally if free and picked up. They abort and signal an error if busy. The fork preserves its state in a single boolean variable.

```
tableware = guardian
    is create
    handles pickup, putdown

    stable busy: atomic_flag     -- Keep the state of the fork on stable storage.

  -- Forks have neither a recovery nor a background section.

    create = creator returns tableware
        busy := atomic_flag$create(false)
        return (self)
    end create

    pickup = handler ( ) signals (already_taken)
        if atomic_flag$test(busy) then
            signal already_taken
        end
        atomic_flag$set(busy, true)
    end pickup

    putdown = handler ( )
        if not atomic_flag$test(busy) then
            abort signal failure ("not picked up")
        end if
        atomic_flag$set(busy,false)
    end putdown
end tableware
```

The following statements create an array of five forks and an array of five philosophers, each indexed starting with 0. (Arrays in Argus are dynamic structures with no upper bounds.) The **for** loops pass the appropriate forks to the appropriate philosophers. Creating the guardians (calling their creators) sets them running.

```
forks  : array[tableware]    := array [tableware]$[0: ]
philos : array[philosopher]  := array [philosopher]$[0: ]
```

```
for i: int in int$from_to(0, 4) do
    array[tableware]$addh(forks, tableware$create( ))
end

for i: int in int$from_to(0, 4) do
    array[philosopher]$addh(philos,
            philosopher$create(forks[i], forks[(i + 1)//5]))    -- // ≡ mod
end
```

Perspective

Argus hones the procedures and procedure entries of conventional distributed programming languages into a tool directed precisely at the problems of distributed information storage systems. The other systems we have studied so far treat communication as the quantum unit of distribution. The programmer is responsible for building these quanta into a coherent algorithmic pattern. Argus identifies a class of conversations (atomic actions) involving many distributed processes and provides specific mechanisms for organizing these actions. A programmer can provide for one action in such a set to terminate the others or can insist that all must complete together. Argus is thus a heuristic approach to distributed computing—a recognition that coordinated problem solving requires tools that are both general and tuned to the issues of distribution.

PROBLEMS

17-1 Transaction A, with timestamp 2880, accesses database record R. If transaction B, with timestamp 2881, now tries to read record R and then update it, what happens? Assume that the system is using the conflict resolution scheme Wait-Die.

17-2 Repeat the previous exercise for Wound-Wait.

17-3 Transaction B, with timestamp 2881, accesses database record R. If transaction A, with timestamp 2880, now tries to read R and then update it, what happens? Assume that the system is using the conflict resolution scheme Wait-Die.

17-4 Repeat the previous exercise for Wound-Wait.

17-5 Could the synchronization mechanisms of timestamps be used to introduce "safe" side-effects to IAP (Chapter 12)?

17-6 In Argus, how can the parent of a subaction abort while the subaction is still running?

17-7 Why do the **sleep** commands in the dining philosophers program include a random value?

17-8 Write an Argus program that books a multiple-segment airline trip by negotiating with the ticket reservation guardian of each airline. Make sure that your program reserves either all the seats for a trip or none of them.

17-9 Often bids for houses are contingent on the sale of the bidder's house. Such contingent bids expire after a specified time. Write an Argus program that mimics the bidding and sales of several house traders. Represent each house by a guardian that is receptive to certain bids. Confirm sales only after all contingencies have been removed.

17-10 Program in Argus a majority-vote commit algorithm. In such a system, a transaction that commits at a majority of sites is deemed to have committed. Thus, the changes made by that transaction are made permanent at those sites that have committed. Bernstein and Goodman's survey article discusses majority voting algorithms in detail [Bernstein 81].

REFERENCES

[**Adiba 80**] Adiba, M. E., and B. G. Lindsay, "Database Snapshots," *Proc. 6th Int. Conf. Very Large Data Bases*, Montreal (October 1980), pp. 86–91. Adiba and Lindsay propose that a database system take "snapshots" of the state of the database, distribute the snapshots, and use them for later processing. A process can use a local snapshot rather than requesting the information from a central repository.

[**Bernstein 81**] Bernstein, P. A., and N. Goodman, "Concurrency Control in Distributed Database Systems," *Comput. Surv.*, vol. 13, no. 2 (June 1981), pp. 185–222. Bernstein and Goodman survey the state of concurrency control for distributed databases. They break concurrency control into two major subproblems, the synchronization of a reader and a writer, and the synchronization of two writers. They state several techniques for each subproblem and show how almost all practical algorithms for synchronization that have appeared in the literature are a selection of one of their techniques for each subproblem.

[**Date 81**] Date, C. J., *An Introduction to Database Systems*, 3d ed., Addison-Wesley, Reading, Massachusetts (1981). Date's book is a good general introduction to database systems. It includes material on the nature of databases and the three major database models: the relational, hierarchical, and network models.

[**Date 83**] Date, C. J., *An Introduction to Database Systems,* vol. II, Addison-Wesley, Reading, Massachusetts (1983). Date's second volume is perhaps the first book on advanced database principles. Of particular interest to coordinated computing are his chapters on concurrency, recovery, and distributed databases. He also covers material such as security, integrity, and database machines.

[**Davies 78**] Davies, C. T., "Data Processing Spheres of Control," *IBM Syst. J.*, vol. 17, no. 2 (1978), pp. 179–198. Davies describes a database organization based on "spheres of control." These spheres effect nested transactions.

[**Eswaran 76**] Eswaran, K. P., J. N. Gray, R. A. Lorie, and I. L. Traiger, "The Notions of Consistency and Predicate Locks in a Database System," *CACM*, vol. 19, no. 11 (November 1976), pp. 624–633. This paper demonstrates that consistency requires two-phase algorithms — a consistent system cannot allow a transaction to acquire new locks after releasing old ones. Eswaran et al. then discuss the nature of locks, arguing that locks must control logical, not physical, sections of databases.

[**Gray 75**] Gray, J. N., R. A. Lorie, and G. R. Putzolu, "Granularity of Locks in a Shared Data Base," *Proc. Int. Conf. Very Large Data Bases*, Framingham, Massachusetts (September 1975), pp. 428–451. In the text we specified that locks are associated with individual records. This paper describes an algorithm for locking sets of resources. The algorithm deals with records and class structures that are related by hierarchies and acyclic graphs. They introduce varieties of locks to achieve class-wide locking.

[**Gray 79**] Gray, J. N., "Notes on Data Base Operating Systems," in R. Bayer, R. M. Graham, and G. Seegmuller (eds.), *Operating Systems: An Advanced Course*, Springer-Verlag, New York (1979), pp. 393–481. Gray focuses on the issues of recovery and locking in transaction systems. He presents a unified database design based on System R [Gray 81].

[**Gray 81**] Gray, J., P. McJones, M. Blasgen, B. Lindsay, R. Lorie, T. Price, F. Putzolu, and I. Traiger, "The Recovery Manager of the System R Database Manager," *Comput. Surv.*, vol. 13, no. 2 (June 1981), pp. 223–242. Gray et al. describe an experimental database system, "System R." System R is based on transactions, recovery protocols for dealing with failures, transaction logs, and saving system checkpoints.

[**Kohler 81**] Kohler, W. H., "A Survey of Techniques for Synchronization and Recovery in Decentralized Computer Systems," *Comput. Surv.*, vol. 13, no. 2 (June 1981), pp. 149–184. Kohler surveys both concurrency control mechanisms for distributed databases and recovery mechanisms for database systems. He first describes locks, timestamps, and several other concurrency control mechanisms. He then deals with the general issue of recovery, which includes both the problems of secure storage and the requirements of recovery procedures.

[**Lamport 78**] Lamport, L., "Time, Clocks, and the Ordering of Events in a Distributed System," *CACM*, vol. 21, no. 7 (July 1978), pp. 558–565. Lamport shows that a process can keep its clock synchronized with the rest of the system if anytime it receives a timestamped communication from another process with a clock time greater than its own, it resets its own clock to that value.

[**Lampson 76**] Lampson, B. W., and H. E. Sturgis, "Crash Recovery in a Distributed Storage System," unnumbered technical report, Computer Science Laboratory, Xerox Palo Alto Research Center, Palo Alto, California (1976). Lampson and Sturgis present an early version of a two-phase commit algorithm in this unpublished paper.

[**Liskov 77**] Liskov, B., A. Snyder, R. R. Atkinson, and J. C. Schaffert, "Abstraction Mechanisms in CLU," *CACM*, vol. 20, no. 8 (August 1977), pp. 564–576. CLU is a programming language based on abstraction—principally data abstraction. CLU provides the syntactic foundation for Argus.

[**Liskov 82**] Liskov, B., "On Linguistic Support for Distributed Programs," *IEEE Trans. Softw. Eng.*, vol. SE-8, no. 3 (May 1982), pp. 203–210. This paper describes a message-based precursor of Argus.

[**Liskov 83**] Liskov, B., and R. Scheifler, "Guardians and Actions: Linguistic Support for Robust, Distributed Programs," *ACM Trans. Program. Lang. Syst.*, vol. 5, no. 3 (July 1983), pp. 381–404. This paper is a preliminary description of Argus. Its major example is a distributed mail system that keeps track of mailboxes and forwards mail to the appropriate destination.

[**Reed 78**] Reed, D. P., "Naming and Synchronization in a Decentralized Computer System," Ph.D. dissertation, M.I.T., Cambridge, Massachusetts (1978). Reprinted as Technical Report TR-205, Laboratory for Computer Science, M.I.T., Cambridge, Massachusetts. Reed introduces a concurrency control scheme based on keeping multiple versions of mutable objects and directing requests at the version with the appropriate timestamp.

[**Rosenkrantz 78**] Rosenkrantz, D. J., R. E. Stearns, and P. M. Lewis, "System Level Concurrency Control for Distributed Database Systems," *ACM Trans. Database Syst.*, vol. 3, no. 2 (June 1978), pp. 178–198. Rosenkrantz et al. present and compare several system-level concurrency control mechanisms based on timestamps. They introduce the Wait-Die and Wound-Wait algorithms.

[**Ullman 82**] Ullman, J. D., *Principles of Database Systems*, 2d ed., Computer Science Press, Potomac, Maryland (1980). This is a text for an introductory database course. Ullman ties his development of database systems to other areas of computer science, such as theory and programming languages.

[**Wiederhold 83**] Wiederhold, G., *Database Design*, 2d ed., McGraw-Hill, New York (1983). In contrast with other introductory books on database systems, Wiederhold concentrates less on the organization of particular databases and more on the quantitative aspects of database performance.

[**Weihl 83**] Weihl, W., and B. Liskov, "Specification and Implementation of Resilient, Atomic Data Types," *SIGPLAN Not.*, vol. 18, no. 6 (June 1983), pp. 53–64. Weihl and Liskov discuss atomic and resilient data types, particularly with respect to the emerging implementation of Argus.

EIGHTEEN

DISTRIBUTED PROBLEM SOLVING

So far in this book we have described several models and languages for under-standing and controlling distribution and presented some (relatively) mature and specific algorithms for distributed database systems. In this section we become highly speculative—describing particular algorithms for organizing nonexistent machines, often to do tasks that we do not know how to do on conventional, sequential machines.

After all, why would anyone want a distributed computing system? Some tasks, such as databases and sensing (which we discuss below), are naturally distributed — they reflect the distribution of their input sources and output destinations. However (to echo one of our earlier themes), the real promise of the megacomputer lies in its potential for vast increases in processing. What tasks require so many cycles? Processing is important for problems involving search, where we use "search" in its broadest sense. That is, an intelligent sys-tem *searches* in the space of possible actions for the solution to its particular problem.

Of course, assignments in an introductory programming course can also in-volve search. In general, search tasks span a range from well-structured domains to ill-structured domains. In a well-structured domain, the computer merely sifts through a mass of data to find an answer. At any point it is clear which oper-ation is to be applied to which data items. The control structure of the search can be predicted before the program is run. Most primitive operations fail and this failure is forgotten. That is, the choice of what to consider next is usually independent of most of what has already been discovered.

In an ill-structured domain there are many potentially useful actions at any point. Selecting the most appropriate direction to follow is itself a problem requiring solution. Distributed computing is most intriguing for this class of problems because of the possibility of *really* pursuing many different paths at the same time, extending those that appear promising while deferring those that seem barren. In effect, this scheme allows the real resource consumption of subgoals to influence the processing agenda.

Of course, distributed systems can be used for well-structured search domains. Such domains allow the task to be decomposed into processor-size pieces before it is run. The processors run in parallel, with only a minimum of communication required to integrate their results.

Ill-structured domains do not provide the luxury of predefined decomposition. Instead, the course of problem solving shapes the future direction of the program. Such ill-structured domains often have multiple knowledge sources, each of which can contribute to the solution of some problems. These sources need to communicate queries, hypotheses, and partial results—to *cooperate* in problem solving.

Functionally Accurate Cooperative Systems

Victor Lesser and Daniel Corkill [Lesser 81] characterize contemporary distributed systems as being "completely accurate, nearly autonomous" systems. These systems are completely accurate because they operate on complete and correct information. They are nearly autonomous because each process has an almost complete database of the information it needs. In completely accurate, nearly autonomous systems, the interprocess relationship is usually that of a calling program and called subroutine (or, more figuratively, *master-slave*).

Lesser and Corkill argue that the best way to solve some problems is by decomposing them into local subproblems that operate on incomplete data. This division seems natural for dealing with problems that use many diverse knowledge sources (such as speech understanding in the Hearsay model [Erman 80]) and for problems involving noisy, distributed data (such as distributed sensing).* They suggest that these systems should be organized as "functionally accurate, cooperative" distributed systems. In such systems, the processing nodes use incomplete data and exchange partial results. Functionally accurate systems produce acceptable, though not perfect, answers. Such systems must deal with uncertainty inherent in both the problem and any intermediate results. Functional accuracy can be achieved by processes

---

* In a *distributed sensing system*, sensing/processing units focus on particular parts of space and cooperate in tracking objects through the whole of the space. For example, a distributed radar system that tracks incoming missiles is a distributed sensing system.

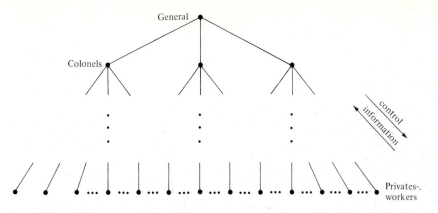

Figure 18-1 A hierarchical control structure.

that act as *iterative coroutines*, communicating partial results and extending the partial results of other processes. These systems are therefore inherently cooperative.

Cooperation structures How can systems be structured to focus control and provide direction? One obvious mechanism is hierarchy — some topmost node (the general) divides the original task into subproblems, and then distributes these subproblems to the second level of command (the colonels). The colonels repeat this subdivision through the ranks until "private-size" tasks reach the nodes that do the primitive work. Figure 18-1 shows a hierarchical control structure. The results of processing progress from the leaves of the hierarchy to the root. At each level, an officer node synthesizes the results of its immediate subordinates. This synthesis may require additional requests of the lower-level processing nodes. Thus, this organization leads naturally to communication up and down the hierarchy, but not across subtrees.

Hierarchical organization has the advantage that there is *some* control path for focusing the system if the problem environment changes radically. However, this organization may prove unwieldy in a distributed system whose elements themselves possess considerable processing ability. The higher-level officer nodes may be a communication bottleneck; the problem may not decompose into nearly-independent subtasks, and the system as a whole is delicately dependent on the health (nonfailure) of the top-level command.

Several alternative *heterarchical* control organizations for distributed systems have been proposed. In this chapter we consider three of these, Distributed Hearsay, Contract Nets, and the Scientific Community Metaphor.

18-1 DISTRIBUTED HEARSAY

The Hearsay-II system [Erman 80] is a speech understanding system.* It synthesizes the partial interpretations of several diverse knowledge sources into a coherent understanding of a spoken sentence. These *knowledge sources* cover domains such as acoustics, phonetics, syntax, and semantics. Each knowledge source iterates through the process of first hypothesizing a possible interpretation of some part of the current data and then testing the plausibility of that hypothesis. The various knowledge sources form new hypotheses by using both a priori knowledge about the problem domain (the information about speech understanding incorporated in the knowledge source when it was created) and those hypotheses already generated in the problem-solving process. Because knowledge sources work with imperfect a priori knowledge and noisy input signals, many of the hypotheses they create are incorrect. Of course, conclusions that other knowledge sources draw from incorrect hypotheses are also suspect. To avoid focusing the system on a single, inappropriate solution path, each knowledge source can generate several possible interpretations of input data, associating a credibility rating with each.

Knowledge sources communicate by reading and writing a global database called the *blackboard.* The blackboard has several distinct levels. Each level holds a different representation of the problem space (Figure 18-2). Typical blackboard levels for speech understanding are sound segments, syllables, words, and phrases. The knowledge sources are pattern-action productions; if the information on the blackboard matches the pattern of a knowledge source then its action can be executed. This action usually writes new hypotheses on the blackboard. Most knowledge source patterns refer to only a few contiguous blackboard levels.

At any time, many knowledge sources are likely to have patterns that match the contents of the blackboard. The *scheduler* decides which knowledge source is to be executed next, choosing the knowledge source whose action has the highest priority. An action's *priority* is an estimate of the impact (reduction in problem uncertainty) of the information generated by executing its pattern. Hearsay-II also has a *focus-of-control* database that contains meta-information about the system's state. This information is used both to estimate the impact of actions and to redirect a stagnating system.

Since many actions are potentially executable at any time, Hearsay-II would seem to be a naturally concurrent system. This proves to be the case. Experiments have shown that a shared-memory, multiprocessor Hearsay-II implemen-

---

* The Hearsay-II architecture has been used for other knowledge-based interpretation tasks, such as sonar interpretation [Nii 78] and image understanding [Hanson 78]. To be accurate, we should distinguish between the architectural organization (knowledge sources, blackboard, etc.) of Hearsay-II and the particular application of Hearsay-II to speech understanding. However, for the sake of simplicity we merge the two, speaking of Hearsay-II as a speech understanding system. We rely on the reader to generalize the concepts to the Hearsay-II architecture.

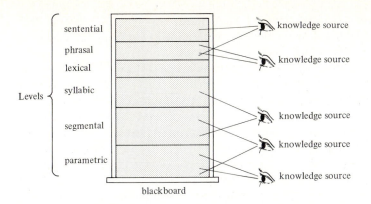

Levels {
sentential
phrasal
lexical
syllabic
segmental
parametric

knowledge source
knowledge source
knowledge source
knowledge source
knowledge source

blackboard

Figure 18-2 Knowledge sources and the levels of the blackboard.

tation runs significantly faster than the original system [Fennell 77]. However, because of its reliance on a centralized, global blackboard, Hearsay-II is not trivial to distribute.

Erman and Lesser's approach to distributing Hearsay-II makes each node of the system a full Hearsay-II system in its own right, complete with knowledge sources, blackboard, scheduler, and focus-of-control database [Lesser 80]. This is possible because speech understanding naturally divides along two dimensions, blackboard level and time. The blackboard has multiple levels, and few knowledge sources mention information on more than two contiguous levels. The speech signal is itself distributed in time—typically, signals a few seconds apart interact only at the highest semantic levels. Thus, by overlapping the signal covered by different nodes, Distributed Hearsay-II systems need to communicate only semantic information. This distribution of tasks by the two-dimensional problem space produces a "near neighbor" communication pattern. The decision of which information to communicate is also entrusted to knowledge sources— particular *transmit* actions are matched by appropriate *receive* patterns.

Erman and Lesser's experiments with a Distributed Hearsay-II system divided the knowledge-level/time space only along the temporal dimension. Each logical node was statically assigned a continuous segment of speech signal, with the segments of neighboring nodes overlapping. Thus, each node had a full set of knowledge sources. Figure 18-3 shows the task division among the nodes. Distributing Hearsay-II prompted a few modifications to the speech understanding knowledge sources. Erman and Lesser added communication knowledge sources, modified those knowledge sources that depended on distant information, and corrected those knowledge sources that contained implicit assumptions about the sequential nature of the overall processing. They discovered that a (simulated) three-node Distributed Hearsay-II system proved accurate on a set of sample utterances and produced a slight (10 percent) improvement in overall system speed. The system was also somewhat immune to communication errors. Even when many internode communications were discarded, it still understood most sample sentences. Distributed Hearsay-II was thus self-correcting and functionally accurate. This result is not surprising; the original Hearsay-II architecture was designed to deal with noisy and incomplete data. This resilience carried over into the distributed environment.

The Hearsay-II speech understanding system was easy to distribute because the problem domain and knowledge sources themselves have a natural distribution. Few knowledge sources reference noncontiguous levels of the blackboard; the understanding of a particular segment of speech is related only semantically to another segment seconds later. Our next two approaches, Contract Nets and the Scientific Community Metaphor, consider the organization of interacting knowledge sources without respect to the geometry of the underlying problem structure.

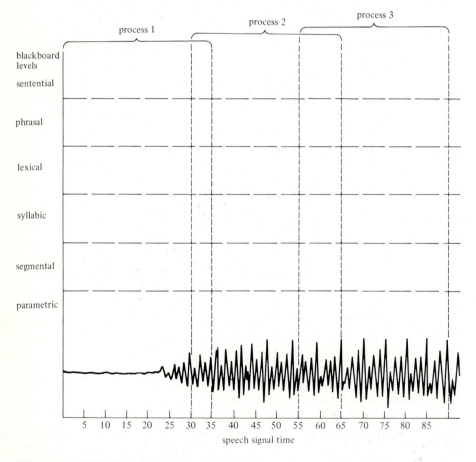

Figure 18-3 Task division in Distributed Hearsay-II.

18-2 CONTRACT NETS

Reid Smith and Randall Davis propose the Contract Net Protocol as an architecture for organizing distributed systems, particularly for the problem of distributing tasks among a set of (potentially heterogeneous) nodes [Smith 78, Smith 81a]. They start with the idea of expert problem solvers who need to communicate tasks and solutions. Smith and Davis argue that such a collection of experts need *problem-solving protocols*, much as computer networks need communication protocols. The Contract Net Protocol draws its inspiration from the activities surrounding the negotiation of commercial contracts.

A *Contract Net* is a set of autonomous processing nodes that communicate according to the rules of the Contract Net Protocol. Individual subtasks of the global problem are called *contracts*. A node that needs a subtask performed advertises (broadcasts) the existence of that task to the other nodes of the network. Those nodes that have the resources or expertise to solve the task *bid* on it, returning the bids to the broadcasting node (the *manager* of the task). On the basis of the information in the bid responses, the manager node *awards* the contract to one of the bidders, the *contractor*. The contractor can then break the task of the contract into further subtasks, letting out contracts on those subtasks.

Unlike hierarchical structures, the Contract Net Protocol calls for negotiation between nodes. Nodes evaluate announcements, bidding only on those of interest. Managers evaluate bids to select the most appropriate bidder. The protocol thus ensures a mutual selection.

A manager with a contract can broadcast the terms of that contract to all other nodes. However, broadcasting wastes precious communication bandwidth. A manager that knows which nodes are potential bidders sends a *limited broadcast* to only those nodes. A manager that can narrow the potential contract to a single node sends just that node a *point-to-point announcement*. The Protocol also allows *directed contracts*, awarded by a manager to a specific node without bidding, and *request-response sequences*, used to obtain immediate information without negotiation.

Task announcements contain three kinds of information. The *task abstraction* is a brief description of the task. The *eligibility specification* lists criteria that potential bidders must meet. And the *bid specification* details the form of desired bids. The bid specification resembles an application form with blanks to be filled in; potential contractors need to return only values for the blanks, instead of retransmitting the entire form.

After a manager has received bids, it selects a successful bidder and awards the contract to that bidder. This award contains a *task description*, a complete specification of the task. On completing the task, the contractor returns a *task report* to the manager, which includes the results of performing the task. Managers may also terminate unfinished contracts still in progress.

Smith and Davis cite distributed sensing as a possible application of Contract Nets. Their hypothetical sensing system has many nodes that communicate over a common broadcast channel. The nodes themselves have sensing or processing capabilities (or both). A *sensing node* detects traffic in its neighborhood and performs low-level feature analysis. A *processing node* integrates and processes the data from sensing nodes. A processing node does not have to be physically near a sensing node to use its results. A single *monitor node* is responsible for managing the entire task and communicating with the outside world. The other nodes are at fixed positions. These nodes know their positions, but this knowledge is not known a priori by the monitor.

Just as the knowledge in speech understanding naturally divides into different levels, distributed sensing has distinct levels: signal processing, signal grouping, vehicle detection, area mapping, and global mapping. Related signals from a single sensor are formed into signal groups; several signal groups detected from different locations compose into a vehicle. Once discovered, vehicles are subject to analysis for type, location, and projected course. From the vehicles in a region the system develops an understanding of the traffic in that region; from regional understanding comes a global understanding. This natural hierarchy leads to a processing hierarchy. Figure 18-4 shows one such organization of nodes.

The first task of the system is to divide the traffic space into areas. The monitor node (knowing the names of potential area processors) broadcasts a task announcement to them, requesting bids on area division. The area processors respond with bids; each bid includes the bidder's location. From the replies, the monitor partitions the space, awarding area contracts to some of the bidders, the area managers. These managers continue this process recursively, seeking signal-group processing nodes. However, since the area nodes do not know which signal-group nodes are in their areas, they must broadcast their task announcements. These announcements require (as an eligibility specification) that the signal-group nodes must be within the area node's area. The process continues through to signals, thus defining the initial state of the sensing tree. Nodes that do not already have tasks (or have the capacity to accommodate additional tasks) continue to listen for task announcements and bid for contracts.

The same organization that is used to create the sensing hierarchy is used during system operation. A signal sensor that detects a signal reports to its group manager. This group manager then integrates this signal with its existing signal group or attempts to form a new signal group. The group manager reports new groups to the area contractor. Using the contract announcement and bidding procedure, the area contractor either finds the vehicle contractor that is already monitoring that signal or creates a new vehicle monitor to do that monitoring. If the vehicle monitoring task requires help with localization or course prediction, the vehicle monitor issues subcontracts.

We introduced distributed problem solving by arguing that in ill-structured, distributed search, dividing the search space is itself a major task. The Contract Net formalism takes this idea to heart, providing mechanisms for distributing tasks. Just as programming languages do not prescribe per se which programs are to be written in them, the Contract Net Protocol does not specify what

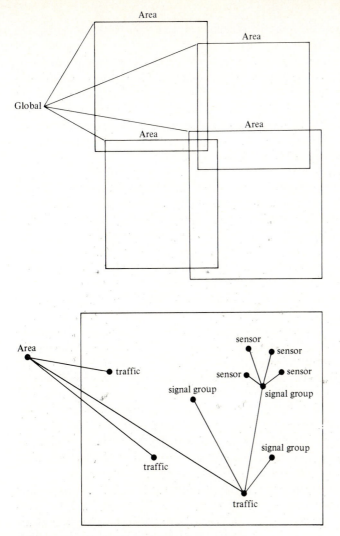

Figure 18-4 The distributed sensing hierarchy.

contracts should be let and bid or how bid specifications should be phrased. Contract Nets provides only the framework for internode negotiations on the problem-solving issues.

18-3 THE SCIENTIFIC COMMUNITY METAPHOR

Paradigms draw their inspiration from analogy—the transfer of the key features of one domain to another. The Hearsay-II architecture is guided by analogy to people who communicate on a shared blackboard; Contract Nets, by analogy to businesses negotiating for subcontracts.

Perhaps the ultimate human refinement of the problem-solving process is the activity of science itself. William Kornfeld and Carl Hewitt have investigated the idea of treating machine problem solving analogically to the problem-solving structure of an idealized scientific community [Kornfeld 81]. Scientists, far more than the knowledge sources of Hearsay-II, incorporate active problem solving. And like the societies of which they are a part, scientific communities use the economics of funding as an essential control mechanism.

Kornfeld and Hewitt identify several aspects of the organization of scientific research that they feel are important to mimic in distributed problem-solving systems: monotonicity, commutativity, parallelism, and pluralism. *Monotonicity* refers to the monotonic increase in the store of scientific knowledge—early results may be later contradicted, but their vestiges remain. For scientific communities, archived journal volumes embody this monotonicity. *Commutativity* is the ability of scientists to draw both on work already completed and on work still to be done. That is, it does not matter which came first, the "answer" or the "question"—the two can be matched in either case. *Parallelism* results from scientists working concurrently, using this concurrence to guide resource allocation and search direction. And *pluralism* refers to the ability of a scientific community to entertain multiple hypotheses at any time, with no hypothesis ever achieving the status of "absolute truth."

Kornfeld and Hewitt have developed the language Ether to express highly parallel, "scientific community" algorithms. Ether is based on the message-passing theme of Actors (Chapter 11) and extends the demon ideas of artificial intelligence languages such as Planner [Hewitt 69] and Micro-Planner [Sussman 70]. These languages revolve around a global database. Each demon has a pattern and an action. The demon "watches" the database, and when the information in the database matches its pattern, it executes its action.*

In Planner, demons recognized only those database changes that happened *after* their creation. Ether proposes a new kind of demon, the sprite. Like Planner demons, sprites recognize database entries that match their patterns. However, unlike demons, sprites are commutative. A sprite that matches a data item matches that item, regardless of whether the sprite was created before or after the data item. Ether systems thus resemble the interaction of scientists and scientific libraries. A researcher interested in a given topic finds papers on that topic regardless of whether the papers were written before or after her interest was aroused. Similarly, a sprite interested in a particular fact in the database finds that fact regardless of when it was created.

---

* Resemblance to the knowledge sources and blackboard of Hearsay-II is not coincidental. Demons have been a recurring A.I. theme with more different instantiations than we care to list. However, Planner was certainly one of the first systems to explicitly support them. *Production systems* are the generalization of pattern/action systems. A good overview of the use of production systems in A.I., circa 1976, is Davis and King [Davis 76].

Since many sprites can be active at any time, Ether is a parallel system. And Ether supports a form of state vector or possible world for dealing with multiple, competing hypotheses, thus providing a mechanism to support pluralism.

Combinatorial implosion Kornfeld presents the example of finding the *covering set* of a predicate using sprites [Kornfeld 82]. We are given a set of propositional predicates, $P = \{p_1, p_2, \ldots, p_k\}$ and a predicate $\mathcal{P}$ such that

$$\mathcal{P} \supset p_1 \vee p_2 \vee \cdots \vee p_k$$

The problem task is to determine all subsets S of P such that:

$$\mathcal{P} \supset S$$

and

there is no proper subset R of S such that $\mathcal{P} \supset R$

That is, we want all the "minimal covering subsets" of P. For example, we imagine our propositions ranging over the base predicates A, B, C, D, and E. If our original set $\{p_1, p_2, p_3, p_4, p_5\}$ is

$$
\begin{aligned}
p_1 &= A \vee B \\
p_2 &= C \vee D \\
p_3 &= A \vee C \\
p_4 &= B \vee D \\
p_5 &= E
\end{aligned}
$$

and our given predicate $\mathcal{P}$ is

$$\mathcal{P} = A \vee B \vee C \vee D \vee E$$

then the minimal subsets, S, are

$$\{p_1, p_2, p_5\}$$

and

$$\{p_3, p_4, p_5\}$$

We say that a set S for which $\mathcal{P} \supset S$ is a *working set*, while a working set with no working, proper subsets is a *minimal set*.

This problem is amenable to both top-down and bottom-up solutions. In the top-down solution, one starts with the entire set, P. We consider all subsets of P formed by removing one element from P. If none of those sets works, then P is a minimal set (and should be added to the set of answers). If any one of those subsets works, then we need to apply the process recursively to each working subset.

This algorithm is easily expressed in Lisp. We represent sets of propositions as lists; the set $\{p_1, p_2, p_4\}$ becomes the list (p1 p2 p4). We imagine having the following auxiliary functions and constant:

(working s)   ≡ is true if s works with respect to the global predicate *P.*
(remove x l)   ≡ is a list of all the elements of l except x.
(result w)   ≡ adds w to the list of answers if it is not already there.
(mapcar f l)   ≡ applies function f to each element of l, returning a list of the
                 results. Mapcar is a standard Lisp function.
(mapc f l)   ≡ applies function f to each element of l, returning nil. Mapc is a
                 standard Lisp function.
(mapconc f l) ≡ applies function f to each element of l. Each application should
                 yield a list of values. These lists are appended together to form
                 the function's result. (Actually, the lists are destructively joined
                 together, an irrelevant detail for our purposes.) Mapconc is a
                 standard Lisp function.
P   ≡ the list that represents the entire set of propositions.

The top-down function is as follows:*

```
(top_down l) ≡
    (top_down_recur l
                    (keep_working (mapcar (lambda (x) (remove x l))
                          l)))

(top_down_recur l w) ≡
    (cond ((null w) (result l))
          (t (mapc top_down w)))

(keep_working m) ≡
    (mapconc (lambda (s)
                 (cond ((working s) (list s))
                       (t nil)))
         m)
```

The program is run as (top_down P). Before running this program the answer
list should be set to nil.

In the bottom-up solution, we successively create all subsets of *P*, from the
empty set to the entirety of *P*. At each stage, we add each set that works and
is not a superset of any minimal set to the collection of minimal sets. For this
program, we need the additional auxiliary functions

(superset_working l) ≡ is true if l is a superset of any already-found answer.

---

 * We have written this program with two auxiliary functions to avoid deluging the reader
with embedded lambda expressions.

(member x l) ≡ is true if x is a (top-level) element of the list l. **Member** is a standard Lisp function.

The bottom-up program is as follows:

```
(bottom_up l) ≡
    (cond ((null l) nil)
          (t (mapc bottom_up_one l)
             (bottom_up (successors l)))))

(bottom_up_one s) ≡
    (cond ((superset_working s) nil)
          ((working s) (result s)))

(successors l) ≡
    (mapconc
        (lambda (m)
            (mapconc
                (lambda (x)
                    (cond ((member x m) nil)
                          (t (list (cons x m)))))
                P))
        l)
```

-- *The embedded mapping functions are the Lisp equivalent to Pascal embedded for loops.*

This program is run as (bottom_up (quote (nil))).

Which program, top_down or bottom_up, is better? The top-down solution is faster if the minimal subsets are large with respect to the original set; the bottom-up solution is faster if they are small.* Each algorithm is already amenable to some immediate concurrent acceleration, because the mapping functions (mapc, mapcar, and mapconc) can apply their functional arguments to the elements of their list arguments in parallel.

Kornfeld observes that a large improvement in execution time can result from running both algorithms concurrently if each passes information about its discoveries to the other. More specifically, when top_down finds that a set does not work, then no subset of that set works; when bottom_up finds that a set works, then no superset of that set is minimal. Many algorithms

---

* These programs are also wasteful, in that many subsets of P are generated repeatedly and some answers are found several times. Exercise 18-5 asks for a modification of the top-down algorithm to avoid generating redundant subsets.

are of exponential complexity — the number of elements that need examining "explodes" (increases exponentially) as the size of the problem increases. The top-down and bottom-up algorithms have this property. If P is a set of size k, then bottom_up considers 2^k different possible sets in its search for minimal sets. However, the combination of several search algorithms, operating cooperatively and in parallel, can eliminate this combinatorial explosion, producing instead a combinatorial implosion. Kornfeld proposes the Ether language as an appropriate vehicle for describing combinatorially implosive algorithms.

Ether is based on sprites. The syntax

$$\text{(when <trigger> <command}_1\text{> ... <command}_k\text{>)}$$

defines the action of a sprite that, when it recognizes database entries that match <trigger>, executes actions <command$_1$> ... <command$_k$>. Function assert enters items into the database. To set a sprite working, it must be activated.

The sprite that recognizes working sets and asserts the nonminimality of their supersets is

```
(not_minimal_upwards) ≡
    (when ⟨Works S⟩
        (foreach q ∈ P
            (if (not (q ∈ S))
                (assert ⟨Works ({q} ∪ S)⟩)))))
```

Similarly, the sprite that asserts that subsets of nonworking sets are nonworking is

```
(not_working_downwards) ≡
    (when ⟨NotWorks S⟩
        (foreach q ∈ S
            (assert ⟨NotWorks (S − {q})⟩))))
```

Of course, the value of working simultaneously from both ends is that redundant searching can be eliminated. Ether provides such a capability with processes that can be explicitly destroyed. Ether calls processes *activities*. Function NewActivity creates a new activity; function Execute starts an activity running a particular piece of code. A *sprite* is an activity that runs a pattern/action program. Executing stifle on an activity aborts it.

In our example, evaluation of (working S) asserts (in the database) either ⟨Works S⟩ or ⟨NotWorks S⟩. Sprites whose pattern refers to one of these assertions will then be able to execute their actions.

```
(top_down S) ≡
    (foreach q ∈ S
```

```
(let ((activity (NewActivity)))             -- Create a new sprite
    (Execute (working (S − {q})) activity)    and call it "activity."
    (when ⟨Works (S − {q})⟩
        (stifle activity)
        (top_down (S − {q}))))
    (when ⟨NotWorks (S − {q})⟩
        (stifle activity)))))
(when (∀ q ∈ S ⟨NotWorks (S − {q})⟩)        -- This sprite has a
    (assert ⟨Minimal S⟩)))                     quantified pattern.
```

Similarly, function bottom_up is

```
(bottom_up S) ≡
    (foreach q ∈ P
        (if (not (q ∈ S))
            (let ((activity (NewActivity)))
                (Execute (working (S ∪ {q})) activity)
                (when ⟨NotWorks (S ∪ {q})⟩
                    (stifle activity)
                    (bottom_up (S ∪ {q})))
                (when ⟨Works (S ∪ {q})⟩
                    (stifle activity)
                    (assert ⟨Minimal (S ∪ {q})⟩)))))))
```

The entire program is run as

```
(progn
    (Execute (top_down P) (NewActivity))
    (Execute (bottom_up { }) (NewActivity))
    (Execute (not_working_downwards) (NewActivity))
    (Execute (not_minimal_upwards) (NewActivity)))
```

which sets four initial sprites running to solve the task. The last two sprites in this list are accelerators facilitating the passing of results through the system. When the activity created by this function has quiesced, the database contains Minimal assertions for exactly the minimal sets.

This example uses a simple structure (database pairs such as ⟨Works x⟩) to encode the information discovered by the sprites. Hewitt, Kornfeld, and de Jong [Kornfeld 81; Hewitt 83] argue that distributed systems based on communication need to be more complex; they must incorporate distinguishable world viewpoints, descriptions of system objects, sponsorship-based control, and elements of self-knowledge and self-reference. They call such systems *Open Systems.*

Viewpoints support the relativization of beliefs. A system with *viewpoints* allows the creation of possible worlds, the assertion of different hypotheses in different worlds, and the deduction of varying conclusions based on these differing hypotheses. A major issue in the construction of such an architecture is the inheritance of properties between subworlds.*

The idea of descriptions is that the description of what something is should be separated from the details of its implemention. This echoes both the abstract data type theme of separating abstract specification from implementation (Section 2-2) and the ancient A.I. debate over procedural and declarative representations [Winograd 75].

A major factor controlling the direction of scientific research is the allocation of research funds by sponsoring organizations. More promising research is more likely to be funded. In Ether, this idea is reflected in the requirement that all sprite triggering is to be performed under the control of a sponsor that is working on a particular goal. An explicit **goal** function associates goals with sponsors. The stifle command of the covering sets program is also an example of sponsor-based control.

Finally, since distributed problem solving involves many elements of negotiation and control, distributed problem-solving systems need to have some elements of self-knowledge and self-reference. When a subsystem is floundering or reaching contradictions, it needs mechanisms to discover and analyze the problem.

In summary, Hewitt and his coworkers propose extending the communication basis of Actor systems (Chapter 11) to distributed problem-solving systems. Their investigation has identified many fundamental aspects of such systems. These include the need to base distributed systems on communication and to model them on sophisticated problem-solving mechanisms.

18-4   SYNTHESIS

Different programming languages have different pragmatic characteristics. Individual languages lend themselves to certain tasks and suggest particular algorithms for those tasks. We find similar specializations in the pragmatics of distributed problem-solving architectures. Distributed Hearsay takes advantage of the regular geometry of certain problem spaces. It divides a task into chunks that overlap on that space and allocates one chunk to each process. An interesting open question is whether the Distributed Hearsay-II architecture can profitably be applied in domains that lack an appropriate geometry. The Contract Net Protocol focuses on the task distribution aspect of problem solving, taking seriously the idea that task distribution is a problem that requires solution as much as any other. The Protocol suggests modeling task distribution on

---

* Possible world semantics is yet another subject with a vast literature, spanning both philosophy and artificial intelligence. Some of the more interesting A.I. ideas are those of Moore [Moore 79] and Weyhrauch [Weyhrauch 80].

a simplified contract economy. The Scientific Community Metaphor argues that the ultimate distributed systems will need to be communication-based reasoning systems. Such systems will require richer representations of data and more complex inference patterns than simple serial systems have so far achieved.

Of course, each of these formalisms has its limitations. Distributed Hearsay-II is still limited by the geometry of the problem space. Contract Nets is a general but low-level tool for organizing systems. It recognizes that the elements of the problem-solving system will not even know *where* to find the expertise they need. Its resolution is to broadcast requests for subtask solution. However, depending on the underlying architecture, broadcasting can be expensive. It may be a mistake to encourage broadcasting at so low a system level. Contract Nets also requires that the solutions of tasks be funneled back to the originator of that task. This precludes continuation-based architectures.

The Scientific Community Metaphor is probably the most advanced in recognizing the attributes required of a coordinated computing system. But that advanced perspective is a major obstacle to using these ideas in the near future. The Metaphor demands knowledge representation and reasoning beyond the capabilities of current systems. Journal articles may be permanent, but typical articles mention a vast volume of bibliographic and documentary evidence in the process of drawing only narrow conclusions. Knowledge representation systems have only begun to deal with issues involved in dependencies and truth maintenance. Adding the complexities of communication complicates matters further. The Metaphor's introduction of sponsors acknowledges that distributed problem-solving systems will need to devote much of their resources to self-monitoring.

Programming languages have evolved in the programming environment, improving on the (perceived) inadequacies of earlier languages and propelled by developments in associated mathematical theories such as formal languages and semantics. We expect that distributed problem-solving architectures will evolve in the same way.

PROBLEMS

† **18-1**   Lesser and Corkill, in a demonstration of the depth of cooperation needed for serious decentralized control, propose the following problem [Lesser 78, p. 8]:

> Consider a demand bus system where a fleet of buses is to serve an urban area. Upon arrival at a bus stop, a customer might dial his desired destination on a selector device and this information would be used to plan bus routing dynamically. There are a number of elements which must be considered in such a system: buses should be kept reasonably full but not overloaded; the total mileage of the fleet should be kept as low as possible; the mean service time (waiting time at the bus stop and riding time) should be kept small; the maximum service time of any one customer should not exceed a reasonable amount (a customer waiting to get to Fifth and Main should not have to ride around all day merely because no one else needs to go near that location); and the system should be able to monitor and respond to special events (e.g., different traffic patterns at different times of

the day, concerts, athletic events, local weather conditions, bus breakdowns, stalled traffic, etc.)

Lesser and Corkill propose that any solution involve a limited broadcast transmitter/microprocessor on each bus and at each bus stop. They argue that such processing elements must not only retain a local view, but must also achieve distributed control to respond to more global conditions.

Using the language or model of your choice, program a solution to the distributed demand-driven bus system problem.

† **18-2** Lesser and Corkill also propose the Distributed Processing Game [Lesser 78] as a vehicle for exploring distributed control. The game they describe is quite general; the rules are parameterized differently for each play. For the sake of simplicity, we present only a single instantiation of the Distributed Processing Game. Also, for simplicity and tractability of implementation, we have modified some of the rules.

The game is a two-team game, played on a finite section of a plane 2000 by 2000 units large [that is, all points (x, y) such that $-1000 \leq x, y \leq 1000$]. Each team has 24 mobile nodes (the rovers) and a single, stationary home node. At the start of the game, random locations are selected for the home nodes and the players distribute their rovers within a 20-unit radius of their home nodes. Each rover has a unique identity (a number from 1 through 24) and knows its own initial location and the location of its home. The object of the game is to destroy the opponent's home node before one's own home is destroyed.

The rovers are equipped with sensors, communication devices, and energy weapons. The game proceeds in discrete steps, which are alternating team's turns. A turn consists of:

(a) Each rover moves to any spot within 10 units of its current location.

(b) Each node senses its environment. It becomes aware of the location and identity of any node within 20 units. It also becomes aware of the number of friendly and the number of unfriendly nodes within 40 units. It does not find out the identity or specific location of any unit more than 20 units away.

(c) Each node broadcasts a communication.

(d) Each node receives the communications of all nodes on its team within 100 units.

(e) Each rover can point its weapon in any direction, focus it to an angle θ, $15° \leq \theta \leq 90°$, and shoot. The weapon covers an area of 36π square units; the smaller the angle θ, the longer the covered range. Any rover that is in the coverage of the firing weapons of two or more rovers is destroyed (removed from the game). (This also includes rovers of the attacking team.) A "last words" message can be left by a rover just before it is annihilated. This message can include the identity and location of its attackers. It is received on its team's next turn. Any rover that is hit by only a single shot is unscathed. Such a rover becomes aware of the location of its attacker.

On the other hand, home nodes accumulate damage. Each rover that attacks a home node adds one damage unit to it. The first home node to accumulate 20 damage units is destroyed (resulting in a loss for that team). Figure 18-5 shows a pair of attacks.

After the completion of one side's turn, control passes to the other team for its five-step turn. Since attacking requires cooperation, this game is a good test of cooperation strategies.

These rules designate a large amount of computation. But it's just as well, because the various nodes are all processes. In particular, each (human) player *programs* her team's nodes. The game is then run free of human intervention.

The advanced version of the game introduces errors into communication and sensing. That is, in the advanced game, there is a finite probability (say, 15 percent) that any sensing or communication message is lost.

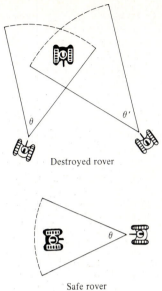

Destroyed rover

Safe rover

Figure 18-5 Attack sectors.

We have selected the above numbers arbitrarily. Clearly, the game can be varied in other ways. For example, instead of alternating, teams could move simultaneously; messages between nodes could be restricted to some particular size; and so forth.

18-3 Compare and contrast demons and guarded statements.

18-4 Modify the Lisp program for the top-down covering set problem so that it deals abstractly with sets, not lists. Invent any set-primitive and set-mapping functions you may need, such as `union`, `subset`, and `mapset`.

18-5 Modify the programs for the top-down covering set problem so that `top_down` is never called on any set more than once. (Hint: Provide an ordering on the elements of the original set. Associate with each recursive subset an element "beyond which that subset does not generate new sets.")

18-6 Does running the `top_down` and `bottom_up` Ether programs concurrently solve the combinatorial explosion problem in all cases?

† **18-7** By the experimental or analytic method of your choice, determine the expected degree of improvement gained by running the two algorithms concurrently.

18-8 What parallels can you draw between the monotonicity of Ether systems and the monotonicity of the increasing fixedness of `frons` lists (Chapter 12)?

† **18-9** Societies develop economic systems to organize, control and distribute the results of economic labor. From the time of Adam Smith to the present day, economic systems have been proposed and analyzed. Three of the most interesting systems (from the point of view of coordinated computing) are centralized, planned economies (the current Soviet model) where a centralized authority distributes all tasks and resources; *laissez faire*, free market economies (the "ideal" of the American economy) where the marketplace is the only control; and mixed planned/decentralized economies (the French and Japanese economies) where the government sets goals and provides incentives to meet them. Clearly, centralized planning is the "subroutine structure" of conventional programming. Contract Nets captures some aspects of economies with the idea of contracts; sponsors in Ether capture another. A *laissez faire* economic model

would merge the two with a real sense of currency. That is, Contract Nets gives us processes that compete for work but have no drive for accumulation (why are all these tasks bidding?); sponsors give us funding agencies but no funds (and no funding action except project cancellation). How would a coordinated computing system organized as a free market be structured? What elements of centralized planning could be introduced into such a system to improve its performance? Consider the ability of a central controller to shift system organization through taxation policy.

† **18-10** Mammalian neural systems (particularly the human neural system) have proved to be ideal distributed problem solvers, combining with great skill distributed sensing, intelligent processing, and effective manipulation. The neural system combines a high degree of redundancy with regularly-patterned control paths. It makes significant use of inhibition to prevent undesired processing. The nervous system is also amazingly complex. Read Kent's book, *The Brains of Men and Machines* [Kent 81], and design a coordinated computing system based on neural principles.

† **18-11** Individual businesses achieve their goals though composed of many independent processing elements (the workers). Mark Fox suggests that business organizations can serve as a model of system design. He develops a design language that incorporates facets of the business organization metaphor [Fox 79; Fox 81]. Design a coordinated computing system based on business and management paradigms. Another possible starting place for working on this problem is Galbraith's *Organizational Design* [Galbraith 77]. That book is a good introduction to management concepts used in business organizations.

REFERENCES

[**Corkill 83**] Corkill, D. D., and V. R. Lesser, "The Use of Meta-level Control for Coordination in a Distributed Problem Solving Network," *Proc. 8th Int. J. Conf. Artif. Intell.*, Karlsruhe, Germany (August 1983), pp. 748–755. In this paper, Corkill and Lesser extend their work on Distributed Hearsay-II, using the problems of distributed sensing as a framework in which to study distributed control.

[**Davis 76**] Davis, R., and J. King, "An Overview of Production Systems," in E. W. Elcock, and D. Michie (eds.), *Machine Intelligence 8*, Wiley, New York (1976), pp. 300–332. Broadly speaking, a production system is a set of pattern-action pairs (productions) and a database. A production system executes by repeatedly (1) finding a production whose pattern matches the database, and (2) executing the action of that production. The matching process on the pattern may bind some of the identifiers of the action, so one can write quantified productions. Production systems are a recurrent theme in A.I., appearing in many different guises. This paper discusses the theoretical nature of production systems and provides examples of systems that use them.

[**Davis 83**] Davis, R., and R. G. Smith, "Negotiation as a Metaphor for Distributed Problem Solving," *Artif. Intell.*, vol. 20, no. 1 (January 1983), pp. 63–109. Davis and Smith argue that negotiation is the appropriate metaphorical foundation of distributed problem solving and that Contract Nets is a good organization for such negotiation.

[**Erman 80**] Erman, L. D., F. Hayes-Roth, V. R. Lesser, and D. R. Reddy, "The Hearsay-II Speech-Understanding System: Integrating Knowledge to Resolve Uncertainty," *Comput. Surv.*, vol. 12, no. 2 (June 1980), pp. 213–253. Hearsay-II is a speech understanding system, developed at Carnegie-Mellon University in the mid 1970s. The system is characterized by many "knowledge sources," each of which is an expert on some aspect that contributes to understanding the spoken sound. These sources communicate their conclusions about an input sound signal by writing messages on a common "blackboard."

[**Fennell 77**] Fennell, R. D., and V. R. Lesser, "Parallelism in AI Problem-Solving: A Case Study of Hearsay-II," *IEEE Trans. Comput.*, vol. C-26, no. 2 (February 1977), pp. 98–111. Fennell and Lesser analyzed the performance of a multiprocessor implementation of

Hearsay-II. They found that the system performance could improve by a factor of 4 to 6 by the use of multiprocessors.

[**Fox 79**] Fox, M. S., "Organization Structuring: Designing Large Complex Software," Technical Report CMU-CS-79-155, Department of Computer Science, Carnegie-Mellon University, Pittsburgh, Pennsylvania (December 1979). Fox surveys organization and economic decision theory as it applies to organizing distributed programs and systems. In the final chapter of this report, he presents an organization design language, ODL.

[**Fox 81**] Fox, M. S., "An Organizational View of Distributed Systems," *IEEE Trans. Syst. Man Cybern.*, vol. SMC-11, no. 1 (January 1981), pp. 70–80. Fox argues that management science has studied the principles of human (business) organizations and that these principles are applicable to organizing distributed problem-solving systems.

[**Galbraith 77**] Galbraith, J., *Organizational Design*, Addison-Wesley, Reading, Massachusetts (1977). Galbraith describes the general management concepts used in business organizations.

[**Hanson 78**] Hanson, A. R., and E. M. Riseman, "VISIONS: A Computer System for Interpreting Scenes," in A. Hanson, and E. Riseman (eds.), *Computer Vision Systems*, Academic Press, New York (1978), pp. 303–333. This paper describes a system that generates a high-level, semantic description of color images of natural scenes. The system architecture was strongly influenced by the design of Hearsay-II.

[**Hewitt 69**] Hewitt, C. E., "PLANNER: A Language for Manipulating Models and Proving Theorems in a Robot," *Proc. 1st Int. J. Conf. Artif. Intell.*, Washington, D.C. (August 1969), pp. 295–302. The problem-solving language Planner was Hewitt's dissertation. Knowledge in Planner was encapsulated in functional, pattern-invoked demons. Micro-Planner [Sussman 70] was an implementation of some of the ideas in Planner.

[**Hewitt 83**] Hewitt, C. E., and P. de Jong, "Message Passing Semantics for Conceptual Modeling," in M. L. Brodie, J. L. Mylopoulos, and J. W. Schmidt (eds.), *Perspectives on Conceptual Modeling*, Springer-Verlag, New York (1983), pp. 147–164. Hewitt and de Jong present the theory of Open Systems.

[**Kent 81**] Kent, E., *The Brains of Men and Machines*, Byte/McGraw-Hill, Peterborough, New Hampshire (1981). In this book, Kent attempts to describe neural function and organization in terms that an electrical engineer can understand. The book is interesting not so much as an exact description of neurophysiology but as a sourcebook of ideas for the possible structure of intelligent systems.

[**Kornfeld 81**] Kornfeld, W. A., and C. E. Hewitt, "The Scientific Community Metaphor," *IEEE Trans. Syst. Man Cybern.*, vol. SMC-11, no. 1 (January 1981), pp. 24–33. This paper projects the traditional paradigms of scientific discovery into an organization for a distributed problem solver.

[**Kornfeld 82**] Kornfeld, W. A., "Combinatorially Implosive Algorithms," *CACM*, vol. 25, no. 10 (October 1982), pp. 934–938. Kornfeld argues that parallel algorithms can form a "best-first" search strategy for search problems.

[**Lesser 78**] Lesser, V. R., and D. D. Corkill, "Cooperative Distributed Problem Solving: A New Approach for Structuring Distributed Systems," Technical Report 78-7, Department of Computer and Information Science, University of Massachusetts, Amherst, Massachusetts (May 1978). This report is an early presentation of the idea of cooperative distributed problem solving. It is the source of the distributed bus problem and the attacking-rovers game.

[**Lesser 80**] Lesser, V. R., and L. D. Erman, "Distributed Interpretation: A Model and Experiment," *IEEE Trans. Comput.*, vol. C-29, no. 12 (December 1980), pp. 1144–1163. Lesser and Erman describe the creation of a "distributed" version of the Hearsay-II speech understanding system.

[**Lesser 81**] Lesser, V. R., and D. D. Corkill, "Functionally Accurate, Cooperative Distributed Systems," *IEEE Trans. Syst. Man Cybern.*, vol. SMC-11, no. 1 (January 1981), pp. 81–99. Lesser and Corkill assert that distributed systems need to treat uncertainty and errors as part of the network problem-solving process, much as some Artificial Intelligence systems treat noisy input data and approximate knowledge in their problem solving. They discuss the paradigm of functionally accurate, cooperative systems in the context of distributed interpretation, distributed traffic control, and distributed planning.

[**Moore 79**] Moore, R. C., "Reasoning About Knowledge and Action," Ph.D. dissertation, M.I.T., Cambridge, Massachusetts (February 1979). Traditionally, reasoning about knowledge deals with determining what an individual could know. Several modal logics have been proposed for this task. Moore axiomatizes the possible-world semantics of modal logic in first-order logic. This leads to reasoning about the worlds that are compatible with an individual's knowledge.

[**Nii 78**] Nii, H. P., and E. A. Feigenbaum, "Rule-Based Understanding of Signals," in D. A. Waterman, and F. Hayes-Roth (eds.), *Pattern Directed Inference Systems*, Academic Press, New York (1978), pp. 483–501. SU/X is a system for interpreting large quantities of "continuous signals produced by objects" (sonar readings). SU/X uses the Hearsay-II architecture, principally the concepts of blackboard and multilevel representation of knowledge.

[**Smith 78**] Smith, R. G., and R. Davis, "Distributed Problem Solving: The Contract Net Approach," *Proc. 2d Natl. Conf. Canadian Soc. Comput. Stud. Intell.*, Toronto (July 1978), pp. 278–287. This paper is an overview of Contract Nets. It describes the distributed-sensing Contract Net.

[**Smith 81a**] Smith, R. G., *A Framework for Distributed Problem Solving*, UMI Research Press, Ann Arbor (1981). This dissertation is a general study of Contract Nets. It includes performance analyses of a simulated Contract Nets system and comparisons with other problem-solving formalisms.

[**Smith 81b**] Smith, R. G., and R. Davis, "Frameworks for Cooperation in Distributed Problem Solving," *IEEE Trans. Syst. Man Cybern.*, vol. SMC-11, no. 1 (January 1981), pp. 61–70. Smith and Davis identify two forms of cooperation in a distributed problem-solving system: task sharing and result sharing. They discuss these two kinds of sharing with respect to Contract Nets.

[**Sussman 70**] Sussman, G. J., T. Winograd, and E. Charniak, "MICRO-PLANNER Reference Manual," Memo 203, Artificial Intelligence Laboratory, M.I.T., Cambridge, Massachusetts (1970). Micro-Planner is an implementation of some of the ideas in Hewitt's thesis [Hewitt 69]. Micro-Planner featured a database of "facts," pattern-directed invocation of demons that matched the facts in that database, and automatic backtracking. Micro-Planner had a period of popularity in the early 1970s. However, the automatic backtracking mechanism proved too cumbersome and the language fell into disuse.

[**Weyhrauch 80**] Weyhrauch, R. W., "Prolegomena to a Theory of Mechanized Formal Reasoning," *Artif. Intell.*, vol. 13, no. 1 (1980), pp. 133–170. Weyhrauch describes the knowledge representation system FOL. FOL encapsulates both collections of facts and rules for manipulating those facts in a single structure. One can both reason in this structure or reason about it.

[**Winograd 75**] Winograd, T., "Frame Representations and the Declarative-Procedural Controversy," in D. G. Bobrow, and A. Collins (eds.), *Representation and Understanding*, Academic Press, New York (1975), pp. 185–210. Prior to Micro-Planner, the mainstream of A.I. knowledge representations was declarative: the facts of the situation were described in a suitable logic and a general-purpose theorem prover sought to prove the desired goals. Micro-Planner represented knowledge in procedural form; knowing something was knowing what to do with it. This dichotomy lead to the "declarative-procedural controversy" as to whether the best method of knowledge representation used axioms or programs. A more modern view is that systems not only need to reason with their knowledge (procedural form) but also to reason about it (declarative form).

FIVE

CONTRASTS AND COMPARISONS

NINETEEN

CONTRASTS AND COMPARISONS

The systems discussed in this book span the important ideas for coordinated computing. The variety of mechanisms and structures in these systems may seem staggering. But as we argued in Chapter 5, most of the important differences can be described as choices in a decision space. This chapter has three sections. In the first, we review the choice dimensions and describe where each system lies in the decision space. We summarize these results in a series of tables. The second section discusses specific common themes in greater detail. Often systems are refinements of earlier ideas; this section conveys some of this historical development. In the last section we propose a unified model, showing how an appropriate set of primitives is sufficient to achieve any of the behaviors.

19-1   GENERAL COMPARISONS

Dimensions of Distribution

In Chapter 5, we identified 12 key dimensions in the design of coordinated computing systems. In this section, we review these dimensions, ascribing to each system its place in the dimension space.* The differences among systems are best summarized in tabular form. Unfortunately, a table of 12 dimensions and 18 systems would be incomprehensible. Instead, we have broken our table into three parts: (1) Table 19-1 examines the general goals and structure of each system, (2) Table 19-2 exhibits aspects of intrasystem communication, and (3) Table 19-3 presents the systems with respect to the remaining dimensions.

---

* Other authors who have pursued the theme of comparisons of concurrent and distributed languages include Andrews and Schneider [Andrews 83], Mohan [Mohan 80], Rao [Rao 80], and Stotts [Stotts 82].

Problem Domain (A) The systems described in this book range from simple models to elaborate languages. Much of this diversity arises from differences in task domains; the different systems are meant to be solutions to different problems. The models tend to be mathematical. For example, Shared Variables is a tool for studying algorithmic analysis and program correctness; Concurrent Processes, program semantics; and Petri Nets, system correctness. The programming languages focus on the problems of writing programs. They divide into the "general-purpose" or *pragmatic* languages (PLITS), programming languages directed at implementing operating systems (Concurrent Pascal, Distributed Processes, SR, and Cell), and languages concerned with the issues of particular subproblems of operating systems (Ada, embedded systems; and Argus, distributed databases). The heuristic systems (Distributed Hearsay-II, Contract Nets, Ether) focus on organizing distributed problem solving.

Some systems assume an intermediate point between these extremes: CSP is not only a language for systems implementation but also a model of both hardware and program semantics; Actors and IAP strive both to have a well defined semantics and to be pragmatic programming environments. And lastly, Exchange Functions, while in many ways similar to the formal Concurrent Processes, is directed toward a completely different goal— requirements specification for program development.

Of course, we mean these distinctions to capture the thrust of a system design, not the minor intentions. Languages for systems implementation must be concerned with the pragmatic problems of programming. Accompanying the design of many new programming languages is an attempt to provide their formal semantics. And good models often correspond to the reality of building the kinds of systems they model. Nevertheless, understanding the differing intentions of the system designers is an essential component for understanding the diversity in the designs.

Explicit Processes (B) These systems all support concurrent computation. One issue for concurrent systems is designating which actions can be executed concurrently. Almost all our systems use explicit processes to show concurrency. In *explicit process systems*, the programmer causes process entities to be created. Once created, these processes compute concurrently (subject to various synchronization constraints). Most systems call their processes, "processes." Occasionally, a system uses another name for the same concept: tasks in Ada, modules in PLITS, actors in Actors, cells in Cell, and sprites in Ether.

Despite the popularity of processes, not all systems use them. Four systems indicate concurrency without processes. In IAP, each call to cons and frons creates a suspension (a form of task) to be resolved by the underlying system. This task will be satisfied either lazily, by otherwise idle resources, or immediately, driven by a demand for its answer. Distributed Hearsay-II combines the pattern-directed invocation of productions with the broadcast communication of blackboards. And Data Flow and Petri Nets abstract concurrency by the independent flow of graph tokens.

For the sake of comparison, we treat concurrency in IAP as the concurrency of the underlying evaluators (communicating through the realization of cell values), concurrency in Distributed Hearsay-II as the concurrency of knowledge sources, and concurrency in Petri Nets and Data Flow as the concurrency of the transitions and actors communicating with tokens.

Process Dynamics (C) Process dynamics describes the change in number and variety of processes through the execution of a program. Some systems allow programs to create new processes during execution. Others require that all processes be defined at system creation (*static processes*). Shared Variables, Exchange Functions, Petri Nets, Data Flow, CSP, Concurrent Pascal, Distributed Processes, SR, Distributed Hearsay-II, and Contract Nets are static process systems.

Two different syntactic mechanisms support dynamic process creation, explicit allocation (*dynamic*) and lexical program elaboration (*lexical*). Systems with explicit allocation have a statement to create a new process, much as Pascal has a statement to allocate a new record. Actors, IAP, Ada, and PLITS have explicit process allocation. Lexical elaboration creates processes by combining declarations with recursive program structures. That is, if procedure P declares process A and then calls itself recursively, the recursive invocation of P creates another copy of A. Concurrent Processes, Ada, PLITS, Cell, Argus, and Ether create new processes by lexical elaboration.

By and large, pragmatic systems more frequently allow dynamic process creation than systems-oriented languages. Systems based on compilation restrict new processes to be described by a "type," though processes may be specialized by parameterization. Some interpreted systems (such as Actors) allow the description of a process to be generated at the time the process is created.

Systems with explicit allocation ought to provide names (pointers) to the newly created processes. These names can then be passed between processes, allowing other processes to become aware of the new processes and send them messages. Lexical process creation often restricts interprocess communication to lexical scopes.

Synchronization (D) The differences that distinguish concurrent computation from simple serial processing center on communication and synchronization among processes. The first notable division between systems is the issue of synchronous versus asynchronous communication. In synchronous communication, both processes "attend" to the communication. Every communication request is matched by a reception; a process cannot send a second communication until the first has been handled. In asynchronous communication, processes send requests without regard to their reception; a process is free to send a request and continue computing.

Ten systems are asynchronous: Shared Variables, Petri Nets, Data Flow, Actors, IAP, Concurrent Pascal, PLITS, Distributed Hearsay-II, Contract Nets, and Ether. SR provides both synchronous and asynchronous communication. The other systems are synchronous.

Table 19-1 Goals and Structures

System	(A) Task domain	(B) Explicit processes	(C) Process dynamics
Shared Variables *Lynch & Fischer*	Analysis, correctness	Processes	Static
Exchange Functions *Fitzwater & Zave*	Requirements specification	Processes	Static
Concurrent Processes *Milne & Milner*	Semantics	Processes	Lexical
Petri Nets *Petri*	Correctness, modeling	Structure	Static
Data Flow *Dennis/Arvind & Gostelow*	Pragmatics	Structure	Static
CSP *Hoare*	Systems, semantics	Processes	Static
Actors **Hewitt**	Pragmatics, semantics	Processes	Dynamic
IAP *Friedman & Wise*	Pragmatics, semantics	Tasks	Dynamic
Concurrent Pascal *Brinch Hansen*	Systems	Processes	Static
Dist. Processes *Brinch Hansen*	Systems	Processes	Static
Ada *DoD*	Systems (embedded)	Processes	Dynamic, lexical
PLITS *Feldman*	Pragmatics	Processes	Dynamic, lexical
SR *Andrews*	Systems	Processes	Static
Cell *Silberschatz*	Systems	Processes	Lexical
Argus *Liskov*	Systems (database)	Processes	Dynamic
Dist. Hearsay-II *Lesser & Corkill*	Problem solving	Productions	Static
Contract Nets *Smith & Davis*	Problem solving	Processes	Static
Ether *Kornfeld & Hewitt*	Problem solving	Processes	Dynamic

Buffering (E) A system's buffer size is the number of messages from a given process that can be pending at one time. The interesting distinction is between systems with *bounded* buffers and systems with *unbounded* buffers—that is, systems for which a process's pending messages can occupy only a limited space in contrast with systems that allow a process to send an unbounded number of messages. Synchronous systems invariably have bounded buffering—a synchronous process can have only a finite number of pending messages.* Message-based, asynchronous systems (Petri Nets, Actors, PLITS, SR, and Contract Nets) have unbounded buffering, as do pattern-invocation systems (Distributed Hearsay-II and Ether). One version of Data Flow uses bounded buffers [Dennis 74], another unbounded [Arvind 77]. Additionally, some systems (Shared Variables, IAP, Concurrent Pascal, Ada, and SR) permit processes to share memory. Shared memory is a form of bounded, asynchronous communication.

Information Flow (F) Interprocess communication is the transfer of information. Clearly, the mere occurrence of a communication is informative. Thus (particularly in synchronous systems), communication provides a synchronization signal. However, it is usually desirable to transmit more than pure synchronization—effectively, to transmit information. The various systems propose different organizations for information flow. For some, communication provides a sender and a receiver; the information flow is unidirectional (*uni*) from the sender to the receiver. Of course, unidirectional communication is a consequence of message-based asynchronous systems (Petri Nets, Data Flow, Actors, PLITS, Contract Nets, and the asynchronous primitive in SR). Only a single synchronous system (CSP) has unidirectional information flow.

Shared memory introduces its own nuances of information flow. Shared memory is naturally asynchronous. In its simplest form, like IAP, Distributed Hearsay-II, and Ether, it is unidirectional, from a "writer" to a "reader." Monitors in Concurrent Pascal structure the exchange to be bidirectional—first, a transfer of information to the monitor and then a reception of return values. In Shared Variables, the exchange is (for read-write processes) somewhat the opposite—first a value is received from the variable and then the variable is set to a new state.

Synchronous communication can be treated either as a single, instantaneous event or as an event that progresses through stages. The first of these is simultaneous, bidirectional communication (*bi-sim*). Exchange Functions and Concurrent Processes have simultaneous, bidirectional communication. The synchronous programming languages have delayed bidirectional communication (*bi-del*). In this organization, processes enter a rendezvous. In *rendezvous*, the requesting process transfers information to the called process. This process then computes

---

* Naively, it would seem that a single-message buffer would suffice for synchronous systems. However, systems with output guards can have a pending message for each guarded output clause.

a response and sends that response back to the original caller. This pattern, the remote procedure call, is a generalization of the procedure call, with its stepwise transfer of query and control to the called procedure, the execution of the body of the procedure, and the return of answers and control to the caller. Distributed Processes, Ada, SR, Cell, and Argus use delayed bidirectional communication.

Strangely, none of the models or languages has generalized the coroutine as a communication model. Such a generalization would provide first an establishment of communication and then an alternation of information transfer and computation through the entire transaction. However, processes are adequate coroutines of and by themselves; in any system that provides some filtering of message reception it is straightforward to obtain this control pattern.

Communication Control (G) The various models and languages show the most diversity in mechanisms for establishing communication. To handle this variety, we break this dimension into two parts, control and connection. Control concerns the actions that processes take to communicate, including the facilities they have for choosing a communication partner. Connection is an issue of naming: to what does a communicating process refer?

Seven systems (Shared Variables, Exchange Functions, Concurrent Processes, CSP, IAP, Concurrent Pascal, and Distributed Hearsay-II) treat communicators as equals (*equal*). In Exchange Functions and Concurrent Processes, communicating processes take identical actions. Exchange Functions allows processes to test whether communication is available and to abort a communication attempt if it is not (*immed. time-out*). CSP treats processes (roughly) as equals. It introduces asymmetry with unidirectional information flow. Input guards (and, extensionally, output guards) provide further concurrency control (*I/O guards*). In Shared Variables, IAP, and Distributed Hearsay-II, communication is anonymous and nondirective. Processes asynchronously read and write shared storage. No process has, a priori, a distinguished role. In Concurrent Pascal, processes communicate through shared monitors. Processes do not address each other directly; hence, communicating processes are equals.

The other systems specify roles for the "calling" and "called" processes. Petri Nets, Data Flow, Actors, Distributed Processes, Argus, and Ether treat the called process as a passive server (*passive*) that accepts requests without controlling the order of their reception. (However, Distributed Processes programs can then use guarded commands to order accepted requests.) Ada, PLITS, SR, Cell, and Contract Nets allow the called process some freedom in choosing which requests to serve (*active*). All segregate requests into groups. In Ada, SR, and Cell, requests are grouped by entry queues; in PLITS, by transaction keys. All but PLITS have input guards to read from one of several queues at once (*i-guard*); all have functions to determine if a particular queue is empty.

Additionally, some languages add their own features for communication control. PLITS, SR, and Cell allow filtering of requests by origin (*send-filt*); SR and Cell, ordering requests by priority (*priority*); and SR, guards that can examine not only the internal state of the process, but also the message (*mess-grd*). Ada allows both input and output guards and permits time-outs by both the calling and called processes. Concurrent Pascal and Cell can suspend processing a request and then later resume it (*suspend*).

Connection (H) These systems use four different syntactic forms to channel communication: ports, names, entries, and pattern-selective broadcast. These syntactic devices can be used by the sender, the receiver, or both the sender and the receiver of the communication.

Communication through a symbol external to communicating processes is communication through a port (*port*). Shared memory systems (Shared Variables, IAP, and Concurrent Pascal) use ports, where the shared memory is the port. Additionally, Exchange Functions and Concurrent Processes use explicit ports. We view the shared places of Petri Nets as another form of port. Data Flow, Actors, and PLITS direct communication at an unmodified process (*name*). None of these systems requires the receiver of a communication to describe the sender. However, PLITS processes can filter requests by transaction keys (*key-filt*), using the transaction keys as a kind of entry mechanism.

Several of the languages (Distributed Processes, Ada, SR, Cell, and Argus) focus communication on an entry (*entry*) in the called process. In Ada, SR, and Cell, a called process can have several entries and accept requests from them in an order determined by program control. In Distributed Processes and Argus, entries are not explicitly referenced by the recipient program. CSP pattern matching serves a similar filtering purpose.

Three heuristic systems, Distributed Hearsay-II, Contract Nets, and Ether, specify subproblems as tasks and distribute these tasks in a broadcastlike fashion. On the basis of the pattern-described interests of the processing elements, the system directs relevant messages to them.

Time (I) Einstein asserted that time is relative. Relativity arises because the information of an event cannot travel faster than the speed of light. Lamport has argued that a similar principle applies to distributed computing systems [Lamport 78]. In a distributed system, it is meaningless to refer to the absolute "time" at which an event happened, particularly from the perspective of a single process. Instead, the information of an event diffuses, through communication, to interested processes. Processes can only be synchronized, not made simultaneous. Whenever a model or language argues that some communication event is to abort because of time-out, it is natural to ask, "Which process timed the time-out?"

This ambiguity about time leads to an ambivalence about time by the more mathematical models and languages. Most of them avoid the subject entirely; the few that mention the problem (such as Shared Variables) discount its significance.

Table 19-2 Communication

System	(D) Synch.	(E) Buffer.	(F) Inform. flow	(G) Commun. control	(H) Commun. Connection send.	rec.
Shar. Var.	Asyn.	Bnded.	Bi-Mem	Equal	Port	Port
Ex. Fun.	Syn.	Bnded.	Bi-Sim	Equal i'm. t.-o.	Port	Port
Con. Proc.	Syn.	Bnded.	Bi-Sim	Equal	Port	Port
Petri Nets	Asyn.	Unbnd.	Uni.	Pass.	Port	Port
Data Flow	Asyn.	Bnded./ Unbnd.	Uni.	Pass.	Name	——
CSP	Syn.	Bnded.	Uni.	Equal I/O-grd.	Name pat.-mat.	Name pat.-mat.
Actors	Asyn.	Unbnd.	Uni.	Pass.	Name	——
IAP	Asyn.	Bnded.	Uni.	Equal	Port	Port
Con. Pas.	Asyn.	Bnded.	Bi-Mem	Equal susp.	Port w/entry	Port w/entry
Dist. Proc.	Syn.	Bnded.	Bi-Del	Pass.	Entry	——
Ada	Syn.	Bnded.	Bi-Del	Act. I/O-grd., time-out	Entry	Entry
PLITS	Asyn.	Unbnd.	Uni.	Act. send-filt.	Name	Key-filt.
SR	Syn./ asyn.	Bnded./ Unbnd.	Bi-Del/ Uni.	Act. I-grd., mess-grd., send-filt., prior.	Entry	Entry
Cell	Syn.	Bnded.	Bi-Del	Act. I-grd., send-filt., prior., susp.	Entry	Entry
Argus	Syn.	Bnded.	Bi-Del	Pass.	Entry	——
DH-II	Asyn.	Unbnd.	Uni.	Equal	Broad.	Pat. mat.
Con. Nets	Asyn.	Unbnd.	Uni.	Act.	Broad.	Pat. mat.
Ether	Asyn.	Unbnd.	Uni.	Pass.	Broad.	Pat. mat

This reflects the attitude that since time is inherently ambiguous any possible formalization is vacuous.

The systems languages, needing to deal with the real world, must take the opposite attitude: "Time may be relative, but if it has been one millisecond (one second, one minute, one day, ...) since I sent that message and I have not received a reply, the other process is not going to respond."* Only three of the systems have mechanisms for direct temporal manipulation: Exchange Functions's immediate exchange function, Ada's delayed input and output select statements, and the ability of Argus actions to first delay and then kill sibling actions. In some ways, Ether is especially atemporal—sprites have access not only to communications sent after their creation but also to those sent before.

Fairness (J) Fairness concerns the bounds on the delay that a process faces before achieving access to a resource. Most of our concerns are with communication fairness, since processes interact through communication. However, there are also fairness considerations involved in processor allocation and peripheral device control. Our systems exhibit three attitudes towards fairness. In an *antifair* system a process can be indefinitely blocked from getting a resource. *Weak fairness* implies that a process is sure to get the resource eventually. *Strong fairness* demands that processes get resources in turn. In a strongly fair system, it is possible to determine a finite upper bound on the number of other requests (of equivalent priority on the given request structure) that will be served before a given request. One common mechanism for enforcing strong fairness is to queue waiting requests. With a queue, a process waits only for those processes ahead of it in line.

Interestingly, there is only a weak correlation between attitudes towards fairness and other dimensions of system organization. Concurrent Processes, Petri Nets, Data Flow with indeterminate-merge,† CSP, Argus, Distributed Hearsay-II, Contract Nets, and Ether are explicitly antifair. Shared Variables, Exchange Functions, IAP, and Actors have weak fairness. For example, in Shared Variables, every process eventually takes another step; in Actors, every message is eventually received and processed. Distributed Processes, Ada, PLITS, SR, and Cell are queue-based systems and are, in some respects, strongly fair.

Failure (K) Most models and languages treat processes as fault-free automata and communication as invariably successful. However, several systems have some mechanisms for dealing with failure. With the **frons** statement, IAP encourages convenient redundancy. Ada has several mechanisms for handling failure and distributed termination, including time-outs and exception handlers. Contract

---

* The software controlling the first flight of the space shuttle Columbia provided a graphic illustration of the difficulties of programming multiprocessor systems that depend on intricate timing relationships [Garman 81]. Because a central clock would send different processors different times, the programmers of the shuttle controller used an ad hoc arrangement to provide processors with identical times. This system had a bug that, with low probability, allowed the processors to initialize to a permanently unsynchronized state. Unfortunately, when the system was brought up for the planned launch, it fell into this state. This forced a delay of the shuttle flight until the bug was found and fixed.

† Fairness is not an issue in determinate systems.

Table 19-3 Other issues

System	(I) Time	(J) Fairness	(K) Failure	(L) Heuristics
Shar. Var.	——	Weak	——	——
Ex. Fun.	Instantaneous time-out	Weak	——	——
Con. Proc.	——	Anti	——	——
Petri Nets	——	Anti	——	——
Data Flow	——	Anti	——	——
CSP	——	Anti	——	——
Actors	——	Weak	——	——
IAP	——	Weak	Convenient redundancy	——
Con. Pas.	——	Anti	——	——
Dist. Proc.	——	Strong	——	——
Ada	Delayed time-out	Strong	Exception handlers, distributed termination	Distributed termination
PLITS	——	Strong	——	——
SR	——	Strong	——	——
Cell	——	Strong	——	——
Argus	Delayed time-out	Anti	Atomic actions, exception handlers	Atomic actions
DH-II	——	Anti	Evidence	Pattern-directed invocation
Con. Nets	——	Anti	Contract managers	Contracts
Ether	Anti-time	Anti	Evidence	Pattern-directed invocation

Nets allows the manager of a contract to monitor its progress. Argus provides perhaps the most comprehensive set of conventional failure mechanisms, wrapping each remote call in an atomic action and allowing exception handlers to deal with the failures of these actions. Distributed Hearsay-II and Ether rely on weighing evidence in drawing conclusions, using the natural redundancy of their processing organization to immunize against failure.

Heuristic Mechanisms (L) Five systems have specific heuristic mechanisms. Ada provides a primitive for coordinating distributed termination of a set of processes. Argus, extending this idea, provides atomic actions. Contract Nets implements the contract mechanism and negotiation as an organizing principle. And Distributed Hearsay-II and Ether each have a version of pattern-directed invocation for communication.

19-2 SPECIFIC COMPARISONS

Many of the themes of particular models and languages are echoed, with variations, in other systems. A set of systems that share several key properties form a family of systems. We find the variations within a family noteworthy. In this section we identify several concepts that define families of systems and note some general metaphors about models and languages.

Communication metaphors Human artifacts parallel human experience. One contention of Chapter 18 is that human organizations are candidate models for coordinated systems. We observe that the interprocess communication mechanisms of most of the systems resemble human communication mechanisms. How do people communicate? Face-to-face, direct communication is the most immediate form, but such proximity is the antithesis of distribution. The primary indirect interpersonal communication media are the telephone and the mail. The directness and immediacy of the telephone parallel synchronous communication. For example, in CSP communicating processes "call" each other. However, CSP conversations differ from human telephone calls in two important respects: (1) once attempted, a call cannot be aborted; and (2) only a single message is sent in a conversation. Guarded commands in CSP allow calling several "phones" at once, waiting for the first to answer. Exchange Functions and Concurrent Processes share the telephonic flavor of CSP, though they direct calls to "central switchboards" (ports) instead of using "direct dialing." In Exchange Functions, a process that would otherwise be required to wait for an answer can "hang up."* The asynchronous communication of Actors and PLITS parallels posting letters. One composes a message, drops it in the mail, and continues one's activities.

The other important human communication media are broadcast (like message boards, radio, and television) and archival (like books, records, and newspapers). The communication medium of Shared Variables is like a bulletin board. Messages are written and overwritten, without specifying for whom they are in-

---

* The synchronous communication of Distributed Processes and its derivatives is unlike this phone metaphor, because the called party can consult arbitrarily many other processes between accepting the call and responding—somewhat like being able to place arbitrarily many callers on hold.

tended. Distributed Hearsay-II and Ether specifically relate their communication organization to blackboards and libraries. No system has explored messages that are generally but only intermittently available.

Functional and applicative formalisms Functional languages describe computation as the result of successive applications of functions to input values. Applicative languages, a close cousin of functional languages, emphasize the binding of values to names along with function application. These languages contrast with the assignment operation of imperative languages like Pascal. Five of the systems (Exchange Functions, Concurrent Processes, Data Flow, Actors, and IAP) are in some way functional or applicative. Exchange Functions and Concurrent Processes center on processes with state. They use applicative syntax only to describe the state-succession functions. The other three systems are inspired by applicative and functional programming (and the earliest applicative programming language, pure Lisp). IAP is a direct extension of pure Lisp to include nonevaluating cons and frons and functional objects. Except for the state mechanisms of impure actors, the Actor model is a direct implementation of the lambda calculus. We can easily program nonevaluating cons and frons operators in Actors. In particular, a nonevaluating cons actor receives messages about potential car and cdr fields, remembers the messages, but does not act on them until receiving the corresponding car and cdr requests.

It may strike the reader as odd that we classify Data Flow as an applicative language. After all, the syntax of Data Flow (as we have described it) is graphical. However, Data Flow graphs (without indeterminate-merge) are isomorphic to applicative notation. The concurrency in Data Flow computations is the same as the concurrency provided by parallel argument evaluation in applicative languages. Therefore, Data Flow is, in some sense, just another syntax for applicative programming. From this perspective, Data Flow is distinctive principally for syntactic reasons. Data Flow has a simple syntax for constructing functions with several outputs, allows infinite structures without a special **letrec** construct, and provides strong data typing. Data Flow suffers from the pragmatic disadvantage that the free form of the Data Flow graphs encourages poorly structured programs. Also, unlike IAP, the "push" of Data Flow tokens causes the computation to be done with call-by-value instead of call-by-need.

Indeterminate-merge transforms data flow in much the same way that frons transforms IAP and amb transforms LISP. Chapter 12 discusses the effect of hypothesizing a split operation in suspending cons. Such an operator resembles the inverse of indeterminate-merge. Instead of taking inputs from several lines and merging them into a single stream, split takes a single stream and parcels it out to several lines, feeding each line as it "needs" another token.

What would a Data Flow split operator be like? The split operator of suspending cons presents the next data item to the output line that "needs" one next. But since Data Flow is call-by-value, its split could not know which line "needs" the next output.

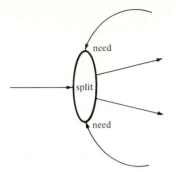

Figure 19-1 Split actor with need lines.

A possible resolution of this difficulty would be to add explicit need inputs to the split actor. Each output line from a split operator would have an associated need input. Split would place a token on that line only if the corresponding need input had a token. In doing so, it would consume the need token. Figure 19-1 shows a split actor with need lines.

Filling split is a possible alternative mechanism for introducing split to Data Flow. Filling split has a single input line and several output lines. It is enabled when there is a token on its input line. On firing, it transfers this token to one of its output lines that does not currently hold a token. Although filling split cannot match split's ability to divide an input stream among several deserving outputs, it can apportion work roughly according to demand among several successors.

Synchronous models One family of models is the systems that communicate by immediate, synchronous messages: Exchange Functions, Concurrent Processes, and CSP. These models differ in details: Concurrent Processes allows dynamic process creation, while Exchange Functions and CSP require static processes. Exchange Functions and Concurrent Processes have bidirectional communication through ports, while CSP uses mutual naming modified by pattern matching. Concurrent Processes was defined to investigate the mathematics of concurrent computation; Exchange Functions, to aid in the design of systems. CSP serves a dual purpose, both as a mathematical model and as a systems implementation language. We find it interesting that such diverse domains give rise to such similar systems.

Perspectives on queue control When several requests are pending for a particular process, the system must decide which request to handle next. Some systems specify that no particular service order is defined: requests are served arbitrarily. Models tend toward this approach, as they are more mathematical, and antifairness is easier to express mathematically. In particular, CSP and Actors treat all waiting requests equally.

Languages designed for systems development tend toward the opposite extreme. These languages often have elaborate rules for deciding the next request to be processed. These mechanisms express the programming tradition of giving the system implementor maximum control of the computing environment, balanced only by the requirements of straightforward implementation and efficient execution. In our systems languages we see a progression of mechanisms for queue control. Our first such language, Distributed Processes, sorted calls only by their destination procedure. Ada and SR developed this idea of grouping calls, resulting in the concept of task entries, that serve, like monitor procedures, as collectors of requests, but can appear in several places in the program. Entries also began to acquire attributes of their own. In particular, a program can count the requests waiting on an entry.

PLITS, a contemporary of Ada, unified all entries into a single queue but provided the first filtering on that queue: processes can select messages by sender or transaction key. Feldman presented the rationale of that decision as [Feldman 79, p. 359]:

> One would like a module to be able to do quite selective **receive**'s and not be bothered with messages that it was not ready to process. For example, one could allow **receive** to take an arbitrary predicate on the values of slots in the message. There are several difficulties. One cannot build into the system all the generality that might ever be required—for example, a module might want to receive that message that has the greatest value for some slot. Another problem is that having very selective **receive**'s puts a great burden on the system for storing, checking, and keeping track of messages. Finally, there are problems of defining the correct sequencing for messages that are being controlled by complex predicates. The definition we have chosen is a compromise. Clearly, having **receive** only specify the source is too restrictive.

He proceeded to show that many different control regimes can be encoded by transaction keys.

SR adapted the PLITS mechanism of sorting messages by sender and added features of its own: guard and priority clauses based on the values in the message itself. Cell extended these mechanisms with provisions for examining a request and returning it to a suspended state. What Feldman feared as too complex (sorting for the message with the greatest value on some slot) has become the routine of later languages.

What is gained by more complex sorting mechanisms? If the system hides a sorting mechanism, some complicated programs are easily expressed. This is particularly so when one wants the request that is extreme in a way that can be mapped onto the sorting mechanism. In such circumstances, a primitive that selects extremities dramatically simplifies the program. Is SR's approach the ultimate in queue control? Feldman hinted at the answer to this question with his mention of arbitrary predicates. We imagine predicates as objects to be applied to the elements of the queue. Additionally, some criteria are attributes of the queue as a whole. For example, on a given entry, a process might want to select a member of the class of requests with the greatest number of pending calls.

Such a decision involves examining not only the individual elements but also the queue as a whole. Such a control structure is a step beyond the current proposals.

Asynchronous message systems Two systems center on asynchronous messages, Actors and PLITS. Though different in appearance (PLITS has an imperative syntax, while Actors is applicative), they are at heart similar. Both systems are based on messages and recognize the importance of being able to pass process names in messages. Both thereby allow a form of continuation. Actors is primarily a model. It provides only a minimal set of primitive mechanisms and rules restricting the behavior of these primitives. PLITS carries the asynchronous message metaphor into practice. It extends this metaphor by adding structure to messages and message receptions. The most important operational difference is that in PLITS, messages sent from the same sender with the same transaction key arrive in the order sent. Actors does not guarantee any such ordering. In practice, the PLITS restriction requires a fairly complicated communication protocol; the Actor perspective may prove more realistic in megacomputing systems. This difference notwithstanding, PLITS can be viewed as a pragmatic, imperative implementation of the actor metaphor.

Processes The process concept is basic to most approaches to distributed computing, but the definition of process varies among systems. All processes have permanent storage and the power to compute. In some systems, processes are objects; they can be dynamically allocated and deleted; they possess names that can be passed in messages. In Cell, processes can even express "last wishes" to be executed before they are deallocated. Other systems, for reasons of philosophy or implementation difficulty, do not provide all these facilities. Limitations include fixing the set of processes at compilation time and failing to provide process names, thereby restricting the potential communication structure.

19-3 BASIS SYSTEMS

The systems have a variety of mechanisms. We are drawn to the question of natural primitives and desirable extensions: What sets of primitives can describe the behavior of our systems? What mechanisms built from these primitives best support coordinated computing? In this section we discuss these two issues.

Seeking a Basis

We seek a primitive model, a *basis* model. We want an *operational* model, one that describes what to do without specifying the details of an implementation. We will not impose a syntax on our model, but we want the primitives of the model to correspond directly to the familiar programming concepts they are meant to emulate.*

Both Milne and Milner and Lynch and Fischer address formal equivalence of concurrent systems. These authors show that a set of concurrent processes is semantically equivalent to a single process with unbounded indeterminacy. Hence, a simple extension of Turing machines will capture the formal semantics of distributed systems. However, we find this formal result unsatisfying; it fails to reflect the operational reality of a distributed environment. Multiple processing agents provide some efficiency advantages, and distribution provides some constraints. We want the basis model to reflect these realities.

Our technique is to go through our list of dimensions, selecting a choice for each dimension that encompasses the others. This results in a basis model; restrictions of this model give us the individual systems discussed in Parts 2, 3, and 4. A key theme of our discussion is protocols—how one system can model another if its processes follow a particular pattern of actions.

Of course, the problem domain of our approach is modeling languages and models. The first real dimension is explicit processes. Almost all the systems use explicit processes. Four systems do not: Petri Nets, Data Flow, IAP, and Distributed Hearsay-II. We can simulate Petri Nets with processes by having a process for each transition and place, Data Flow by having a process for each actor, IAP by creating new processes for each cons or frons, and Distributed Hearsay-II by creating a process for each entry and knowledge source. Thus, explicit processes are adequate to model any of our systems. Some systems allow processes to be (externally) suspended or destroyed. We can model this by requiring processes to check between other communications to see if they should spin or die.

Though a single process with unbounded indeterminacy can simulate any number of other processes, it seems most natural to give our model dynamic process creation. We identified two syntactic mechanisms for creating new processes: lexical elaboration and explicit creation. Clearly, a system that creates new processes by explicit command subsumes lexical elaboration. To model lexical elaboration, we execute "create" instructions in place of process declarations. To model a system of static processes, one merely fails to create any new processes not required by the rest of the model.

Which is more primitive, synchronous or asynchronous communication? We can easily model synchronous communication with asynchronous communication—processes obey a protocol that requires the sender of a message to wait for an acknowledgment and the recipient of a message to send such an acknowledgment. A system with static processes, textually guarded output statements,

---

* Reid's dissertation [Reid 82] is an attempt similar to this one. Its approach and its conclusions are both more comprehensive and more complex than the theme developed in this section.

and synchronous communication cannot model asynchronous communication. This is because an asynchronous message-based system can create an unbounded number of pending messages, while a synchronous system with static processes cannot have more than one pending message per process per output guard at any time. A system with dynamic process creation and synchronous communication could mimic asynchronous communication by creating a "secretary" process for each message and making that secretary responsible for completing the communication.

We choose asynchronous communication for our model because it is easier to express protocols asynchronously. Along the same lines, we give our model unbounded buffers and unidirectional information flow. Unbounded buffers can certainly model bounded ones; bidirectional information flow can be simulated by a protocol of exchanged messages.

We identified four varieties of interprocess connection: name, entry, port, and broadcast. Typically, a process with a single code point for receiving messages uses names, and a process with several reception points uses entries. Ports are used to target messages that are not necessarily addressed to a particular process. Broadcasting mechanisms distribute a single message to many "appropriate" recipients.

Entries serve to sort and filter messages and to direct messages to particular segments of code. Names and entries are equivalent: a system that uses names can be modeled as a single-entry process, and a system with entries can be modeled as a single name process with a "computed goto" after that name. This goto would jump to the code originally associated with the entry name. This latter modeling requires some facility for filtering requests, such as secretaries or PLITS-like transaction keys.

Ports differ from names and entries in that several processes can share a port. The simplest variety of port receives messages of two kinds: insertions and removals. An insertion adds a message to the port's set of pending messages; a removal deletes a message and responds with that message.

Broadcasting takes several forms. The simplest form of broadcasting is a message directed at a specific finite set of recipients. This is equivalent to a program that loops, sending one message at each step. A second form of broadcasting resembles shared memory—information is available to processes but not channeled directly to them. This can be modeled as a port or, in the unbounded case, as a sequence of ports. A process seeking the latest broadcast could ask a broadcast port and be told both the information itself and the name of the successor broadcast port. The most complicated form of broadcast ties broadcast dispatch with pattern-directed reception. Here, processes specify a message pattern, and the system directs all broadcast messages that match that pattern to the process. We can model this arrangement by giving each process a secretary process that scans all broadcasts and forwards the appropriate ones to its executive.

For the moment, we observe that ports model entries by handling insertion and deletion requests, and that ports model broadcasts by accepting insertions and responding to requests with both information and the names of successor ports. Since ports allow message sharing that is unavailable to entries, we give our basis model ports.*

Communication control presents the widest variety of mechanisms. These mechanisms are used for three purposes: indeterminacy, filters, and time-outs. To handle them, our ports become more active agents — they need programs of their own. Indeterminacy is usually shown by guarded statements. Our port has several ways to select a guard clause. For example, it could choose one at random, survey them in some fixed priority order, or select the earliest arrival. Our port may need a random-number generator to imitate the first mechanism, but in any case, these can all be expressed by programs within the port.†

Programs use filters to select the desired message from among the waiting requests. Typical filters are the message-sender and transaction-key filters in PLITS, the sender and priority filters of SR and Cell, and the pattern-matching of Ether. Of course, if messages are to be filtered by sender, then message senders must decorate messages with their identities. To expect the port to do this filtering requires sending the port a more detailed request. Nevertheless, such filtering is still easily accommodated in our model.

Three systems have time-out mechanisms. Receiver time-outs (Exchange Functions and Ada) require either that the port respond immediately if it is empty (Exchange Functions and Ada conditional select/entry statements) or that it be prepared for a second message from the receiver, telling the port to ignore the initial request (Ada timed select/entry statement). Sender time-outs (Ada and Argus) permit the sender of a message to remove it from the port. Thus, "ports that served as entries" (which we originally presumed would allow only a single process to remove messages) turn out, in certain circumstances, to allow multiple message removers.

Fairness is a subtle issue. Shared Variables provides a convenient formalism for illustrating some of the difficulties in producing a fair implementation. If two processes compete to write a variable, the first may always write just before the second. Thus, the second's writing may prevent any other process from reading the value written by the first. The timing and actions of these two processes may be so regular that this sequencing continues arbitrarily into

---

* We will later retreat from this assertion back to a simpler name mechanism.

† Two processes can simulate an unbounded random-number generator in the following fashion: the first sends a message asking for a reply to the second process and starts counting. The first process counts until it receives the reply. The usual rules of the temporal independence of processes imply that a sequence of such counts is both unbounded and random.

the future. We can avoid this dilemma by polling — providing each process with a variable that it alone writes and having the message receiver check, in turn, each variable that might contain a message to it. In a dynamic system, a process that created other processes would be responsible for polling them.*

The polling argument shows that if each process continues to make computational progress, strong fairness can be achieved (albeit at the cost of great synchronization). However, the assumption of computational progress is itself an assumption of weak fairness. Thus, achieving strong fairness requires assuming a weakly fair implementation, and a weakly fair implementation can simulate strong fairness.

A weakly fair implementation that wishes to imitate the potential "unfairness" of an antifair system can randomly select particular messages for delayed processing. Hence, weak fairness suffices for imitating the other two kinds of fairness.

What is the computational meaning of time? Good clocks exhibit certain behavior. Specifically, they produce a monotonically increasing sequence of values, where these values have a rough correspondence to both the internal clocks of people and noncomputer clocks. A computer clock thus can be implemented as a counter that is repeatedly incremented. It may be necessary to occasionally adjust the values on this clock to reflect the clocks of the other processes of a system or external clocks. (Lamport has proposed one algorithm for such synchronization [Lamport 78].) Therefore, we see that temporal constructs do not have to be primitive in the model, but can be simulated by counting, "clock" processes.

Similarly, each of the mechanisms for dealing with failure is an algorithm relying on more primitive events. When presenting a system with failure mechanisms, the authors take pains to describe the algorithms of the failure mechanisms in terms of more basic notions. In particular, the most fundamental failure notion is that of failure to receive a reply within a specified time. The basis model can simulate these time-outs with alarm processes.

Our ports have progressed from simple message repositories to elaborate message handlers, complete with facilities for storing, sorting, and organizing messages. Thus, the ports themselves have become processes. Who handles messages for our port/processes? It is inappropriate to imagine, for this port/process, a port/process of its own. This would create an infinite regress of port/processes. Instead, let the port/process handle the messages that come to it in a first-come, first-served order, at a single entry point. With this observation we see that the port/process is just an ordinary process. We have eliminated the need for a spe-

---

* In his paper on time and clocks, Lamport presents an algorithm for ensuring strong fairness [Lamport 78]. Unfortunately, his algorithm requires a broadcast to all other processes at each significant event.

cial variety of port. Instead, processes that require a special kind of filtering declare a secretary process to do that filtering for them and have their messages directed to the secretary.

In summary, our basis has dynamic creation of explicit processes. These processes communicate asynchronously, receive messages at a single entry, and enforce weak fairness. It has little else in the way of queue organization. We have shown how this organization is primitive and natural; it can directly model each of the other models and languages.

Ideal Language and Heuristic Systems

The discussion of the basis model argued that the appropriate set of primitives could model any of our systems. In this section we consider the opposite side of the design question: Which macro operations, built from these primitives, should an "ideal" system provide? Once again, our discussion parallels our dimensions.

In one sense, such an ideal system leaves the programmer unaware of the lower-level concepts of programming, such as the existence of processes. Instead, the programmer describes tasks, and the system arranges its resources to carry out those tasks concurrently. This resembles the goals of the heuristic systems of Chapter 18. Those proposals are clearly heading toward the successors of programming languages. However, the systems described in that section represent only the infancy of that technology.

Though it may be pleasant to contemplate the demise of explicit processes, we recognize that processes are the mainstream of current distributed language design. If we take it as given that our system must resemble a language, what features do we give this "ideal language"? Clearly, we want it to have the flexibility that comes from dynamic process creation. Asynchronous communication is (in a naive sense) more general than synchronous, but many process requests require an answer, much as many procedure calls require that a value be returned. The syntax of our language should provide a macro operation (send and immediate receive) to express this variety of interaction. Similarly, the multiple choice of guarded commands should expand into a "multiple send, receive the first answer, and cancel the remaining requests." In an inherently asynchronous system, information flow at the primitive level is unidirectional. These macros build bidirectional information flow into the system.

Naming and access mechanisms mark communication control. Providing processes with explicit entries serves a preliminary sorting function. The various selection mechanisms (filters, guards) are all variations of programs that run through the current input queue to select a particular element. The resolution of this theme is to turn the entries into explicit objects that respond to insertions and comparisons. Transaction and priority filters and guards then become simple programs over these queues. That is, we observe that clever ports can simulate filter and control mechanisms and provide clever ports as part of the language.

So far our ideal language is notably similar to our basis model. We diverge with the items of our third table — time, failure, and fairness. The queueing mechanism of the ideal language encourages a stronger form of fairness than weak fairness, though we do not demand a fairness that corresponds with external time.

Internal time should be implemented with explicit clock processes. A process that wishes to time-out a request should be able to do so by sending a "withdrawal" request to the destination port. If the port has not yet sent the request to the destination process, it should remove that message from the queue and return an acknowledgment to the original requestor.

A process can recognize a failure in one of two ways. Either a process explicitly fails (like the **self destruct** statement in PLITS) or failure can be inferred from the lack of response to a request. Explicit failure is a variety of message that a process sends in response to a request. It can be so encoded. Failure from a lack of response arises when a request does not receive a response within some program-determined duration. Such a limit should be potentially explicit in every request that demands a response. The concurrent subactions of Argus provide a particularly elegant integration of failure and time-outs. The ideal language should provide a library of such algorithms, not limited to atomicity, but also including the portlike processes discussed above and the resource allocation algorithms discussed in Chapter 18. Textually, such a language must simplify the task of interrupting the flow of program control to handle unusual messages, much as exception handlers in conventional languages deal with system exceptions. Our ideal language will profit if it is able to treat its program state as an object to be manipulated, delayed, and resumed on request.

PROBLEMS

19-1 Identify another common theme in the systems studied and analyze the perspectives on that theme.

19-2 Design a distributed language or model. Analyze your system in terms of the dimensions discussed in Section 19-1.

19-3 Design a distributed language or model by "making a choice" for each of the columns of Tables 19-1, 19-2 and 19-3. Besides syntax, what else do you need to specify for your system?

† **19-4** Implement your language or model design from Exercise 19-3.

19-5 To what extent can the effect of filling split be imitated with an indeterminate-merge, a demultiplexer, and an (implicit) queue? What are the limitations of such a solution?

19-6 To what extent does the basis model resemble Actors? How and where does it differ?

19-7 The previous question suggests that an Actor-like system can model the other systems. Select another one of the systems described in this book and show that that system can serve as a basis for the others.

19-8 Which systems cannot serve as a basis, and why not?

[**Ackerman 79**] Ackerman, W. B., and J. B. Dennis, "VAL — A Value-Oriented Algorithmic Language: Preliminary Reference Manual," Technical Report TR-218, Computation Structures Group, Laboratory for Computer Science, M.I.T., Cambridge, Massachusetts (June 1979).

[**Adams 68**] Adams, D. A., "A Computation Model with Data Flow Sequencing," Technical Report TR-CS 117, Computer Science Department, Stanford University, Stanford, California (December 1968).

[**Adiba 80**] Adiba, M. E., and B. G. Lindsay, "Database Snapshots," *Proc. 6th Int. Conf. Very Large Data Bases*, Montreal (October 1980), pp. 86–91.

[**Agerwala 82**] Agerwala, T., and Arvind, "Data Flow Systems," *Comput.*, vol. 15, no. 2 (February 1982).

[**Aho 74**] Aho, A. V., J. E. Hopcroft, and J. D. Ullman, *The Design and Analysis of Computer Algorithms*, Addison-Wesley, Reading, Massachusetts (1974).

[**Ahuja 82**] Ahuja, V., *Design and Analysis of Computer Communication Networks*, McGraw-Hill, New York (1982).

[**Alagic 78**] Alagic, S., and M. A. Arbib, *The Design of Well-Structured and Correct Programs*, Springer-Verlag, New York (1978).

[**Allen 78**] Allen, J., *The Anatomy of LISP*, McGraw-Hill, New York (1978).

[**Andrews 81a**] Andrews, G. R., "Synchronizing Resources," *ACM Trans. Program. Lang. Syst.*, vol. 3, no. 4 (October 1981), pp. 405–430.

[**Andrews 81b**] Andrews, G. R., "SR: A Language for Distributed Programming," Technical Report TR81-14, Computer Science Department, University of Arizona, Tucson, Arizona (October 1981).

[**Andrews 82**] Andrews, G. R., "The Distributed Programming Language SR—Mechanisms, Design and Implementation," *Softw. Pract. Exper.*, vol. 12, no. 8 (1982), pp. 719–753.

[**Andrews 83**] Andrews, G. R., and F. B. Schneider, "Concepts and Notations for Concurrent Programming," *Comput. Surv.*, vol. 15, no. 1 (March 1983), pp. 3–43.

[**Apt 80**] Apt, K. R., N. Francez, and W. P. de Roever, "A Proof System for Communicating Sequential Processes," *ACM Trans. Program. Lang. Syst.*, vol. 2, no. 3 (July 1980), pp. 359–385.

[**Arvind 77**] Arvind, and K. P. Gostelow, "A Computer Capable of Exchanging Processors for Time," in B. Gilchrist (ed.), *Information Processing 77: Proceedings of the IFIP Congress 77*, North Holland, Amsterdam (1977), pp. 849–854.

[**Ashcroft 77**] Ashcroft, E. A., and W. W. Wadge, "Lucid, a Nonprocedural Language with Iteration," *CACM*, vol. 20, no. 7 (July 1977), pp. 519–526.

[**Backus 78**] Backus, J., "Can Programming be Liberated from the von Neumann Style? A Functional Style and Its Algebra of Programs," *CACM*, vol. 21, no. 8 (August 1978), pp. 613–641.

[**Berger 82**] Berger, P., D. Comte, N. Hifdi, B. Perlois, and J.-C. Syre, "Le Système LAU: Un Multiprocesseur à Assignation Unique," *Tech. Sci. Inf.*, vol. 1, no. 1 (1982).

[**Bernstein 80**] Bernstein, A. J., "Output Guards and Nondeterminism in 'Communicating Sequential Processes,'" *ACM Trans. Program. Lang. Syst.*, vol. 2, no. 2 (April 1980), pp. 234–238.

[**Bernstein 81**] Bernstein, P. A., and N. Goodman, "Concurrency Control in Distributed Database Systems," *Comput. Surv.*, vol. 13, no. 2 (June 1981), pp. 185–222.

[**Birtwistle 73**] Birtwistle, G. M., O.-J. Dahl, B. Myhrhaug, and K. Nygaard, *Simula Begin*, Auerbach, Philadelphia (1973).

[**Brinch Hansen 75**] Brinch Hansen, P., "The Programming Language Concurrent Pascal," *IEEE Trans. Softw. Eng.*, vol. SE-1, no. 2 (June 1975), pp. 199–207.

[**Brinch Hansen 77**] Brinch Hansen, P., *The Architecture of Concurrent Programs*, Prentice-Hall, Englewood Cliffs, New Jersey (1977).

[**Brinch Hansen 78**] Brinch Hansen, P., "Distributed Processes: A Concurrent Programming Concept," *CACM*, vol. 21, no. 11 (November 1978), pp. 934–941.

[**Brinch Hansen 81**] Brinch Hansen, P., "The Design of Edison," *Softw. Pract. Exper.*, vol. 11, no. 4 (April 1981), pp. 363–396.

[**Buckley 83**] Buckley, G., and A. Silberschatz, "An Effective Implementation for the Generalized Input-Output Construct of CSP," *ACM Trans. Program. Lang. Syst.*, vol. 5, no. 2 (April 1983), pp. 223–235.

[**Burns 80a**] Burns, J. E., personal communication, 1980.

[**Burns 80b**] Burns, J. E., P. Jackson, N. A. Lynch, M. J. Fischer, and G. L. Peterson, "Data Requirements for Implementation of N-Process Mutual Exclusion Using a Single Shared Variable," *JACM*, vol. 29, no. 1 (January 1982), pp. 183–205.

[**Carlson 81**] Carlson, W. E., "Ada: A Promising Beginning," *Comput.*, vol. 14, no. 6 (June 1981), pp. 13–15.

[**Church 36**] Church, A., "An Unsolvable Problem of Elementary Number Theory," *Am. J. Math.*, vol. 58 (1936), pp. 345–363.

[**Church 41**] Church, A., *The Calculi of Lambda Conversion*, Annals of Mathematical Studies 6, Princeton University Press, Princeton, New Jersey (1941).

[**Clark 81**] Clark, K. L., and S. Gregory, "A Relational Language for Parallel Programming," *ACM Proc. 1981 Conf. Func. Program. Lang. Comput. Archit.*, Portsmith, New Hampshire (October 1981), pp. 171–178.

[**Clinger 81**] Clinger, W., "Foundations of Actor Semantics," Ph.D. dissertation, M.I.T., Cambridge, Massachusetts (May 1981).

[**Comte 79**] Comte, D., and N. Hifdi, "LAU Multiprocessor: Microfunctional Description and Technological Choices," *Proc. 1st Eur. Conf. Parallel and Distrib. Proc.*, Toulouse, France (February 1979), pp. 8–15.

[**Conway 63a**] Conway, M. E., "Design of a Separable Transition-Diagram Compiler," *CACM*, vol. 6, no. 7 (July 1963), pp. 396–408.

[**Conway 63b**] Conway, M. E., "A Multiprocessor System Design," *Proceedings AFIPS 1963 Fall Joint Computer Conference*, AFIPS Conference Proceedings vol. 27, Spartan Books, New York (1963), pp. 139–146.

[**Cook 83**] Cook, S. A., "An Overview of Computational Complexity," *CACM*, vol. 26, no. 6 (June 1983), pp. 400–408.

[**Corkill 83**] Corkill, D. D., and V. R. Lesser, "The Use of Meta-level Control for Coordination in a Distributed Problem Solving Network," *Proc. 8th Int. J. Conf. Artif. Intell.*, Karlsruhe, Germany (August 1983), pp. 748–755.

[**Courtois 71**] Courtois, P. J., F. Heymans, and D. L. Parnas, "Concurrent Control with 'Readers' and 'Writers,'" *CACM*, vol. 14, no. 10 (October 1971), pp. 667–668.

[**Cremers 79**] Cremers, A., and T. Hibbard, "Arbitration and Queueing under Limited Shared Storage Requirements," Forschungsbericht 83, University of Dortmund, Dortmund, Germany (1979).

[**Date 81**] Date, C. J., *An Introduction to Database Systems*, 3d ed., Addison-Wesley, Reading, Massachusetts (1981).

[**Date 83**] Date, C. J., *An Introduction to Database Systems*, vol. II, Addison-Wesley, Reading, Massachusetts (1983).

[**Davies 78**] Davies, C. T., "Data Processing Spheres of Control," *IBM Syst. J.*, vol. 17, no. 2 (1978), pp. 179–198.

[**Davis 78**] Davis, A. L., "The Architecture and System Method of DDM1: A Recursively Structured Data Driven Machine," *Proc. 5th Annu. Symp. Comput. Archit.*, IEEE (April 1978), pp. 210–215.

[**Davis 76**] Davis, R., and J. King, "An Overview of Production Systems," in E. W. Elcock, and D. Michie (eds.), *Machine Intelligence 8*, Wiley, New York (1976), pp. 300–332.

[**Davis 83**] Davis, R., and R. G. Smith, "Negotiation as a Metaphor for Distributed Problem Solving," *Artif. Intell.*, vol. 20, no. 1 (January 1983), pp. 63–109.

[**Dennis 66**] Dennis, J. B., and E. C. Van Horn, "Programming Semantics for Multiprogrammed Computations," *CACM*, vol. 9, no. 3 (March 1966), pp. 143–155.

[**Dennis 74**] Dennis, J. B., "First Version of a Data Flow Procedure Language," in B. Robinet (ed.), *Proceedings, Colloque sur la Programmation*, Lecture Notes in Computer Science 19, Springer-Verlag, Berlin (1974), pp. 362–376.

[**Dennis 77**] Dennis, J. B., "A Language for Structured Concurrency," in J. H. Williams, and D. A. Fisher (eds.), *Design and Implementation of Programming Languages*, Lecture Notes in Computer Science 54, Springer-Verlag, Berlin (1977), pp. 231–242.

[**Dijkstra 68**] Dijkstra, E. W., "Co-operating Sequential Processes," in F. Genuys (ed.), *Programming Languages: NATO Advanced Study Institute*, Academic Press, London (1968), pp. 43–112.

[**Dijkstra 72a**] Dijkstra, E. W., "Hierarchical Ordering of Sequential Processes," in C.A.R. Hoare, and R. H. Perrott (eds.), *Operating Systems Techniques*, Academic Press, New York (1972), pp. 72–93.

[**Dijkstra 72b**] Dijkstra, E. W., "Notes on Structured Programming," in O.-J. Dahl, E. W. Dijkstra, and C.A.R. Hoare, *Structured Programming*, Academic Press, London (1972), pp. 1–82.

[**Dijkstra 75**] Dijkstra, E. W., "Guarded Commands, Nondeterminacy, and Formal Derivation of Programs," *CACM*, vol. 18, no. 8 (August 1975), pp. 453–457.

[**Dijkstra 76**] Dijkstra, E. W., *A Discipline of Programming*, Prentice-Hall, New Jersey, Englewood Cliffs (1976).

[**DoD 80**] Department of Defense, "Military Standard Ada Programming Language," Report MIL-STD-1815, Naval Publications and Forms Center, Philadelphia, Pennsylvania (December 1980).

[**Donzeau-Gouge 80**] Donzeau-Gouge, V., G. Kahn, and B. Lang, "Formal Definition of the Ada Programming Language: Preliminary Version for Public Review," unnumbered technical report, INRIA (November 1980).

[**Dwyer 81**] Dwyer, R. A., and R. K. Dybvig, "A SCHEME for Distributed Processes," Technical Report 107, Computer Science Department, Indiana University, Bloomington, Indiana (April 1981).

[**Erman 80**] Erman, L. D., F. Hayes-Roth, V. R. Lesser, and D. R. Reddy, "The Hearsay-II Speech-Understanding System: Integrating Knowledge to Resolve Uncertainty," *Comput. Surv.*, vol. 12, no. 2 (June 1980), pp. 213–253.

[**Eswaran 76**] Eswaran, K. P., J. N. Gray, R. A. Lorie, and I. L. Traiger, "The Notions of Consistency and Predicate Locks in a Database System," *CACM*, vol. 19, no. 11 (November 1976), pp. 624–633.

[**Feldman 79**] Feldman, J. A., "High Level Programming for Distributed Computing," *CACM*, vol. 22, no. 6 (June 1979), pp. 353–368.

[**Fennell 77**] Fennell, R. D., and V. R. Lesser, "Parallelism in AI Problem-Solving: A Case Study of Hearsay-II," *IEEE Trans. Comput.*, vol. C-26, no. 2 (February 1977), pp. 98–111.

[**Filman 80**] Filman, R. E., and D. P. Friedman, "Inspiring Distribution in Distributed Computing," *Working Papers ACM SIGOPS/SIGPLAN Workshop Fundam. Issues Distrib. Comput.*, Fallbrook, California (December 1980), pp. 53–59.

[**Filman 82**] Filman, R. E., and D. P. Friedman, "Models, Languages, and Heuristics for Distributed Computing," *1982 National Computer Conference*, AFIPS Conference Proceedings vol. 51, AFIPS Press, Arlington, Virginia (1982), pp. 671–678.

[**Fisher 78**] Fisher, D. A., "DoD's Common Programming Language Effort," *Comput.*, vol. 11, no. 3 (March 1978), pp. 24–33.

[**Fitzwater 77**] Fitzwater, D. R., and P. Zave, "The Use of Formal Asynchronous Process Specifications in a System Development Process," *Proc. 6th Texas Conf. Comp. Syst.*, The University of Texas at Austin (November 1977), pp. 2B-21:2B-30.

[**Fosseen 72**] Fosseen, J. B., "Representation of Algorithms by Maximally Parallel Schemata," Masters thesis, M.I.T., Cambridge, Massachusetts (1972).

[**Fox 79**] Fox, M. S., "Organization Structuring: Designing Large Complex Software," Technical Report CMU-CS-79-155, Department of Computer Science, Carnegie-Mellon University, Pittsburgh, Pennsylvania (December 1979).

[**Fox 81**] Fox, M. S., "An Organizational View of Distributed Systems," *IEEE Trans. Syst. Man Cybern.*, vol. SMC-11, no. 1 (January 1981), pp. 70–80.

[**Francez 80**] Francez, N., D. J. Lehmann, and A. Pnueli, "A Linear History Semantics for Distributed Languages," *21st Annu. Symp. Found. Comput. Sci.*, Syracuse, New York (October 1980), pp. 143–151.

[**Friedman 76**] Friedman, D. P., and D. S. Wise, "CONS Should Not Evaluate its Arguments," in S. Michaelson, and R. Milner (eds.), *Automata, Languages and Programming*, Edinburgh University Press, Edinburgh (1976), pp. 257–284.

[**Friedman 77**] Friedman, D. P., and D. S. Wise, "Aspects of Applicative Programming for File Systems," *Proc. ACM Conf. Lang. Des. Rel. Softw.*, North Carolina (1977), pp. 41–55.

[**Friedman 78a**] Friedman, D. P., and D. S. Wise, "A Note on Conditional Expressions," *CACM*, vol. 21, no. 11 (November 1978), pp. 931–933.

[**Friedman 78b**] Friedman, D. P., and D. S. Wise, "Unbounded Computational Structures," *Softw. Pract. Exper.*, vol. 8, no. 4 (August 1978), pp. 407–416.

[**Friedman 79**] Friedman, D. P., and D. S. Wise, "An Approach to Fair Applicative Multiprograming," in G. Kahn (ed.), *Semantics of Concurrent Computation*, Lecture Notes in Computer Science 70, Springer-Verlag, New York (1979), pp. 203–225.

[**Friedman 80**] Friedman, D. P., and D. S. Wise, "An Indeterminate Constructor for Applicative Programming," *Conf. Rec. 7th ACM Symp. Princ. Program. Lang.*, Las Vegas, Nevada (January 1980), pp. 245–250.

[**Galbraith 77**] Galbraith, J., *Organizational Design*, Addison-Wesley, Reading, Massachusetts (1977).

[**Garman 81**] Garman, J. R., "The 'Bug' Heard 'Round the World," *Softw. Eng. Notes*, vol. 6, no. 5 (October 1981), pp. 3–10.

[**Goldberg 83**] Goldberg, A., and D. Robson, *Smalltalk-80: The Language and its Implementation*, Addison-Wesley, New York (1983).

[**Gordon 79**] Gordon, M.J.C., *The Denotational Description of Programming Languages*, Springer-Verlag, New York (1979).

[**Gordon 81**] Gordon, M., "A Very Simple Model of Sequential Behavior of nMOS," *Proc. VLSI 81 Int. Conf.*, Edinburgh, Scotland (August 1981), pp. 18–21.

[**Gray 75**] Gray, J. N., R. A. Lorie, and G. R. Putzolu, "Granularity of Locks in a Shared Data Base," *Proc. Int. Conf. Very Large Data Bases*, Framingham, Massachusetts (September 1975), pp. 428–451.

[**Gray 79**] Gray, J. N., "Notes on Data Base Operating Systems," in R. Bayer, R. M. Graham, and G. Seegmuller (eds.), *Operating Systems: An Advanced Course*, Springer-Verlag, New York (1979), pp. 393–481.

[**Gray 81**] Gray, J., P. McJones, M. Blasgen, B. Lindsay, R. Lorie, T. Price, F. Putzolu, and I. Traiger, "The Recovery Manager of the System R Database Manager," *Comput. Surv.*, vol. 13, no. 2 (June 1981), pp. 223–242.

[**Greif 75**] Greif, I., and C. E. Hewitt, "Actor Semantics of Planner-73," *Conf. Rec. 2d ACM Symp. Princ. Program. Lang.*, Palo Alto, California (January 1975), pp. 67–77.

[**Gries 81**] Gries, D., *The Science of Programming*, Springer-Verlag, New York (1981).

[**Hanson 78**] Hanson, A. R., and E. M. Riseman, "VISIONS: A Computer System for Interpreting Scenes," in A. Hanson, and E. Riseman (eds.), *Computer Vision Systems*, Academic Press, New York (1978), pp. 303–333.

[**Henderson 76**] Henderson, P., and J. H. Morris, "A Lazy Evaluator," *Conf. Rec. 3d ACM Symp. Princ. Program. Lang.*, Atlanta, Georgia (January 1976), pp. 95–103.

[**Henderson 82**] Henderson, P., "Purely Functional Operating Systems," in J. Darlington, P. Henderson, and D. A. Turner, *Functional Programming and its Applications*, Cambridge University Press, Cambridge (1982), pp. 177–192.

[**Hewitt 69**] Hewitt, C. E., "PLANNER: A Language for Manipulating Models and Proving Theorems in a Robot," *Proc. 1st Int. J. Conf. Artif. Intell.*, Washington, D.C. (August 1969), pp. 295–302.

[**Hewitt 77a**] Hewitt C. E., "Viewing Control Structures as Patterns of Passing Messages," *Artif. Intell.*, vol. 8, no. 3 (June 1977), pp. 323–364.

[**Hewitt 77b**] Hewitt, C. E., and H. Baker, "Laws for Communicating Parallel Processes," in B. Gilchrist (ed.), *Information Processing 77: Proceedings of the IFIP Congress 77*, North Holland, Amsterdam (1977), pp. 987–992.

[**Hewitt 79**] Hewitt, C. E., G. Attardi, and H. Lieberman, "Specifying and Proving Properties of Guardians for Distributed Systems," in G. Kahn (ed.), *Semantics of Concurrent Computation*, Lecture Notes in Computer Science 70, Springer-Verlag, New York (1979), pp. 316–336.

[**Hewitt 80**] Hewitt, C. E., G. Attardi, and M. Simi, "Knowledge Embedding in the Description System Omega," *Proc. 1st Annu. Natl. Conf. Artif. Intell.*, Stanford, California (August 1980), pp. 157–164.

[**Hewitt 82**] Hewitt, C. E., personal communication, 1982.

[**Hewitt 83**] Hewitt, C. E., and P. de Jong, "Message Passing Semantics for Conceptual Modeling," in M. L. Brodie, J. L. Mylopoulos, and J. W. Schmidt (eds.), *Perspectives on Conceptual Modeling*, Springer-Verlag, New York (1983), pp. 147–164.

[**Hirschberg 80**] Hirschberg, D. S., and J. B. Sinclair, "Decentralized Extrema-Finding in Circular Configurations of Processors," *CACM*, vol. 23, no. 11 (November 1980), pp. 627–628.

[**Hoare 72**] Hoare, C.A.R., and D.C.S. Allison, "Incomputability," *Comput. Surv.*, vol. 4, no. 3 (September 1972), pp. 169–178.

[**Hoare 74**] Hoare, C.A.R., "Monitors: An Operating System Structuring Concept," *CACM*, vol. 17, no. 10 (October 1974), pp. 549–557.

[**Hoare 78**] Hoare, C.A.R., "Communicating Sequential Processes," *CACM*, vol. 21, no. 8 (August 1978), pp. 666–677.

[**Hoare 81**] Hoare, C.A.R., "The Emperor's Old Clothes," *CACM*, vol. 24, no. 2 (March 1981), pp. 75–83.

[**Holt 68**] Holt, A. W., H. Saint, R. Shapiro, and S. Warshall, "Final Report of the Information System Theory Project," Report TRRADC-TR-68-305, Rome Air Development Center, Griffiss Air Force Base, New York (1968).

[**Hopcroft 79**] Hopcroft, J. E., and J. D. Ullman, *Introduction to Automata Theory, Languages and Computation*, Addison-Wesley, Reading, Massachusetts (1979).

[**Ingerman 61**] Ingerman, P., "Thunks," *CACM*, vol. 4, no. 1 (January 1961), pp. 55–58.

[**Johnson 81**] Johnson, S. D., and A. T. Kohlstaedt, "DSI Program Description," Technical Report 120, Computer Science Department, Indiana University, Bloomington, Indiana (December 1981).

[**Johnson 84**] Johnson, S. D., "Circuits and Systems: Implementing Communication with Streams," in M. Ruschitzka, M. Christensen, W. F. Ames, and R. Vichnevetsky, R. (eds.), *Parallel and Large-Scale Computers: Performance, Architecture, Applications*, vol. 2 IMACS Transactions on Scientific Computation, North-Holland, Amsterdam (1984), pp. 311–319.

[**Kahn 74**] Kahn, G., "The Semantics of a Simple Language for Parallel Programming," in J. L. Rosenfeld (ed.), *Information Processing 74: Proceedings of the IFIP Congress 74*, North Holland, Amsterdam (1974), pp. 471–475.

[**Kahn 77**] Kahn, G., and D. B. MacQueen, "Coroutines and Networks of Parallel Processes," in B. Gilchrist (ed.), *Information Processing 77: Proceedings of the IFIP Congress 77*, North Holland, Amsterdam (1977), pp. 993–998.

[**Karp 66**] Karp, R. M., and R. E. Miller, "Properties of a Model for Parallel Computations: Determinacy, Termination, Queueing," *SIAM J. Appl. Math.*, vol. 14, no. 6 (November 1966), pp. 1390–1411.

[**Keller 81**] Keller, R. M., and G. Lindstrom, "Applications of Feedback in Functional Programming," *ACM Proc. 1981 Conf. Func. Program. Lang. Comput. Archit.*, Portsmith, Hew Hampshire (October 1981), pp. 171–178.

[**Kent 81**] Kent, E., *The Brains of Men and Machines*, Byte/McGraw-Hill, Peterborough, New Hampshire (1981).

[**Kessels 77**] Kessels, J.L.W., "An Alternative to Event Queues for Synchronization in Monitors," *CACM*, vol. 20, no. 7 (July 1977), pp. 500–503.

[**Kieburtz 79**] Kieburtz, R. B., and A. Silberschatz, "Comments on 'Communicating Sequential Processes,'" *ACM Trans. Program. Lang. Syst.*, vol. 1, no. 2 (January 1979), pp. 218–225.

[**Knuth 73**] Knuth, D. E., *The Art of Computer Programming*, vol. 3: *Sorting and Searching*, Addison-Wesley, Reading, Massachusetts (1973).

[**Kohler 81**] Kohler, W. H., "A Survey of Techniques for Synchronization and Recovery in Decentralized Computer Systems," *Comput. Surv.*, vol. 13, no. 2 (June 1981), pp. 149–184.

[**Kornfeld 81**] Kornfeld, W. A., and C. E. Hewitt, "The Scientific Community Metaphor," *IEEE Trans. Syst. Man Cybern.*, vol. SMC-11, no. 1 (January 1981), pp. 24–33.

[**Kornfeld 82**] Kornfeld, W. A., "Combinatorially Implosive Algorithms," *CACM*, vol. 25, no. 10 (October 1982), pp. 934–938.

[**Kosaraju 82**] Kosaraju, S. R., "Decidability of Reachability in Vector Addition Systems," *Proc. 14th Annu. ACM Symp. Theory Comp.*, San Francisco (May 1982), pp. 267–281.

[**Lamport 78**] Lamport, L., "Time, Clocks, and the Ordering of Events in a Distributed System," *CACM*, vol. 21, no. 7 (July 1978), pp. 558–565.

[**Lamport 80**] Lamport, L., "The 'Hoare Logic' of Concurrent Programs," *Acta Informa.*, vol. 14, no. 1 (1980), pp. 21–37.

[**Lampson 76**] Lampson, B. W., and H. E. Sturgis, "Crash Recovery in a Distributed Storage System," unnumbered technical report, Computer Science Laboratory, Xerox Palo Alto Research Center, Palo Alto, California (1976).

[**Landin 65**] Landin, P., "A Correspondence Between ALGOL 60 and Church's Lambda Notation: Part I," *CACM*, vol. 8, no. 2 (February 1965), pp. 89–101.

[**Lauer 78**] Lauer, H. C., and R. M. Needham, "On the Duality of Operating Systems Structures," *Proc. 2d Int. Symp. Oper. Syst.*, IRIA (October 1978).

[**Ledgard 81**] Ledgard, H., and M. Marcotty, *The Programming Language Landscape*, Science Research Associates, Chicago (1981).

[**Lesser 78**] Lesser, V. R., and D. D. Corkill, "Cooperative Distributed Problem Solving: A New Approach for Structuring Distributed Systems," Technical Report 78-7, Department of Computer and Information Science, University of Massachusetts, Amherst, Massachusetts (May 1978).

[**Lesser 80**] Lesser, V. R., and L. D. Erman, "Distributed Interpretation: A Model and Experiment," *IEEE Trans. Comput.*, vol. C-29, no. 12 (December 1980), pp. 1144–1163.

[**Lesser 81**] Lesser, V. R., and D. D. Corkill, "Functionally Accurate, Cooperative Distributed Systems," *IEEE Trans. Syst. Man Cybern.*, vol. SMC-11, no. 1 (January 1981), pp. 81–99.

[**Levin 81**] Levin, G. M., and D. Gries, "A Proof Technique for Communicating Sequential Processes," *Acta Informa.*, vol. 15, no. 3 (June 1981), pp. 281–302.

[**Li 81**] Li, C.-M., and M. T. Liu, "Dislang: A Distributed Programming Language/System," *Proc. 2d Int. Conf. Distrib. Comput. Syst.*, Paris (April 1981), pp. 162–172.

[**Liskov 77**] Liskov, B., A. Snyder, R. R. Atkinson, and J. C. Schaffert, "Abstraction Mechanisms in CLU," *CACM*, vol. 20, no. 8 (August 1977), pp. 564–576.

[**Liskov 82**] Liskov, B., "On Linguistic Support for Distributed Programs," *IEEE Trans. Softw. Eng.*, vol. SE-8, no. 3 (May 1982), pp. 203–210.

[**Liskov 83**] Liskov, B., and R. Scheifler, "Guardians and Actions: Linguistic Support for Robust, Distributed Programs," *ACM Trans. Program. Lang. Syst.*, vol. 5, no. 3 (July 1983), pp. 381–404.

[**Loveland 78**] Loveland, D. W., *Automated Theorem Proving: A Logical Basis*, North-Holland, Amsterdam (1978).

[**Lynch 81**] Lynch, N. A., and M. J. Fischer, "On Describing the Behavior and Implementation of Distributed Systems," *Theoret. Comp. Sci.*, vol. 13, no. 1 (1981), pp. 17–43.

[**McCarthy 60**] McCarthy, J., "Recursive Functions of Symbolic Expressions and Their Computation by Machine," *CACM*, vol. 3, no. 4 (April 1960), pp. 184–195.

[**McCarthy 63**] McCarthy, J., "A Basis for a Mathematical Theory of Computation," in P. Braffort, and D. Hirschberg (eds.), *Computer Programming and Formal Systems*, North Holland, Amsterdam (1963), pp. 33–70.

[**McCarthy 65**] McCarthy, J., P. W. Abrahams, D. J. Edwards, T. P. Hart, and M. I. Levin, *Lisp 1.5 Programmer's Manual*, M.I.T. Press, Cambridge, Massachusetts (1965).

[**McGraw 82**] McGraw, J. R., "The VAL Language: Description and Analysis," *ACM Trans. Program. Lang. Syst.*, vol. 4, no. 1 (January 1982), pp. 44–82.

[**MacQueen 79**] MacQueen, D. B., "Models for Distributed Computing," Rapport de Recherche 351, INRIA, Le Chesnay, France (April 1979).

[**Mayr 81**] Mayr, E. W., "An Algorithm for the General Petri Net Reachability Problem," *Proc. 13th Annu. ACM Symp. Theory Comp.*, Milwaukee (May 1981), pp. 238–246.

[**Mead 80**] Mead, C., and L. Conway, *Introduction to VLSI Systems*, Addison-Wesley, Reading, Massachusetts (1980).

[**Metcalfe 76**] Metcalfe, R. M., and D. R. Boggs, "Ethernet: Distributed Packet Switching for Local Computer Networks," *CACM*, vol. 19, no. 7 (July 1976), pp. 395–404.

[**Milne 78**] Milne, G. J., "A Mathematical Model of Concurrent Computation," Ph.D. dissertation, University of Edinburgh, Edinburgh (1978).

[**Milne 79**] Milne, G., and R. Milner, "Concurrent Processes and Their Syntax," *JACM*, vol. 26, no. 2 (April 1979), pp. 302–321.

[**Milner 80**] Milner, R., *A Calculus of Communicating Systems*, Lecture Notes in Computer Science 92, Springer-Verlag, New York (1980).

[**Milner 83**] Milner, R., "Calculi for Synchrony and Asynchrony," *Theoret. Comp. Sci.*, vol. 25, no. 3 (1983), pp. 267–310.

[**Minsky 67**] Minsky, M., *Computation: Finite and Infinite Machines*, Prentice-Hall, Englewood Cliffs, New Jersey (1967).

[**Mohan 80**] Mohan, C., "A Perspective of Distributed Computing: Models, Languages, Issues and Applications," Working Paper DSG-8001, Department of Computer Science, The University of Texas, Austin, Texas (March 1980).

[**Moore 79**] Moore, R. C., "Reasoning About Knowledge and Action," Ph.D. dissertation, M.I.T., Cambridge, Massachusetts (February 1979).

[**Nelson 81**] Nelson, B. J., "Remote Procedure Call," Ph.D. dissertation, Carnegie-Mellon University, Pittsburgh (1981).

[**Nii 78**] Nii, H. P., and E. A. Feigenbaum, "Rule-Based Understanding of Signals," in D. A. Waterman, and F. Hayes-Roth (eds.), *Pattern Directed Inference Systems*, Academic Press, New York (1978), pp. 483–501.

[**Organick 75**] Organick, E. I., A. I. Forsythe, and R. P. Plummer, *Programming Language Structures*, Academic Press, New York (1975).

[**Perlis 82**] Perlis, A. J., "Epigrams on Programming," *SIGPLAN Not.*, vol. 17, no. 9 (September 1982), pp. 7–13.

[**Peterossi 81**] Peterossi, A., "An Approach to Communications and Parallelism in Applicative Languages," *International Conference on Automata, Languages, and Programming*, Lecture Notes in Computer Science 107, Springer-Verlag, New York (1981), pp. 432–446.

[**Peterson 81**] Peterson, G. L., "Myths about the Mutual Exclusion Problem," *Inf. Proc. Lett.*, vol. 12, no. 3 (June 1981), pp. 115–116.

[**Peterson 77**] Peterson, J. L., "Petri Nets," *Comput. Surv.*, vol. 9, no. 3 (September 1977), pp. 223–252.

[**Peterson 81**] Peterson, J. L., *Petri Net Theory and the Modeling of Systems*, Prentice-Hall, Englewood Cliffs, New Jersey (1981).

[**Petri 62**] Petri, C. A., "Kommunikation mit Automaten," Ph.D. dissertation, University of Bonn, Bonn (1962).

[**Pratt 75**] Pratt, T. W., *Programming Languages: Design and Implementation*, Prentice-Hall, Englewood Cliffs, New Jersey (1975).

[**Pyle 81**] Pyle, I. C., *The Ada Programming Language*, Prentice-Hall International, Englewood Cliffs, New Jersey (1981).

[**Rao 80**] Rao, R., "Design and Evaluation of Distributed Communication Primitives," Technical Report 80-04-01, Department of Computer Science, University of Washington, Seattle, Washington (April 1980).

[**Reed 78**] Reed, D. P., "Naming and Synchronization in a Decentralized Computer System," Ph.D. dissertation, M.I.T., Cambridge, Massachusetts (1978).

[**Reid 82**] Reid, L. G., *Control and Communication in Programs*, UMI Research Press, Ann Arbor (1982).

[**Reynolds 65**] Reynolds, J. C., "COGENT," Report ANL-7022, Argonne National Laboratory, Argonne, Illinois (1965).

[**Reynolds 72**] Reynolds, J. C., "Definitional Interpreters for Higher-Order Programming Languages," *Proc. 25th ACM Natl. Conf.*, Boston (1972), pp. 717–740.

[**Robinson 79**] Robinson, J. A., *Logic: Form and Function*, North Holland, New York (1979).

[**Rodriguez-Bezos 69**] Rodriguez-Bezos, J. E., "A Graph Model for Parallel Computation," Report MAC-TR-64, Project MAC, M.I.T., Cambridge, Massachusetts (September 1969).

[**Rosenkrantz 78**] Rosenkrantz, D. J., R. E. Stearns, and P. M. Lewis, "System Level Concurrency Control for Distributed Database Systems," *ACM Trans. Database Syst.*, vol. 3, no. 2 (June 1978), pp. 178–198.

[**Sacerdote 77**] Sacerdote, G. S., and R. L. Tenney, "The Decidability of the Reachability Problem for Vector Addition Systems," *Proc. 9th Annu. ACM Symp. Theory Comp.*, Boulder, Colorado (May 1977), pp. 61–76.

[**Shaw 74**] Shaw, A. C., *The Logical Design of Operating Systems*, Prentice-Hall, Englewood Cliffs, New Jersey (1974).

[**Shaw 81**] Shaw, M. (ed.), *Alphard: Form and Content*, Springer-Verlag, New York (1981).

[**Siewiorek 82**] Siewiorek, D. C., G. Bell, and A. Newell, *Computer Structures: Principles and Examples*, McGraw-Hill, New York (1982).

[**SIGPLAN 79**] SIGPLAN Notices, "Ada Manual and Rationale," *SIGPLAN Not.*, vol. 14, no. 6 (June 1979).

[**Silberschatz 79**] Silberschatz, A., "Communication and Synchronization in Distributed Systems," *IEEE Trans. Softw. Eng.*, vol. 5, no. 6 (November 1979), pp. 542–547.

[**Silberschatz 80**] Silberschatz, A., "Cell: A Distributed Computing Modularization Concept," Technical Report 155, Department of Computer Science, The University of Texas, Austin, Texas (September 1980). (To appear March 1984, *IEEE Trans. Softw. Eng.*).

[**Smith 78**] Smith, R. G., and R. Davis, "Distributed Problem Solving: The Contract Net Approach," *Proc. 2d Natl. Conf. Canadian Soc. Comput. Stud. Intell.*, Toronto (July 1978), pp. 278–287.

[**Smith 81a**] Smith, R. G., *A Framework for Distributed Problem Solving*, UMI Research Press, Ann Arbor (1981).

[**Smith 81b**] Smith, R. G., and R. Davis, "Frameworks for Cooperation in Distributed Problem Solving," *IEEE Trans. Syst. Man Cybern.*, vol. SMC-11, no. 1 (January 1981), pp. 61–70.

[**Smyth 78**] Smyth, M. B., "Powerdomains," *J. Comput. Syst. Sci.*, vol. 16, no. 1 (February 1978), pp. 23–36.

[**Stark 82**] Stark, E. W., "Semaphore Primitives and Starvation-Free Mutual Exclusion," *JACM*, vol. 29, no. 4 (October 1982), pp. 1049–1072.

[**Steele 76**] Steele, G. L., Jr., "Lambda: The Ultimate Declarative," Memo 379, Artificial Intelligence Laboratory, M.I.T., Cambridge, Massachusetts (November 1976).

[**Steele 77**] Steele, G. L., Jr., "Debunking the 'Expensive Procedure Call' Myth," *Proc. 30th ACM Natl. Conf.*, Seattle (October 1977), pp. 153–162.

[**Steele 78**] Steele, G. L., Jr., and G. J. Sussman, "The Revised Report on SCHEME, a Dialect of LISP," Memo 452, Artificial Intelligence Laboratory, M.I.T., Cambridge, Massachusetts (January 1978).

[**Stotts 82**] Stotts, P. D., "A Comparative Study of Concurrent Programming Languages," *SIGPLAN Not.*, vol. 17, no. 10 (October 1982), pp. 50–61.

[**Stoy 77**] Stoy, J. E., *Denotational Semantics: The Scott-Strachey Approach to Programming Language Theory*, M.I.T. Press, Cambridge, Massachusetts (1977).

[**Strachey 74**] Strachey, C., and C. P. Wadsworth, "Continuations—a Mathematical Semantics for Handling Full Jumps," Technical Monograph TRG-11, Programming Research Group, Oxford University, Oxford, England (1974).

[**Sussman 70**] Sussman, G. J., T. Winograd, and E. Charniak, "MICRO-PLANNER Reference Manual," Memo 203, Artificial Intelligence Laboratory, M.I.T., Cambridge, Massachusetts (1970).

[**Sussman 75**] Sussman, G. J., and G. L. Steele, Jr., "SCHEME: An Interpreter for Extended Lambda Calculus," Memo 349, Artificial Intelligence Laboratory, M.I.T., Cambridge, Massachusetts (December 1975).

[**Tanenbaum 81**] Tanenbaum, A. S., *Computer Networks*, Prentice-Hall, Englewood Cliffs, New Jersey (1981).

[**Tesler 68**] Tesler, L. G., and H. J. Enea, "A Language Design for Concurrent Processes," *Proceedings of the 1968 Spring Joint Computer Conference*, AFIPS Conference Proceedings vol. 32, AFIPS Press, Arlington, Virginia (1968), pp. 403–408.

[**Treleaven 82**] Treleaven, P. C., D. R. Brownbridge, and R. P. Hopkins, "Data-Driven and Demand-Driven Computer Architecture," *Comput. Surv.*, vol. 14, no. 1 (March 1982), pp. 93–145.

[**Turing 36**] Turing, A., "On Computable Numbers, with an Application to the Entscheidungs-Problem," *Proc. London Math. Soc.*, ser. 2-42 (1936), pp. 230–265.

[**Turner 80**] Turner, D. A., personal communication, 1980.

[**Ullman 80**] Ullman, J. D., *Principles of Database Systems*, 2d ed., Computer Science Press, Potomac, Maryland (1980).

[**Vuillemin 74**] Vuillemin, J., "Correct and Optimal Implementation of Recursion in a Simple Programming Language," *J. Comput. Syst. Sci.*, vol. 9, no. 3 (June 1974), pp. 332–354.

[**Wadsworth 71**] Wadsworth, C., "Semantics and Pragmatics of the Lambda-calculus," Ph.D. dissertation, Oxford University (1971).

[**Wand 80**] Wand, M., *Induction, Recursion, and Programming*, North Holland, New York (1980).

[**Watson 82**] Watson, I., and J. Gurd, "A Practical Data Flow Computer," *Comput.*, vol. 15, no. 2 (February 1982), pp. 51–57.

[**Wegner 68**] Wegner, P., *Programming Languages, Information Structures, and Machine Organization*, McGraw-Hill, New York (1968).

[**Wegner 81**] Wegner, P., "Self-Assessment Procedure VIII," *CACM*, vol. 24, no. 10 (October 1981), pp. 647–677.

[**Weyhrauch 80**] Weyhrauch, R. W., "Prolegomena to a Theory of Mechanized Formal Reasoning," *Artif. Intell.*, vol. 13, no. 1 (1980), pp. 133–170.

[**Weihl 83**] Weihl, W., and B. Liskov, "Specification and Implementation of Resilient, Atomic Data Types," *Proc. SIGPLAN '83 Symp. Program. Lang. Issues Softw. Syst.*, San Francisco, California (June 1983), pp. 53–64.

[**Wiederhold 83**] Wiederhold, G., *Database Design*, 2d ed., McGraw-Hill, New York (1983).

[**Williams 64**] Williams J.W.J., "Algorithm 232 Heapsort," *CACM*, vol. 7, no. 6 (June 1964), pp. 347–348.

[**Winograd 75**] Winograd, T., "Frame Representations and the Declarative-Procedural Controversy," in D. G. Bobrow, and A. Collins (eds.), *Representation and Understanding*, Academic Press, New York (1975), pp. 185–210.

[**Winston 81**] Winston, P. H., and B.K.P. Horn, *LISP*, Addison-Wesley, Reading, Massachusetts (1981).

[**Wirth 76**] Wirth, N., *Algorithms + Data Structures = Programs*, Prentice-Hall, Englewood Cliffs, New Jersey (1976).

[**Wirth 77**] Wirth, N., "Toward a Discipline of Real-time Programming," *CACM*, vol. 20, no. 8 (August 1977), pp. 577–583.

[**Wirth 82**] Wirth, N., *Programming in Modula-2*, Springer-Verlag, New York (1982).

[**Wolynes 80**] Wolynes, G. P., J. R. Ginder, B. Roitblat, and V. Roland, "SPLITS: An Experiment in Scheme-Based Distributed Processing," Technical Report 97, Computer Science Department, Indiana University, Bloomington, Indiana (August 1980).

[**Zave 77**] Zave, P., and D. R. Fitzwater, "Specification of Asynchronous Interactions using Primitive Functions," Technical Report 598, Department of Computer Science, University of Maryland, College Park, Maryland (1977).

[**Zave 82**] Zave, P., "An Operational Approach to Requirements Specification for Embedded Systems," *IEEE Trans. Softw. Eng.*, vol. SE-8, no. 3 (May 1982), pp. 250–269.

[**Zave 83**] Zave, P., personal communication, 1983.